D0940737

Women in Psychiatry

Personal Perspectives

Editorial Advisory Board

Elissa P. Benedek, M.D.
Past President, American Psychiatric Association; Adjunct Professor of Psychiatry, University of Michigan Medical School

Michelle O. Clark, M.D.
Medical Director, West Central Family Health Center, Los Angeles, California

Leah J. Dickstein, M.D., M.A.
Professor Emerita, University of Louisville School of Medicine; Lecturer, Department of Psychiatry, Tufts University School of Medicine

Marcia K. Goin, M.D., Ph.D.
Professor of Clinical Psychiatry, Keck School of Medicine, University of Southern California; Past President, American Psychiatric Association

Maria T. Lymberis, M.D.
Clinical Professor of Psychiatry, University of California, Los Angeles; Founder and Past President, Hellenic American Psychiatric Association

Asha S. Mishra, M.D.
Professor of Psychiatry, Virginia Commonwealth University Hospital System; Past President, Indo-American Psychiatric Association

Patricia Ordorica, M.D.
President, Association of Women Psychiatrists; Board Member and Scientific Consultant, The Roskamp Institute

Marilyn Price, M.D., C.M.
Vice President, American Academy of Psychiatry and the Law; Clinical Instructor, Department of Psychiatry, Harvard Medical School

Michelle B. Riba, M.D., M.S.
Professor, Department of Psychiatry, University of Michigan; Past President, American Psychiatric Association

Carolyn B. Robinowitz, M.D.
Clinical Professor of Psychiatry and Behavioral Science, George Washington University School of Medicine; Clinical Professor of Psychiatry, Georgetown University School of Medicine; Past President, American Psychiatric Association

Gail E. Robinson, M.D.
Professor of Psychiatry and Obstetrics/Gynecology, University of Toronto Faculty of Medicine; Director, Women's Mental Health Program, University Health Network, Toronto General Hospital

Altha J. Stewart, M.D.
Past President, Black Psychiatrists of America; Past President, Association of Women Psychiatrists

Sandra C. Walker, M.D.
Courtesy Clinical Associate Professor, Psychiatry and Behavioral Sciences, University of Washington; Chair, American Psychiatric Association Council on Minority Mental Health and Health Disparities

Women in Psychiatry
Personal Perspectives

■|■

Edited by

Donna M. Norris, M.D.
Assistant Clinical Professor,
Department of Psychiatry, Harvard Medical School

Geetha Jayaram, M.D., M.B.A.
Associate Professor, Departments of Psychiatry and Health Policy
and Management, The Johns Hopkins University School of Medicine

Annelle B. Primm, M.D., M.P.H.
Deputy Medical Director and Director, Minority/National Affairs,
American Psychiatric Association

American Psychiatric Publishing
A Division of American Psychiatric Association

Washington, DC
London, England

Note: The authors have worked to ensure that all information in this book is accurate at the time of publication and consistent with general psychiatric and medical standards. As medical research and practice continue to advance, however, therapeutic standards may change. Moreover, specific situations may require a specific therapeutic response not included in this book. For these reasons and because human and mechanical errors sometimes occur, we recommend that readers follow the advice of physicians directly involved in their care or the care of a member of their family.

Books published by American Psychiatric Publishing (APP) represent the findings, conclusions, and views of the individual authors and do not necessarily represent the policies and opinions of APP or the American Psychiatric Association.

Purchases of 25–99 copies of this or any other APP title are eligible for a 20% discount; contact Customer Service at appi@psych.org or 800–368–5777. If purchasing 100 or more copies of the same title, please e-mail us at bulksales@psych.org for a price quote.

Copyright © 2012 American Psychiatric Association
ALL RIGHTS RESERVED
Manufactured in the United States of America on acid-free paper
16   15   14   13   12   5   4   3   2   1

First Edition
Typeset in Baskerville and Briem

American Psychiatric Publishing
a Division of American Psychiatric Association
1000 Wilson Boulevard
Arlington, VA 22209–3901
www.appi.org

Library of Congress Cataloging-in-Publication Data
Women in psychiatry : personal perspectives / edited by Donna M. Norris, Geetha Jayaram, Annelle B. Primm. — 1st ed.
    p. ; cm.
  Includes bibliographical references and index.
  ISBN 978-1-58562-408-9 (pbk. : alk. paper)
    I. Norris, Donna M., 1943- II. Jayaram, Geetha. III. Primm, Annelle. IV. American Psychiatric Publishing.
  [DNLM: 1. Psychiatry—Autobiography. 2. Women, Working—Autobiography. 3. Career Choice 0150Autobiography. WZ 112.5.P6]
  616.890092'52—dc23
                              2012003522

British Library Cataloguing in Publication Data
A CIP record is available from the British Library.

Contents

Part I
The Early Years

Part II
Mid-Career and Beyond: A Mosaic

Contributors

Andrea M. Brownridge, J.D., M.S., M.D.
Resident Physician (PGY-2), Department of Psychiatry, Morehouse School of Medicine, Atlanta, Georgia

Mary E. Barber, M.D.
Clinical Director, Rockland Psychiatric Center, Orangeburg, New York; Clinical Assistant Professor, Department of Psychiatry, Columbia University College of Physicians and Surgeons, New York, New York

Crystal R. Bullard, M.D.
Child and Adolescent Psychiatry Fellow, University of South Carolina School of Medicine, Columbia, South Carolina

Hind Benjelloun, M.D.
Assistant Professor of Clinical Psychiatry, Associate Psychiatry Residency Training Director, and Associate Medical Director, Inpatient Psychiatry Unit, Georgetown University Hospital, Washington, D.C.

Deborah Deas, M.D., M.P.H.
Professor, Department of Psychiatry and Behavioral Sciences, and Senior Associate Dean for Medical Education, College of Medicine, Medical University of South Carolina, Charleston, South Carolina

Esperanza Díaz, M.D.
Associate Professor of Psychiatry and Associate Residency Program Director, Yale School of Medicine, Yale University, New Haven, Connecticut; Medical Director, Hispanic Clinic, Connecticut Mental Health Center, New Haven, Connecticut

M. J. Doherty, Ph.D.
Special Assistant to the President, Regis College, Weston, Massachusetts

Mary Jane England, M.D.
President, Regis College, Weston, Massachusetts

Anita S. Everett, M.D.
Section Director, Community and General Psychiatry, Johns Hopkins Bayview Medical Center, Baltimore, Maryland

Ellen Haller, M.D.
Professor of Clinical Psychiatry, University of California, San Francisco, School of Medicine

Geetha Jayaram, M.D., M.B.A.
Associate Professor, Departments of Psychiatry and Health Policy and Management, The Johns Hopkins University School of Medicine, Baltimore, Maryland

Surinder Nand, M.D.
Professor of Clinical Psychiatry and Associate Director, Psychiatry Residency Training Program, Department of Psychiatry, University of Illinois College of Medicine at Chicago

Cassandra F. Newkirk, M.D., M.B.A.
Vice President of Correctional Mental Health Services and Chief Medical Officer, GEO Care Inc., Boca Raton, Florida

Donna M. Norris, M.D.
Assistant Clinical Professor of Psychiatry, Department of Psychiatry, Harvard Medical School; Program in Psychiatry and the Law, Beth Israel Deaconess Medical Center; Adjunct Faculty, Department of Psychiatry, Children's Hospital Boston, Boston, Massachusetts

Annelle B. Primm, M.D., M.P.H.
Deputy Medical Director and Director, Office of Minority/National Affairs, American Psychiatric Association, Arlington, Virginia

Patricia R. Recupero, J.D., M.D.
Clinical Professor of Psychiatry and Human Behavior, Warren Alpert Medical School of Brown University; President and CEO, Butler Hospital, Providence, Rhode Island

Elspeth Cameron Ritchie, M.D., M.P.H.
Professor of Psychiatry, Uniformed Services University of the Health Sciences, Bethesda, Maryland; Chief Medical Officer, Department of Mental Health of Washington, D.C.

Gail E. Robinson, M.D.

Professor of Psychiatry and of Obstetrics and Gynecology, University of Toronto Faculty of Medicine; Director, Women's Mental Health Program, University Health Network, Toronto General Hospital, Toronto, Ontario, Canada

Jo-Ellyn M. Ryall, M.D.

Associate Professor of Clinical Psychiatry, Washington University School of Medicine in St. Louis, Missouri

Altha J. Stewart, M.D.

President, Stewart Behavioral Health Associates, Memphis, Tennessee; Medical Director, Women's National Basketball Association

Ann Marie Sullivan, M.D.

Clinical Professor, Department of Psychiatry, Mount Sinai School of Medicine, New York, New York; Senior Vice President, Queens Health Network, New York City Health and Hospitals Corporation, New York, New York

Amy Ursano, M.D.

Associate Training Director for Child and Adolescent Psychiatry, University of North Carolina at Chapel Hill School of Medicine, Chapel Hill, North Carolina

Disclosure of Interests

The contributors to this book have indicated a financial interest in or other affiliation with a commercial supporter, a manufacturer of a commercial product, a provider of a commercial service, a nongovernmental organization, and/or a government agency, as listed below:

Andrea M. Brownridge, J.D., M.S., M.D.—*Affiliation:* America Women's Medical Association Resident Division, Treasurer.

Deborah Deas, M.D., M.P.H.—*Speaker's Bureau/Consultant:* Eli Lilly.

Mary Jane England, M.D.—*Board of Directors:* Healthways, Nashville, TN; WSF, Ann Arbor, MI.

Geetha Jayaram, M.D., M.B.A.—*Consultant:* One-time consultation on community psychiatry for Janssen Pharmaceutica.

Donna M. Norris, M.D.—*Board of Directors:* Coverys, a medical professional mutual insurance company.

Elspeth Cameron Ritchie, M.D., M.P.H.—*Consultant:* Consultation on posttraumatic stress disorder for Major League Baseball. *Speaker's Honoraria:* Institute of Disaster Mental Health, Las Vegas Psychiatry Society, Missouri School of Social Work.

Altha J. Stewart, M.D.—*Consultant:* Selection Committee for Fellowship in Health Disparities, Pfizer, Inc.

The following contributors to this volume indicated that they had no competing interests during the year preceding manuscript submission.

Mary E. Barber, M.D.
Crystal R. Bullard, M.D.
Esperanza Díaz, M.D.
M. J. Doherty, Ph.D.
Anita S. Everett, M.D.
Ellen Haller, M.D.
Carol C. Nadelson, M.D.
Surinder Nand, M.D.
Cassandra F. Newkirk, M.D., M.B.A.
Patricia R. Recupero, J.D., M.D.
Vivian W. Pinn, M.D.
Annelle B. Primm, M.D., M.P.H.
Gail E. Robinson, M.D.
Jo-Ellyn M. Ryall, M.D.
Ann Marie Sullivan, M.D.
Amy Ursano, M.D.

Preface

WOMEN *in Psychiatry: Personal Perspectives* chronicles the personal journeys of twenty-one women physicians as they pursue psychiatric training, develop professionally, and attain leadership in psychiatry across a broad spectrum of the field, including clinical practice, research, medical education, and administration.

This book grew out of a 2007 American Psychiatric Association (APA) Special Presidential Symposium: *Women Leaders in the APA and Beyond.* The presenters, all women from varied backgrounds and areas of expertise, spoke candidly and personally about their life experiences as women and as psychiatrists. This symposium generated extensive audience participation. The editors, also participants in the symposium, recognized the need for more opportunities to explore and understand the depth and breadth of the challenges that women face in psychiatry. At that same time, the editors were struck by these women's willingness to share personal narratives about their lives in such a public venue.

Based on the positive audience response to this successful symposium, the editors invited a group of women psychiatrists representing various psychiatric career stages, including medical student, resident, early career, mid-career, and senior psychiatrist, to contribute chapters for this book. These women are distinguished in their diverse professional areas of expertise and they represent a wide range of backgrounds prior to entering psychiatry. These twenty-one chapter authors represent only a subset of the many women leaders in psychiatry.

Approximately 31% of all physicians and surgeons in the United States are women and approximately 34% of psychiatrists are women, according to the U.S. Department of Labor and the American Medical Association. Significantly, the APA has experienced a nearly fourfold increase in the number of women in the organization since the mid-1970s. In 1975, 12% of APA members were women; in 2009, that number had increased to 35%. More than half of psychiatry residents are women; in the past fifteen years the percentage of women psychiatry residents increased from 45% to 55%. This changing presence of women in medicine necessitates more resources to assist women in considering their choices and addressing challenges within the field. This book is a contribution toward fulfilling that need.

When we began this book, some questioned the requirement for the personal nature of the narratives. For some, this expectation contradicted the orthodoxy of psychiatric training to be less self-disclosing. Several women whom we contacted suggested that meeting this request for candor would be too risky, with such personal exposure possibly placing their professional careers in jeopardy. As a result, several women chose not to participate in this book project.

The authors provide synopses of their professional and life challenges, with special reflections on personal and family life decisions that influenced their careers. In addition, they discuss the impact that their identities and background have had on their careers in psychiatry. Factors addressed include cultural and linguistic background, race, ethnicity, sexual orientation, religion, marital status, subspecialty, place of employment, and work setting. The authors reflect on the challenges associated with being a woman psychiatrist and their pursuit of life and work balance. All share the lessons they learned and provide recommendations on what they found helpful in achieving their goals of personal and professional fulfillment.

These chapters present several common themes among women professionals both within and outside the field of psychiatry, including handling pregnancy and motherhood in training and in professional life and the challenges associated with aspirations of career advancement while juggling work and family priorities. Another common theme was strain between women and men in a field dominated by men. This was particularly pronounced among women from diverse cultural backgrounds.

The authors describe various styles of leadership that provide a range of different strategies to accomplish goals. A surprise to the editors was the number of authors who were active in or who lived through the struggle for civil rights in this country. Their consciousness and conscientiousness exemplify the important role of women in correcting inequities in our society, utilizing leadership with a humanistic approach. This focus on the human condition is in alignment with a career in psychiatric medicine.

This is a book for women who are considering a career in psychiatry or other areas of medicine. It is also a book for spouses and partners of women in medicine and psychiatry. Each story is special in its narrative style and content. We, the editors, are indebted to the contributing authors for embracing the opportunity to tell their stories so that others might benefit from learning about the early life of each psychiatrist and how she chose her path, surmounted obstacles, and managed challenges along the way.

Donna M. Norris, M.D.
Geetha Jayaram, M.D., M.B.A.
Annelle B. Primm, M.D., M.P.H.

Acknowledgments

WE wish to express our sincerest gratitude to the members of our distinguished editorial advisory board, who are outstanding psychiatrist leaders and mentors in their own right. Their names are listed on page ii.

We are indebted to Alison Bondurant, M.A., Associate Director of the American Psychiatric Association Office of Minority and National Affairs, whose coordinating talent and gentle persistence were vital in bringing this book to fruition. Also, the completion of *Women in Psychiatry* would not have been possible without the research and editorial assistance of Rosa Bracey, M.S., Executive Assistant, and Deborah Cohen, M.B.A., Research Projects Manager, both of the APA Office of Minority and National Affairs.

Foreword

THROUGH the achievements and reflections of accomplished women psychiatrists in private practice, teaching institutions, hospitals, public health treatment programs, and leadership positions, this book illustrates the wide array of professional positions and activities open to women in a career in psychiatry. In addition, the frankly presented personal stories of the twenty-one women featured in this book illustrate a variety of strategies these women have used to meet the challenges they faced in balancing their private lives with their professional lives and in overcoming barriers to their development and advancement as women professionals in medical careers.

The featured women represent diverse backgrounds, ethnicities, positions, career pathways, and accomplishments. They were asked to lend insight into their career paths by describing pivotal events and decisions that shaped their careers as scientists, commenting on mentoring experiences, and discussing their perspective on how to balance personal and professional responsibilities. Some women also provide details on their career milestones, scientific accomplishments, or other inspirational observations about being a woman in science. These personal profiles represent perspectives throughout their life cycles.

The autobiographical information indicates where an interest in science or medicine can lead when combined with determination, guidance, experience, mentoring, perseverance, and organizational support. Many of these women have served as mentors to other women and men, in addition to having benefited from mentoring themselves, which, in many cases, led to their pursuit of a career in psychiatry and to advancement in their profession.

These women have earned the respect with which they are regarded, as their personal profiles demonstrate. That respect was not always granted to women in psychiatry and other medical fields. The historical context is important in understanding that until recent decades, despite irrefutable evidence that women in the biomedical professions are capable, they were few in most fields with the exceptions of nursing, dental hygiene, and elementary science teaching.

With the swelling of the women's movement in the 1980s, government agencies, universities, and other sectors began to question why there were so few women in medical fields. In 1992, one of the first meetings on the status of women in science and health careers was convened by the newly established Office of Research on Women's Health of the National Institutes of Health (NIH). The public hearing and workshop of that meeting, Recruitment, Retention, Reentry, and Advancement of Women in Biomedical Careers,[1] gave credibility to the importance of improving the representation of women in medicine and other health and research sciences. At that workshop, the dual roles of women in their professional and personal lives, and the need for mentoring, role models, and equity of professional rewards (e.g., salaries, promotions, advancement opportunities) were emphasized as concerns, and continue to be foremost in discussions of supporting women in medicine today.

The NIH and the medical and professional communities have directed continuous efforts toward inspiring women to enter medical and scientific fields and to redress the discriminatory climate that many women have experienced in their attempts to succeed and advance professionally with fulfilling personal lives. These efforts have met with much success in some fields but lesser, although still hopeful, achievements for women in other biomedical fields. During the past forty years, there has been steady growth in the number of women entering biomedical careers, and entering classes for medical studies and other life science doctoral programs now are composed of about fifty percent women. In 2008, about one-third of physicians who identified themselves as practicing psychiatry in the United States were women, and the diversity of their approaches to the practice of psychiatry is encouragingly illustrated by the women represented in this book.

In spite of the increased entry of women into medicine and science, there has not been a corresponding increase in women in leadership positions; there are still challenges for women in demanding medical careers in the context of organizational structures that have not all evolved to support the somewhat unique realities for women who more often have multiple demanding responsibilities as physicians, scientists, and family care providers. As emphasized in a 2007 report by the National Academies, *Beyond Bias and Barriers: Fulfilling the Potential of Women in Academic Science and Engineering,* there continues to be a loss of women from along the career pipeline in medicine and science.[2] The National Academies report challenged universities, professional societies, federal agencies, and Congress to take action to address these issues. NIH, in its role as the lead agency in the U.S. Department of Health and Human Services supporting biomedical

---

[1]Summarized in the report *Women in Biomedical Careers: Dynamics of Change* (NIH Publ No 95-3565). Bethesda, MD, Office of Research on Women's Health, National Institutes of Health, 1995.

research, has established a Working Group on Women in Biomedical Careers to develop meaningful and tangible actions that can assist women in fulfilling their potential in biomedical careers (http://womeninscience .nih.gov/). This working group has sponsored several conferences to determine and illustrate successful strategies to promote the advancement of women, including a workshop titled *National Leadership Workshop on Mentoring Women in Biomedical Careers,* which reemphasized the importance of being a mentor and having a mentor, and of having an identifiable role model or models.[3]

The women in this book provide advice to women in psychiatric careers. Many emphasize the importance of finding a mentor because mentoring was a major aid to them at all levels of their career development. That these women represent the continuum from early career stages to advanced leadership roles, sharing what has inspired as well as what has challenged them, provides a wealth of personal perspectives that readers can enjoy as well as learn from. This is an inspirational and educational document that women and men, including those in medicine and those in other careers, can value through an appreciation of the recounting of personal and professional experiences that made a difference.

Vivian W. Pinn, M.D.
Associate Director for Research on Women's Health
Director, Office of Research on Women's Health
National Institutes of Health
U.S. Department of Health and Human Services

---

[2]Committee on Maximizing the Potential of Women in Academic Science and Engineering, National Academy of Sciences, National Academy of Engineering, and Institute of Medicine: *Beyond Bias and Barriers: Fulfilling the Potential of Women in Academic Science and Engineering.* Washington, DC, The National Academies Press, 2007.

[3]National Institutes of Health Working Group on Women in Biomedical Careers and the Office of Research on Women's Health: Meeting proceedings of the National Leadership Workshop on Mentoring Women in Biomedical Careers, Bethesda, MD, November 2007 (NIH Publ No 09-6364). Available at: http:// womeninscience.nih.gov/mentoring. Accessed September 26, 2011.

Introduction

THROUGHOUT history, women's accomplishments have more often been connected with their relationships with men or to their childbearing functions than based on their own efforts. Their achievements have often been ignored by historians, attributed to husbands, brothers, or sons or to anonymous sources. Women's roles in health care throughout history, however, have been as healers, caretakers, midwives, pharmacists, abortionists, physicians, witches, nurses, counselors, and "wise women."

For as long as 6,000 years there has been evidence of women's roles as priestess-physicians. There were women physicians in ancient Egypt, Greece, and Rome. As early as 400 C.E., women founded hospitals and worked in public health, but the Church soon silenced them. However, there are reports dating back to at least the eleventh century of women studying and practicing medicine, and even assuming leadership positions. Trotula, an eleventh-century physician at the University of Salerno, Italy, was the author of important obstetrics and gynecology texts and headed a department of diseases of women. Her work was, until recently, more often attributed to her husband or sons. At about the same time, Hildegard of Bingen was well known as an abbess philosopher, composer, and scientific scholar who wrote medical textbooks, including in them concepts of normal and abnormal psychology. Women became physicians and practiced medicine in medieval Europe, but the Inquisition eliminated them from higher education and careers. Women doctors, women pharmacists, and other medical women were accused of witchcraft and were severely punished.

By the sixteenth century women again became active in health care. The need for attention to people with mental illness began to be acknowledged at this time, and the Sisters of Charity cared for them. Soon French institutions began to train nurses to care for mental patients. The connection between physical and mental health was made in the seventeenth century by a Swiss woman, Barbara von Roll, who pioneered in "psychosomatic medicine." By the mid-nineteenth century many wives of asylum superintendents (the first psychiatrists) began to open their homes to entertain asylum patients to "calm a fevered mind." This "moral treatment" reformation was led by Dorothea Dix, whose efforts brought a new era of reform in the treatment of people with mental illness.

During the early years of the U.S. colonies and until the mid-nineteenth century, women were midwives and in "irregular" practices of medicine, since they did not have formal training or degrees. When, in 1765, the first medical school in the colonies was opened at the University of Pennsylvania, it did not admit women. In 1847 Elizabeth Blackwell became the first woman admitted to a "regular" medical school in the United States (Geneva Medical College in western New York), and in 1850 a group of Quakers founded the first women's medical college in the world, the Female (later *Woman's*) Medical College of Pennsylvania. Ann Preston enrolled in the first class and later became the first woman dean. Shortly thereafter, there were three all-women's medical colleges in the United States: Boston Female Medical College (which is now Boston University), Woman's Medical College of Pennsylvania (now Drexel University), and one at the University of Cincinnati. The first European medical schools to accept women were the University of Zurich (1864) and the University of Paris (1868).

The idea that women weren't suited to medicine persisted despite their increasing presence in the profession. Even in 1873, Harvard Professor Edward Clarke stated that "higher education for women produces monstrous brains and puny bodies" in their offspring. Despite this belief, women persevered and leaders emerged. Mary Putnam Jacobi was elected to the New York Academy of Medicine in 1871, and in 1875, Emeline Cleveland, the dean of the Woman's Medical College of Pennsylvania, was the first known woman physician to perform major surgery in the United States. The American Medical Association admitted a woman to membership in 1876, and by 1890 thirty-five U.S. medical schools admitted women. By 1900, six percent of U.S. physicians were women. The Johns Hopkins School of Medicine was able to open its doors in 1893 when prominent women provided financing with the agreement that women be admitted using the same criteria as for men.

Despite their increasing acceptance by the latter part of the nineteenth century, women continued to have difficulty obtaining hospital admitting privileges and difficulty joining medical societies. This led to the movement to start their own hospitals, medical societies, and a medical school. Elizabeth Blackwell and her sister Emily, also a physician, had opened the New York Infirmary for Women and Children in 1856, and its Women's Medical College in 1868. Women, however, continued to be marginalized and isolated, so in 1915 the American Medical Women's Association was founded by Dr. Bertha Van Hoosen. Even in 1925, only twenty-four percent of U.S. hospitals with internships approved by the American Medical Association accepted women.

Currently women constitute half of all medical students and one-third of academic medical faculties, but only a small percentage are leaders in academic professional organizations. Women are slowly moving into traditionally male-dominated fields of medicine, but even in those specialties with a substantial percentage of women trainees and practitioners (pediatrics, ob-gyn, and internal medicine) they do not hold many department chairs or other leadership positions. Many hypotheses have been proposed to explain this apparent paradox. They include the structure of the system (by and for men), gender bias/discrimination, socialization, work-family balance, preference, and biology/genetics. As in most situations, there is no one explanation, but many variables contribute.

My own leadership in medicine and psychiatry began early in my life but the civil rights movement, the rise of feminism, and the Vietnam War protests in the United States in the 1960s and 1970s fueled societal changes and social consciousness. When I entered medical school in 1957, there were two women in my class, and four out of twenty-four in my residency program. But I was fortunate to have Dr. Grete Bibring, the first woman chair of a Harvard medical department, as a supervisor. There were several important women in the department, including Dr. Malkah Notman, who became a supervisor and then a collaborator for the rest of our careers. Our commitment to women's reproductive rights and the issue of violence against women sparked work in the areas of abortion and rape crisis intervention.

The contribution of mentors, mostly males, to my career has been immeasurable. I was appointed to the Harvard Medical School Admissions Committee by one and nominated to be an officer in the Massachusetts Psychiatric Society by another. Their early support and my decision to take risks led to other leadership positions in academic and organizational psychiatry, including my winning the APA presidency in 1984, as the first woman and 114th president of the APA.

It was not easy or seamless, but the support and encouragement of my family, mentors, colleagues, friends, and children propelled me. At a large international meeting in Mexico City when I was APA president, the male presidents of psychiatric organizations from around the world were taking turns delivering greetings. When I was to speak, the last speaker of the group, the lights suddenly dimmed and everyone disappeared from the room. The opening session had ended. Perhaps I didn't look like a president! Over and over my women colleagues and I have heard "you don't look like"—a president, a dean, a chair, a chief executive officer (CEO), a governor, an NIMH director. We understood that attributes that are valued in men—assertiveness, ambition, tenacity—although viewed as positive for men, are viewed as negative for women.

My appointment as editor-in-chief and later CEO of American Psychiatric Publishing, Inc. (APPI) was viewed as risky even though I had no more or less experience than the men being considered. I knew that failure was not an option, and I persevered. APPI flourished.

This book is testimony to the progress that women have made in many areas of psychiatry since the beginning of the feminist movement of the 1970s. The authors of these chapters have had rich and diverse careers and life experiences, as well as many leadership positions. Some have led medical organizations, some have chaired departments, and some have become deans, CEOs, and leaders in education and research. The stories told by each author are moving and inspirational. These women have changed the face of psychiatry!

I say this with cautious optimism. History teaches us that progress is not made smoothly or continuously. With each step forward, we often move another backward before we move ahead more definitively. Those starting on this journey must learn from the past, and we must all continue to support the development of future women leaders, not yielding to societal ambivalence toward them. As Nancy Andrews, M.D., Ph.D., Dean of Duke University School of Medicine, has said: "If we can find cures to cancer and understand the human genome, why should it be hard to believe that we can fix the culture of our profession?"

Carol C. Nadelson, M.D.
Professor of Psychiatry
Harvard Medical School

Bibliography

Boulis AK, Jacobs JA: The Changing Face of Medicine: Women Doctors and the Evolution of Health Care in America. Ithaca, NY, Cornell University Press, 2008

Dickstein L, Nadelson C: Women Physicians in Leadership Roles. Washington, DC, American Psychiatric Press, 1986

Drachman V: Hospital With a Heart. Ithaca, NY, Cornell University Press, 1984

More E: Restoring the Balance. Cambridge, MA, Harvard University Press, 1999

More E, Fee E, Parry M: Women Physicians and the Cultures of Medicine. Baltimore, MD, Johns Hopkins Press, 2009

Nadelson C: Breaking the barriers: the first woman APA president. Presented at the annual meeting of the American Psychiatric Association, San Francisco, CA, May 2009

Nadelson C: Organizational strategies to develop the careers of women physicians. Presented at the Pioneering Women Physicians conference sponsored by the Massachusetts Medical Society, Waltham, MA, June 2009

Nadelson C: Women in medicine: pathways to leadership. Alma Dea Morani Award Lecture for Renaissance Woman Award presented by the Foundation for the History of Women in Medicine, Countway Library, Harvard Medical School, 10/9/08

Nadelson C, Notman M: Women as health care professionals, in Encyclopedia of Bioethics. Edited by Reich WT. New York, Macmillan, 1978, pp 1713–1720

Part I
The Early Years

■|■

Chapter 1

Embarking on a Career Path

Persistence, Process, and Psychiatry

Andrea M. Brownridge, J.D., M.S., M.D.

As A FIFTEEN-YEAR-OLD, while ambling along the aisles of a local flea market in my hometown of Atlanta, Georgia, with my mother, I uncovered the following Calvin Coolidge quote, laid out on Egyptian-style parchment paper:

> Nothing in this world can take the place of persistence. Talent will not; nothing is more common than unsuccessful people with talent. Genius will not; unrewarded genius is almost a proverb. Education will not; the world is full of educated derelicts. Persistence and determination alone are omnipotent.

President Coolidge was the only U.S. president (1923–1929) to be born on the Fourth of July, and his published views reflect a man ahead of his time who freely expressed his independence. In 1924, he spoke out in favor of the civil rights of African Americans, denouncing a claim that the United States was a "white man's country." As a teenager, I had not a clue as to the astounding impact his legendary quote would have on my life. For many years I reflected on his choice of words, seeking to appreciate the underlying meaning on a higher level. In fact, I still ruminate over the genius of his declaration, pursuing greater significance all the while.

As I embark on a promising career in psychiatry, today I truly appreciate the role that persistence has played in realizing my lifelong dream to serve as a physician. As early as five years of age, I was heard to say "I want to be a doctor when I grow up." I frankly have no recollection of reciting this ambition, but I do know that for as long as I can recall, I envisioned a life in medicine.

Less than stellar grades in the life sciences never detracted from my aspiration. While I had a mastery of the applied sciences of chemistry, physics, and engineering, the rote memorization required to excel in the biological sciences eluded me. Following high school, I attended Georgia Institute of Technology in my hometown of Atlanta. Interestingly, I had absolutely no plans to study engineering; medicine was in my future, and the premedical track of biology was the natural choice. However, no sooner had I declared my major than I got the word from my mother, a physician, that I should consider a major I "could fall back on." I am still amazed by my mother's uncanny ability to gently steer me along life's journey, all the time celebrating my strengths and challenging my faults. And I do believe it was in recognition of my need for continued growth in the life sciences that she "recommended" I consider an undergraduate pursuit more in line with my talent and interests at the time. Sure enough, industrial engineering and its solid corollary in health systems was the perfect fold for my growing interest in business and management and my ultimate ambition to practice medicine.

Plan B

As usually happens when one pursues her passion, I excelled at my engineering coursework as I simultaneously pursued premedical coursework. When I was not accepted into medical school in two consecutive years, I was very disappointed. After graduating from Georgia Tech in 1995, I was fortunate to work as an office manager in my mother's family practice clinic, and my success at managing the office (thanks to my undergraduate certification in health systems) was rewarding as I prepared to define and execute Plan B—attain my law degree. Certain that Plan B was simply a temporary detour along the path to medicine, I would be remiss if I failed to disclose that my mother, too, is a dual doctorate holder in law and medicine. I can scarcely credit my academic successes to my own ingenuity;

instead, I was most certainly blessed to have such ambitious steps in which to follow. James Baldwin (1961/1993, p. 61) remarked, "Children have never been very good at listening to their elders, but they have never failed to imitate them."

In 1996 after the two unsuccessful attempts at medical school admission, I determined that rather than growing increasingly discouraged by these setbacks, I would pursue what I knew to be a rewarding academic pursuit. As a student of the law, I grew immensely both personally and academically. I uncovered new gifts as a result of my participation in moot court, whereby law students compete in simulated court proceedings, drafting legal briefs and crafting persuasive oral arguments to be presented before a panel of judges. I also began to try my hand at advanced leadership opportunities by serving on my local chapter's executive board of the Black Law Students Association and being vice president of moot court competitions at my law school. Until this point in time, I had traditionally served as a fiscal officer in the majority of my extracurricular affiliations; however, with increased confidence and cultivation of newly realized talents I set out to expand my horizons on multiple fronts.

Through the age of twenty-five, obesity had been a great personal obstacle for me. For the majority of my teen years I was emotionally comfortable with my more than voluptuous frame. Whittling down to a healthier size was a noble aspiration, but certainly not one over which I ruminated. Despite my physician-mother's consistent reminders of the sequelae of obesity, including hypertension and diabetes, I continued my indulgences paying little heed to her very real concerns. And frankly, there was no shocking day of reckoning for me that heralded my triumph over obesity. The story goes as follows: While preparing to sit for the bar exam, I knew that I needed to execute to the highest degree of academic discipline if I were to pass on my first attempt. So in addition to my ten-hour-a-day study regimen and for the purpose of alleviating stress, I hit the gym and began a cardiovascular and strength training regimen which left me sixty-seven pounds lighter one year later. But like so many, I discovered that much of my success had more to do with *emotions* than the actual *motion* itself. I began to exercise more for my emotional well-being than even my physical well-being, and soon learned that unhinged emotions were the root of many of my feeding overindulgences. Of course, to this day I continue to fight the good fight, and simply count my blessings that I have more good days than bad.

Lesson Learned

In 2000 I commenced my law practice, and my first job was with a workers' compensation insurance defense firm. This was yet another ironic moment, as I distinctly recall declining to enroll in a workers' compensation course in law school through adamant lack of interest. Sound familiar? The story of my life…visceral disdain *equals* future course! For the next five years I would hone my legal skills investigating insurance claims, deposing employees and physicians, and defending insurance companies at trial. Because the focal point of any workers' compensation matter typically revolves around the physical injuries alleged by the employee and subsequent medical care and treatment, I spent a good deal of time examining medical records in preparation of a sustainable defense. One experience that was particularly challenging involved an employee who sustained a back injury. Because the employee was without legal counsel, I had the opportunity to communicate with her directly on behalf of my client, the insurer. What made this case so peculiar was the inconsistency between the symptoms the employee reported and the medical findings. After her extensive diagnostic testing, physical therapy, and pharmacological therapy, the treating providers were drawing a blank as to the cause of her increasingly worsening symptoms, because the radiography, computed tomography, and electromyography results were negative. Over a five-month period her symptoms progressed from low back muscle spasms to incontinence, lower extremity weakness, and excruciating low back pain. It was only after the patient was evaluated by a second neurologist that magnetic resonance imaging revealed the presence of a thoracic tumor impinging on the spinal cord. Soon thereafter, the patient underwent emergency surgery to remove the tumor. I, the claims adjuster, and certainly the patient were stunned by this turn of events. While there was no doubt that the tumor was unrelated to her original injury, it was also clear that a multitude of medical providers had missed the mark of accurate diagnosis in the face of the patient's increasingly worsening symptoms. For my part, I too grew frustrated in working with this unrepresented employee because I had only the opinions of the authorized treating providers on which to rely in refusing unauthorized diagnostic tests. Fortunately, the patient fully recovered and the insurer was not held liable for medical expenses unrelated to the original injury. And I learned a valuable lesson: Never be so overconfident or so reticent that you fail to challenge yourself or others in the face of incongruity.

Back on Track

After completing law school and passing the bar exam, I set out to practice law for no less than two years. I have always held some regret that I never worked as an industrial engineer after college. I did apply my knowledge in my work as office manager at my mother's family practice clinic, but

I would have valued an authentic experience as an engineer. Seeking not to relive that regret, I concentrated solely on sharpening my legal skills for three years. At that point, I became determined to apply to medical school again. As one would expect, I am often questioned about the reason behind my transition from law to medicine. The simple truth is that while I enjoyed the practice of law, for me medicine was a calling. With this insight, I forged ahead and, with the strong support of my family, close friends, and law colleagues, I reapplied to medical school. I cannot explain the immense joy I experienced when I was accepted by Chicago Medical School at Rosalind Franklin University of Medicine and Science. Poet Jack Gilbert (2005) asked, "Why do so many settle for so little? I don't understand why they're not greedy for what's inside them." My relentless pursuit of a career in medicine was derived solely from a profound conviction that long ago God buried in me a yearning to be a physician and my assignment was to take the necessary steps to realize this vision.

I would love to share that I graduated at the top of my class and never doubted my capacity to be a successful student of medicine. However, the first year of basic sciences was difficult as I made the mental adjustment from professional to student. I recall that my first medical school lecture in physiology was strikingly reminiscent of a physics lecture at Georgia Tech. For the life of me, I could not quite make the connection between electric potential and the human body. But of course I would soon come to learn that ions count everywhere, whether it be in the human heart or in solution. Even so, as my first year drew to a close, I was keenly aware that a piece of the puzzle was missing. No longer operating under the misguided belief that I would be transformed instantaneously into über student upon medical school acceptance, I pondered how to right my academic course and strike a balance that maximized my strengths. Seeking to connect with the campus community, I involved myself in the Christian Medical and Dental Association and the Student National Medical Association. It was not long before I grew comfortable in my new student skin.

In conjunction with my medical studies, I enrolled in a dual-degree healthcare administration and management master of science program. This was just one of the exceptional opportunities afforded by attending an institution dedicated to interprofessional medical and health care education. Learning alongside future podiatrists, nurse anesthetists, physical therapists, pathology assistants, nutritionists, and business people, I advanced my knowledge and skills in collaborative interprofessional practice. Moreover, I gained an appreciation of the academic rigors of other health care disciplines and how, collectively, an interprofessional team enhances the care and treatment of the patient. During the summer following the first year of study, I learned of an exceptional experience in addiction psychiatry. Looking back, it is difficult to say when I began to seriously contemplate psychiatry. While my mother often alluded to my possessing the makings of a good psychiatrist, I regularly dismissed psychiatry as an option, believing the field to be not only emotionally overwhelming, but also a bit boring—can you imagine? But recall my mother's uncanny gift…she hit the nail on the head; for after my summer experience at the Circle Program, I was sold on my future as a psychiatrist.

Round and Round

The Circle Program at the Colorado Mental Health Institute at Pueblo is a fully integrated dual-diagnosis ninety-day inpatient treatment program for men and women, ages eighteen to sixty-five, who have failed to respond to all other treatments. Diagnosed with an Axis I mental illness and substance dependence, all Circle Program patients are expected to participate in an intensive cognitive-behavioral program involving more than forty weekly hours of group therapy, homework assignments, and peer-led therapeutic community groups. Sponsored by the Annenberg Physician Training Program in Addictive Disease, two students had the unprecedented opportunity to step into the role of patients in this program. I was one such student. As an experiential learning exercise, my tenure at the Circle Program was unparalleled.

One of the mainstays of the program was the peer-led therapeutic community treatment, in which patients met four days per week. Patients write up themselves and their peers for rule violations in the form of "gifts." All "gifts" are written up on a small slip of paper folded up and signed by the giver. The first "gift" I received read: "Andrea failed to push her chair in at breakfast." The idea behind "gifts" was to hold one another accountable for even the most trivial transgressions. Patients move up through the levels of the system, based on their participation in the program and their "gifts." It stands to reason that "gift-giving" was one of the more precarious tasks within our small community. First, in order to "gift" another, one really had to acknowledge one's own shortcomings. Second, conflicts could often arise following gift-giving, as I would soon learn.

Like the Circle Program patients, I underwent a search of all my personal possessions and was only granted a weekend pass as I advanced up the Circle level system by demonstrating appropriate behavior with active participation. I cannot overemphasize the authenticity of this experience; two public phones with calls limited to ten minutes duration, no Internet access, clothing quotas (seven to ten pairs of underwear), no Listerine or any other alcohol-containing personal products, and assigned shower times. During check-in when my possessions were inventoried (so long,

Listerine), staff members remarked that I was very brave to be living on the wards. Certainly, this gave me pause. Fortunately, Dr. Libby Stuyt, an addiction psychiatrist and the medical director, was on hand to quell my increasing anxiety by explaining that there were no acute cases on the unit, although there were some "cutters." By day three, I melded into the Circle Program flow and was growing quite comfortable socializing with my peers. Besides some early skepticism as to why a student would *voluntarily commit* herself to a drug treatment program, generally I was well received for my candor and nonjudgmental listening ear as we all shared our life experiences with addiction. Coincidentally, I had recently learned that a close family member was battling a cocaine addiction. The range of dual diagnoses at Circle included alcohol, heroin, cocaine, and methamphetamine dependence, and the psychiatric diagnoses of schizophrenia, schizoaffective disorder, anxiety, depression, and bipolar disorders as well as personality disorders. Generally, more than seventy percent of Circle patients had an Axis II personality disorder, with antisocial and borderline personality disorders being the most common. And for me, this is where the real challenge began.

In hindsight, many of the striking behaviors that I witnessed now seem curiously appropriate considering the probable diagnoses of my Circle peers; however, as a rising second-year medical student, I was completely undone by what seemed to be acts of callous cruelty and untenable attention seeking and grandiosity. During a behavior awareness group, one patient self-reported that she was coming to terms with how evil and malicious she really was, yet she was not sure how to fix it. "Personality disorders are the easiest to treat, but the hardest to cure," the group therapist offered. And this certainly hit home by week two as I strived to manage a personal conflict with one resident in particular. From day one, it was clear that this female resident was the "queen bee" of the Circle Program, if only in her own mind. While I would later learn that she had significant character pathology, as a novice student my first impression was that she simply desired a healthy dose of attention. It was not long before I realized she demanded a *toxic* dose of attention and, like my peers, I grew exhausted by her manipulative antics. With nothing to lose (in my mind), I challenged her via the gift system to cease her cruel comments directed at a fellow peer suffering from the most profound melancholic depression I have ever seen. No sooner had I "gifted" Queen Bee than I became her target. Not one to stray from a valid and mature exchange of positions, I was soon engaged in an active verbal hallway discussion with her as she proclaimed that it was my fault she did not receive her weekend pass—of course.

The dust eventually settled, and true to experiential learning, I met with the program's medical director to review and evaluate my personal progression. In encouraging me to process the unique nature of my situation, Dr. Stuyt called on me to embrace the overall experience, positive and negative, and grow from it. She reminded me that if I should indeed pursue a career in psychiatry I would be one of the few who could attest to the extreme patience and fortitude required when treating personality disorders, let alone living with them. I am incredibly proud that I not only survived thirty days at Circle but also gained an insider's view of addiction and the positive impact of cognitive-behavioral therapy in the management of disease.

Perfect Fit

At the close of the Circle Program I knew psychiatry was the perfect fit for my core values and skill set—something my mother apparently recognized long before I even fathomed a value system. While I cannot be certain, I would imagine that no other field of medicine is viewed with both apprehension and curiosity to the extent that psychiatry is. In my brief tenure as a psychiatry resident I have been regularly quizzed with the question "Why psychiatry?" Some speculate that I must be able to read minds and am reading theirs at that very moment; others assume I must have had a personal experience with mental illness; and of course a few, who require educating, say they did not know "psychologists" went to medical school. In explaining my career path in the simplest terms, I usually offer "What does one have without a sound mind?" Depression and other mood disorders are only the presenting symptom in many medical disorders, but they can be a dominant factor in the progression of medical comorbidities including coronary artery disease, cerebrovascular disease, and diabetes mellitus. Rather than being dismayed by the minority who attempt to delegitimize our profession, I instead am empowered by the reality that the body takes its direction from the mind and am encouraged that I have the good fortune to practice in a field that embraces the science and art of medicine.

    Witnessing my family's own battle with addiction certainly played its role in my early thoughts of pursuing a career in addiction psychiatry. I have always been keenly aware that for most, the decision to even try an illicit substance is not sheer whim but has more to do with some form of escape from their present circumstances. Even with this perspective, however, I could not help but wonder why my loved one would even have a trial run with a drug known to lead to such devastating consequences. While the reasons remain unclear in the ongoing battle, I am reassured by my Circle experience that with more than a little soul searching and earnest effort, people with addictions have a fighting chance with the support of family and friends and professional assistance.

There is no doubt that my protracted journey to medicine was by design—just not my design. In the thirty-two years that preceded my matriculation, each experience, each trial, and certainly every tribulation molded me into the woman I am today and the psychiatrist I will be tomorrow.

PRACTICAL TIPS FOR WOMEN IN PSYCHIATRY

- No one can do "you" better than you. Keep your vision out front and make your decisions as congruent with your priorities as possible.
- It's not about me. Everyone is important, but no one is indispensable.
- It's always darkest just before dawn.
- Sometimes tomorrow never comes! Enjoy the journey along the way. It may turn out to be even more important than the destination.
- It's not our circumstances that matter; it's our perspective.

References

Baldwin J: Fifth avenue, uptown: a letter from Harlem, in Nobody Knows My Name: More Notes of a Native Son (1961). New York, Vintage, 1993

Gilbert J: Jack Gilbert, The Art of Poetry No 91 (interview by Fay S). The Paris Review No 175, Fall/Winter 2005. Available at: http://www.theparisreview.org/back-issues/175. Accessed October 4, 2011.

Chapter 2

A Woman of Culture
and Compassion
From the Carolinas

Crystal R. Bullard, M.D.

I STAND AMAZED at how far I have come professionally as I begin the first year of my child and adolescent fellowship program at the University of South Carolina (USC). When I was approached about writing this chapter I was honored, yet in the next moment I began to think I did not have much to contribute as a thirty-year-old who has not begun her career. I then stopped and pondered my life over the past ten years and the challenges, successes, and opportunities I have had as a single Native American woman, and I realized that my story is quite interesting, to say the least! I am so grateful for the many doors of opportunity that have been opened to me. My desire to pursue psychiatry came to fruition from four influences in my life: my heritage, my family, my education, and my faith. These influences have significantly shaped my journey and represent my life's foundation. They have contributed to who I am today and will continue to guide my future.

My Heritage and Culture

I was born in December of 1980 to two of the most loving and supportive parents. I am the second oldest daughter of four girls. Many lightheartedly have pity for my father for having to be surrounded by so much estrogen. My parents were both public school educators. My father was a high school agriculture teacher and a farmer. He continues to farm 200 to 300 acres of land, cultivating corn, wheat, and soy beans. My mother is a retired elementary school teacher. After my birth, Mom left work to be a housewife and stay-at-home mother for nine years. My parents believed that the role of a wife and mother was significant in the home especially during early childhood and hence this decision was made. Every day, Mom took considerable time to teach us preschool material such as the ABCs, numbers, and nursery rhymes, as well as good manners, morals, and biblical principles. My parents are Christians and have always demonstrated their strong faith in God. They are my role models—the most influential people in my life.

My parents are both Native American. We are members of the Lumbee tribe. Our tribe is unique in comparison to others. The Lumbee nation is not well known in the United States. There are over 50,000 Lumbee Indians, the largest tribe east of the Mississippi River, and the majority of the tribe lives in southeastern North Carolina. The origin of the Lumbee is somewhat mysterious. There are several theories. One of the most accepted is that the Lumbee are descendants of the Lost Colony of English settlers that mysteriously disappeared from Roanoke Island in the early 1500s. Based on archeological, anthropological, and historical research, it is believed that the Europeans intermingled with local natives called Croatans on the coast of Virginia and migrated south. They eventually settled along the Lumber River in Robeson County, North Carolina. Some say the Lumbee derived from a mixture of various tribes, including the Cherokee and the Tuscarora. The federal government initially called our tribe Croatan. Later, further research changed what the government would name our tribe, and therefore the tribe was given several names, including Croatan, Cherokee Indians of Robeson County, and Cheraw. In 1950, the tribe organized a tribal government and voted to change the name of the tribe to *Lumbee*.

Many people assume that all Native American tribes live on a reservation, but this is not so with the Lumbee people. Over time the Lumbee became assimilated into European culture as a way of life. We adopted the European style of dress and the English language and Christian religion, among many other things. Specifically, by the late 1800s, most Lumbee were either of the Methodist or Baptist denomination. Even though the

Lumbee people had adopted the European culture, there was a distinct separation between the white race, Native Americans, and other minorities. Hence we were oppressed by the state and federal government, as many other Native American tribes were. For example, North Carolina passed a law in 1835 to prevent all members of Indian tribes from voting or owning firearms. We were greatly affected by this because we were incapable of influencing political power and unable to defend ourselves. During this time the Lumbee rebelled against the government, created conflicts, and gained the reputation of being rebels. The Lumbee people were also segregated from the whites. My dad remembers how the public restrooms were labeled in town: White, Black, or Indian.

Although it seems apparent that the federal government considered our ancestors Native Americans, they later denied, and still deny, that we are entitled to the rights of true Native Americans. Our tribe is recognized by North Carolina and by the federal government as American Indians. In 1956, the U.S. Congress passed the Lumbee Act, officially recognizing the natives of Robeson County and surrounding counties as the Lumbee Indians of North Carolina. However, in this bill, there is language that makes the Lumbee ineligible for financial support and services administered by the Bureau of Indian Affairs. Today, the Lumbee tribe continues to fight for full federal recognition.

We are grateful for the support we do receive through federal grant funding and state support, which have facilitated the establishment of many programs to improve our health care and education systems. Yet there still remains an unmet need. In Robeson County thirty percent of the population is below poverty level, and this includes a majority of the Lumbee. Unfortunately, the poverty is associated with a multitude of problems due to illicit drug use and associated crimes and violence. Of the 100 counties in North Carolina, our school systems are ranked at the bottom of the list. This is evident as our student's scores on standardized tests are compared to others across the nation. Most Lumbee people are accustomed to an unhealthy diet and get very little exercise. Heart disease, diabetes, and hypertension are rampant. There is a shortage of primary care physicians, and a much greater shortage of mental health providers and services compared to the need for them. Due to the strong religious influence in Lumbee communities, people often associate mental illness with their spiritual state. They seek either spiritual guidance and healing or none at all and often fear being labeled as "crazy" if they seek help from a psychiatrist.

One of my aspirations is to educate the public about mental illness. This includes encouraging pastors and other clergy to refer people to mental health professionals when it is appropriate. Another goal, held dear to my heart, is to make the public aware of the signs and symptoms of child abuse. I envision working with the school systems and organizations, such as parent-teacher associations, encouraging them to get involved in rescuing innocent children. With full federal recognition, our tribe plans to improve access to health care and enhance the education system.

My tribe is proud of its heritage. Our ancestors were forerunners who fought for equality and stood united for what was right. They believed that neither Native Americans nor African Americans should be oppressed. One of the most interesting events in Lumbee history actually gave us national and international media attention in 1958.

The Ku Klux Klan had organized a rally to be held in Maxton, North Carolina, a small town in Robeson County. Prior to the rally, the Klan burned a cross on the lawn of a Lumbee woman's home, a woman whom they claimed was having an affair with a white man. Prior to the rally, my father says he remembers how the word had spread throughout the community. His father refused to participate in this possibly dangerous encounter. The night of the rally, approximately fifty to a hundred Klansmen assembled. When Klan leader James "Catfish" Cole began to speak, a Lumbee man hidden in the swamps shot the one light burning at the meeting. Over 500 Lumbee men were surrounding the Ku Klux Klan. They began yelling and firing their guns into the air, then attacked the Klan with the intention of scaring them away from Lumbee territory. Most of the Klansmen fled into the swamps and only two were wounded. No one was killed. Following the attack, the Lumbee people celebrated by burning Ku Klux Klan regalia. Local, national, and international newspapers and magazines, including *Life* magazine, covered the story capturing pictures of the Lumbee people celebrating this victory.

A Proud Accomplishment

The Lumbee people are proud to be among the first tribes to build a college with the express purpose of educating Native Americans about how to become educators themselves. Founded and supported by the state of North Carolina, it was built in 1887 and was called Croatan Normal School. The college afforded the Lumbee people the opportunity to teach their own race. The name of the college changed many times; today it is known as the University of North Carolina at Pembroke, and it is the university where I received my bachelor's degree. It is one of the sixteen institutions that make up the University of North Carolina system. Due to the opportunity for many Lumbee Indians to receive a college degree, the Lumbee are some of the most highly educated Native Americans in our country. Numerous Lumbee Indians today have college, master's, and doctoral degrees.

I have always believed that education is the key to success. Education opens the mind to new possibilities, which therefore lead to more opportunities that might not otherwise be granted. As a tribe, we should be very grateful for the opportunity to become educated. As I mentioned, our tribe is unique in that the percentage of those educated in comparison to other tribes is impressive; yet there are still large numbers who have no desire to become educated.

The oppression of my ancestors affected tribal members in one of two ways; they either succumbed to their limited resources or were determined to persevere. I was blessed to be born into a family that fell into the latter category and were filled with determination. Their circumstances didn't hold them back. I remember my Grandmother Rose saying, "We were poor, but didn't realize we were poor." This was because the entire community was of the same socioeconomic status.

Grandmother Rose's dream was to receive an education. Her determination helped her persevere. With the support of her husband (my Grandfather Harvey) she would leave their home in the country and hitch a ride with someone going to Pembroke. She would then stay in Pembroke with her sister for the week, returning home to her family on the weekends. Today, this is only a short ride in an automobile, but at that time it was a longer journey with a mule and buggy. Through this she was able to see her dream achieved, and she became an elementary school teacher. My maternal grandfather, Conrad Oxendine, also received a college degree and later became a high school math teacher and a coach.

It is uncommon among the Lumbee to have two grandparents who graduated with a college degree. I often think my innate drive to push myself for success was inherited through both my paternal and maternal lineages. My grandparents made sacrifices to get a college degree just as I have persevered through college and medical school to obtain a doctorate. I am the first physician in my family and will be the second psychiatrist in the Lumbee tribe.

Present-Day Lumbee Culture at a Glance

Although the Lumbee tribe does not have reservation land, we are a people who stick together. Take a ride through the small rural town of Pembroke, North Carolina, and it will be evident that Pembroke is home of the Lumbee. Most of the tribal members continue to live very close to one another in a specific region along the Lumber River. The tribal council, organized in 1950, is also located in Pembroke. Each year the Lumbee tribe unites with other local tribes to host powwows and celebrate our heritage.

The largest cultural event of the year is Lumbee Homecoming, which is held during the week of the Fourth of July. There are many events including the Miss Lumbee pageant, in which the winner becomes an ambassador for the tribe for one year, doing public speaking and wearing a native crown and Lumbee regalia in powwows across the state. On the last day, approximately 25,000 Lumbee people gather together on the streets of Pembroke for a full day of festivities. Events include a five-kilometer race, a parade, a car show, and a powwow, with numerous vendors selling native jewelry, T-shirts, accessories, and various forms of native artwork such as the pine needle baskets that are specific to the Lumbee. The day ends with fireworks to celebrate both our culture and our nation's Independence Day.

I was raised in a small Lumbee community near the town of Pembroke. As a child, I attended an elementary school that was ninety-nine percent Lumbee; in high school the Lumbee students consisted of about eighty percent of the student population. For most of my life I have been surrounded by my own fellow native people. No one questioned my ethnicity. After I graduated from college and moved away from home for medical school, I began to be questioned quite often about my identity as Native American. I rarely use the term *American Indian* due to the large Indian American population (of South Asian ancestry) and the possibility of confusion. Several people have assumed I am Hispanic or white, but many have just asked me "Where are you from?"

As a third-year medical student, I realized that with each new rotation I was bound to meet someone who would question my identity. Fortunately, most people are very interested and begin asking more questions about my heritage. Instead of feeling offended or annoyed I view this as an opportunity to educate others about current-day Native Americans. It was interesting from my perspective because I finally realized as an adult that my background was quite different from "the norm."

As a physician, I am able to understand how cultural differences can affect the doctor-patient relationship. In my hometown, most of the Lumbee people flock to the Lumbee physicians. Many of our physicians are overworked, trying to provide services for such a large population. I can relate to patients who want a doctor that understands their cultural background. This is particularly important to patients receiving psychiatric services, and I value the interest in training culturally competent physicians.

Education

I graduated from the University of North Carolina at Pembroke, a small university which is now very racially and culturally diverse. There continues to be a significant population of Native American students, mostly Lumbee, but also students from other tribes in North Carolina. During my years in college, 25% of the student population was Native American. This is, however, a distorted view of the actual Native American population across the United States, which is only 1.4% of the U.S. population. In North Carolina overall, the Native American population is only 1%, yet this is still a larger percentage than in about three-quarters of the other U.S. states.

During my sophomore year, I pledged to a sorority called Alpha Pi Omega. It was established on September 1, 1994, and became the first Native American Greek letter organization founded in the United States. The vision for its foundation began in the hearts of four native women at the University of North Carolina at Chapel Hill. The mission of the sorority is "to create a strong sisterhood that will serve as a support for college women in today's society." Even though my sorority sisters and I came from various tribes, we had a strong bond to one another. It was as though we were all family even though I had never met some of those girls before. Now, seventeen years later, the sorority has spread westward to include thirteen chartered chapters with women representing more than seventy tribes nationwide. Therefore, since my social circle continued to be mostly Native American, I never felt much distinction as a minority.

Striving to do my best in school was a consistent goal throughout my life. Since both my parents have a college degree, I considered achieving an undergraduate education to be my minimum goal. I set out to realize my greatest potential and to really apply myself. It was my ambition to pursue graduate education and to make my parents proud. To become a leader in my community, be able to give back to my people, and set an example for the youth were other heartfelt desires. Through my Christian faith, the help of my supportive family, and my innate drive for success, I would achieve my goals.

While I was in high school, I enjoyed studying both math and science. I also had a love of art; drawing and painting continue to be among my pastimes. However, in thinking about a stable future career, I looked toward the sciences. In the eleventh grade I thought I might like to become a pharmacist, but through further research I changed my mind due to the limited interpersonal interactions pharmacists have with the public. As a relational person, I realized I would not enjoy a career that would not allow for one-on-one interaction. I find that I am often intrigued by others' life experiences.

I began to contemplate the idea of the medical field. Mind you, there are no doctors in my family and the thought of medical school seemed insurmountable. It brought about feelings of inadequacy. As a freshman in college, I thought "I will pursue the profession of a physician assistant." Not to undermine this profession, but I felt that this career path would be less intimidating, less demanding, and less challenging.

The Road to Psychiatry and My Mentors Along the Way

During the summer after my freshman year, I participated in a six-week summer program that placed me in a local family medicine practice to shadow both the physicians and physician assistants. I am so thankful for this summer experience because it finalized my decision to go to medical school.

At the practice, I met a family medicine physician named Dr. Robin Peace, a graduate of Brody School of Medicine at East Carolina University in North Carolina. Dr. Peace was a young African American woman truly admired by her patients. She was confident and intelligent, a woman who had overcome obstacles as a minority. Her patients often bragged about her and sometimes patients brought her small gifts such as baked goods or vegetables from their gardens to show their appreciation. I admired her interpersonal skills and I longed to become a physician just like her. One day, Dr. Peace inquired about my interest in medicine and my grades in school. She said to me, "Crystal, you have the potential to go to medical school, so why not do it?" I began to realize that if I became a physician's assistant, I might not reach my greatest potential and could possibly live my life regretting that decision. Talking about this with Dr. Peace gave me the confidence I needed to pursue medical school, and I will always be grateful for her support and encouragement.

Shortly after making the decision to apply to medical school, I was talking with my parents about my career goals. It was disappointing to hear the hesitation in their comments. My mother was concerned; how could I be a good wife and mother in the future while working in such a demanding, time-consuming career? Although they valued education and a rewarding, successful career, marriage, motherhood and faith/commitment to your local church were of equal importance. Worry filled my heart; I doubted they would support my decision to go to medical school. Regardless, I had a made-up mind and was determined to pursue my career dream.

Prior to my senior year in college, I participated in the Summer Program for Future Doctors at East Carolina University Brody School of Medicine. To my surprise, the director of the program was another young, successful African American woman who happened to be Dr. Robin Peace's close college friend. When I struggled with the demands of the program, she pulled me aside to encourage me to stay strong and work hard. She, too, became a mentor supporting me along this difficult journey.

Preparation for the Medical College Admissions Test (MCAT) was not easy. I had never been a person who scored well on standardized tests. My MCAT scores were low, but I did not give up. I dedicated many long hours in the library that summer studying to improve my scores. I had to sacrifice hanging out with friends and even family vacations. I remember one summer when my family went on a vacation to the Appalachian Mountains without me. My sisters felt sorry for me and made a video to show me how nice it was in their rented cabin. (Did my sisters really believe this would cover the sadness I felt from the loss of a much-needed vacation that I believed I deserved over them? Staying focused on a very-long-term goal is not easy.) During the moments of headaches and boredom from my eyes being glued to the books, I sometimes doubted that I would ever get into a medical school with such low scores. After many long hours of preparation, I retook the exam. My scores improved, but I still didn't consider them to be competitive.

In May 2003, I graduated from college, magna cum laude, with a degree in biology and chemistry with a biomedical emphasis. The day after graduation, I received a letter from the Brody School of Medicine stating I had not been accepted, but was placed on the waiting list. Several other medical schools had also denied my acceptance. I was heartbroken. I did not know what I would do for work, but I knew I would apply again to medical school the next year. (That's what you call determination—I was going to be the first doctor in my family.) Thankfully, I was hired by a local family medicine practice. The nursing staff trained me to take patients' signs, conduct various laboratory tasks such as identifying microscopic cells, and assist the physicians with minor procedures. The doctors often brought me in the exam rooms to see patients with interesting pathology. I used my time there to take in all I could, grow through every new experience, learn much with every patient complication, and, yes, reapply to medical school.

The time between submitting my applications and hearing the results seemed never-ending. I often prayed, asking God to direct my path. I wanted to be certain that being a physician was in God's plan for my life. I knew that my parents were praying for me. But one day in particular, my dad told me he had been praying all day for me. That day, while driving down the road he noticed a vehicle with a license plate that said *Revelation 3:8*. He expressed how eager he was to get home and read this scripture in his Bible. He was certain this was the answer to his prayer regarding my future. The scripture read "I know thy works: behold, I have set before thee an open door, and no man can shut it: for thou hast a little strength, and hast kept my word, and hast not denied my name." Finally, a package came in the mail. This was it—my acceptance letter to the Brody School of Medicine and the opportunity that would change my life and allow me to help change the lives of others. It was also striking that this was the same medical school my mentor Dr. Peace had graduated from several years earlier. Excitement overwhelmed me. I felt ten feet tall (although I am only five feet, three inches), proud and blessed. Although I did not know at that time where my life would lead me, I believed that this was an open door that no man could shut, as the scripture given to my dad had said.

Just four days prior to the first day of medical school, I was diagnosed with a medical condition that required immediate surgery. I first met with the surgeon in his office to be evaluated and examined. He told me there was a five percent chance that a nerve could be damaged and I would lose bowel and bladder function. Then, near the end of the appointment, the surgeon asked "What kind of work do you do?" I said, "Sir, I am supposed to start medical school in just four days." His demeanor changed as he looked at me with greater interest and concern. He decided in that moment that he would get me into the operating room the very next morning, working me into his busy schedule. I was honored that he would make special arrangements for me, but I could not stop wondering whether things would have been different had I not been a future physician. I told the surgeon how important it was for me to attend my white coat ceremony, which was on the last day of orientation. He promised me I would feel well enough to attend. Even though I missed the entire first week of orientation at medical school, the surgeon was right and I was able to attend my white coat ceremony. Although I was physically weak, it did not stop me from walking proudly across the stage to receive my white coat.

Brody School of Medicine is well known for its mission to train physicians to practice primary care in rural eastern North Carolina. This was my heartfelt passion and career goal. At that time, my plan was to become a family physician. Prior to medical school, most of my exposure to physicians was in primary care. I was less familiar with other areas of medicine and never aspired to practice in a different specialty. I worked diligently in medical school for the program, and it was a very challenging experience. It was as though medical school were my life. My personal life suffered somewhat, but I did make time for dating and for important family events such as birthdays, holidays, and my sisters' weddings. I often felt guilty when I was taking time off and not studying. My family was extremely supportive, and my parents dedicated themselves to helping me make it through. I'll never forget how, during exam weeks, they would come and stay with me for several nights to lighten my load. They cooked my meals and kept my apartment spotless (oh, my poor parents). On a serious note, I could focus on my studies and had no other worries. (Thank you, Mom and Dad!)

During my third year of medical school (the clinical rotations), I experienced a change in my course. Until this point, I was certain I would become a primary care physician. Surprisingly, I felt disappointed after completing my first two rotations in pediatrics and family medicine. I had been more seriously considering pediatrics, but I found myself less interested in pediatric illnesses and more interested in the patients' family dynamics. There are five specific cases that I can't erase from my mind that influenced my decision to pursue psychiatry as a specialty: a sick child with a parent with an unknown mental illness; a victim of child abuse; a Vietnam veteran with survivor guilt; a patient who had attempted suicide; and a patient with a somatization disorder.

Finally, I began my psychiatry rotation—and *loved* it. Truly, psychiatry is my niche. I find so much enjoyment in being able to take more time with each patient and get involved on a personal level. Psychiatry is it—the perfect specialty for me. Psychiatry is the only field of medicine that significantly involves treatment of all aspects of a human being; the physical, mental, and spiritual/emotional; it's a thrill to be able to treat each area. It's so amazing how improving a patient's mental state can powerfully affect their physical health. I enjoy acknowledging a patient's spiritual life in their psychiatric treatment, which often encourages them.

One night, I called my mother to tell her I had changed my mind: I no longer wanted to be a primary care physician; instead, I had chosen the field of psychiatry. I was not sure how she would respond but knew she and my father would be supportive. My mother had just retired as an elementary school teacher, prior to completing thirty years of service to get full benefits and retirement income, because she was compelled to fulfill her calling from God to begin Christian counseling for people in the church and community. My mom has a heart for the hurting, and to hear I had chosen a similar path gave Mom tears of joy. She was thrilled I had chosen psychiatry and believed there was a divine reason for the change in my path. The extensive need for psychiatrists in our local communities and the shortage of professional mental health specialists was now evident to Mom and she felt relief that I would be able to help our tribe in this way. As in my rural hometown, this shortage spans most areas of the country.

Residency

The next step, of course, was the application process for residency programs. I decided to apply to programs in the southeastern part of the United States. I only applied to general psychiatry residency programs that also have a child and adolescent fellowship program. Even though I had decided not to specialize in pediatrics, I continued to have an interest in working with children and teenagers. I believe that early psychiatric intervention can change the future for a child suffering with mental illness or social stressors, especially child abuse. I applied to eight residency programs and interviewed with each of them. I was astounded by the in-depth interest the interviewers had in my native heritage. At one program, I was probed with more questions about my tribe than about my interest in psychiatry. I considered it a privilege to be a representative for my people, educating others about the origin and current state of the tribe. It often surprises me that people living in states adjacent to North Carolina know very little about Native Americans and specifically a tribe as large as the Lumbee. As people in each program learned more about me, I learned more about each program. I had hoped there would be one that would separate itself from the others and that I would quickly discover which residency program was right for me.

The day I interviewed at USC in Columbia, South Carolina, I felt an immediate connection to both the residents and the faculty. This program is one that has an emphasis in psychotherapy, which I believe continues to be important in psychiatry. It was located in a midsize city, which was perfect for me. And Columbia is only 140 miles from my hometown, which meant it was a short drive home to see my family and to be there for important events. Before finalizing my decision and rank list of preferred schools, I went back to USC for a second look at the program.

I was interviewed by one unique individual, Dr. Craig Stuck, a psychiatrist and the director of the child and adolescent psychiatry program. Dr. Stuck and I had a very casual conversation in which he shared with me his path to becoming a psychiatrist. Originally trained as a family physician, Dr. Stuck was also strong in his Christian faith, had many interests, and was very service minded. He and his family were long-term medical missionaries and provided medical care in Pakistan for seven years. After several successful, spiritually fulfilling mission trips, Dr. Stuck decided to change his specialty to psychiatry. He went back to residency training and subspecialized in child and adolescent psychiatry. I was totally engulfed in his stories as he shared at length his medical mission experiences. What was so special was that I had often thought about doing some medical missionary work in my career, also. I am forever grateful for the day I met Dr. Stuck. He has become the most significant mentor in my training thus far. Through our talk, it was confirmed that USC was where I wanted to be trained. I ranked USC at the top of my list of residency programs. Anxiously, I waited for match day—the special day that medical schools reveal the residency program where you have matched. I was thrilled to learn that USC was just as interested in me as I was in them. (Go Gamecocks!)

I graduated from medical school in May 2008. I knew I would soon become the second Lumbee psychiatrist. Dr. Theresa Bullard, a very distant relative who also trained at USC, was the first. Our medical school class was unique in that it had five Lumbee Indian students from Robeson County. We were the largest group of Native American students in one class in the history of the school. They each decided to specialize in family medicine. We all looked forward to our future careers in medicine and the opportunity to have a positive impact on the patients we would treat and the communities in which we would live.

During my internship year as a general psychiatry resident, my passion for psychiatry continued to grow. Although I am biased, I believe psychiatry is the most rewarding, fulfilling specialty of medicine. However, there are some inevitable issues such as patients who refuse your help, do not adhere to treatment, and misuse the mental health system for their own personal gain. In child and adolescent psychiatry, we often find parents who have poor parenting skills and innocent children suffer in such circumstances. On a personal note, I am sometimes annoyed when patients assume I am a nurse or say I look too young to be a doctor. Yet the positives at the end of each day far exceed the negatives. As patients receive mental health treatment, I witness family and interpersonal relationships improving and patients experiencing relief, making it possible for some to return to work. Many patients express their gratefulness as their treatment makes them feel much better. Being part of a patient's progress is such a joy.

Faith and the Future

I have a significant interest in mental illness among Native Americans as well as a special interest in religion and spirituality in psychiatry. My plan is to incorporate both in my future career. I was amazed when I discovered that an opportunity to provide hands-on, spirituality-based psychiatric care to a native tribe would not only present itself in the future, but was right around the corner. I was honored when Dr. Stuck asked me to join him and several others on a mission to Alberta, Canada, for one week to work with the Cree Indians on the Hobbema Reserve. (In the United States we use the term *reservation,* but Canadians use the term *reserve.* A reserve or reservation is an area of land occupied and managed by a specific tribe.) This experience was directly related to both of my interests in psychiatry: religion and native peoples.

Dr. Stuck is a member of the Presbyterian Church in America (PCA). Mission to the World is a Christian mission–sending agency of the PCA and our trip was organized by this agency. Mission to the World sponsors a missionary named Marcus Toole who lives in Wetaskiwin, a small town near the Hobbema reserve. There is also a small church on the reserve called *Jesus Church.* This is the name given to the church by some of the

Christian members of the tribe. The church building was built by former missionaries. Its beautiful architectural design has a steeple in the shape of praying hands and a white cross at the peak of the steeple.

The Cree Indians of Hobbema historically roamed freely, hunting buffalo in various northern parts of North America. Beginning in the 1840s, many of the children ages six to fifteen were forcibly removed from their families to live in residential schools, stripping them of their language and culture. They had no contact with their families for up to ten months at a time. Most of the schools were initially operated by churches: sixty percent by the Roman Catholic Church and thirty percent by the Anglican Church of Canada. Most of the residential schools were closed in the 1940s and 1950s when the government revised the Indian Act.

Now the Cree are confined to a reserve that has oil deposits, and their oil deposits are gradually being depleted. Today, they are plagued with gangs, violence, drugs, and alcohol problems. Due to their short lifespans, an elder is considered to be someone older than fifty years old. More than ninety-eight percent of students who attend school on the reserve drop out of high school, and most girls have babies before they are eighteen years old. Many infants are born with fetal alcohol syndrome, and children suffer from neglect and child abuse. The rates of sexual and physical abuse are difficult to fathom.

Our mission team consisted of nine people, including two retired nurses, a marriage and family therapist, a college student, and several church members, each with different talents. Our purpose was to organize a three-day seminar for couples, youth, and children of all ages. We provided the adults tips and tools to have better communication and enhance their relationships. When the Cree members realized I was Native American also, they honored me with gifts and the opportunity to be interviewed on a local Cree radio station. I was asked several questions about the Lumbee tribe, and I shared with them information about the upcoming seminar and invited the listeners to come and participate.

Also, the team participated in the children's Sunday morning service. In preparation for the service, one of the volunteers assisting our mission's team drove a van through the reserve and picked up the children who wanted to attend. There were approximately fifty children in attendance, three to ten years old. Few of them sang and danced to the children's worship songs and listened quietly to the Bible story, while the others enjoyed crawling over and under the pews playing with each other. At first I was shocked, then I realized that although these children had come eagerly, there was a lack of parental support and supervision. I knew that our compassion, along with the continuous support from Pastor Marcus Toole, would make a difference in their lives. It was a pleasure to see the smiles and laughs on their faces. The children's service ended with refreshments and crafts.

We walked door to door to advertise for the couples and youth seminar. We had a great turnout and the seminar was a big hit. One night, we separated the men from the women. I led a group discussion on domestic violence for the women. Several women shared personal stories of physical abuse, sexual abuse, and neglect, which allowed them to open up and disclose the hurt in their lives. The act of disclosure is critical in the process of emotional healing and with this talk I could see their hearts were uplifted, and can only hope for total healing in due time.

Other activities during our mission trip included learning about Cree culture through home visits with the elders and making *banac*, a traditional Cree fried bread. I also had the opportunity to work with the adolescents. We used artwork as a means to indirectly open the lines of communication. In just three nights, their desire was evident for direction, attention, compassion, and someone to simply listen to them. We were often welcomed into their homes and occasionally had the opportunity to pray with them for their physical, emotional, and spiritual needs. One couple even requested a home visit for Christian-based marriage counseling.

On the last night, as the adolescents said their goodbyes, it was obvious they were sad to see us go (and so too was I sad to leave them). They hugged us and asked if we would ever come back to Hobbema. Unlike before, I now know you can impact others' lives even in such a short period of time. As I've often heard others say, "it is not always about our abilities, but more importantly, our *availability*."

The memories and impact of this mission trip will go forward with me into my career. I will never forget them. Even though challenging at times, it was spiritually uplifting and encouraging, much like my career in psychiatry. It was also an opportunity to share the love of Jesus Christ and his message of hope. I feel inspired to continue participating in mission trips and outreach programs throughout my life. I challenge myself and others to be more available and willing to go share hope and encouragement with people who are less fortunate. Remember, when you encourage others, you are encouraged yourself.

We plan to repeat this mission trip annually and are currently planning the next trip with the focus on parenting issues. As we continue to build relationships with the Cree Indians of Hobbema, we will continue to encourage change and instill hope.

Change: On a National Level

I have often pondered over ways to use psychiatry to positively affect masses of people instead of just one patient at a time. My thoughts have included educating teachers and church organizations about the signs and symptoms of child abuse, substance use disorders, and childhood and adult psychiatric disorders. My hope is to change the stigma about mental illness through educating the public.

I had not yet seriously considered getting involved with change on a national level. Then, the next door of opportunity opened and I was awarded the American Psychiatric Association (APA) Diversity Leadership Fellowship. This is a two-year fellowship awarded to minority psychiatry residents who have a vested interest in using their career in psychiatry to work with some particular minority group. I was honored to attend the APA September Component Meeting in Washington, D.C., in 2010. During this conference I learned much more about the APA's operations and functions. The APA plays a vital role in influencing the federal government regarding policies that affect psychiatrists and our patients. Along with a colleague, we went to Capitol Hill to meet with one of the South Carolina senators to lobby in support of several bills affecting the field of psychiatry and mental health. I was assigned to the APA's Council on Minority Mental Health and Health Disparities and continue to participate in their council meetings, discussing issues affecting minority groups across the nation.

Looking Into the Future

As I journey through my fellowship in child and adolescent psychiatry, I realize how much I have already been affected personally by psychiatry. Many psychiatry residents enter this field of medicine eager to learn how to more deeply understand patients so that they will be capable of providing the best possible treatment. Along with learning about a patient, I have learned more about myself. As humans, we all experience hurt, pain, and fear. Some suffer to greater depths. Yet we can all relate to one another to some degree. Many people have asked me how I can listen to patients' problems and hear so many sad stories and not let it take away my own happiness and joy. I personally think the ability to be a good psychiatrist requires more than good training. It is more like a gift or talent. A former Psychiatry chair in the USC–Palmetto graduate medical education program once said, "A good psychiatrist is born, not made." Psychiatrists must be mentally and emotionally stable to receive the burdens of others while not allowing those burdens to incapacitate themselves. When I feel burdened by the horrific stories from some of my patients, I remind myself that this patient has made the first step to recovery by seeking treatment. Each patient I meet presents me an opportunity to make a difference, one life at a time. Human beings are composed of mind, body, and soul, yet many people only seek treatment for the mind and body. I believe that complete healing must also include spiritual healing.

Although naturally I am biased on this topic, I believe women often make excellent psychiatrists. Women are generally known to have the qualities necessary for motherhood. We express compassion, gentleness, and kindness that can be therapeutic for psychiatric patients. I would encourage any man or woman with a strong interest in psychiatry to pursue this field of medicine. As a female, I have occasionally felt superiority from my male counterparts, but as society continues to change, women experience more equality in our professions. Whatever oppression, inhibitions, or limitations exist in your life, anything is possible if you just believe in yourself.

PRACTICAL TIPS FOR WOMEN IN PSYCHIATRY

For any future psychiatrist, my advice is to learn your strengths and your weaknesses; then you can expand on your strengths and learn to understand and accept your weaknesses. Over the past ten years, I have learned that when an opportunity presents itself, I should not let it pass me by. Occasionally a door may close in front of me, but I am learning each day to accept that a closed door does not imply failure, but a change of direction. Some people say "follow your heart," for the heart of a person is your soul, and it will guide you. I do believe I am following my heart, and today I am convinced that being a psychiatrist is more than just my job, it is also my calling. I have much more to learn about the field of psychiatry and will continue to create new goals for my career. I embrace the future challenges and I am determined to continue making a difference in this world—one life at a time.

Chapter 3

Emerging From the Shadow and Exposed to the Light

Hind Benjelloun, M.D.

Under a Shadow

My impression of my role as a woman is strongly shaped by my upbringing. The Moroccan culture, as many Arab cultures do, places a great emphasis on the first-born child; the first son in particular grants great pride and esteem to a family. Although the legal-religious organization of no two Arab countries is identical, women are stereotypically represented as oppressed and subordinate. This perception is reinforced by a patriarchal class system that has dominated the Arab world for thousands of years. Unlike in the West where the individual is the basic unit of the state, it is the family that is the basis of Arab states. Within this framework, the rights of women are expressed solely in their roles as wives and mothers (Handal 2000; Sebbar 2000). And within this framework I was raised.

In 1971, my mother, a beautiful nineteen-year-old girl from a well-known family in Fez, Morocco, married my father, a young, esteemed, intelligent banker living and working in Casablanca. In 1974, my parents moved to the United States after my father accepted a prestigious position at the Moroccan Embassy in Washington, D.C. My brother was born in 1974. I was born in 1975; we were only twenty months apart. The story was traditionally perfect.

From the time of my earliest memories, I felt inadequate to my older brother in a multitude of ways. Although we were extremely close in age, as we were growing up the power differential was palpable. And to me, it felt clear that my deficiencies were because I was a girl. Culturally, that was the accepted standard. In my superficial child's mind, my brother was bigger, stronger, meaner, and faster. And he was obviously smarter than I was. I was *just* a girl.

My self-esteem suffered enormous consequences because of this perceived shadow that I lived under. I became isolative in my elementary school years, finding the most pleasure immersing myself in the life of another. I was particularly intrigued with the mystery novel character Nancy Drew; I fantasized being like her, but understood that I never would. My impression was that she was a *girl* who was capable of doing whatever a *boy* can do. Of course to me, the concept was absolutely fictitious; I thought, "a girl could never really do the things Nancy Drew did."

Nancy Drew's spirit stayed with me throughout my childhood and adolescent years. I started to slowly believe that a girl, or woman, could accomplish whatever she sets her mind to accomplish. Nancy Drew fueled the curiosity I developed in myself and encouraged me to expand my dreams.

I am not alone in my admiration of Nancy Drew. Her most vocal fans are international female leaders. Recently, U.S. Supreme Court Justice Sonia Sotomayor said that Nancy Drew represented "boldness and intelligence." And among the series' fans are the likes of Oprah Winfrey, Laura Bush, Hillary Rodham Clinton, Diane Sawyer, Nancy Pelosi, and Ruth Bader Ginsburg (Shipman 2009).

In high school, I began to develop a greater vision for myself in life. I was a straight-A student and in every honor society. As expected of me culturally, I never dated and was home with my family during most of my free time. As senior year was coming to a close, classmates were planning international excursions and choosing outfits for their prom nights. But not me. It started becoming more evident that I had missed out on exploring life, and I was continuing to miss out.

I was introduced to the poetry of Khalil Gibran that year. *The Prophet* is the piece of literature that continues to have an unmatched impact on my life. Gibran wrote a chapter on self-knowledge that profoundly touched me and made me question my concepts of self-worth. Here is an excerpt (Gibran 1923, p. 54):

The hidden well-spring of your soul must needs rise and run murmuring
    to the sea;
And the treasure of your infinite depths would be revealed to your eyes.
But let there be no scales to weigh your unknown treasure;
And seek not the depths of your knowledge with staff or sounding line.
For self is a sea boundless and measureless.

The only apparent way to escape the life that I for years had conformed to and accepted was to go away to college. The following year, despite resistance from my parents to letting me loose, I started my new life at the University of Virginia.

Blackjack

Blackjack became my sanctuary as I embarked on my adult life. I carry both pride and shame with this admission. The blackjack table is where I matured the most as a human being; it's where I matured as a woman.

Early in my junior year in college, during their twenty-fifth year of marriage, my parents decided to get a divorce. It hit me incredibly hard and it was unexpected. As my parents became engrossed with the details of the divorce, I felt a sense of freedom. My being away at college created an "out of sight, out of mind" mentality in my preoccupied parents, and their interest in my day-to-day life was down to a minimum. The idea of shedding the obligations of uncomfortable family holidays and the expected daily phone check-ins was heavenly. Was it actually true that I no longer needed to report to anyone? Yes, it was true. Hallelujah!

Through a friend, I learned about a variety of venues in southern Maryland where blackjack was dealt. I was immediately intrigued. "Gambling? Me? I don't drink, I don't smoke, I don't have sex; I'm a good girl. I come from a good Moroccan family. Me?" I recall now the immediate, intense feeling almost a decade and a half ago: a sense of much-needed rebellion. My mother always reminded me that gambling was for "the big boys" and was "bad." However, gamblers, in my mind, seemed streetsmart, strong, confident. Could I be that? I wanted to be that. The mere suggestion was intoxicating.

My beginners' luck created an itch that, to this day, I feel. I was intrigued by deep-rooted intellectualization of blackjack. I spent months researching blackjack, attempting to get a good grasp of the game from a scientific perspective, learning the subtleties to increase my edge, and working to master the various blackjack counting systems (Uston, Thorpe, Revere, etc.) (Humble 1987). Feeling equipped, I moved on to gambling in Atlantic City casinos. Hours to days to weeks I spent playing blackjack and establishing a name and a rating for myself. It was invigorating.

I have met unique, extraordinary people at the blackjack table. Blackjack is nondiscriminatory. It sees no color, no gender, no sexual orientation, no culture, and no upbringing. It attracts folks from all parts of the world and all walks of life. I have found a striking curiosity among people at the blackjack table. I've met taxi drivers, movie stars, Harvard professors, janitors, chief executive officers, tattoo artists, boxers, teachers, ex-cons, doctors, lawyers; you name it. I found my voice at the blackjack table. It became second nature to probe into the life of a fellow blackjack player. People, and all their complexities, became more and more fascinating to me. The foundation of my interest in psychiatry was developing.

The life lessons learned from the blackjack table are deep and sophisticated, and they influenced significantly my notion of being a street-smart, strong, confident person. In particular, I made a few notable conclusions from the way players approach blackjack. One example is the complete distinction I observed between a novice and an expert blackjack player. Almost customarily, novice blackjack players play too conservatively, overlooking the most fruitful opportunities. Experts, on the contrary, take substantial but calculated risks. On the blackjack table as in the game of life, it is about the quality of your successes and failures; not at all the quantity. When conditions in life are favorable for seeking out opportunities instead of waiting for them to arrive, be proactive! And when you begin to obtain positive consequences to your efforts and the odds are in your favor, take advantage of the situation and push ahead as if there is no limit. Of course, the circumstances of life aren't always conducive to chasing every opportunity. There may even be a struggle to maintain what exists or to catch up on what has fallen behind. In life, we must be patient and persevere. These themes of life set a precedent for how I have lived life from that point forward.

Awakening

I fled to New York City immediately after college to escape the potential grips of my culturally conservative life back in the D.C. area. I was young, energetic, naive, and rebellious. I was fueled by Khalil Gibran and the themes of life explored within *The Prophet,* in addition to a newfound confidence from the casinos. My parents were still consumed by their divorce and I was empowered by the concept of *enough is enough*; I wanted out of the sheltered life. With less than a hundred dollars in my pocket and a small suitcase of personal belongings, I stepped out into an unknown city.

I had a solid résumé in hand with a reputable degree under my belt, and I felt ready to conquer the world. I jumped from sublet to sublet for a few weeks between places, traveling across the NYC boroughs in addition to Hoboken, New Jersey. I was like a vagabond. Door after door slammed in my face following interview after interview. How could this be? I had a master's degree that I initially believed put me in a prime position to land a job as an editor-writer. Why were things so hard? Why did I feel so unprepared for this wake-up call?

And as many things are, it was a matter of perseverance. If you fail, try, try again. As arrogant as I was about my educational background and imaginary earning potential, with time my arrogance turned to contemplation. Success seemed to be founded on more than just a notable degree or two. Fearing failure and finding the idea of returning to Washington, D.C. intolerable, I trekked along for a year until I found myself in an apartment in midtown Manhattan with a senior editor position working for a pharmaceutical marketing company. And because I was finally making a reasonable NYC income, I carried an internal smugness that would come back to haunt me. I had broken free from the chains that limited my life throughout the first two decades of my life. Now that my foot was in the door, I want to make sure I kicked the door open.

On January 16, 1999, my life was irreversibly transformed. While on a trip back to northern Virginia to visit my mother, whom I was becoming increasingly close with, I learned of a tragic situation. My eleven-year-old sister Sonia was hit head-on by a van while crossing the street in front of her school. That night in the pediatrics intensive care unit at Fairfax Hospital, the neurologists indicated the prognosis was poor. They said her brain would continue its inflammatory reaction to the multiple frontal lobe hemorrhages clearly identified on head imaging. That night, she was physically unrecognizable; the left side of her face had taken a brutal blow. Sonia's prospects for recovery were poor.

Somehow she lived through the next few weeks, emerged from a coma, and ultimately was transferred to the Kennedy Krieger Institute in Baltimore, Maryland, for weeks and weeks of rehabilitation. I left everything behind in New York temporarily after that miserable, unforgettable day in January. I was granted medical/family leave for two months.

From the moment I learned of her accident, I dedicated my life to taking care of my sister. I took on the major responsibilities of communicating with physicians and sifting through bills and insurance paperwork. As the first few weeks drifted by, Sonia slept deeply within her coma. I would stare at her for hours on end pondering the fragility of life. Everything can come, as everything can go.

As she progressed through the scores on the Glasgow Coma Scale, there emerged a peculiar irritability, impulsivity, and disinhibition that were uncharacteristic of my sweet, well-mannered Sonia. Within a week of her first sign of consciousness, she was behaving as if possessed by the devil. Sonia was uncontrolled, erratic, and aggressive, and her language was offensive and vulgar. She frequently required physical and chemical restraints. A psychiatric consultation was critical.

The psychiatry consultation team explained Sonia's behavior was a frontal lobe phenomenon and her experience was characteristic of pediatric frontal lobe traumatic brain injuries. Psychotropic medications were needed and were incredibly effective.

During her recovery, I became fascinated with the connection between the brain and behavior. This is the period in my life when I became most intrigued by psychiatry. The field appeared so innovative, so stimulatingly puzzling, with vast room for breakthroughs! In psychiatry, we are just at the beginning of discovery and we have a tremendous way to go. Sonia finally was discharged home following a seemingly miraculous recovery.

During Sonia's long hospitalization, I read widely in the writings of the great humanitarian Dr. Albert Schweitzer. He wrote (Schweitzer 1949, p. 321):

> Just as the wave cannot exist for itself, but is ever a part of the heaving surface of the ocean, so must I never live my life for itself, but always in the experience which is going on around me.

This experience fully transformed me.

I returned to NYC soon after to find my not-so-missed apartment and my uninspiring life as an editor. Things felt different. My purpose no longer brought me excitement. I felt embarrassed for boasting about my new impressive salary only a short time ago. I had let money take on a value that now made me feel selfish and basically I was disgusted with myself. I decided it was time to pursue the field about which I had recently developed an unsurpassed passion: I wanted to study the mind.

Hello, Stigma

I started medical school in 2001 with the intent to become a psychiatrist. My life's unfortunate but highly rewarding experiences had made me view the field of psychiatry as the mystery I wanted to explore thoroughly. I felt psychiatry offered me the opportunity to be at the forefront of discovery. It was the Nancy Drew in me emerging.

It was surprising to discover that a majority of my fellow medical students did not view the study of psychiatry the way that I did. I was alone in discussions of the brain as an organ and disease processes manifesting themselves behaviorally. Medical students were much more interested in digging into the gross anatomy cadaver or practicing suturing on a suturing game kit. There existed an underlying disdain for psychiatry, and those passionate about psychiatry seemed timid and less vocal about their interest. In my intern year, the medical school psychiatry interest group had five members, myself included.

I recall a professor in my medical school who was a mentor to all. He was a fantastic, whimsical, elderly fellow and I absolutely adored this man. He mentored many students one-on-one and I decided that it would be beneficial to meet with him early in my medical school career. This first formal meeting started out as lovely. He picked one of my favorite topics, travel, and I did not hesitate to expand on my desire to visit Japan. We spoke at length about the terrorist attacks of September 11, 2001, months earlier, and the fears of future attacks. He told me about his children and grandchildren and a little of his history in the medical school.

"So, Hind? What do you want to be when you grow up?" he asked. I smiled, allowing him, because of his age, the luxury of a well-known and pretty condescending question.

"Of course, a psychiatrist. That's why I came to medical school."

He laughed hard, with the final part of the laugh ending in a strong and loud wheeze. I didn't know how to react.

"Hind. Are you kidding?"

"No, I'm not. I am going to be a psychiatrist."

"Did you choose to go into psychiatry because you want to be somebody's friend…or is it because you want to be a pill pusher?"

There was a silence. I couldn't believe what I was hearing.

"I don't mean to discourage you. But what about pediatrics? Or maybe even geriatrics so that you can take care of old guys like me." He chuckled.

"I'm not sure what to say to your comments," I said in a bewildered tone. "But I am going to be a psychiatrist!"

He continued staring in silence.

I asked, "Is this the response I should be prepared to expect from the medical community?"

He paused briefly and then answered, "Well, I think you should be prepared."

He was right. As the months progressed, I was oddly enough thankful for that awkward yet telling interaction. The three years that followed this conversation were entirely peppered with the stigmatization of psychiatry. I encountered the heaviest disregard for the profession in a handful of clerkship rotations where I would be routinely singled out as "the psychiatry one." I was robustly challenged on multiple occasions to explain why I wanted to enter psychiatry; other times, I would receive an "Oh, psychiatry" remark followed by a certain look of dismay, and then silence. It was surprising and rare when there was a positive, motivating response.

There was a blunt stigma associated with the profession. I realized that medical students who show an interest in psychiatry were often scrutinized by their peers, family, and even the educators they depend on for guidance. It became clear that without a solid, indestructible desire to enter the field, the stigma posed the risk of redirecting energetic minds interested in psychiatry into another specialty.

The term *stigma* arises from the visually oriented Greeks. Stigma referred to cuts or burns on the body created to reveal one's moral status, such as being a thief or a traitor. The Christians later expanded the term to include both bodily signs of the holy grace and bodily signs of a physical disorder. In 1963, Goffman defined stigma as "a trait, which is deeply discredited." In current terms, stigma refers to the dishonor itself, rather then the bodily evidence of such (Goffman 1986).

The repercussions of stigma are elegantly described in the 1956 publication *Clinical Studies in Psychiatry* (Sullivan 1956):

> The awareness of inferiority means that one is unable to keep out of consciousness the formulation of some chronic feelings of the worst sort of insecurity. The fear that others can disrespect a person because of something he shows means that he is always insecure in his contact with other people; and this insecurity arises, not from the mysterious and somewhat disguised sources, as a great deal of our anxiety does, but from something which he knows he cannot fix. Now that represents an almost fatal deficiency of the self-system.

Fortunately, the present fight against the stigmatization of mental illness is vigorous, as witnessed, for example, in the unprecedented efforts toward health care parity. And this arguably is reflected in the 2009 increase in the total number of U.S. medical school graduates entering psychiatry residency programs, from 595 in 2008 to 656 in 2009. That represents an 11% increase, which reverses the three-year decline that started in 2005. The percentage of U.S. medical graduates choosing to match into psychiatry remained stable at 4.5% of the 14,566 who matched across the board (Moran 2009).

Mentorship is thus essential at all levels. It is critical to mentor those interested in psychiatry from the outset of their medical school careers. Many brilliant, inquisitive medical students may begin with a trivial consideration of the field that, with mentorship, can be expanded to create a firm desire to explore a career in psychiatry.

The Mentors in My Life

In my last year of medical school, I was granted the American Psychiatric Association (APA) Minority Medical Student Scholarship to travel to the APA meeting in Atlanta, Georgia, in May 2005. It was there that I met an inspirational mentor, Dr. Constance Dunlap. At the time, she was the president of the D.C. Psychiatric Society, a chapter of the Washington Psychiatric Society. That summer, I began my intern year at the Georgetown University Department of Psychiatry in July. I accepted Dr. Dunlap's invitation to join the chapter council, and I attended monthly meetings religiously. Dr. Dunlap is a young African American woman whose demeanor is breathtaking and commands authority. I gained a great deal observing her leadership of the chapter and her proactivity for change in the community.

I also met Dr. Eliot Sorel, who would later become my most cherished mentor. In fact, in September 2005 during my intern year, Dr. Sorel hosted and led the first gathering of Washington, D.C., postgraduate year 1 (PGY1) and PGY2 residents from all of the area's psychiatry residency programs. Dr. Sorel indicated that this ongoing collaborative effort was designed to bring area psychiatry residents together, raise awareness, foster mentor-mentee relationships, and provide insight.

I have great respect and esteem for Dr. Sorel, who has made mentorship a lifetime endeavor. He is particularly passionate about nurturing young psychiatrists, and he recognizes medical students, residents, and early career psychiatrists as the future leaders of our field. In January 2008, together we started the Washington Psychiatric Society Career, Leadership, and Mentorship (CLM) initiative, funded by an APA Area 3 grant that has been renewed three years in a row. This initiative serves as a model that has the potential to inspire residents across the United States to establish similar enterprises within their district branches and to seek available funding for such initiatives. It has spread successfully to New Jersey and is heading for Virginia and California in the very near future. The opportunities for career development, leadership, and mentorship for medical students, residents, and early career psychiatrists within the APA are extensive and extraordinary. Our CLM project exposes those opportunities and encourages involvement early in our careers (Benjelloun et al. 2009).

In a 2007 study in the *Journal of General Internal Medicine*, scientific findings confirmed the importance of mentoring to medical residents and identified a relationship between mentoring and perceived career preparation. However, of the 329 intern and resident respondents (65%), 93% reported the importance of a mentor during residency, but only half of those identified a current or past mentor (Ramanan et al. 2006). Mentors and mentees alike must be proactive in seeking out mentorship. Psychiatric communities, both academic and organizational, must invest in creating and maintaining mentorship as a formalized, structured priority. Mentorship is an unending commitment.

I graduated from the Georgetown University Hospital's Department of Psychiatry Residency Training Program in June 2009. After a year as the hospital's chief resident, I had become addicted to the hustle and bustle of acute psychiatric care and the excitement of the academic world. I continued on at Georgetown as Associate Medical Director of the Inpatient Unit and the Associate Residency Training Director. I thrive being surrounded by medical students and residents throughout my day. I am revitalized by them moment after moment.

Mentorship comes in many forms. Although I will be forever a mentee, I now consider myself an apprentice mentor. My guiding principle is the unshaken desire to give to my mentees the knowledge, wisdom, and foresight to excel further than I have excelled. This is the selfless act that my mentors have shown me.

In particular, the women that I have met through the APA have been tremendous inspirations, mentors, and friends. As Dr. Anna Lembke (2004, p. 275) observed, "Women in power have the ability to create opportunity and advantage for other capable and qualified women coming up through the ranks. Women mentors also may change a woman's internal sense of what she is capable of doing." On a personal note, the female mentors in my life have been instrumental in guiding me through the process of my own evolution as a leader. A local icon in the Washington Psychiatric Society, Dr. Catherine May, has been priceless, continuing to guide me through my first few years in leadership at this district branch. On the national level, Dr. Annelle Primm, APA Deputy Medical Director, has taught me to embrace who I am and to cherish my unique features, culture, and traits. And finally, Dr. Donna Norris, who embodies perseverance and vision, encourages me to make every obstacle a stepping stone.

Women and Leadership

There remains a strong, unspoken differential in the impressions and expectations of women versus men as leaders. Hillary Clinton and her pursuit of the U.S. presidency is a recent example that outlines various discrepancies. It was a struggle for Clinton throughout her scrutinized campaign to remain within the narrowly defined boundaries for her behavior as a powerful woman leader. As Hilary Lips, Ph.D. (2009, p. 16), an expert in gender studies, indicated, "It appears that the acceptable scripts for women in powerful public...roles are still rigidly defined and easy to violate—by being too 'pushy' or too 'soft,' too 'strident' or too accommodating, too sexless or too sexual." A woman, because of predefined and learned perspectives, will encounter a variety of forces that challenge her desire to be viewed as a competent, valuable, and potent leader.

In particular, in the transition out of my training years (from resident, to chief resident, to attending physician), I have been increasingly mindful of this phenomenon. It remains a struggle for me to find my individual equilibrium, especially in the academic world at Georgetown. I am more and more aware of opinions and critiques about my teaching and leadership style that seem related in many ways to my gender. I consider myself extremely honest and direct. I am less likely to sugarcoat things, and I consider constructive, direct criticism to be at the forefront of teaching. In an age of continued discrimination against female leaders, we are provoked to be increasingly assertive and to tone down femininity. Yet women who act more confident and appropriately aggressive run a significant risk of disapproval.

Furthermore, I am wary of self-promotion because it can be precarious for women. As Dr. Lips noted, research clearly demonstrates that women who promote their accomplishments, although viewed as more competent, are "less likeable." However, for men, self-promotion brings higher acceptance and likeability (Lips 2009). I witness this throughout the academic world and remain attentive to this as I develop my professional reputation.

The balance between personal and professional life is a critical issue that every woman must contemplate endlessly. Undoubtedly, learning how to manage this balance increases motivation, career fulfillment, and productivity. For me, as a woman in a transitional period of both her career and her personal life, the balance becomes dependent on establishing limits. As the career opportunities for leadership and advancement multiply, so does the potential to become overwhelmed or exploited. Catherine May taught me that "learning how to say *no*" is a skill that I must adopt and perfect early in my leadership career. Although I initially believed that saying *no* would make me appear ineffective or weak, it is an essential component to success. Feeling overworked, overwhelmed, overstressed, and overcommitted leads to an unproductive, fruitless life.

And I am learning that there is a graceful, respectful, and diplomatic way to say *no*. Efficiently creating a team and delegating tasks accordingly is a necessity.

PRACTICAL TIPS FOR WOMEN IN PSYCHIATRY

As a nascent mentor in the field, I have geared my practical tips toward women at the outset of their careers, who are progressing through their training or are very early in their professional lives. These tips come from my personal experiences and the wisdom shared with me by my mentors.

- Be prepared to combat the stigma against our profession and our patients.
- Don't be discouraged by failures. Persevere and try, try again.
- Learn how to say *no*.
- Delegate effectively.
- Find a mentor early in your career.
- Become a mentor early in your career.
- Get involved with the APA at the local and national level.
- Find your passions and pursue them.
- Find your voice.
- Reach out when you need guidance. There is a wonderful community ready to lend wisdom and advice.
- Be proud to be a female leader in psychiatry.
- And a final quote:

> A true leader has the confidence to stand alone, the courage to make tough decisions, and the compassion and wisdom to listen to the needs of others. He does not set out to be a leader, but becomes one by the quality of his actions and the integrity of his intent.
> —Anonymous

References

Benjelloun H (ed): Career and Leadership Development: Making It Our Priority (special issue). Am J Psychiatry Residents' Journal 4(1):1–7, 2009

Gibran K: The Prophet. New York, Knopf, 1923

Goffman E: Stigma: Notes on the Management of Spoiled Identity. New York, Simon & Schuster, 1986

Handal N: The Poetry of Arab Women. New York, Interlink Books, 2000

Humble L: The World's Greatest Blackjack Book. New York, Broadway Books, 1987

Lembke A: Why is this special issue on women's professional development in psychiatry necessary? Acad Psychiatry 28:275–277, 2004

Lips H: Women and leadership: delicate balancing act. Women's Media. April 2, 2009. Available at: http://www.womensmedia.com/lead/88-women-and-leadership-delicate-balancing-act.html. Accessed September 23, 2011.

Moran M: More med students choose psychiatry, reversing recent-year declines. Psychiatr News 44(8):2, 2009

Ramanan RA, Taylor WC, Davis RB, et al: Mentoring matters. Mentoring and career preparation in internal medicine residency training. J Gen Intern Med 21:340–345, 2006

Schweitzer A: The Philosophy of Civilization, Part II: Civilization and Ethics. New York, Macmillan, 1949

Sebbar L: Sherazade. London, Quartet Books, 2000

Shipman C, Rucci S: Nancy Drew: the smart woman's role model. ABC News, Good Morning America, July 9, 2009. Available at: http://abcnews.go.com/GMA/story?id=8034954&page=1. Accessed January 10, 2012.

Sullivan HS: Clinical Studies in Psychiatry. Edited by Perry HS, Gawel ML, Gibbon M. New York, WW Norton, 1956

Chapter 4

An Early-Career Perspective on Work, Parenthood, and Leadership

You Can Have It All, You Just Can't Have It All Right Now

Amy Ursano, M.D.

THE SUBTITLE OF THIS CHAPTER, *You Can Have It All, You Just Can't Have It All Right Now,* was one of the pearls shared with me by my division director early in my child and adolescent psychiatry fellowship. While it seemed clever and amusing at first, I've come to appreciate how frequently this saying provides reassurance and guidance as I face career and family decisions on a daily basis.

As the daughter of a psychiatrist and writer-turned-social worker, I always considered medicine and psychiatry as a possible career. Of course,

I also considered acting and writing as a career at some point, but didn't think I was good enough to make a living doing those things. Much of my youth and adolescence was spent in the Maryland suburbs of Washington, D.C., an area of the country where it seemed many of my friends had a parent or two who were psychiatrists. I did not experience the stigma associated with a focus on mental illness that often creates barriers to choosing a career in psychiatry. In fact, it wasn't until I went to college and saw the trepidation on my friends' faces when I told them what my father did that I realized firsthand the powerful fear with which many approach mental illness. Majoring in English in college, I returned to the idea of psychiatry and medicine following graduation. I completed my premedical courses and then worked in pediatric clinical research for a year prior to entering medical school. I enjoyed thinking and talking about child development and the concept of preventive care and early intervention in pediatric populations. Throughout medical school I vacillated between pediatrics and psychiatry. Child psychiatry encompassed aspects of both that I most enjoyed. It allowed me time with my patients, access to their stories, and a chance to intervene early in their development. After completing my general and child psychiatry training at the University of North Carolina at Chapel Hill, I elected to stay as a member of the faculty there.

Currently, my interest is in medical education and residency training. I accepted a position as a clinician educator, teaching and supervising trainees of all levels in multiple settings: small group, lecture, inpatient, outpatient, and psychotherapy. I was named to the medical school admissions committee and increased my involvement in organizations like the American Psychiatric Association and the American Academy of Child and Adolescent Psychiatry. Around the time that I joined the faculty, my husband and I decided to have a baby. I thought to myself, other women have done this, and have even done this in more challenging ways. It seemed quite feasible at the time. That was about seven years ago.

Let me make clear that I recognize what a privilege it is to have the opportunity to struggle with this balancing act. I know that to have been limited to just a career or only motherhood would have been a far greater hardship for me. That being said, I will try to share some of the lessons I've acquired being a mom and an early-career psychiatrist in an academic setting.

First of all, this is hard. There are exceptional pioneering women who managed this before many of the advantages that I take for granted were available. Also, there are women who manage to have children during medical school or postgraduate training and contend with much greater struggles than I am experiencing currently (Goodwin 2004). Yet some days, I recognize that this life is chaotic—and those are the good days. Other days, it can be downright absurd.

It has been critical on this journey to recognize that I certainly don't have all the answers. And that is OK. On many days I have more questions than answers, and I am beginning to get used to that. I am often faced with recurrent questions such as, Should I work less and, if so, how? If I do cut back, will I simply be another part-time mom working full-time hours with part-time pay in academics? Was a nanny the right decision for our family? Will my children think the nanny is their mommy? Would I have been happier with the more diffuse attachment setting of a good day care facility? How do people provide good clinical care, remember to teach pearls of wisdom to trainees, make their publishing deadlines, use a breast pump, get children to school and themselves to work on time and not forget to shower each day?

I cried a lot when I returned to work after my maternity leave. I cried when I left the house, as I climbed from the parking lot to my office, and again as I entered my friend's office to try to "pull it together." It got better, but not quickly. Many friends and colleagues told me it would be easier with the second child. And in some ways, I suppose it has been. I am familiar with the pain of separating from my children and returning to work, but my days contain so much more now. My time is reduced. I already feel split in two pieces, or three or four.

There are times that I welcome going to work, having the opportunity to think about nonfamily things: how to help my patients, how to help my team run better, how to be a better teacher of the residents and medical students I supervise. It can be quite rewarding to work on a committee project or a book chapter, to feel like I am accomplishing something professionally, actually producing something. It is an opportunity to feel fulfilled and appreciated in a way that is complementary to the personal fulfillment that comes from my time with my family. But on the tough days, I've come to learn that it is acceptable to like and not always love going to work; just as it is also acceptable to love and not always like all aspects of your children.

Women in psychiatry balance multiple roles in their personal and professional lives. As a child and adolescent psychiatrist, I think about things in terms of development. I catch myself thinking a lot about Erikson's "identity versus role confusion." Is my dual career "role confusion"? Certainly some of the challenges are the same. If it were simply about multitasking, it may not seem so daunting. But at this stage of life, we are defining and growing in two important roles at the same time—as new physician and as new parent. The temptation might be to attempt to do these sequentially and master one before taking on the other, if you have the biological clock on your side. This isn't always possible. There may be implications for promotion and career advancement or that bane of the professional woman, fertility.

The peak childbearing years coincide with the years of medical school, residency and fellowship training, and early career (Fox et al. 2006). According to the American Medical Association (2008), between 1970 and 2006 the percentage of women physicians more than tripled, from 7.6% to 27.8%. In 2006, 25% of these women were less than thirty-five years old and 51% were less than forty-five years old. According to the Association of American Medical Colleges (AAMC), in 2007–2008, women received 49.3% of the medical degrees awarded in U.S. medical schools. This represented the largest number of women earning an M.D. of any national graduating class to date (AAMC 2010). There are choices women are making about career and family, how to balance them and what to prioritize. Their decisions have implications for the individual and also for medical training and faculty development.

Learning to Say No

In my efforts to try to balance work and family, I have had to make the decision to give some things up. In fact, it was noted that beginning in the late 1990s, women showed significantly diminished interest in academic careers in medicine (Nonnemaker 2000). Friends and colleagues have often remarked that having a part-time private practice would be a more efficient or profitable way to make a living. One can certainly argue for the truth of such assertions. However, my strong desire to be a teacher and leader of a team has kept me in academics. The collision between biological clock and tenure clock has been cited many times in the literature (Bickel 2004; Fox et al. 2006; Verlander 2004). The issue of the tenure track for female faculty is an interesting one. In a study at the University of Illinois College of Medicine at Chicago, it was postulated that full-time junior faculty members may preferentially select a nontenure track in an effort to set reasonable career expectations while meeting the demands of a young family (Fox et al. 2006).

In my case, I did decide to step off the tenure track around the time of the birth of my first child. I felt that if my interest in writing and publishing continued then I would do it without an externally imposed timetable. And I have. Some would make different choices, seeing this as a sign of the losses incurred by women in academics. And in some ways it is. You can't have it all right now. When embarking on the unknown path of motherhood, I didn't need any more *should*'s or *ought to*'s in my life. These were things that needed to take place on my time line, on my family's time line, and not according to the tenure clock.

I have gone through most of my life saying *yes* to jobs and opportunities. And it is flattering to be needed, to be included on a committee or in a project. But all those *yes*'s that came at little cost prior to children, now are increasingly expensive. The time and the energy spent in extra projects takes away from the time and energy I want and need to spend with my children. Becoming a mother has required me to learn how to say *no*. I have not yet fully experienced the emotional part of saying *no,* or *not now,* to a project or opportunity. There may be worry that no other opportunity will be available when I am ready. There is also the real experience that one doesn't talk about of watching someone else enjoy what I have passed up. Part of the balancing act of career and family includes prioritizing both at work and at home. It often means focusing on the immediate needs at work and forgoing longer-term planning. At home, it has meant less time for my own pursuits and interests.

Men, of course, also make choices and sacrifices when raising a family. Interestingly, the needs of men and women in academic positions may actually be the same. A faculty needs survey of men and women in the Department of Psychiatry and Behavioral Sciences at the University of California at Davis found the following to be very important to faculty: finding meaning in one's work, maintaining integrity and ethics, maintaining one's values and academic vitality, balancing personal and professional demands, finding a flexible work environment, and preventing and handling burnout. These results were similar across gender and rank. Clearly, however, the path to achieving these goals and the definitions of such achievement may be different between genders (Seritan et al. 2010).

In our family, I have not been the only one who has made difficult choices and sacrifices. In an effort to balance our family needs, my husband elected to leave academics to work at a state hospital as a child and adolescent psychiatrist and adjunct faculty member. He was still able to teach, but not to the degree that he had or as much as he would have liked. It provided us more income and better flexibility, which, ironically, was necessary for me to maintain my appointment and make decisions so we could afford our choices about child care for our growing family.

Women in Academic Medicine

Advancing in academic medicine is like ascending a mountain. Certainly having children has changed my approach but there are multiple approaches to any peak. Some approaches are steeper and thus more direct; others are less direct but require more time and less singular effort. Women faculty leave full-time appointments more often than men do (Association of American Medical Colleges 2002). Women tend to choose part-time career paths or tenure stoppage to help with child-rearing whereas men tend to choose part-time academic status for outside employment (Fox et al. 2006).

These decisions, the juggling and the conflict between family and career have ramifications for achieving tenure and advancement into leadership positions in academics for women. The phenomenon is not limited to medical faculty. Mason and Goulden (2004) noted that when comparing men and women who have children within five years of earning their Ph.D. degrees, women are almost 20% less likely to achieve tenure.

Female medical school faculty members are less likely to achieve academic promotion than are male faculty members with similar durations of faculty appointments, and there is reason to believe that sex-based differences in promotion continue (Nattinger 2007). Despite the increased number of women in medicine over the last several decades, the percentage of women faculty holding full professor rank has risen slowly, from 7% in 1978 to 19% in 2010, while the percentage of male faculty holding the rank of full professor has remained steady at 30% (AAMC 2010). Only 11% of department chair positions were held by women in 2005 (Nattinger 2007). Psychiatry lags behind other disciplines. According to the AAMC, in 2010, 17% of full professors of psychiatry were women as compared with 26% in pediatrics, 23% in dermatology, and 21% in family medicine (AAMC 2010). In 2009, only 10% of women in psychiatry were full professors while 27.6% of men held that position. System changes are necessary in order for faculty members who care about the work-family balance to reach senior positions to help junior faculty who follow them (Fox et al. 2006).

Mentorship

Much of life can be understood through a children's book. People with children have probably read, and others may remember, *Are You My Mother?*, a story in which a baby bird falls from the nest and searches for his mother (Eastman 1960). He surveys everyone and everything around him, even inanimate objects, looking for what he needs to find. This reminds me of my experience, always looking at others around me, surveying what they have done to be a good-enough parent and a good-enough psychiatrist. Some days I really want to know how they handled a specific situation and how they structured their jobs when their children were in preschool. Other days, I just need to know that they seem to have managed it and it reassures me.

Mentoring is essential to survival when one is juggling career and family (Olarte 2004). The challenge I encountered was the paucity of women within the department who had attempted like me, to have children while working as full-time faculty member and had remained in academic medicine. For the most part, there were very few senior women faculty. It is hard to imagine a successful path when there are not many available and accessible models. Thankfully, there have been a couple of colleagues just a step or two ahead of me on this path. I work with several women in similar structures with respect to career and family. We are able to provide support and advice to one another regarding our careers. Peer mentorship can be quite effective (Files et al. 2008).

Mentorship can come in many forms—both formal and informal. There is top-down mentoring from a senior faculty member to a junior faculty member, but there is also a type of what I will call *bottom-up mentoring*, particularly in issues of mothering. Some of the best advice and support I have received have been from my fellows or residents who were moms long before I was. Of course, mentors may also be men. I have male mentors who have been essential teachers for me throughout my development and continue to be sounding boards for issues of career and family. It is important to remember that there may not be just one mentor that fits all of one's needs all of the time.

Good mentoring should include emotional support as well as instrumental support. As in business, effective mentoring must incorporate an aspect of advocacy or sponsorship in areas like promotion (Ibarra et al. 2010). And for women in academia, mentoring is especially important for the practical issues of promotion, publication, and professional development as well as for advice about achieving balance, having time with family, and finding creative ways to negotiate your job during the time your children are young. As a mentor said to me, "You may have to make a few ultimatums."

As a mentor now for residents, fellows, and medical students, my identity as a woman has played a significant role. It recently became evident to me that my position as a woman, a mother of young children, in academics, with an interest in clinical teaching and in local and national organizational medicine, is critical to those physicians that are following me. People ask me straightforward questions such as how do I get involved, apply for a fellowship, or make connections. The questions can also be highly complicated ones, such as how do you do this—kids, work, career? The challenge has become how to help people make the decision that is right for them at a given time, and how to help them recognize that their answers are unlikely to be the same for very long, because interests and careers develop, children grow, and everyone's desires and needs change.

Leadership

Leadership comes in many different forms. My models for leadership come from women and men I work with in my department as well as those in organizations such as the American Psychiatric Association and American Academy of Child and Adolescent Psychiatry. Much has been written about leadership styles and the differences between men and women. There is some research to support that women leaders are most successful when they pair stereotypic male behaviors (being tough, direct, and transparent) with stereotypic female behaviors (building power through consensus) (Isaac et al. 2010). Leadership is often taking on the task that you want to accomplish because it matters to you, when no one else will do it; you draw others in to join. My style includes thinking out loud with residents and multidisciplinary teams, inviting comment and full participation. I expect discussion and tend to empower those around me. I am willing to acknowledge errors and areas of weakness, and I strive to demonstrate my own learning. Sometimes leadership means stepping forward and being the one to make tough decisions. It also means taking responsibility for those decisions whether they are right or wrong in the long run. It is an important developmental step in your early career to practice being in a position in which not everyone will like your decisions. To make unpopular choices and maintain good working relationships even with those that opposed you is critical to one's own learning. It doesn't hurt one's parenting, either.

Conclusion

There are many decisions I have to make about how to balance career and family. It is remarkable to me that prior to having children I naively thought that once I made a decision about how to juggle or balance work and motherhood, life would proceed smoothly. I find that like many things in life, this is not one decision but a series of decisions. There are days when I can look years ahead and set a goal for my career or family, but there are other days when the best I can do is to make decisions for that week or sometimes only for that day. Many days, I question whether I am doing this the "right" way. Carrying with me role models of what the best mother does for her children and her family and what the best academic psychiatrist does for her students and her patients can be a heavy burden. It is sometimes difficult to remember that one cannot be all things to all people all at once. Perhaps in any moment, you are giving more in one area or another. Chaos and change are the only constants. It is a challenging task to become a mother and a new faculty member, though the hope is that each informs the other, that time is on your side, and that decisions come in small steps. Learn to be patient and know there will be many chances to adjust your path. Be reassured that you can have it all, but you just can't have it all at once.

PRACTICAL TIPS FOR WOMEN IN PSYCHIATRY

- Allow yourself to recognize how very hard this journey is. No matter who has done it before or how well or easily it seems they have managed it, it is always difficult. It is always different.
- Use humor as often as you can. Find others to laugh with you about the absurdity of this juggling act.
- Sleep as much as you can, when you can.
- It is OK to like and not always love all aspects of your work, just as it is OK to love and not always like all aspects of your children.
- Get help with child rearing—it does take a village. For those with family close by, use them; for those without family nearby, get a nanny or good day care. Find support in friends, and other toddlers' parents.
- Travel to meetings with children. We have been very lucky to do this, and my children have been on many airplanes in their short lives, and have seen some great places.
- Take extra time at the end of a trip to be at home with the children prior to returning to work. It helps all of us with the transition and particularly helps me when I have spent significant time on the trip in meetings.
- Consider a regular date night with your mate, which can be hard to do if you already feel you don't get enough time with your children. But we use it for reconnecting, having adult conversations, and sometimes even for exercise.
- Be flexible. Cancel a trip if you need to—especially if a child or children are sick and you want to be the one there to help them feel better.
- Try to work in a place where you feel you can contribute and in which you can be vulnerable enough to ask for help when you need it.
- Recognize that decisions are made over and over again. There will be many opportunities to adjust and perfect your course.

References

American Medical Association: Statistics history: physicians by gender. 2008. Available at: http://www.ama-assn.org/ama/pub/about-ama/our-people/member-groups-sections/women-physicians-congress/statistics-history/table-1-physicians-gender-excludes-students.page. Accessed December 1, 2011.

Association of American Medical Colleges: Women in U.S. academic medicine: statistics and medical school benchmarking report, 2009–2010. Available at: https://www.aamc.org/download/170248/data/2010_table1.pdf; https://www.aamc.org/download/170252/data/2009_table03.pdf; and https://www.aamc.org/download /170254/data/2009_table04a.pdf. Accessed December 1, 2011.

Bickel J: Women in academic psychiatry. Acad Psychiatry 28:285–291, 2004

Eastman PD: Are You My Mother? New York, Random House, 1960

Files JA, Blair JE, Mayer AP, et al: Facilitated peer mentorship: a pilot program for academic advancement of female medical faculty. J Womens Health (Larchmt) 17:1009–1015, 2008

Ibarra H, Carter NM, Silva C: Why men still get more promotions than women. Harv Bus Rev 88:80–85, 2010

Fox G, Schwartz A, Hart KM: Work-family balance and academic advancement in medical schools. Acad Psychiatry 30:227–234, 2006

Goodwin JP: Autumn: thoughts on commencing a fourth decade in academic psychiatry. Acad Psychiatry 28:325–330, 2004

Ibarra H, Carter NM, Silva C: Why men still get more promotions than women. Harv Bus Rev 88:80–85, 2010

Isaac C, Griffin L, Carnes M: A qualitative study of faculty members' views of women chairs. J Womens Health (Larchmt) 19:533–546, 2010

Mason MA, Goulden M: Do babies matter (part II)?: closing the baby gap. Academe 90(Nov-Dec), 2004. Available at: www.aaup.org/AAUP/pubsres/academe/2004/ND/Feat/04ndmaso.htm. Accessed September 22, 2011.

Nattinger A: Promoting the career development of women in academic medicine. Arch Intern Med 167:323–324, 2007

Nonnemaker L: Women physicians in academic medicine: new insights from cohort studies. N Engl J Med 342:399–405, 2000

Olarte SW: Women psychiatrists: personal and professional choices: a survey. Acad Psychiatry 28:321–324, 2004

Seritan AL, Iosif AM, Hyvonen S, et al: Gender differences in faculty development: a faculty needs survey. Acad Psychiatry 34:136–140, 2010

Verlander G: Female physicians: balancing career and family. Acad Psychiatry 28:331–336, 2004

Part II
Mid-Career and Beyond: A Mosaic

Chapter 5

Farmer's Daughter Excels in Psychiatry

Deborah Deas, M.D., M.P.H.

THIRTY MILES SOUTH OF CHARLESTON, South Carolina, sits the town of Adams Run, a rural community nestled among ageless oak trees and beautiful azaleas. While farmland generally rested on the perimeter of the community, it was an extension of the homes of the farmers. My father, Mike Deas, was a well-known farmer in Adams Run and my mother, Carrie Deas, an anchor for the community. She had a self-effacing personality and a generosity that was never-ending, extending to family, friends, and strangers who crossed her path.

Some of my favorite pastimes in my country town were riding my bicycle, sharing a long Sunday walk with my girlfriends, and sitting on the front porch with my parents and grandfather. The hours I spent on the front porch in the rocking chair, carefully listening and frequently offering

I wish to thank Dr. Emmett Michael Lampkin and Ms. Marshelle Grant for their manuscript preparation and editorial assistance. This work is dedicated to my daughters, Nasim and Tahirih Nesmith.

my opinions to the elders proved to be more beneficial than any college course I have taken. They usually started with stories of the past, deviating to what life would look like if things were different and admonishing me not to squander opportunities. They emphasized the importance of setting goals and keeping your eyes on the prize. Service was important and the ways that one could serve were numerous.

They frequently said "We all stand on someone else's shoulders." The notion that one should learn from others, as well as teach others, was as common as baked bread. These experiences shaped me and led me to the establishment of the guiding principles that chartered the course of my professional development. Those principles emerging for me were: establishing of goals, engaging in service, seeking and obtaining mentorship, networking, refining leadership skills, and taking care of yourself and your loved ones. These principles were not necessarily implemented in a hierarchical or stepwise fashion, but maintained a fluidity throughout my professional development, sometimes occurring simultaneously and in concert, while other times shifting out of necessity.

My parents instilled in me that education is the key to a fruitful future and that it is something no one can take away from you. Toward that end, they were motivational and encouraged excellence in all things. After graduating from high school at the age of sixteen, I attended the College of Charleston, thirty miles north of my rural hometown. I received a bachelor of science degree in biology and immediately began graduate school at the University of South Carolina, where I received a master of public health degree. Shortly after completing graduate school, I married Alonzo Nesmith Jr. and we moved to Iowa City, Iowa, where he pursued a master's degree in hospital administration at the University of Iowa. I worked at the University of Iowa in research, investigating the role of the renin-kallikrein system in hypertension. After two years in Iowa, we returned to Charleston. I then worked at the Medical University of South Carolina (MUSC) in the Department of Microbiology and Immunology and for several years did research that explored the role of autoantibodies in infertility.

Medical School Years: Embracing Psychiatry

After several years of research I returned to my dream of becoming a physician, applying and being accepted to medical school at MUSC. When I entered medical school, I felt with utmost certainty that I would pursue a career in family medicine and one day return to my hometown of Adams Run to care for people who are poor and underserved. Once I began my clinical clerkships, that certainty of choosing family medicine had dampened, and I was mesmerized by several of the other specialties. While I enjoyed all of the clinical rotations, I was struck by the lack of attention paid to fairly obvious psychological and social issues affecting the patients. In fact, when I attempted to introduce these issues during my presentation of the patient, they were readily dismissed most of the time. In spite of these dismissals, it became quite apparent to me that the clinical outcomes of the majority of patients were influenced by psychological and social issues.

When I started my psychiatry rotation I was intrigued by the emphasis on the biological, psychological, and social aspects of the patient. I felt that I had found what I was searching for in medicine. There was a part of me that was concerned about whether I would be considered a "real doctor" if I chose psychiatry as my field of specialty. Despite the concern, it was so rewarding to be able to attend to the entire patient. My psychiatry rotation was at the Ralph H. Johnson Veterans Affairs Medical Center (VAMC) in Charleston, where I saw patients with multiple medical illnesses as well as psychiatric illnesses. I quickly recognized that I really had to know and understand what I learned during my internal medicine rotation in order to be a competent psychiatrist. Much to my surprise, I felt comfortable and at home in the field of psychiatry. Moreover, my mentor, Dr. Miriam DeAntonio, an attending physician at the VAMC, encouraged me to take notice of the joy that I was getting out of the psychiatry clinical clerkship. She was always willing to have a conversation about a future career in psychiatry and share how much satisfaction she got from her career as a psychiatrist.

During my fourth year of medical school, I chose to do a psychiatry externship that had a different dimension. I worked with Dr. Stephen McLeod-Bryant, an attending psychiatrist at the MUSC Institute of Psychiatry, on a project that explored the process of deinstitutionalization of psychiatric patients. This project involved visits to community mental health centers and the state hospital, as well as the administrative offices of the commissioner of mental health for the state of South Carolina. At that time, the commissioner was Dr. Joseph Bevilacqua, and his director of children's services was Dr. Jerome Hanley. Meetings with Drs. Bevilacqua and Hanley enlightened me on the operations of a mental health system on the state level. Throughout the externship, I met regularly with Dr. McLeod-Bryant. At the end of my externship we wrote the paper "Psychiatric Deinstitutionalization and Its Cultural Insensitivity: Consequences and Recommendations for the Future" (Deas and McLeod-Bryant 1992). Not only was the paper published, it was pivotal to my interest in psychiatric research. As a fourth-year medical student, I submitted this paper in the student and resident competition of the National Medical Association and in May 1989 was awarded the Annual Chester M. Pierce, M.D., Resident and Medical Student Research Symposium Award. For the remainder of the fourth year of medical school I focused on choosing the right place for my residency. Although I interviewed at several programs for residency, I chose to stay at MUSC because of its stellar reputation, my spouse's job, and the closeness of family.

Residency match day rolled around in no time, and my spouse and six-year-old daughter, Nasim, accompanied me to open the envelope to see where we would spend the next four years. When I opened my envelope and saw that I would be in the MUSC psychiatry program I jumped for joy. The excitement of the year 1989 was just getting started. At graduation, I was flanked by my parents, spouse, daughter, and a host of family members and friends, including many from my small hometown, all supportive and excited about my receiving my medical degree.

Residency Years

A month later, the National Council of Women recognized me for my leadership and community involvement by honoring me with the Young Woman Achievement Award. Shortly thereafter, the Omega Psi Phi fraternity presented me with their Achievement in Medicine Award. The week after I started my internship, my parents called to inform me that I was on the front page of our local newspaper, *The Post and Courier.* The article highlighted the farm girl from rural Adams Run, South Carolina, becoming the first physician in her family. Other highlights of 1989 included Hurricane Hugo, which forced me to leave Charleston the evening before Hugo struck and to return the following morning to be on call at the Charleston Memorial Hospital. The trauma of the hurricane exacerbated some of the patients' illnesses. As a resident, I slept on the inpatient unit for two nights. Later during the same year we had one of the biggest snowstorms in over twenty-five years.

The atmosphere of residency training was much like that of medical school. When I arrived at MUSC for residency training orientation, I quickly learned that I was one of two African Americans among the 500 residents at MUSC. It was not uncommon for me to be mistaken by many to be a social worker, a secretary, or a ward clerk despite wearing my white coat with *Deborah Deas, M.D.,* written on it. This mistake was even made by some of my fellow M.D. peers. I found that the best response was to ask "And just why do you think I am a social worker?" That question was always met with a foot-in-the-mouth response, especially when they looked and saw that I had a long white coat on and a stethoscope in my pocket. Within the Department of Psychiatry and Behavioral Sciences, I was the only African American psychiatry resident among the fifty-five residents in training. I later learned that there had not been an African American resident in ten years, when Dr. Mike Lampkin was the first African American resident in psychiatry at MUSC.

Residency training was very rewarding, and I sought to learn from many people. I recognized that mentors were important, and I carefully chose several mentors, namely Drs. Stephen McLeod-Bryant, Kathleen Brady, William (Bill) Carson, and Carrie Randall. They were my primary mentors, but I learned so much from other attending physicians as well. Much to my surprise, although I thought I would not have a research interest while in residency, as I continued to ask specific questions several mentors responded with "We have not looked at that; maybe you should put a study together to explore it." One such question was whether the medication fluoxetine (Prozac) would be effective for psychogenic polydipsia. In my exploration of this question, I worked with Dr. Timothy Brewerton and we published a case report, *A Case of Fluoxetine-Responsive Psychogenic Polydipsia: A Variant of Obsessive-Compulsive Disorder?* (Deas-Nesmith and Brewerton 1992). The following year, I received a travel award to attend the American College of Neuropsychopharmacology (ACNP) annual meeting. During that meeting I was thoroughly convinced that I would augment my clinical skills in psychiatry with research. I later garnered the Charter Fellow Leadership Award from the American Academy of Child and Adolescent Psychiatry (AACAP), and had the good fortune of meeting Dr. Jeanne Spurlock, former deputy medical director of the American Psychiatric Association's Office of Minority/National Affairs and a child psychiatrist, who later became one of my mentors. Dr. Spurlock spent time with me during the annual AACAP meetings and over breakfast encouraged me to think seriously about a career as a child and adolescent psychiatrist. Virginia Anthony, Executive Director of AACAP, echoed Dr. Spurlock's sentiments. These two individuals paved the way for me to network at AACAP's annual meetings and suggested I attend sessions that provided information about the various opportunities and paths one might venture as a child and adolescent psychiatrist. When I attended the AACAP annual meeting during my third year of residency training, I had no doubt that I would pursue a child and adolescent psychiatry fellowship.

Residency training encompassed successes and challenges. I held several leadership positions as a resident, including class representative, resident representative on the Residency Selection Committee, and member of the On-call Reorganization Committee, to name a few. Multiple national awards were within my reach, and Dr. Alberto Santos, the psychiatry residency training director, often nominated me as well as others for these awards. I never failed to win a national award for which I was nominated. Some of the awards included the National Institute of Mental Health Outstanding Resident Award, the National Medical Association Outstanding

Resident Award, the National Council of Women Award, the Laughlin Fellow Award of The American College of Psychiatrists, National Institute of Mental Health Selected Seminar Participant award, National Medical Association Chester Pierce, M.D., Research Award, the Young Women's Christian Association (YWCA) Tribute to Women in Leadership Award, the American Psychiatric Association Resident Travel Award, and the ACNP Travel Award. Surprisingly, near the end of the third year of residency training, a few of my fellow residents met with the training director to complain that I was being nominated for too many national awards, and at least a couple of them implied that I got the awards because I am African American. Although hurtful, it just confirmed what my parents told me years ago on the front porch in Adams Run, South Carolina, "Regardless of how intelligent you might be, you will always have to work twice as hard...."

During residency training, my mother had a second cerebrovascular accident, and although her recovery was remarkable, she was plagued by complications from chronic illnesses such as diabetes, hypertension, and hypercholesterolemia. We lived about five miles from my parents, which provided the comfort that we were available at a moment's notice. There were multiple transports by ambulance to the emergency department, several medical admissions, and a lengthy stay at a transition facility. I will never forget the phone call from my mother's physician at 5:10 A.M. informing me that my mother had passed away. I took two days off to plan and attend the funeral, and on the third day I returned to my duties on the inpatient adult psychiatry unit. For several weeks I would awaken intermittently at 5:10 A.M., grieving my loss. The prayers and loving support of my spouse and three dear friends in my residency program, Drs. Shannon Little, Kimberly White, and Mark Wagner provided scaffolding for me. Additionally, as a child my parents grounded me in the Baha'i Faith, a world religion founded by Baha'u'llah (Glory of God) and based on the principles of One God, One Mankind, and One Religion. The teachings of the Baha'i Faith and the prayers are my guiding posts throughout life. The Baha'i prayers for assistance and for the departed revealed in me a level of resiliency that I had no idea I possessed.

The end of the third year of residency was fast approaching, and it was time for the selection of the chief resident. In years past, the chief resident was always chosen from the rising fourth-year residency class. Most of my faculty mentors had no doubt that I would be chosen as chief resident. One faculty member said, "You are the most obvious amongst your cohort to be chosen as chief resident—you have held multiple leadership positions; you have won several national awards which brought notoriety to our psychiatry program; you have a master's degree in administration and chaired the resident finance committee and served in many administrative positions as a resident; you are a team player and constantly try to advance others—need I say more?" Much to my surprise, the department chair told me six months prior to the selection process that I was his first choice. Not only was I not chosen as chief resident, a fifth-year resident (a fellow) was chosen. It was unprecedented for the chief resident to be chosen from outside the fourth-year residency class. To my knowledge, this has not since been the case for the chief resident selection in the department. I guess this must have been the kind of example my parents referred to when they told me, "Desperate times call for desperate measures."

The not-so-transparent process prompted me to have a face-to-face meeting with the chair of the department. My purpose being to ascertain whether this was to be an example of what I might expect if I remained in MUSC's psychiatry department as a child and adolescent psychiatry fellow or as a future faculty member. My chair assured me that I had a bright future in the department, and he wanted me to remain there as a child and adolescent psychiatry fellow and a future faculty member. Although apologetic, he in no way adequately explained the logic of this chief resident selection.

I began my child and adolescent psychiatry fellowship (at MUSC) during my fourth year of residency, and combined it with a National Institute of Alcohol Abuse and Alcoholism (NIAAA) research fellowship focusing on adolescent substance abuse (alcohol). My mentors in the child and adolescent psychiatry fellowship were Drs. Donald Carek, Lisa Hand, and Katherine Outz. A community experience was integrated into my fellowship training, allowing me to spend one day a week at a community mental health center caring for children and their families while working with a case management team.

Ultimately my research focus shifted to adolescents with substance abuse as well as other psychiatric disorders. Dr. Carrie Randall was my primary mentor for the NIAAA research fellowship, and by the end of my first year in the fellowship we had written a small National Institutes of Health grant proposal, *Substance-Abusing Adolescents: HIV/AIDS Intervention*, which was funded by the NIAAA. Dr. Randall taught me to think critically, evaluate existing scientific literature, design research studies, and write research grant proposals. I continued to attend the AACAP annual meetings, where I frequently met with Dr. Spurlock and Virginia Anthony. The potential for being a child and adolescent psychiatrist with a research career became clearer.

The meetings at the ACNP were instrumental and offered me the opportunity of having a mentor there. I took full advantage of the mentor-mentee relationship. Dr. Myra Weissman was assigned as my mentor at the ACNP. When she learned of my research interest in adolescent substance abuse, as well as clinical work in child and adolescent psychiatry, she allotted time for us to meet during the meeting to design my first inpatient adolescent research study. We designed a study to explore the prevalence of substance use disorders in an adolescent inpatient sample. This study was conducted in the final year of my fellowship and our findings revealed that thirty percent of adolescents admitted to the youth inpatient unit at the Institute of Psychiatry at MUSC had a substance use disorder (Deas-Nesmith et al. 1998). This study provided the impetus for me to join the MUSC Department of Psychiatry and Behavioral Sciences faculty and develop an adolescent substance abuse program at the Institute of Psychiatry.

Charting My Career Path

There was another saying that I heard from my parents, "Don't put all your eggs in one basket." Therefore, in preparation for an academic position, I interviewed at Vanderbilt University, Yale University, and the University of Kentucky. With several great offers, I had to weigh all options to make the best decision. Some of the important things considered were my spouse's employment, our daughter's education and her contact with extended family, and our parents' health and well-being, particularly that of my elderly father (then eighty-eight years old), who was a bit anxious about us leaving the Charleston area. My husband had recently received a great promotion, and his parents were retiring. We made a decision to stay in Charleston, and I joined the MUSC psychiatry faculty as assistant professor and director of the Adolescent Substance Abuse Program, which I would develop.

My chairman charged me with developing an adolescent substance abuse program, giving me a timeline of four to five years. I thought he was a bit generous, knowing that I would not take that long to develop the program. While developing the program I worked as an inpatient attending physician in the Youth Division of the Department of Psychiatry and Behavioral Sciences, maintained an outpatient case load, and continued my research projects. By the end of the first year on faculty, I had established a small dual-diagnosis inpatient unit for adolescents with psychiatric and substance use disorders. Two years later, the inpatient dual-diagnosis program had expanded with the addition of an intensive outpatient after-school program. The Adolescent Substance Abuse Program ballooned into a comprehensive program that included services across the continuum of inpatient and outpatient services as well as research and educational training. Our program joined forces with the Addiction Psychiatry Fellowship to provide adolescent substance abuse training to fellows in the addiction fellowship as well as training for child and adolescent psychiatry fellows who had an interest in substance abuse. The program was one of the five accredited programs nationally that provided adolescent substance abuse training. Needless to say, interested candidates from across the country sought fellowship training at MUSC in substance abuse.

The wisdom of our decision to remain in Charleston became clear when my father fell ill at my kitchen table and required hospitalization. He was treated for atrial fibrillation and six months later a pacemaker was placed. We celebrated his eighty-ninth birthday in September 1994 surrounded by his family and friends. His smile seemed to light up the room, and the memory is indelibly marked. He passed away in November 1994. I often remind myself how glad I was about not moving out of state for another job.

In 1995 our younger daughter, Tahirih, was born, twelve years after her sister Nasim, and I quickly learned how to balance an infant and a full-time career. I had lots of support systems in place to manage my career and a newborn. My mother-in-law, Amelia Nesmith, having retired, was always willing to lend a hand and Willie Mae Brodrick (Grandma Brodrick) was Tahirih's primary care giver when we were at work.

During my third year as an inpatient attending, Dr. Randall suggested that if I was going to be an expert in child and adolescent substance abuse, I should get more mentored research training and work toward becoming an independent investigator. We began work on a National Institutes of Health Mentored Career Development Award application, which consumed many nights and parts of my weekends. Much to our liking, the Mentored Career Development Award (K24) was funded by NIAAA on its first submission, and funding was provided for career development and research for five years at the level of seventy-five percent effort. During the career development period, I was fortunate to have an apprenticeship with Dr. James Roberts, statistician for the Charleston Alcohol Research Center, who taught me statistical analyses, database development, and writing of the data analysis section of manuscripts. The training further solidified my research skills as an academic clinician. Dr. Raymond Anton mentored me on conducting clinical trials and managing a research team. My research expanded to conducting other clinical trials in the adolescent population. I was successful in obtaining industry funding to conduct clinical trials in the areas of adolescent depression, anxiety, and substance abuse.

Dr. Himanshu Upadhyaya joined the child and adolescent psychiatry fellowship at MUSC and later completed an addiction fellowship in adolescent substance abuse. He became one of my closest friends and collaborators. Once he joined the department's faculty, we worked closely on research studies in adolescents and I learned much from him about research on nicotine use in adolescents.

I never forgot the importance of mentorship, and as a result I have reached out to students, residents, and junior faculty to provide mentorship. Several medical students worked with me on research projects in the Jeanne Spurlock Minority Medical Student Research Fellowship in Substance Abuse and Addiction, jointly sponsored by AACAP and the National Institute on Drug Abuse. Over the years, I mentored more than ten medical student recipients of the fellowship. The fellowship provided them a summer research opportunity, attendance at the annual AACAP meeting, and an opportunity to present their research at the meeting. As a result, the AACAP has awarded me the Outstanding Mentor Award on many occasions. Likewise, I mentored more than fifteen child psychiatry fellows during their training. Several of the child psychiatry mentees received "best paper" awards for their work and I was honored with the Golden Apple Award for Teaching in Child/Adolescent Psychiatry, by the child and adolescent psychiatry fellows at MUSC.

I quickly climbed the academic ladder at MUSC, rising to associate professor of psychiatry and behavioral sciences within five years of joining the faculty, and becoming a tenured faculty member the year after reaching the associate level. I became an independent researcher and was awarded an independent research award (R01), for a study titled *Naltrexone Treatment of Adolescent Alcoholics*, funded by NIAAA. Over several years, my research funding totaled more than seven million dollars. Four years after becoming an associate professor, I was promoted to professor of psychiatry and behavioral sciences, and became the first African American, tenured, full professor on faculty at MUSC. Additionally, the number of my accumulated publications in scientific journals reached almost seventy.

My career in psychiatry has always been rewarding, and most days are filled with excitement and enthusiasm. I have received great satisfaction from teaching, mentoring medical students, residents, and junior faculty, caring for my patients, and conducting research. I became an expert in adolescent substance abuse treatment and was frequently asked to present at national and international meetings. My work has taken me to countries such as Japan, Sweden, France, India, Turkey, the Czech Republic, and throughout the United States. Oftentimes, Nasim and Tahirih would accompany me on the international trips. I attended the meetings, and afterward we extended our stay to vacation and enjoy each other. Rest and recreation have always been integral components of my life, and I manage to continue fun activities throughout my career.

Throughout medical school, my family and I had a standing dinner outing every Friday evening. We have continued this tradition, which allows us to decompress into the weekend. Exercise has been an important staple for me, although during medical school I only got a chance to work out two to three times a week. When I started my residency program, a wellness center membership was part of the benefits package for residents, and I took full advantage by increasing my routine exercise to four times a week at the wellness center. Over the past ten years, I have been exercising at the Harper Student Wellness Center at least five times a week and meeting with a personal trainer twice a week. I noticed quickly that the increase in my exercise routine enhanced my productivity in all areas.

I enjoy the arts and have always attended dance and jazz performances regularly. Charleston has been the host city for almost twenty-five years of Spoleto Festival USA, the international arts festival that originated in Spoleto, Italy. Over the past fifteen years I have purchased season tickets for the Spoleto Festival, and cherished this time to enjoy the activities with family and friends. Charleston also hosts the Family Circle Cup (a women's professional tennis tournament) during the spring, and I have been a season ticket holder for more than a decade. I also enjoy travel outside the context of work. Thus, I have traveled throughout the United States with my children and friends, as well as going to South Africa, Botswana, Zimbabwe, France, Belgium, England, Germany, Costa Rica, and other countries.

Administration has been involved in my professional career, beginning with the development of the Adolescent Substance Abuse Program when I joined the MUSC faculty, and including managing my research programs. Several of my colleagues thought I had a knack for administration, and I suppose this was enhanced by my master of public health degree in administration and epidemiology. I envisioned a goal of doing more administrative work once I reached the rank of professor.

During the year 2000, I began to explore administrative opportunities in the field of psychiatry and interviewed at three universities, two of which offered me positions. During the decision-making process, I was approached by Dr. Layton McCurdy, former dean of the College of Medicine at MUSC, who was about to retire within six months. Dr. McCurdy was one of my mentors and I served on his National Board of Examiners team. He counseled me to explore administrative opportunities at MUSC before making a decision to accept a job elsewhere. The new dean who would replace Dr. McCurdy was to arrive in July 2001, and there was no certainty that there would be an available administrative position in the dean's office. Dr. McCurdy asked me to postpone my decision until the new dean arrived and to make a decision after having a formal meeting with the dean.

Dr. Jerry Reves was appointed dean of the College of Medicine at MUSC on July 1, 2001. I met with Dr. Reves a month later and he shared his vision for the College of Medicine, and discussed leadership opportunities within the college. I expressed interest in the area of admissions for medical students. In September, I was appointed associate dean for admissions for the College of Medicine. In this role, I had oversight of all medical school applications, student interviews, the admissions committee, and the acceptance of medical students to MUSC. Dr. Reves also asked me to assist him in the area of diversity in the college. He expressed his desire to have a College of Medicine Diversity Committee that would develop a strategic diversity plan for the college. While I accepted this job, I also informed him that the diversity work was much larger than "an assistant" role. He replied, "We will expand as we go along, and I am willing to put resources in the area of diversity."

Dr. Reves and I carefully selected members from the College of Medicine faculty to serve on the College of Medicine Diversity Committee. As a group, the members of this committee solidly supported the vision for diversity, so we were off to an excellent start. Before developing the College of Medicine diversity plan, our committee assessed the state of diversity in the College of Medicine. The assessment revealed that in medicine, there were 35 members of underrepresented groups (African American, Hispanic, and Native American) among the 800 faculty members and 16 underrepresented-in-medicine residents among the 522 house staff members. Underrepresented medical students constituted 10% of the student body. Additionally, the assessment revealed that fewer than 20 underrepresented-in-medicine individuals were invited to present grand rounds or participate in seminar series in the College of Medicine over the previous several years. Each department in the College of Medicine was asked to develop a diversity plan to meet its needs but maintain consistency with the College of Medicine's diversity plan. All departments developed their diversity plans and the college launched the College of Medicine Six-Year (2003–2009) Diversity Plan. An assessment tool was developed to evaluate progress by each department on an annual basis.

In the midst of my medical school admissions and diversity work, I completed the Hedwig van Ameringen Executive Leadership in Academic Medicine (ELAM) program for women. ELAM is an in-depth, year-long program that prepares senior women faculty members for leadership positions in academic health centers. My capstone project was to develop a comprehensive diversity program for MUSC's College of Medicine. This project complemented our ongoing diversity work.

Over the six-year period of careful implementation and evaluation of the College of Medicine and departmental diversity plans, we made unprecedented progress. The number of underrepresented-in-medicine faculty members increased from thirty-five to sixty-seven. By 2008, we almost quadrupled the number of underrepresented-in-medicine residents with growth from sixteen to sixty-one and underrepresented individuals consti-tuted eighteen percent of our medical student body. Over a three-year pe-riod, more than 200 underrepresented-in-medicine individuals were invited to speak at grand rounds and seminar series. We developed several pipeline programs as well as mentoring programs for students and resi-dents. The Association of American Medical Colleges (AAMC) recog-nized MUSC's College of Medicine with the AAMC Institutional Diversity Leadership Award. We were able to recruit and matriculate ten African American males to the graduating class for four consecutive years. These African American males developed the A Gentleman and a Scholar Mentoring Program, which focuses on high school and undergraduate Af-rican American males interested in the field of medicine. The AAMC rec-ognized the A Gentleman and a Scholar Mentoring Program in its *AAMC Reporter* in 2009 (Harris 2009).

Dr. Reves was set to retire from the dean's position in July 2010 and to remain on faculty at MUSC. Prior to Dr. Reves' departure, our University Medical Associates faculty practice plan contributed one million dollars to a diversity scholarship endowment in honor of Dr. Reves, and the faculty members through their departments matched it with one million dollars. Dr. Reves was presented with the Jenny and Jerry Reves Diversity Schol-arship Endowment in the spring before his departure. Funds from this two million dollar endowment will be used to provide scholarships for under-represented-in-medicine medical students entering the College of Medi-cine at MUSC.

Fortunately, I was asked by Dr. Raymond Greenberg, the president of MUSC, to serve on the selection committee for the dean who would replace Dr. Reves. There were several well-qualified candidates for the po-sition, all of whom I interviewed. Needless to say, I explored the can-didates' vision for diversity and inclusion in the College of Medicine. We selected Dr. Etta Pisano, an internationally renowned radiologist and former vice dean of academic affairs at the University of North Carolina, to join MUSC as the College of Medicine dean and vice president for medical affairs.

One of Dr. Pisano's first orders of business was to endorse the diversity work in the College of Medicine and expand the diversity plan to focus on: the promotion of racial/ethnic and gender diversity in leadership; the pro-motion of cultural understanding and cultural competency; and the expan-sion and enhancement of opportunities for individuals of all backgrounds. She charged all departments to develop a five-year diversity plan (2010–2015). Dr. Pisano invited me to be on her team and I accepted my new role as senior associate dean for medical education. In this role, I have over-sight of medical school education (undergraduate medical education for medical students, graduate medical education for residents, and continuing medical education for faculty), medical school admissions, diversity, and student affairs.

Throughout my life, service has been of utmost importance and my parents placed great emphasis on serving humanity and uplifting others. They frequently reminded me of the writing of the Baha'i Faith, "Man's merit lieth in service and virtue and not in the pageantry of wealth and riches." As such, my service extended beyond the realms of my university into the community. Throughout residency, I served as an on-call physician for the emergency mobile crisis psychiatric team, and was a frequent speaker for Career Day and Parent Day at local schools. I participated in community health fairs and the YWCA, and presented youth seminars at local churches. High school students often sought me to mentor them on senior theses and college students pursued me for career and educational advisement. On any given day, I agreed to be a guest on radio and television programs aimed to educate the community, especially teens, about mental health and substance use issues.

Within MUSC, my service on departmental and university committees has been extensive as a participating member and frequently as the committee chair. My expertise in adolescent substance abuse has been sought by national committees, resulting in service on committees of The American College of Psychiatrists, the American Psychiatric Association, and the American Academy of Addiction Psychiatry.

PRACTICAL TIPS FOR WOMEN IN PSYCHIATRY

As I reflect on my career path, I am completely satisfied with the road I've traveled, which at times had crises, but I recognized many victories in those crises. My guiding principles rested in an abiding faith, and preparation for what was to come. My advice to others would be:

- Establish goals (short-term and long-term).
- Seek and obtain mentorship.
- Refine your leadership skills.
- Engage in service.
- Take care of yourself and your loved ones.

In summary, the farmer's daughter has come a long way. I have stood on the shoulders of many, pushing forward with an abiding faith that there was nothing that I could not accomplish.

References

Deas-Nesmith D, Brewerton TD: A case of fluoxetine-responsive psychogenic polydipsia: a variant of obsessive-compulsive disorder? J Nerv Ment Dis 180:338–339, 1992

Deas-Nesmith D, McLeod-Bryant S: Psychiatric deinstitutionalization and its cultural insensitivity: consequences and recommendations for the future. J Natl Med Assoc 84:1036–1040, 1992

Deas-Nesmith D, Campbell S, Brady KT: Substance use disorders in an adolescent inpatient psychiatric population. J Natl Med Assoc 90: 233–238, 1998

Harris S: Man to man, students inspire youth. AAMC Reporter, October 2009. Available at: https://www.aamc.org/newsroom/reporter/oct09/88608/oct09_youth.html. Accessed October 5, 2011.

Chapter 6

Finding My Way

A Nontraditional Career in Psychiatry

Mary E. Barber, M.D.

LET ME INTRODUCE MYSELF. I am a psychiatrist, a wife, and a mother. I am also a lesbian and a white person in a black family. In some ways my life is conventional, and in some ways it is not so conventional. My career is similar. I have an academic appointment, I write, and I lecture at meetings. Yet as an administrator in a state psychiatric hospital, I do these things outside of the usual academic medical center environment. My job as a psychiatric administrator and my academic role as an expert on lesbian, gay, bisexual, and transgender (LGBT) mental health share many philosophical commonalities, such as a belief in people's individuality and autonomy, and in a person-centered approach to treatment. Yet the two parts of my career don't often overlap.

There was no roadmap for the career I have built, and I did not know that my life would turn out as it has when I started my psychiatry residency. Yet I'm very happy with how the different parts of my life and work fit together and complement each other. I was attracted to medicine and psychiatry partly for the varied experiences I could have, and I have found a way to achieve that variety that is uniquely my own.

The Early Years

My mother, famous in her classroom and at home for her provocative sayings, used to say "Better to have a drink than to have to see a shrink." (She also said, "A bop on the head once in a while can't hurt.") Although she was joking, and I might add was by no means a drinker, there was an underlying message that people should solve their problems on their own.

My father had similar biases. I remember a time when I was fourteen years old and reading Jonathan Miller's *States of Mind* (Miller 1983) after seeing an interview with Miller on PBS (yes, I was always a bit nerdy). Excited by what I was reading, I came downstairs from my room and told my father that I wanted to be a psychiatrist. He said, "People usually go into that field because they have their own problems." I remember thinking, "Then I'll do it anyway, but I won't tell you about it." You see, my parents may have had their ideas about mental health and psychiatry, but they also taught me to be curious and engaged and to have my own opinions.

I'm sure I was also born with a rebellious streak. Another thing my teacher parents often said was, "You can do anything you want, but please, don't be a teacher." They both loved the art of teaching but wanted something more prestigious and respected for their children. So, naturally, I gravitated to a field that is very close to teaching.

I grew up in Oswego, New York, a small town far upstate, north of Syracuse on Lake Ontario. My father taught math at the state university and my mother taught math at the high school. I have always loved math, loved reading, and loved learning generally. In Oswego, it was not "cool" to be smart or to like school. It was not cool to be different in any way in this very homogeneous town, and once my girlfriends started going crazy about boys, I had an inkling that I was different in more ways than just being smart and nerdy. Although I had several close friends, I often felt stifled and alienated growing up in a small town.

Eventually, I escaped to college at Cornell University, which was just a couple of hours' drive from Oswego but felt like Disneyland to me. In college I met all different kinds of people, very smart people who all loved school. I finally felt as though I could breathe.

When I started college, becoming an engineer seemed to make sense given my interest in math and science. But as classes progressed from the basic sciences to the applied ones, a career in engineering seemed less appealing. I started volunteering in the campus gynecology clinic; it seemed medical school might be a good career. As a student medical assistant, I helped women choose birth control methods and learn how to use diaphragms. This work was enjoyable, and my volunteer time extended beyond the expected tenure. When it came time to declare a major, I decided to switch to math and be a premed student.

During the summer after college and the first two summers of medical school, I worked as a medical assistant in the local obstetrics and gynecology practice in Oswego. My duties included conducting "urine checks" and, as the medical assistant, talking to the patients about the results and follow-up. This visit did not include an opportunity for the patient to see the doctor.

One day I went to the waiting room to get a patient who had one of these urine check appointments. When I brought her back into the office and told her that her test was negative, she was irate. She had not been clearly told the purpose of the visit, and she knew that she didn't have a urinary tract infection, and what kind of office were we running anyway, and on and on, in escalating intensity. I was taken aback but answered that I was very sorry that this mix-up had occurred and that she had been misinformed about the type of appointment she had been given. Her affect immediately changed; her anger evaporated and she became tearful. She started telling me her actual symptoms, which sounded like symptoms of menopause. These symptoms were scaring her, and she had hoped to see a doctor because she had a lot of questions. I had her wait in the office while I got the doctor to agree to fit her in for a visit that day. It was an important lesson for me about the power of simply listening to a patient.

I have since experienced many other times when listening was as important as any medical test or technology. And I think it was this understanding, coupled with my eventual realization that I had very little interest in the surgical aspects of ob-gyn, that led me back to my adolescent interest in psychiatry.

Becoming a Community Psychiatrist

If you had asked me what I wanted to do when I was in residency, I would have said I wanted to be a clinician-researcher, like the attending psychiatrists I admired at the Payne Whitney Clinic. I couldn't have imagined my career in public psychiatry, and I'm not sure I would have wanted it. Yet now that I am where I am, I am happy I didn't take the other path. I am grateful that I let my career happen step by step, not completely sure at each point where I would end up.

When I went to interview for a psychiatry residency at Payne Whitney, one of my interviewers looked at my resume—which listed rotations in epidemiology research at the Centers for Disease Control and community medicine and family practice with the Indian Health Service—and said, "You seem to have an interest in community psychiatry." I had no idea what community psychiatry was, or that it was a specialty. I had just been doing things that interested me.

As a result of these experiences, my residency program director recommended me for the Mead Johnson Fellowship, an American Psychiatric Association (APA) award that is now called the APA Public Psychiatry Fellowship. That enabled me to go to APA meetings and meet leaders in community psychiatry. It also got me noticed near the end of my residency by the leaders of the Columbia University Public Psychiatry Fellowship, who invited me to come for an interview.

Again, I heard negativity about a possible career path, this time not from my parents but from my colleagues. "You don't need to do a fellowship to do community psychiatry," I heard from another resident, who no doubt had heard it from an attending physician. "You can just get a job." I thought it wouldn't hurt to have the interview, since I hadn't yet decided what to do after my residency. And I was very impressed by the fellowship, with its mix of academics and field placement (Ranz 1996). I was offered a few possible field placement sites to consider, including the one I eventually chose, Ulster County Mental Health Services. I was told about Ulster, "It's a CMHC." I had no idea what those initials meant (community mental health center), and I realized I would learn a lot in the fellowship.

And learn I did. Through the Columbia Public Psychiatry Fellowship, I developed the beginnings of a framework for how to be a manager and to think in terms of systems and not just individual patients. I learned too about evidence-based treatments for people with serious mental illness and substance use disorders, and, at the same time, I treated patients at my field placement site. Perhaps most important, I acquired a lifetime network of community psychiatrists in the other fellows, alumni, and faculty of the program. I still call the fellowship director, Jules Ranz, M.D., whenever I have a need for supervision. So, instead of "just getting a job," I was able to develop a professional identity as a public psychiatrist.

Gender and Sexuality

I emerged from college with a good awareness of gender bias in science, largely thanks to the teaching of Sandra Bem, Ph.D. (1993). In Professor Bem's *Psychology of Sex Roles* course at Cornell, we looked critically at studies purporting to show gender differences and attribute them to biology. One famously cited study is the study of girls with congenital adrenal hyperplasia that documented the presence of increased testosterone in utero

(Money and Ehrhardt 1972). The study found these girls to prefer boys' toys over dolls and to show little interest in having children, compared to girls without this condition. This is a widely referenced study even today for demonstrating how biology affects gender roles; however, Professor Bem described to us several problems with the study's conclusion, noting that the parents, and often the children as well, were not blind to the girls' condition. There is a possibility that the parents, knowing that their daughters were "different," could have tolerated or even encouraged more cross-gender behavior. The condition includes sterility, so it is possible that some of the girls knew they would not be able to have children and were therefore less interested in dolls. And the condition also requires treatment with cortisol, which can have its own masculinizing effects.

The ability to think critically about research was important then and continues to be important today. In my view, sex roles are more rigidly regarded today than they were in the 1970s when I was growing up. The proliferation of princess movies and attire for little girls is one manifestation of this, but for boys the rules seem even more binding. When my older daughter was three years old, I remember picking her up from daycare one day and witnessing another mother running to pull her son away from a play kitchen sink, crying in horror, "No, sweetie!! That's a *girl's* toy!"

In science and medicine, the pendulum seems to have swung fully in the direction of magnifying every gender difference and attributing each one to biology. Yet even obviously biological differences are less absolute than we make them out to be. We have to be cautious and a little skeptical whenever we encounter absolute statements about gender. Some writers talk about gender in a more nuanced way, and discuss the intertwining of biology and the environment, and their interaction. It is often difficult to determine how much of a characteristic is genetic and how much is linked to the environment (Fausto-Sterling 1992, 2000). Yet authors with this opinion seemingly receive less attention than those who give genetic reasons for there being fewer women scientists (Bombardieri 2005). Understanding genetic and environmental interactions requires very complex analyses.

Gender bias is so embedded in our culture that it was impossible not to encounter it in medical school. In our dissection manual in anatomy lab, we read "The perineum forms a closed sac, except in the female." My fellow women medical students and I had a good laugh about this, but didn't complain or point it out to our professors. We also noticed that in small group interactions with professors such as in labs or on rounds, if a woman student didn't know the answer to a question the professor or attending physician posed, she would usually say "I don't know." But a male student would often repeat part of the question, saying, "Hmm…the most com-

mon causes of dyspnea, that would be, hmmm, dyspnea causes, are…."
and while he was clearly stalling, the attending would nod encouragingly
and start feeding him clues. We would be dumbfounded and annoyed at
this tactic and its effectiveness, but somehow we could never bring ourselves to use it.

When we got to surgery rotation, the sexism became less subtle. The
group of students that preceded my group on the surgery rotation had had
a very negative experience, with male attending physicians making inappropriate sexual comments about the students and the sedated patients on
whom they were operating. When the students complained to the medical
school, the attendings stopped making the comments but instead informed
us that "We can't make any funny jokes any more because the *female medical students* complained." The residents always seemed to jump to the conclusion that their female surgery patients were faking their abdominal
pain, nausea, constipation, or other symptoms and needed a "punitive" diagnostic or interventional procedure. Being aware of the response to the
previous group's complaints, we did not complain ourselves, but suffered
through the rotation. I felt especially bad for one of my female classmates,
who wanted to become a surgeon.

In psychiatry residency I was initially not open about being gay, except with some of my close friends. In my second year, something happened that prompted a very public disclosure. One of the senior residents,
who had been taking time off for illness, made an announcement to all the
residents that he had HIV. Not only did he have HIV, he had cytomega-
lovirus retinitis, at that time a late complication of AIDS. At the same
meeting, the resident came out to his fellow housestaff as gay.

We had a subsequent meeting with attending physicians and without
the resident to process our feelings about these disclosures. I was shocked
that being a gay psychiatry resident would be such a taboo that it would
take a terminal illness to get someone to talk about it. As residents discussed their feelings, my shock and anger about this just kept rising, until I
said something about it, saying I was speaking "as one of the gay residents
here." It was a very public statement; essentially, I "came out" to the whole
hospital community.

A couple of fellow residents, both gay and straight, gave supportive
comments to me after the meeting. My expressing concerns about how
open the program was to talking about gay residents sparked a discussion
of how much residents were taught about sexuality in general. As a result,
a small lecture series on lesbian and gay patients was added to the curriculum. Closely following this time, I was given gay therapy patients and was
assigned Richard Isay, M.D., who has written two books about being homosexual (Isay 1989, 1996), as a therapy supervisor.

There were some negative aspects to being an openly gay resident. These were less than obvious or easy to measure. One supervisor walked into my office one day to find me looking at a flyer announcing a gay residents' supervision group. He glanced at the flyer and his whole manner changed. From that day forward he was cold and distant in his supervision, and he gave me a very negative evaluation at the end of our time together. Toward the end of my fourth year of residency, I was discussing with a new supervisor how to transition my therapy patients. I mentioned that I was having a hard time finding someone to treat a gay male patient, who had requested a gay therapist. "Isn't that interesting," she said, "that he would want a gay therapist, when he has had a…a…rr…I mean nn…I mean…." She was searching for a word—I think it was "regular" or "normal"— but, realizing she didn't know I was gay, I jumped in to help her, explaining that he had felt well connected to me and wanted another openly gay therapist. She appeared shocked that my patient would know my sexual identity. This was a disclosure my previous supervisor and I had discussed and agreed would be fine provided there was a subsequent discussion between the patient and me. Whatever her feelings, the new supervisor found a reason why we could not meet for the rest of the semester.

A Typical Two-Mom Family

My partner Alleyne and I have sometimes joked that we are a typical two-mom, two-physician, interracial couple living in the country. Our home life is pretty typical—boring, routine, sometimes hectic and crazy, just as it is for most families. We are just an atypical demographic.

Alleyne and I met at a party for gay physicians in New York City. At the time, Alleyne was a neurosurgery resident at Mount Sinai Medical Center while I was in my psychiatry residency at the Payne Whitney Clinic. Attractive, petite, quiet, and serious, Alleyne drew my interest right away. I wrote my number down for her, something I had never done before. Unfortunately, I used my bad doctor-handwriting and the number was illegible. A few days later, I was on call in the hospital when a call came in from "Dr. Fraser." Alleyne had given up on figuring out my handwriting to call me at home, and had tracked me down instead in the hospital. I had to admire her persistence. We talked easily, and at the end of the call she asked me out on a date. It was a big date, to Carnegie Hall to see the New York City Gay Men's Chorus. She had season tickets. This was another point in her favor, since I, too, love music.

During that week and the next, we seemed to run into each other everywhere. We met by chance again at a lecture, and while talking afterward we learned that we had both practiced the same form of Tae Kwon

Do. She said she might stop by my karate school sometime, and appeared at the very next class to watch. Usually when people say "sometime," they mean never, so this also scored points with me.

It was a conventional dating and falling-in-love scenario. Yes, there are differences between us—she is a neurosurgeon, I am a psychiatrist; she is black, and I am white. But we are both opinionated, Ivy-League elitist intellectuals with teacher parents who instilled in us a love of learning, books, and music. Fast-forward a few years. She moved out of the city to start a solo private practice in Middletown, New York. I had come to love the city after having stayed for medical school and residency, but I followed her after finishing my residency a year later. The Columbia fellowship allowed me to have a foot in both places for another year as I readjusted to rural life. We had a commitment ceremony in a big church on Park Avenue, followed by a reception on a boat sailing around Manhattan. Our parents walked us each down the aisle, and our siblings were the attendants. This ceremony preceded same-sex marriage or civil union rights in any state, so it was purely a symbolic event, yet nonetheless beautiful and meaningful.

Oh, yes, and she was five months pregnant at our ceremony. We had talked about having children from early in our dating period—we both wanted them. Alleyne was thirty-nine by the time we were planning our commitment ceremony, while I was twenty-nine and seemingly had plenty of childbearing years left. We went to an ob-gyn just to explore the idea of Alleyne trying to get pregnant, and she told us there was not a moment to spare: It might take a while for her to get pregnant, and meanwhile her fertile time was ticking away. Alleyne explained, "But we're planning a commitment ceremony now, what if I get pregnant before the ceremony?" and the doctor retorted, "Don't you think pregnant women are pretty?" So we started out trying with donor insemination right away and, sure enough, Alleyne got pregnant on our first try. This eventually led to a very amusing encounter with a bunch of tailors, who were very attentive in letting out Alleyne's tuxedo so it would fit properly for the ceremony. We were fairly certain it was the first time they had dealt with that situation!

And that's how we got our first daughter, Kennedy. We were immediately introduced to the world of diapers, worrying, sleeplessness, and joy that is parenting. We both found out quickly how much being a parent focuses one's priorities. We also learned that although some knew us as a gay couple, there was a new group, including day care providers, pediatricians, teachers, and other parents, who did not know us as a couple. "Coming out" in these situations was about being authentic and being able to talk about our lives openly. It was absolutely essential for the safety of our child for it to be known that we were both her parents. After coming out to numerous people for our commitment ceremony, we generally had positive experiences as a couple and in parenting situations. We always attend parent-teacher conferences together, saying "we're the moms."

It turns out we are well suited to keeping house together and raising children. Alleyne has no interest in cooking, while I love to cook but have no interest or aptitude in laundry or ironing, while she excels in these skills. Our jobs are well matched for juggling kids. As a government employee, I have regular hours, holidays off, and paid sick time. She has her own office where she can bring a mildly sick or off-from-school kid for a day if she chooses.

A couple of years after Kennedy was born, we decided to try to add to our family. Neither of us was an only child, and we could not see having Kennedy grow up without any siblings. So I started trying to get pregnant. After two years and a series of escalating interventions and tests, it became clear that it was not happening. In a way this was a difficult realization for me, since I had really wanted to experience pregnancy and nursing a baby. It was actually the first major thing I had set out to do and failed to accomplish. Yet I also realized that I had experienced pregnancy, if not firsthand, then at least close up, and this may have been the first time I thought of being a lesbian as not just what I am but as a distinct advantage.

Toward the end of my attempts to get pregnant, we started exploring public adoption. We had actually talked about doing this later, when we were "done" with having children through pregnancy, so it was not too much of a stretch. We got the strangest reactions from friends and family about this. Some said how wonderful and altruistic we were to consider taking in a child in this way. Others expressed concern: Why would we risk messing up our family by having a kid with baggage join us? Of course, we were not altruistic at all, just trying to add another child to our family, and if we had wanted to avoid risk, we wouldn't have had any kids in the first place. And that's how our second daughter, Trinity, came to us. Our family was complete.

Compartmentalization

In 2010 I attended a memorial service for Bertram Schaffner, M.D. (Drescher 2010; Merlino 2001). He was a pioneer as an openly gay psychiatrist, brilliant and accomplished in many ways, and a role model for many of us. Yet many in attendance knew only one aspect of Bert, because he kept the parts of his life very separate. The Asian art colleagues knew him as an avid and knowledgeable collector and museum benefactor; a colleague who helped him research his family roots knew him as a genealogist and historian; those of us who came out and became comfortable with ourselves in meetings in his apartment knew him as an openly gay psychiatrist, but, modest as he was, we didn't know the other parts. It is understandable that the other folks didn't know or acknowledge the gay part because of Bert's generation (he was ninety-seven when he died in 2010). In that cohort, even if you were out, you didn't talk about it much.

Yet, professionally, this is still true to a great extent, and I have my own compartmentalization. I have gotten the message many times, sometimes directly and sometimes indirectly, that while it is acceptable to be openly lesbian, it is not acceptable to be "too out," or to try to "make a career out of being gay." This means it is best not to have your résumé stack up too many LGBT organizations, publications, or activities. It means it is better to concentrate on more legitimate specialties with more prestige.

I have always sought out the gay activities in the APA, the Association of Gay and Lesbian Psychiatrists (AGLP), and the LGBT committee of the Group for the Advancement of Psychiatry. I am now co–editor-in-chief of the *Journal of Gay & Lesbian Mental Health,* AGLP's journal. My curriculum vitae is really, really gay. Maybe this is my rebelliousness again—doing what I have been advised against. Doubtless it is also because I have found these activities to be stimulating and supportive, and they keep me motivated to do my "day" job. Ah, yes, and of course I have a day job, a "legit" career as a public psychiatrist and psychiatric administrator.

For a long time, my public psychiatry career and gay psychiatry career were kept almost completely separate. While I was at AGLP and APA meetings, I seldom even mentioned my job as a clinical director at a county department of mental health. Similarly, my colleagues and boss at the mental health department were mostly unaware of my election as AGLP president and my publications in LGBT psychiatry. I think this separation was partly due to fear of discomfort from my straight colleagues, internal antigay bias, and the work ethic in public settings. If you appeared to be involved in a lot of outside activities, people might think you were spending government time on irrelevant work. Rather than national activities being considered good for the positive exposure of the government agency and its employees, such activities, whether gay-related or not, were generally regarded with suspicion and considered a waste of time. So I usually practically sneaked out of the office to attend conferences and said little about them when I returned. Why did I not talk about the day job to the gay psychiatrists? I think because most of them are in private practice, and my job seemed less legitimate in that arena. I do not have a private practice treating lesbian and gay patients; in fact, at this point in my career, I have no caseload at all. That doesn't mean I haven't seen many LGBT patients over my career, but somehow I felt less qualified as a psychiatrist talking about LGBT clinical issues because of the administrative focus of my work.

To further compartmentalize, I have mostly dealt with balancing my family life and work by keeping the family life under the radar at work.

This has become trickier because my older daughter has an interest in being on Broadway. She takes voice and dance lessons, acts in professional-level plays, has an agent, and sometimes gets auditions. The invitations for Broadway auditions are usually within New York City, which is a ninety-minute drive from our home. This is a challenge given my work responsibilities.

Nonetheless, because I didn't listen to those cautioning me against the gay activities, in fact I have forged two careers: one in public psychiatry, and one in LGBT psychiatry. And the career in LGBT psychiatry has enhanced my career in general. For several years I was working in a county mental health department, miles away from any academic medical center. At the time I didn't even have access to a medical library. I had no academic affiliation. Yet in those years I continued to lecture at the Columbia fellowship program, gave talks at APA meetings, published (Barber 2000, 2003, 2007, 2008a; Barber et al. 1998, 2001; Group for Advancement of Psychiatry 2007), and ultimately became an APA distinguished fellow. Through these opportunities, my work in AGLP, and my colleagues in LGBT psychiatry, I have made "a career" out of being gay.

Additionally, I received terrific leadership training through my work in these groups, which helped me as a psychiatric administrator. In turn, my leadership training as an administrator helped me to better manage my AGLP responsibilities. I am very proud and happy about my career path and choices.

My two career worlds were brought together a few years ago when Jules Ranz, M.D., asked me to lecture to the Columbia fellows about my work in AGLP. I spoke about my work as president of the organization, during which we wrote a mission statement, created a new logo, redesigned the website, wrote our first successful foundation grant applications, produced a documentary film (Barber and Scasta 2006), and funded a new APA award for contributions to LGBT mental health (Barber 2006). The Columbia talk was well received and led to a publication (Barber 2008b). Since then I have gone back to the fellows yearly to give the same lecture. Later, the two parts of my career were brought together in a different way, when I wrote a book chapter (Barber 2010) and article (Barber 2009) about LGBT people with serious mental illness.

Leadership and Saying Yes

At this point in my career, I have held significant leadership positions in a local government department (clinical director of Ulster County Mental Health Department in Ulster County, New York), a state psychiatric hospital (clinical director of Rockland Psychiatric Center [RPC], a New York state hospital), and a nonprofit organization (president of AGLP and now co-editor of the *Journal of Gay & Lesbian Mental Health*). I didn't plan it to happen that way, and while I was getting this varied experience I didn't think of it all as significant. My career was the result of saying *yes* to one thing at a time.

After I finished the Columbia fellowship, I stayed on at Ulster County Mental Health, first as a staff psychiatrist, then as associate medical director, then as medical and clinical director. Although I had trained for a leadership position with the Columbia fellowship, I did have some misgivings as I transitioned from direct patient care to more and more, and eventually full-time, administration. Ernest Townsend, D.C.S.W., the mental health commissioner of Ulster County during my early years, provided mentorship. About leaving direct patient care, Ernie said, "You can have a private practice or work in a clinic and help a few hundred patients, or you can lead the system in a way that affects many more."

After I'd spent a few years as clinical director of the Ulster County Mental Health Department, a position directing outpatient services at RPC opened up, and I decided to try working and learning in a newer and larger system. When the clinical director position at RPC became available, I was less certain about my interest in and ability to do the job. As outpatient director, I was in a new system but doing familiar outpatient administration. In contrast, the clinical director is responsible for a 450-bed hospital. I hadn't done inpatient work since residency and wasn't sure I would like or be good at overseeing the hospital. Yet, with encouragement from some of the hospital managers, I sought and obtained the position.

In my career in LGBT psychiatry, I have Jack Drescher, M.D. (who wrote a book about psychoanalytic therapy and homosexuality; Drescher 1998), to thank for leading me to many of the opportunities that have come my way. Jack first approached me when I was a resident, at a party for gay doctors in New York City, to ask whether I would join the APA's New York City District Branch Committee on Gay, Lesbian, and Bisexual Issues. It was the first time of many that I said *yes* to him. What followed was participation in workshops at APA, then joining the executive board of AGLP, first as secretary, then vice president, and then president. Jack asked me to review books for the *Journal of Gay & Lesbian Mental Health.* He had to keep asking me for about a year to take over from him as editor, because I didn't think I was qualified to edit a journal.

There is a theme here. Although I have been pushing boldly forward in both of my careers, I have nonetheless had doubts at certain points about my own abilities. If there is anything I would do differently or caution others against, it is wasting too much energy on self-doubt. Remember those male medical students rotating in surgery with me who had not the slightest idea of the answer to the attending physician's question, yet jumped in anyway? Women can learn something from that—not to go blindly into a situation with no idea of what we are doing, but to trust that we know a little more than we think we do, and that we can learn systems and skills as we go along.

Certainly in my first years as clinical director of RPC, I have learned an enormous amount and have gained confidence about what unique skills and characteristics I can bring to the role. My outpatient orientation can actually be an asset, since I don't see things as inevitably having to happen in the same way they have always been done. Similarly, in my first two years as journal editor, both my co-editor Alan Schwartz, M.D., and I have had a steep learning curve, *and* we have put our own style and stamp on its content (Schwartz and Barber 2010).

It's important to consider not just what a position or role will do for you, but what you will do with opportunities you are given. Stepping into a position and not having your own vision or goals for the role may maintain the status quo, but it will not lead to much growth or innovation. If I had become president of AGLP after being secretary and vice president, and taken the role for what it had been previously, that would have been a line on my CV and something to say I had done. I might have been proud of the good meetings we put on and the new members we had nurtured. And that would have been a success.

Instead, I led a two-year process of reenvisioning and reinvigorating the organization. After securing foundation grants for AGLP, the organization successfully raised $50,000, endowing the John E. Fryer, M.D., Award, an APA award for LGBT mental health practitioners. Furthermore, my leadership experiences include producing an award-winning documentary film, *Abomination*, on sexual conversion therapies. As a result of all of this, I have gained many valuable skills that translate into other parts of my life, and I have much more than one line on my CV that I can attribute to my time as AGLP president.

I have tried to take this philosophy into every project or position I undertake, and to put something of my own vision into everything. That doesn't mean I just ram my ideas through, or that the ideas and work are only mine. In any organization, major projects or changes are group efforts, with lots of people having input. Yet someone has to provide direction and lead everyone there.

One important management saying I've kept, "Go and see," dates back to my earliest days as an intern on the medical wards. Nurses would call me to report a patient having symptoms or in distress. The nurse usually wanted an order given over the phone, but when I instead went to see the patient, I often had a different idea of what to do than I would have had from just the phone message. Sometimes the patient's condition was more serious than it had sounded in the nurse's report, sometimes it seemed milder, and sometimes the symptoms were different entirely than what I had heard in the report. It wasn't a matter of whether the nurse was competent, but that the message, and my interpretation of it, had been changed by one or more translations. Going and seeing could make all the difference, preventing a catastrophic mistake such as ordering a benzodiazepine for someone breathing fast, thinking it sounded like mild anxiety, when it was actually a person in acute respiratory distress from a pulmonary embolism. The further removed one gets from direct clinical care, the easier it is to not go and see, but it is still very important.

Systems change is another touchstone that I bring to any leadership role I undertake. It has certainly been discussed in theory (Anthony and Huckshorn 2008; Collins 2001), and I have found over and over in practice that if you want to change an organization, you need to not only educate clinicians but change the systems and the structure within that organization. This is akin to taking a broader public health approach to behavior change, rather than trying to get patients to make changes through personal education alone. That is, telling people to quit smoking is much more effective when taxes are also increased on cigarettes, just as counseling people about the importance of exercise is more effective when sidewalks are improved to allow people to walk more.

At the Ulster County Mental Health Department we held many training sessions on integrating substance use disorder treatment and mental health treatment, but real change happened when we sat substance abuse counselors next to mental health counselors in our intake unit, both filling out the same intake form, and conducted universal drug testing on all people coming to the clinic. On the RPC inpatient units, levels of observation (such as one-to-one observation or constant observation by a staff member) decreased dramatically when we tightened up the documentation required to continue the existing levels. Education, keeping up with the literature, and clinical case reviews are all important and are needed to inform change to a system, but unless we change people's routine procedures, they are likely to keep doing what has been comfortable despite new evidence or training. When administrators get pegged as evil bureaucrats, there may have been systems change without adequate education behind it. On the other hand, administrators who get burned out and frustrated by lack of change may have relied too much on education and clinicians' personal efforts, while failing to modify the system to facilitate that change.

Above all, it's important to surround yourself with great people and to have fun. In all my public psychiatry positions and in my LGBT organizations, I have been fortunate to work with terrific people and to have enjoyed myself while making a difference.

Recovery and Person-Centered Medicine

I came to psychiatry partly because of realizing how transformative it is to listen to the patient. Currently, person-centered medicine and the recovery movement in psychiatry are being widely discussed, but these are values I have held for a long time.

Doing psychiatry training in a psychodynamically oriented residency program has helped me keep in mind the importance of clinician-patient interactions even as our field has become so medication focused. It also gave me an acceptance of patients as autonomous individuals who are allowed to make decisions and live their own lives. For example, as a resident I had been seeing a young woman for psychotherapy for over a year, and our relationship was becoming rocky. We were getting into some difficult issues, she was unhappy with me, and in the middle of one session she just stood up and walked out of my office. I never heard from her again. When I told my supervisor, Lawrence Jacobsberg, M.D., Ph.D., about this, I was feeling pretty foolish and embarrassed, but he smiled. "Well, you know what that is, don't you?," he asked. I had no idea what he was talking about. He answered for me, "That's a cure." At the time, I thought he was simply making a joke to help me feel better, but as time went on I realized he was right. The patient had gotten what she needed out of that course of psychotherapy, had had enough, and had voted with her feet. Perhaps she would seek treatment again at some later point, or perhaps not. Neither I nor she needed to see what happened as a failure.

I frequently hear people contrast working within a recovery framework to the "medical model." I bristle a little at the two being placed in opposition to each other, because there is really nothing contradictory about these approaches. Recovery does not mean throwing out our professional knowledge or expertise. Seeing patients as partners in care, shared decision-making, and treating the whole person rather than just the illness are changes that have been happening in other areas of medicine for decades (Barber, in press). These changes have been most notable in ob-gyn and cancer care (Ragins 2010).

When my mother was having children in the late 1960s and early 1970s, it was common practice for the woman giving birth to be under general anesthesia. Forceps deliveries were common. The husband or partner was not allowed in the delivery room, and neither of the parents-to-be were given choices about delivery preferences such as whether to have an episiotomy. It is completely different now, with women and their partners having lots of input into the birth process and being expected to be actively involved. Obstetricians still intervene when complications necessitate it, and the woman's medical condition still determines the range of choices available. Just as is happening now in mental health, these changes came about because patients and patient advocacy groups demanded them.

Recovery does not mean that we need to throw out research evidence. In fact, longitudinal studies indicate that people with schizophrenia achieve medical remission or at least partial remission much more frequently than we think they do (Davidson et al. 2005). It has been hard for us to accept this evidence, perhaps because recovered patients leave our care. Those whom we continue to see, we talk about sometimes as being "burned out," rather than realizing that they are in recovery.

Wanting to be a doctor who listens to patients was what drew me to psychiatry in the first place. Thinking about and developing my philosophy on recovery and person-centered care—whether the work is clinical or administrative, and whether I'm talking about people with serious mental illness or sexual and gender minorities—continues to guide me in the various parts of my career.

PRACTICAL TIPS FOR WOMEN IN PSYCHIATRY

- Don't undersell yourself. Know who you are and what your talents and expertise are.

- Don't be afraid to say *yes* because you think the project or assignment is too big or you are "not ready."

- Go toward career moves and projects that captivate you, whether they are the most prestigious or mainstream or not.

References

Anthony WA, Huckshorn KA: Principled Leadership in Mental Health Systems and Programs. Boston, MA, Boston University Center for Psychiatric Rehabilitation, 2008

Barber ME: Examining differences in sexual expression and coming out between lesbians and gay men. J Gay Lesbian Med Assoc 4:167–174, 2000

Barber ME: An interview with Nanette Gartrell, MD. Journal of Gay & Lesbian Psychotherapy 7:35–47, 2003

Barber ME: Honoring John Fryer's legacy. Behav Healthc 26:14–15, 2006

Barber ME: Today and tomorrow, in American Psychiatry and Homosexuality: An Oral History. Edited by Drescher J, Merlino JP. New York, Haworth, 2007

Barber ME: An interview with David R. Kessler, MD. Journal of Gay & Lesbian Mental Health 12:245–257, 2008a

Barber ME: The role of the psychiatrist as advocate. Psychiatr Q 79:287–292, 2008b

Barber ME: Lesbian, gay, and bisexual people with severe mental illness. Journal of Gay & Lesbian Mental Health 13:133–142, 2009

Barber ME: "Where are these voices coming from?": serious mental illness among lesbians, in Lesbian Health 101: A Clinician's Guide. Edited by Dibble SL, Robertson P. San Francisco, UCSF Nursing Press, 2010, pp 293–304

Barber ME: Recovery as the new medical model for psychiatry. Psychiatr Serv (in press)

Barber ME, Marzuk PM, Leon AC, et al: Aborted suicide attempts: a new classification of suicidal behavior. Am J Psychiatry 155:385–389, 1998

Barber ME, Marzuk PM, Leon AC, et al: Gate questions in psychiatric interviewing: the case of suicide assessment. J Psychiatr Res 35:67–69, 2001

Barber ME, Scasta DL (cochairs, production team), Salzer A (director and producer), et al: Abomination: Homosexuality and the Ex-Gay Movement. Documentary, DVD format, 35 min. Frameline (distributor), 2006

Bem SL: The lenses of gender: transforming the debate on sexual inequality. New Haven, CT, Yale University Press, 1993

Bombardieri M: Summers' remarks on women draw fire. The Boston Globe, January 17, 2005. Available at: http://www.boston.com/news/local/articles/2005/01/17/summers_remarks_on_women_draw_fire. Accessed May 17, 2010.

Collins J: Good to Great: Why Some Companies Make the Leap…and Others Don't. New York, HarperCollins, 2001

Davidson L, Harding C, Spaniol L (eds): Recovery From Severe Mental Illness: Research Evidence and Implications for Practice. Boston, MA, Boston University Center for Psychiatric Rehabilitation, 2005

Drescher J: Psychoanalytic Therapy and the Gay Man. Hillsdale, NJ, Analytic Press, 1998

Drescher J: In memoriam: Bertram H. Schaffner, MD. Journal of Gay & Lesbian Mental Health 14:251–256, 2010

Fausto-Sterling A: Myths of Gender: Biological Theories About Women and Men. New York, Basic Books, 1992

Fausto-Sterling A: Sexing the Body: Gender Politics and the Construction of Sexuality. New York, Basic Books, 2000

Group for Advancement of Psychiatry, Committee on LGBT Issues: LGBT Mental Health Syllabus. 2007. Available at: http://www.aglp.org/gap. Accessed December 1, 2011.

Isay R: Being Homosexual: Gay Men and Their Development. New York, Farrar, Straus & Giroux, 1989

Isay R: Becoming Gay: The Journey to Self-Acceptance. New York, Pantheon, 1996

Merlino J: An interview with Bertram H. Schaffner, MD. Journal of Gay & Lesbian Psychotherapy 5:85–99, 2001

Miller J: States of Mind: Conversations With Psychological Investigators. London, BBC/Random House, 1983

Money J, Ehrhardt A: Man and Woman, Boy and Girl. Baltimore, Johns Hopkins Press, 1972

Ragins M: Road to Recovery. Available at: http://www.village-isa.org/
    Ragin's%20Papers/Road%20to%20Recovery.htm. Accessed June 15, 2010.
Ranz JM, Rosenheck S, Deakins S: Columbia University's fellowship in public
    psychiatry. Psychiatr Serv 47:512–516, 1996
Schwartz A, Barber ME: Reflecting. Journal of Gay & Lesbian Mental Health
    14:173–175, 2010

Chapter 7

Getting to the Inner Circle

The Long, Hard Road

Jo-Ellyn M. Ryall, M.D.

MY NAME IS JO-ELLYN M. RYALL, M.D., and I was asked to participate in this book because I am addicted to medical politics.

I do have a story. I grew up in Irvington, New Jersey, as the oldest child, with two younger brothers. My parish had a grade school and a high school that I attended. I discovered that I enjoyed the sciences. I went to Douglass College, a women's college, in the state university system. I was the first member of my family to go to college. At first, I was going to be a medical technologist, but the course load was the same as the premed curriculum. In sophomore year I got "chicken" and decided that medical school was too far a reach, so I switched to chemistry so that I could have a job in a laboratory when I finished college. I was one of thirteen chemistry majors. In junior year, I decided to take the Medical College Admissions Test for medical school. I got a decent score and was on the dean's list, so I applied. Among the women I knew, all of us who applied to medical school had multiple acceptances. The guys at Rutgers were hurting; they were not getting these multiple acceptances. This was back in the early 1970s.

One of the best parts of my undergraduate education at a women's college was the chance to experience the birth of the women's movement. I also learned tolerance and acceptance of minorities. As a chemistry major, I did not have time for a lot of extra reading but I did read *The Feminine Mystique* by Betty Friedan (1963) and *Sexual Politics* by Kate Millett (1969). During sociology, a mandated course, I wrote a paper on how only seven percent of medical doctors were women. By 1971, the percentage of females accepted in medical school classes was rising to ten percent. Kate Millett was our commencement speaker. Brave new horizons and women power infused my brain.

I went to Washington University School of Medicine in St. Louis, Missouri, as one of the ten percent quota for women. When I was a medical student, I studied, learned to cook, kept my head above water, and graduated. I knew nothing about medical politics. After receiving some information about AMSA, the American Medical Student Association, I joined. Dues were five dollars, not a large expense, and that was the extent of my participation. During medical school I volunteered once at a people's clinic. Basically, I lived in the library. I studied, did my rotations, and didn't get involved in organized medicine. I'm so delighted that there are so many medical students in the American Medical Association (AMA) medical student section, who then go on to the resident fellow section, and then on to the young physician section. These AMA sections started long before I even learned about organized medicine.

Following graduation, I stayed at Washington University in St. Louis for a psychiatry residency. During my second year of residency, I married a man who was pursuing a degree in electrical engineering and bioscience. He was on the cutting edge of the research that led to computer-assisted tomography scans. We seemed to be a perfect couple; however, it took forever for him to finish his doctorate and I tired of being the breadwinner, and we parted ways after almost five years. We did not have any children because I refused to be a single working mother. I had enough trouble managing my work and my political activities with my local district branches of the Eastern Missouri Psychiatric Society and American Medical Women's Association.

During the residency years, a girlfriend and I decided to go to Eastern Missouri Psychiatric Society (EMPS) meetings. They held about six continuing medical education (CME) meetings a year. We didn't need the CME credit, but we went because we were curious. Every month we went to the medical society building to have the same dinner of steak, potatoes, salad, cheesecake, open bar, and no condiments. The second month we attended the dinner, I brought the plastic lime for the gin and tonics, and she brought the A-1 sauce. Immediately we were accepted by the older male doctors. They wanted us to sit at their table. Why? Because we came, we were interested, and we brought condiments. So the first piece of advice is, show up, volunteer, and bring something of use.

The second event that happened in St. Louis is that we had a committee of women in the EMPS, with the main goal of getting a woman on the dais. There was only one woman officer, and she was the Secretary. She performed very well in that position, but she never reached a higher one. I was the Secretary of this little committee, and the best part was that the superintendent of my hospital, the Malcolm Bliss Mental Health Center, was also a member of the committee. She had a vision problem, so I drove her to the lunch meetings. While we were driving I learned a great deal about my boss, Dr. Kathleen Smith, a woman pioneer in psychiatry.

The work product of the committee was that the nominating committee included a woman candidate for president-elect. In 1981, Dr. Maria Manion became the first female president of EMPS, and I was rewarded by becoming her program chair. That was quite a job—more than I expected it to be. I had to find speakers for those six meetings. That was tougher than bringing condiments. I looked through the American Psychiatric Association (APA) annual meeting program and found six interesting speakers, called them, and arranged for their visits and the Society paid the expenses. This was before pharmaceutical money helped pay for the meetings. Members paid twenty-five dollars for the dinner and we received CME credit from the local medical society.

In 1979, I also joined the American Medical Women's Association (AMWA), and in 1980 we started our local branch again, reviving it after a period of dormancy. A group of us began rousing women to form an executive committee. I became president-elect and then president; which was pretty good for a young physician. By going to the national meeting of AMWA in 1980, as president-elect, I discovered a whole new world of mentors and women who were pioneers in medicine. I went to those meetings to feed my own needs of friendship and education. I also started to do needlepoint at meetings because the House of Delegates could be boring at times, rewriting the bylaws one line at a time to make the medical students full members. I thought, who needs these fine details? Little did I know that I would have a knack for bylaws and would become a member and a chair of the bylaws committee of every organization I joined.

In 1979 I also made a very important decision and joined my local and state medical societies, and the AMA. The state medical meeting was in St. Louis in 1979. I attended the psychiatric part of the meeting because that was the only part in which I was interested (who cared about all that other stuff?). The following year, we went to the psychiatric CME meeting in Kansas City. Someone at the meeting said "Oh, and by the way, there's an opening for a delegate from St. Louis because we didn't fill our delegate slots, because they didn't all come. So, please be a delegate." Thus I immediately became a delegate to the state medical meeting, and I've been a delegate ever since. It's very easy: show up, volunteer…get there and do a good job.

My father had died of lung cancer in December of 1977, and I grieved for him for years. It was the first time that I wished I'd had a child so that I could have given him a grandchild, but it was too late. I also watched him scrimp and save so that he could travel after he retired. Since he died at age fifty-eight, he never saw retirement. I made a decision to travel more and save less. Consequently, I have set foot in all fifty states and several countries. Live your dreams or they will get away from you.

In 1981 I was divorced and learned that dating as a female doctor was much harder than dating as a male doctor. I had guys suggest I could not be a doctor because I was female. If I said I worked in a hospital, they guessed nurse, lab technician, or secretary. It was getting frustrating, so I devoted myself to work and medical politics. However, I like to have fun. My one brother, Paul, was in the U.S. Air Force and was stationed at Ramstein Air Force Base in Germany. He invited me to learn how to ski in Austria in January 1982. My ski instructor, Peter, was a sixty-five-year-old Austrian who gave bilingual lessons. I learned that the hardest thing about skiing was to stay upright, so I developed a tremendous sense of balance and did not fall for several days. On the last day we went up higher on the mountain than usual, and I fell during a turn. My nylon ski pants and orange ski jacket made a great toboggan, and I slid down at least 100 yards. I lost both skis and poles, with a "yard sale" array of items scattered along the slope. People uphill kindly brought the lost items and checked to see if I was OK. Fortunately, only my pride was hurt. I decided that if my instructor could ski at age sixty-five, I should be able to ski, also. I am well on my way to being a sixty-five-year-old skier. The one concession is that now I wear a helmet. I also met a major in the U.S. Air Force and had a long-distance romance for years. That seemed to be the best relationship for me. We had long phone calls, but I had lots of time for my practice and political activities.

In 1983 I was still a young psychiatrist, and moved on from being program chair to EMPS president-elect. The reason for my elevation was that the doctor ahead of me was in his last year of psychoanalytic training and he didn't have time to be president-elect. I jumped ahead to become president-elect and later president. This was the same year I decided to learn to fly a plane. That was a very exciting year. Eventually, I got an instrument license and had lots of fun in the clouds. I recommend avoiding thunderclouds because even dissipating thunderstorms make the Screamin' Eagle roller coaster at Six Flags amusement park in St. Louis seem tame.

After I was EMPS president, I had a very sad time in organized medicine. I was chair of the insurance committee, when managed care raised its ugly head. This was tough for me because I'm a patient advocate and managed care was the enemy. They wanted to cut us! They wanted to cut coverage from no-limit psychiatric inpatient days to 21 inpatient days a year. Trying to safely treat suicidal depression with tricyclic antidepressants in three weeks of inpatient treatment per year just doesn't work. I got to advocate for mental health parity in the 1980s.

The following year, I got to do something I really enjoyed. While serving as chair of the Public Affairs Committee, I participated in creating a mental illness awareness coalition that existed for eighteen years. The coalition, at that time, consisted of the National Alliance for the Mentally Ill (now known as the National Alliance on Mental Illness); the Mental Health Association (now Mental Health America); the National Depressive and Manic Depressive Association (now the Depression and Bipolar Support Alliance); several hospitals, all of whom were competitors; Recovery Inc., and The OCD Group. We managed to have this group teach the public about mental illness and have all sorts of activities. This coalition went through the forming, norming, storming, and reforming stages, and then it finally died when those of us who were still on it said, "We are doing all the work and no one, even members of our committee, cares." The coalition ceased to function in 2003. I was given the Golden Couch Award for my eighteen years of participation, an honor that still hangs on the wall of my office. During the same time period, I was a member of the Joint Commission of Public Affairs of the APA. We learned about how to deal with the media—television, radio, and print.

In 1985, I became speaker-elect of the Missouri State Medical Association (MSMA). I knew nothing about parliamentary procedure, but I got into my airplane and flew over to Kansas City, and talked with Dr. Barbara Buchanan, one of my mentors, who is a child psychiatrist and past speaker of MSMA.

I said, "Barbara, what do you have to do [as speaker]?"

She said, "You just have to run the meeting."

I asked, "How many meetings do I have to go to?"

"Oh, just the annual meeting," she said.

To which I responded, "Hey, that sounds like an easy job."

So you learn *Robert's Rules of Order* (Robert et al. 1986), or Sturgis's (2000) *Standard Code of Parliamentary Procedure*; I did, and ran the meeting. I was elected to be vice speaker and then speaker of MSMA for a total of six years. I have been the parliamentarian of MSMA since that time. Still later, I had the opportunity to expand my involvement in organized psychiatry and medical practices to the national level. Barbara Buchanan had been in the APA on the section council to the AMA. When she needed to withdraw from that role she submitted my name to the APA, because she knew me, and I started going to AMA meetings in 1986.

The first AMA meeting I went to was a very enlightening experience. This was an unbelievable kind of business meeting. I was hooked. Dr. Ron Shellow, a psychiatrist who died in 2007, was my mentor there. Ron taught me everything I know about the AMA. I found out about five years ago that he had been to only one meeting more than I had. But he taught me everything I needed to know. He was a very good mentor because he had it all figured out. As a result, I went to forty-six semiannual AMA meetings. It doesn't seem like much, but when you think about it, it's a lifetime. I've seen a number of organizations from the inside. So what I've learned is, show up, volunteer, do a good job, and they'll ask you to do another job. In these volunteer organizations, what one has to worry about is doing too much, because one can get totally burned out.

When I was almost forty years old, I met a man who seemed perfect, and I saw this as my last chance to have a child. The marriage was short and stormy and fortunately I did not become pregnant, which meant that after the divorce I never had to deal with him. The one good thing about the marriage was that I started to take bridge lessons with my husband. It was one of the few things we could do without arguing. Since then, I have met other people who play duplicate bridge, and I found my new addiction. I worked on my life master level. One needs 300 points and at least 25 gold points, so I became a "gold digger." In 2010, after one year, I achieved the status of life master. My social life now consists of bridge games and parties.

I ran for election to the AMA Council on Constitution and Bylaws. This is an easy election compared to APA elections, because only members of the House of Delegates vote for the candidates. It made national politics look easy, or so I thought. But I rapidly learned that there are so many deals struck in these elections. Five people were running for three slots, and the politics were hot and heavy. My principal opponent, a man from North Carolina, was part of a large caucus. I was part of a much smaller caucus and was a total unknown. I simply went around and asked everyone to vote for me. I managed to force a run-off between us, and the vote then went 60%–40%, with his large caucus voting for him and my small caucus for me. The next year, I won a seat on the council by a landslide—so you just need to show up and let them get to know you. It helped that no one from his caucus ran that second year.

As part of my term with the Constitution and Bylaws Council, we rewrote the entire constitution and bylaws. We reduced the volume by a third and said "Now, this is a very readable document; you can actually find things in it." That was accomplished under my watch as chair.

I have learned to have a tough skin and to realize that in a contested election there is one winner and one or more losers. During one of the contested AMWA elections in which I ran, my opponent for the post of vice president was Dr. Roz Epps, the first African American president of AMWA. I was told by several of the senior women that I was a good candidate, but "it is just not your time yet." I did not win an election in AMWA until they asked me to run unopposed for the first speaker of their House of Delegates in 1993. I was going through a terrible divorce at that time and had told them that I could not handle another loss just then. They understood, and I ran unopposed and became the first Speaker of the House of AMWA.

The AMWA national meetings rotated around the country. I was the Local Arrangements Committee chair for the 1986 meeting in St. Louis. Working with the program chair, Dr. Eugenia Marcus, a pediatrician from Newton, Massachusetts, we planned the meeting; this was the year that Dr. Mary Jane England was inaugurated into the association. I had a wonderful time being involved. I went to the airport to pick up our keynote speaker, the columnist Ellen Goodman and made her acquaintance on the fifteen-mile trip to the hotel. Hobnobbing with celebrities, WOW! The best part was that Eugenia and I became the best of friends and roomed together at AMA meetings for years. Show up, have a car, know directions, and doors open.

I have been a member of the APA Assembly since 1993, when I was the deputy representative from EMPS. Later I was elected to deputy representative and representative of APA Area IV, the midwestern states. During my tenure in the assembly, I tried to change the way business was done. Dr. Dale Walker, the speaker, asked Dr. Priscilla Ray (from Texas) and me to give him a template for the Reference Committees. We worked on this project and it changed how business was done. Change is hard, and I am sure there were members of the assembly who did not like the changes. As chair of the Procedures Committee, I changed the format of the action papers so they read like resolutions of state medical societies or the AMA rather than essays.

In 2004, I ran for the office of speaker-elect of the assembly against Dr. Jim Nininger, the recorder from Area II, New York. I lost, but I knew that I was an unknown and I needed to introduce myself to the assembly members. The following year, I ran for the office of recorder of the assembly against Dr. Michael Blumenfield, also from New York, who was term-limited out of the assembly. I was the deputy representative of Area IV at the time, and I heard echoes of "It is not your time yet" as I lost. I continued in my role as representative of Area IV. In 2008, after having lost the 2007 Board of Trustees election in the AMA, I decided to run for recorder of the assembly on a three-person slate. Again I lost. Licking my wounds, I sat out a year and in 2010 I ran for recorder for the last time, since I was term limited at the end of the meeting. I either had too much ego or not enough sense to discontinue my quest to become the speaker of the assembly. It was my goal in 1993 and I had hoped to attain it. The position of recorder is a stepping stone. Alas, I lost. Could this be a door closing and another opening? Time will tell. In 2011, I was elected as president of the newly created Missouri Psychiatric Association.

So how am I able to do all this? First of all, I don't have any children, so I had to find something with which to occupy myself. Second of all, I've had a lot of friends and mentors who have guided me along the way. One of my favorite mentors is Dr. Nada Stotland, past president of the APA. I met Nada when I was a member of the Public Affairs Network and she was the head of the Joint Commission of Public Affairs in the 1980s. I watched Nada run for president-elect and lose and continue to be gracious. Nada was the representative of the Women's Caucus, a minority and underrepresented group. Since she was from Chicago, she was a member of Area IV. When I became the deputy representative from EMPS in 1993, I saw her in action in the assembly and on the Board of Trustees, culminating as president of the APA. In 2007, I honored her as my mentor at the Women's Congress of the AMA. In 2009, I accompanied Nada on a People to People Ambassador Program trip to Russia, where twenty-eight psychiatrists from the United States, Canada, and Australia met with psychiatrists in Moscow and St. Petersburg.

When I was in college, I worked in the Essex County, New Jersey, chief medical examiner's laboratory during the summers. I said to my father, "I think I'll be a medical technologist." He said, "Why don't you be the pathologist and run the lab?" And I thought, "What a great idea! Dad, thank you!" My mother, on the other hand, would say "Don't bite off more than you can chew." I stayed in medical school the entire four difficult years because I wasn't going to prove that my mother was right in cautioning me to lower my aim. My dad was right. I am glad that I decided to become a doctor, a psychiatrist, and involved in medical politics.

When I was in medical school, I was trying to decide what to be when I grew up. Originally, I wanted to go into obstetrics and gynecology. I did subinternships and externships in ob-gyn (got a small paycheck for working during my six-week vacation) in addition to my regular rotation. I learned something: I needed regular sleep, and babies come in the middle of the night. I also learned that my lordosis and scoliosis did not like long stretches of standing at the operating table. Then there was *Roe v. Wade* (1973), and that caused me to ponder how I would reconcile my religion and my basic pro-choice positions. To choose not to have or not to perform an abortion is a choice, too. I had to change my career goals quickly. What to do? The last rotation of my junior year was in psychiatry. I was prepared not to like it. I didn't like internal medicine, I hated pediatrics, my back did not like surgery, and I was too weak to do orthopedics (no upper arm strength). Neurology was too depressing with all the strokes and tumors. I did not have an elective rotation in dermatology, radiology, or occupational medicine. I did not like the idea of psychoanalysis (Woody Allen on the couch for 20 years throughout 20 movies was scary). To battle boredom, I used to carry a fiction paperback book in my white coat pocket at all times, and I crocheted during lectures in the dark lecture hall in order to stay awake. Ready to hate psychiatry, I started the rotation.

The first three weeks of my psychiatry rotation were at Renard Hospital in affiliation with Washington University School of Medicine in St. Louis. I drew a resident from Taiwan. He had a strong accent and the patients could not understand him. (I could barely understand him.) I accompanied him in the initial interviews and repeated the questions he asked if the patient could not comprehend him. I learned to interview patients. The Department of Psychiatry at Washington University in St. Louis bases its training on the medical model and careful diagnosis. The Feighner diagnostic criteria (Feighner et al. 1972) predated DSM-III (American Psychiatric Association 1980). This was active psychiatry and not just saying "uh-huh." I spent the next three weeks at an inpatient community psychiatric hospital, Malcolm Bliss Mental Health Center. We saw patients with schizophrenia, patients with bipolar disorders, and those who were suicidal. We were exposed to patients with alcoholism as well as violent offenders. This was not your father's psychiatric couch! I loved the action. I knew it was a sign when I read more than was included on the syllabus. I was hooked. I had to scramble, since the rotation was in May and we had to interview for residency slots starting in the summer. After speaking to several members of the Department of Psychiatry at Washington University in St. Louis, I decided to list Washington University as my first (and only) choice. I matched, and my psychiatry career started. I moved to St. Louis for medical school and never left. I became a big fish in a little pond.

I was married more than once, and now I am divorced and footloose and fancy-free. I learned that I am a great friend but a lousy spouse. I have owned some cats, and had three dogs. My last dog died at sixteen years old and I never replaced her, so now I really don't have to go home for lunch; I can get a lot of work done. But you have to make choices. Find something you like and say *yes* to it.

I realize that my philosophy of life changed from that of a protected, conservative Catholic-school girl (I voted for Barry Goldwater in our mock presidential election, after I had voted for the Republican female candidate, Margaret Chase Smith, in the primary) to that of a fearless feminist who is more liberal. I believe that the eight years of an all-girls high school and a women's college molded my character. I have done things that I only dreamed of in my youth. Recently I reread the December 1999/January 2000 edition of *Ms.* magazine, dedicated to the first 100 years of feminism. Fortunately for me, I grew up in the age of feminism.

My dad used to take my brother and me on Sunday drives in New Jersey. We would go past the golf course, where he wanted to be. We sat and watched private planes land at a small airport in Hanover, New Jersey. Years later, after obtaining my private pilot's license, I flew over Hanover before landing at Essex County Airport on one of my cross-country flights. I enjoyed flying from 1983, when I took my first lesson, until 2004, when I piloted a plane out of Anchorage, Alaska, while my friend and the flight instructor looked for moose, sheep, goats, and bears in the mountains. I believed that women could do anything that men could do—except urinate without removing undergarments. So there are limitations.

I considered Amelia Earhart my heroine. I was glad that I did not fly over vast expanses of water, because it was easy enough to get lost over land. I learned that I do well in emergencies, such as the time in the early 1990s that my single-engine airplane lost electrical power on a night flight to Nashville, Tennessee, for an AMWA meeting. I resourcefully landed at Paducah, Kentucky, one of the airports that I had visited on a long cross-country flight during training in the dark without lights. I got a plane to Nashville from Paducah (American Airlines' American Eagle network flew nonstop on that route). I flew American Eagle back to Paducah after the meeting and then, during the day, flew my plane with no alternator but with a fully charged battery back to St. Louis, following the Mississippi river, truly IFR (I follow the river). That was a real adventure. In 1999, I was flying with a friend to the Lake of the Ozarks in Missouri for lunch. The three-hour drive took only one hour by single-engine plane. Unfortunately, as we were flying over Rolla, Missouri, about 100 miles from St. Louis, the engine started to sound as though someone had pulled the plug. I immediately realized I had to land at the small airport we had just passed or end up in a tree. I was losing engine power and declared an emergency and radioed the other pilots with power to stay out of the way. I managed to do a perfect landing on the runway and turned off onto the taxiway, and the engine died. I felt angels' wings under my plane. Luckily, there were people at the airport and they came out with a Chevy Suburban and a tow rope and towed the plane to the parking area. I broke out in sweat after the emergency. I guess it was not my day to die. I had some posttraumatic stress disorder symptoms when I flew in that plane again, even after the mechanic fixed the engine. But I flew in it again. So don't let adversity keep you from your goals. Try to think things through, and do them anyway.

Remember that you're not alone. Organized medicine is really important. I'm not just talking about the APA; I'm talking about the AMA also. You will be able to change some policy. You will be able to influence some legislators. We have psychologist prescribing bills. In Missouri, I went to a committee hearing on the bill to promote psychologist prescribing and testified. They asked, "Don't you think there's an access problem?" I replied "Yes, there's an access problem. But the psychologists are in the same locations as the psychiatrists. The pattern is one of rifles hitting a target in five spots, meaning the big cities. The family doctors are all over the state like birdshot." I got the data from the Department of Government Relations of the APA. This is a red state; they liked the gun analogy. It is important to speak their language, have a sense of humor, and smile.

I attended the 2007 AMA advocacy meeting in Washington, D.C., the day that the Mental Health Parity bill was introduced in the Senate. I visited both of my senators and told them to vote for the parity bill. It was hot off the press. The AMA and APA can help get background information so that we can lobby for our patients and our profession.

At times I have wanted to clone myself in order to get everything done. There are times when I have wondered whether I was going to be sleep deprived. What I've learned is, start early in your career. Say *yes* to the volunteer opportunities that interest you. Say *no* to those that don't. If you appear at meetings and are interested, you'll get a job. If you do a good job, you'll get another job. Choose wisely, but choose to join and support with your money, if not your time and talent, because organized medicine provides a framework in which we can help ourselves and help our patients. By the way, if you're not a member of the APA, please join, and consider joining the AMA and your state medical society, which advocate for us at the federal and state legislatures.

PRACTICAL TIPS FOR WOMEN IN PSYCHIATRY

Some of the take-home messages are:

- Show up, volunteer, and bring something useful.
- Show up, volunteer, and do a good job.
- Show up, let them get to know you, and you will succeed.
- Show up, have a car, know directions, and doors will open.
- You have to make choices. Find something you like and say *yes* to it.
- Don't let adversity keep you from your goals. Try to think things through and do them anyway.

- Remember that you are not alone. Reach out to medical organizations.
- When speaking with legislators, speak their language, have a sense of humor, and smile.
- Start early in your career. Say *yes* to the volunteer opportunities that interest you and say *no* to those that don't. Avoid burnout.
- Follow your dreams or they may disappear.
- Face the opportunities that life gives you; be fearless, but wise. Seize the golden ring. Sometimes you win and sometimes you lose. The important thing to remember is that "Life is a game and bridge is serious."

References

American Psychiatric Association: Diagnostic and Statistical Manual of Mental Disorders, 3rd Edition. Washington, DC, American Psychiatric Association, 1980

Feighner JP, Robins E, Guze SB, et al: Diagnostic criteria for use in psychiatric research. Arch Gen Psychiatry 26:57–63, 1972

Friedan B: The Feminine Mystique. New York, WW Norton, 1963

Millett K: Sexual Politics. New York, Doubleday, 1969

Ms. magazine: Celebrating feminism, the first century. Ms., December 1999/January 2000

Robert HM, Robert SC, Evans WJ: The Scott, Foresman Robert's Rules of Order Newly Revised. Pearson Scott Foresman, 1986

Sturgis AF: Standard Code of Parliamentary Procedure, 4th Edition. New York, McGraw-Hill, 2000

Chapter 8

An Adventurous Journey

From the Holy City to the Windy City

Surinder Nand, M.D.

Interest in Medicine and Psychiatry: Exchanging Ankle Bells for the Stethoscope

I was the oldest of six daughters and a son. My father, a major in the Indian Army, was a doting parent who was also a strict disciplinarian. His job took him away from home a lot. My mother, a housewife, was a caring person who was always there for us. Both espoused high standards for our education. Although I was a straight-A student, I was more interested in becoming a dancer in the classical Indian tradition; this interest was inspired by the very talented dance teachers in my school as well as the encouragement of my parents, who would take us to watch dance performances by leading dancers in India. As one of the top dancers in my school, I had dreams of pursuing higher studies at Shantiniketan, an institution founded by Rabindra Nath Tagore, the 1913 Nobel Prize recipient for literature.

This dream was never to turn into a reality. During one of the visits to my maternal grandparents' home, a long discussion with one of my aunts, a godmother to many of her nieces and nephews, turned into a wake-up call. She suggested that I pursue dance as a hobby and focus my attention on pursuing my academic studies to help build a career. Career paths in India then were not chosen and decided by the student; such paths were shown and decided by one's elders—parents and other family members or close family friends. For women in India, postpartition in the 1950s to 1960s, there were limited career options. At the top of the list of careers for women were medicine, law, teaching, and nursing.

Indian women have had a long history of serving as physicians; Anandi Gopal Joshi and Kadambini Ganguly received their medical degrees through training in Western medicine in the 1880s, about forty years after Elizabeth Blackwell became the first woman in the United States to receive her medical degree.

Women patients in India have a strong preference for female physicians. Female physicians are held in high esteem and are in high demand by their female patients, while the field of medicine is otherwise dominated by men. The majority of women physicians are in obstetrics and gynecology and pediatrics, although some are internists, surgeons, and pathologists. Not only does the medical profession pay well, the future marriage prospects for women physicians in India are very bright. Most of them marry physicians.

Although all of the options presented by my aunt appealed to me, the fact that there was no physician in my nuclear family as well as in my extended family was another factor to be considered. A physician in the family bestowed a special status to the person as well as to the family. Thus was made the decision when I was in high school for me to pursue medicine as a career.

After a premedical year in a women's college, I enrolled in the Government Medical College in Amritsar, India, the holy city of the Sikhs. I found many of the subjects fascinating. During the clinical clerkships, in addition to learning about history taking and physical examinations, what caught my attention most was the psychosocial realm—how the person was dealing with his illness, what he found to be emotionally supportive, how his family was handling his illness, etc. During down time between didactics and clinical rotations, my three friends and I would visit the mental hospital near the medical college. Our first few excursions were out of simple curiosity. Psychiatry was one of the areas of medicine to which medical students had very little exposure. Once the administrator of the hospital found out that we were medical students, he assigned a volunteer, a former patient, to escort us on the campus of the hospital. It was an eye-opening experience that left a deep impression on me. While we talked to a woman who believed that she was a top Bollywood star, we also saw men and women in small rooms in restraints. These visits left us all bewildered and made us all the more inquisitive about the patients in this hospital, leading to more visits there. But soon our explorations ended. We passed our final exams and were on our road to internship and housejobs (residencies).

Precipitating Events Contributing to Career Choice: Pediatrics to Psychiatry

Before coming to the United States, I completed a year-long housejob in pediatrics and then started working with a general practitioner. The practitioner put up a large sign outside his clinic: *Lady Doctor Surinder Giani* (my maiden name). Although his practice already included women and children, the fact that now he also had a "lady doctor" started attracting large numbers of women and children, both from the city he practiced in and from neighboring towns and villages. Most of the women from the villages would come accompanied by their husbands and would not utter a word. I was supposed to figure out what their ailments were by checking their pulses—something that my medical training had not prepared me for. Within a year, I got married to a physician, one of my classmates. My husband wanted to pursue further studies in the United States, and after another year we moved to this country. While my husband entered his internal medicine residency, I started studying to pass the required examinations (i.e., the Educational Council for Foreign Medical Graduates [ECFMG]).

It was while studying for the examinations that my interest in psychiatry started to resurface. I found various psychiatric conditions intriguing. I realized that this was one area of medicine where the physician spent a good deal of time listening to the patient and used not only medications but also psychotherapy to help the patient get better. It was around the same time that I noticed that among our friends pursuing different residencies, ranging from internal medicine to surgery, the ones in a psychiatry residency seemed to not only enjoy their residencies but to live a more balanced life. After the death of our first child soon after birth, I could not see myself practicing pediatrics. Unlike women in western countries, women physicians in India usually do not pursue a career in psychiatry (Sood and Chadda 2009). This was uncharted territory for me.

The desire to start a family and to balance career goals and family life were two main forces that helped me decide that I would apply to a psychiatry residency program. Similar observations have been made by

Potter (1983), who noted that the possibility of regular hours and flexible schedules and the nature of the work are some of the reasons that women physicians choose psychiatry as a career.

Soon after passing my required examinations, I started applying to psychiatry residency programs. Since my husband was already in a residency program in Chicago, I limited my inquiries to the programs in Chicago. What a rude awakening this process was! I was not prepared for the difficulties my status as an international medical graduate, or IMG, would pose in getting into a residency program.

Large numbers of IMGs were coming to the United States in the early 1970s (they were referred to as FMGs, foreign medical graduates). These graduates, after their residencies, practiced in underserved areas where most American graduates did not want to go. Although they filled a major gap in medical services, they were not considered on par with their American peers. Cultural barriers, English being a second language, and inadequate medical training at the medical schools in their countries of origin were some of the reasons cited for discriminatory practices. Gaining acceptance into a psychiatry residency program became a major challenge. As soon as I made a telephone call, my accent would give me away and I was politely informed that the training program was not accepting any applications. As much as I did not want to believe that there was a bias against me because of my IMG status, I could not ignore the hard facts. Similar possible bias has been found by Nasir (1994) in his study of hiring IMGs in family practice residencies and by Balon et al. (1997) in the recruitment of psychiatry residents.

I was very fortunate to get a call for an interview from one of the psychiatry residency programs, and to my utter surprise and joy, I was selected as a first-year psychiatry resident in the program. And I took my first step toward my path of becoming a psychiatrist—not any psychiatrist, but a really good one.

Residency and Pregnancy

About three months before starting my residency, I found out that I was pregnant. In a survey conducted by Phelan in 1988, of female residents in psychiatry, obstetrics and gynecology, and surgery, almost half of married female residents become pregnant during their residency. Many female physicians give birth to their first child during their residencies (Bickel 2000). The majority of such pregnancies among psychiatry residents occur in the third and fourth years of residency, a period when residents have to take fewer night calls. I, however, became pregnant during my *first* year of residency!

Since our first child, a daughter, had died soon after birth, my husband and I were thrilled to know that I was pregnant again. I was, however, also concerned how my pregnancy might affect my residency and vice-versa. The residency was physically and intellectually very demanding. Long working hours, night calls every three days, a large case load, competing demands by various attending psychiatrists, an extensive amount of reading, and the desire to excel in my clinical rotations were extremely stressful. Although most of the attending psychiatrists, who were men, were supportive, there was no senior female resident or a female attending physician in the residency program with whom I could share my concerns.

Not only was I unaware of the program's maternity leave policies, I was too afraid to ask. Coming from a culture where one does not question authority, it did not even occur to me that I should at least inquire how much maternity leave I was entitled to. I worked until the day of my delivery and returned to work within two weeks. My return to work in such a short time was in contrast to the extended postpartum period of forty days that is traditionally practiced in many nonwestern cultures, including India (Lauderdale 1999). In most nonwestern cultures, female relatives help new mothers at home during that period. New mothers are advised to not engage in strenuous physical work and to get plenty of rest (Holroyd et al. 1997). My natal and postnatal periods in the United States can be best described as aseptic with excellent medical care, but lacking in the nurturance afforded the new mother in India (Choudhry 1997; Kim-Godwin 2003). We were not able to afford a full-time nanny, nor could our mothers come to help us during the postpartum period (Stewart and Robinson 1985).

Although I wanted to spend more time with my baby, neither taking unpaid leave nor working part-time was financially feasible—and I was not aware of these two possibilities (Shapiro 1982; Young-Shumate et al. 1993). I was also concerned that my fellow residents would have to take care of my clinical responsibilities in addition to their own (Rodgers et al. 1994). We were able to find a caring elderly couple near the medical center to babysit our son. And although we wanted to have another child, we decided to wait until after both of us completed our residencies.

Relationship Between Identity as a Woman and Work as a Psychiatrist

I believe that my identity as a woman helped me in my choice of career as a psychiatrist. Psychiatry has afforded me the advantage of regular hours, working with interesting patients, and opportunities to teach and conduct clinical research. With my patients, I have found that as a female psychiatrist, I am empathic, warm, and caring. Working in teams gives me the sense of affiliation and shared responsibility. As a team leader, my collaborative style and the ability to empower others help other team members feel valued.

After my residency, when my second son was born, I was able to take six weeks off and later I was able to work part-time for a few years. Psychiatry afforded me that flexibility. I started teaching in both clinical and classroom settings. In that capacity, I became an advisor and mentor to many male and female medical students and residents; it is a role that I have enjoyed tremendously.

Challenges Faced Professionally

There is a growing body of literature about the challenges faced by IMGs as they navigate their path through the American system of medical education, residencies, and careers (Haveliwala 1979; Rao 2007). Compounding their struggle through the medical system is the fact that they are also immigrants who are trying to adapt to a new culture. As with other immigrants, I went through a process of culture shock when I arrived in Chicago, the Windy City, from my home town of Amritsar, the Holy City. Initially I was fascinated by the novelty of a new place with tall buildings, long and wide roads, a beautiful lakefront, and food from every imaginable place in the world. Soon, though, I started missing India: my family and friends, the aroma of Indian food, the usual sights of the trees and flowers and sounds of chatter and Indian music. This phase was similar to the one described by Akhtar (1999) and Desai and Coehlo (1980). The longing for India and the associated nostalgia were similar to the feelings expressed in the beautiful poem by Nishat Akhtar (1999, p. 20). Although most immigrants who are fluent in English do well, American English is very different from the English I had learned in India. I had to pay attention to various dialects, the use of certain words, and different spellings. My husband, who had arrived six months before I did, and a small group of our friends were my teachers and guides during this initial time. Later, television and radio became my sources of learning the intricacies of idioms, slang, and the culture. I was expected to know the new culture, its customs and its values. Wearing western clothes and incorporating other foods in our meals was a welcome change. Over time, the acculturation and adaptation process became easier and smoother such that I consider myself quite well integrated in the new society now.

The challenges I faced as an IMG were in some ways similar to those of other new immigrants in this country. The practice of medicine was very different from what I was used to in India, where physicians are put on a high pedestal. A physician there is someone whose advice one follows without question and who becomes part of your extended family, getting invited to major family events and so on. In hospital settings in India, because of a clear hierarchy, the physician is the highest on the totem pole and all other health care professionals follow his commands. Switching to a more democratic and egalitarian American system required a basic shift in my thinking. Similarly, having addressed my superiors as *Sir* or *Madam*, to address my supervisors here by their first name was not easy. The prejudice toward IMGs became very evident when the residency training director of another specialty referred to IMGs as "those aliens." Over the years, such prejudices have become less blatant as the understanding of various cultures and tolerance for differences have increased.

Challenges in Balancing Personal and Professional Life

Although Indian women have been entering the medical profession in increasing numbers, Indian society expects them to be the main person responsible for taking care of children, family, and home (Juthani 2004). In our dual-career home, my husband was the one who brought home the bread and I the butter, and we could always do without the butter!

As new immigrants, we led a hectic life. At work I was a psychiatrist, chief of psychiatry at West Side VA Medical Center, and residency training director at the Department of Psychiatry, University of Illinois at Chicago. At home I was a wife and a mother with main responsibility for the home. Levinson (1996) perhaps, would have found ours to be a modified "traditional marriage enterprise." Initially, the drive home from work was the time I would try to figure out whether I would pick up dinner from McDonald's, Kentucky Fried Chicken, or Pizza Hut. Later, I started listening to soothing Indian music in my car as I drove home, to help me relax. Buying groceries and planning home-cooked meals was how I spent my weekends. Over time, the roles of a working woman, wife, and mother became more integrated. Eating dinner together as a family unit was one time when we all would share our day and unwind together. Both my husband and I made a concerted effort to attend all parent-teacher association meetings, our sons' school performances, and their baseball practices and games. We also took at least one vacation a year as a family.

At one point in my career, when I was acting chief of psychiatry at the Veterans Administration (VA) and the director of the Psychiatry Residency Training Program at the University of Illinois, I could see that I was ignoring my personal needs as well as my family's needs. That is when I decided to make major changes in my professional life. I decided to step down as the residency training director so that I could devote more time to myself and my family.

Style of Leadership and Leadership Roles

I have had the good fortune of serving in several leadership positions. Over the span of thirty years, my leadership potential and leadership style have continuously evolved. My abilities of anticipating and proactively finding solutions for problems, and the ability to form a team of people with diverse viewpoints to work together and remain calm in the midst of a crisis, have helped me execute well my authority as a leader. As the first-born child in my family, I had been used to taking charge and leading my five sisters and a brother; this translated to my professional life easily.

Many authors have noted that men and women have different leadership styles. While men leaders are seen as hierarchical, aggressive, forceful, and competitive, women leaders are seen as less hierarchical, cooperative, democratic, collaborative, and nurturing. Leadership styles have also been described as authoritarian, participatory, and laissez-faire—with men using the authoritarian and laissez-faire styles more often and women, the participatory styles.

I would describe my leadership style as participatory, delegative, and to some extent transformational, although I had to work hard to be able to delegate at work. My assessment of my style is based on looking back at my leadership positions, the leadership assessments I underwent, and responses from some of the people I have worked with. "*Always do the right thing*" and "*Action! Action!*" were two mantras that one of my mentors professed often and tried to instill in me. In a performance-driven Western world it was at times very hard, but a shloka in the Bhagavad Gita, the holy book of the Hindus, has also served as a guiding principle for me: it roughly translates into "Your right is to work only, but never to the fruit of that. Let not the fruit of action be your object, nor let your attachment be in inaction."

In two of my leadership positions I was given the charge of bringing about mergers. Being a leader is a challenge in itself, but to be responsible for a merger or integration can really test the mettle of a leader.

My first experience with a merger or integration was as residency training director in the Department of Psychiatry at the University of Illinois at Chicago. Soon after I was appointed as the residency training program director (I was the first woman and the first IMG in this role in the department's history), I was given the task of merging two residency programs at other institutions in Chicago with the one at the University of

Illinois. Whereas the program at the university had attracted U.S. medical graduates almost exclusively, the other two had more IMGs. The technical part of the integration was extremely detailed and time-consuming. It involved ensuring that the curriculum promised to the residents from the other two programs would continue for them, receiving approval for the merger from the Accreditation Council for Graduate Medical Education and Residency Review Committee, arranging the transfer of stipends and the allotment of office space, and so on. Tasman and Riba (1993) noted the following factors that must be attended to for a successful merger of residency training programs: educational philosophy, program implementation, resources, impact on faculty, organizational culture, and governance. It was the people part of the integration that was daunting and needed enormous attention. The residents and faculty at the university program were worried that such a large number of IMGs might affect future recruitment negatively. The residents from the other two programs on one hand were happy to have access to a larger number of teaching and research faculty; they also mourned the loss of the culture of the program to which they had grown accustomed. Ongoing and clear communications with all parties, listening to their concerns, being as candid and as transparent as possible, and treating all with respect were some key elements of the successful merger.

When I was charged with the merger of psychiatric services of two VA medical centers (while I was director of the Mental Health Service Line at the Jesse Brown VA Medical Center, formerly West Side VA Medical Center), several meetings were held with the staff of both services. It soon became clear that the staff of the service that was to move to the west-side campus considered this merger a hostile take-over. With such strong feelings in the air, it also became evident that there was an ongoing need for clear communication to address and allay the insecurities experienced by the staff of both services. While no major workforce reduction in mental health services was planned, there were concerns about changes in roles and cultural transformation (Kay and Sheldon 2000). The focus became providing a smoother transition of patient care as well as staff. My team of incredibly smart section heads made this process as streamlined as possible for both the patients and the staff. This was one of the many times I felt good about having surrounded myself with a team of extremely competent and dedicated mental health professionals.

Serving as the president of the Illinois Psychiatric Society and as the president of the Indo-American Psychiatric Association were somewhat different experiences. Working together with one's colleagues as a team toward the same goals was less of a burden than these two positions entailed. Both of these offices required more public appearances and the ability to quickly think on my feet when a microphone was suddenly and unexpectedly thrust in front of me.

Leading a not-for-profit charitable organization like Apna Ghar (Our Home), which serves victims of domestic violence, a cause I passionately believe in, has been a totally different experience. I have served in a variety of roles in this organization including as volunteer, consultant, executive committee member, and interim executive director. These roles have given me enormous satisfaction and limitless pleasure in spite of their requiring long hours and high energy.

Mentorship

As John Crosby said, "Mentoring is a brain to pick, an ear to listen, and a push in the right direction." All of us need mentors to help us grow and develop. Mentors provide role modeling, coaching, networking, and sponsorship. They accept you for who you are, recognize your potential, and help you use your positive attributes to develop your career. Good mentors not only help you with your professional goals but also help you become a better human being. Mentoring relationships can help women advance in their chosen careers (Kupersanin 2001). Some believe that mentoring relationships are more important for women than men (Logan 1994). There are differing opinions about whether one's mentor should be of the same gender or not; many profess that female psychiatrists must have female mentors, while others underscore the importance of good mentoring over the gender of the mentor.

Two women, my mother and my maternal aunt, were my personal role models. My mother with her unparalleled, no-nonsense style of nurturance and her exceptional organizational skills built a solid foundation for me and my aunt with her unconditional love and guidance showed me the path I would take. Professionally, however, my situation was unique. Over the long course of my academic career, I had the good fortune of having had three male mentors. The male gender was the common factor; otherwise, they were quite different.

In the 1980s, the Department of Psychiatry at the University of Illinois had only a handful of female psychiatrists. My chief at the VA medical center, Dr. Prakash Desai, a male Indian psychiatrist, became my mentor. His was the brain I picked; he lent me his ear and, when I needed it, gave me a gentle push. As a mentor, he not only shepherded my career in the right direction, he also was my guide for my cultural adaptation to this new homeland. From the time I entered the VA system as a staff psychiatrist on the inpatient unit until my retirement as the Director of the Mental Health Service Line at the same VA twenty-four years later, he was my advocate, my cheerleader, my guide, and a harsh critic! Although we both have re-tired from the VA, we have continued our friendship, and when I need a word of advice, I call him.

Dr. Boris Astrachan appointed me director of the Psychiatry Resi-dency Training Program when he came to the University of Illinois as chair of the Department of Psychiatry in 1990. My appointment told vol-umes about his belief that women would bring value to the department and showed that he did not discriminate against the IMGs. A visionary with an astute business sense who believed in building effective systems, he took me under his wings. My relationship with him was almost like a father and daughter relationship—warm and friendly. He paved the way for me to re-ceive executive training at Harvard's Executive Program for Physician Leaders and encouraged me to present at national conferences and to get more involved with organized psychiatry. He taught me about mergers of residency programs and effective leadership. He helped me understand the difference between power and authority and how best to exert my au-thority as a new residency training director.

My third mentor, another male psychiatrist, Dr. Ivan Pavkovic, came into my professional life much later, when I was facing the prospect of merging the psychiatric services of two VA medical centers. With exten-sive experience running large systems of mental health care, he was held in high esteem by his peers and subordinates. I found his mentorship ex-tremely challenging. Not one to give advice, he helped me look at my strengths and limitations in a most critical manner—a process that was quite nerve-wracking at times! Someone who believed in adages like "Never be mean to anyone; be generous," "You will make mistakes; learn from those and move on," and "Forgive yourself and then others," he had a major impact on my developing into a better human being.

Just as these three mentors shaped my professional and personal life, I have tried to convey some of their principles when I mentor others. Of all my professional roles, the one I enjoy the most is that of a mentor. In the course of my academic career I have mentored male as well as female medical students, residents, junior faculty, and other health care profes-sionals, many of whom have gone on to take leadership roles in other fields of medicine as well as in mental health. Recently, while mentoring a stu-dent, I found myself using the same language and words that my mentors had used to encourage me; a clear indication that I had internalized the good values of my mentors.

I can say without any hesitation that who I am today is to a large extent because of my mentors. As I look back on my life, I can truly say that it has been an interesting and adventurous journey.

PRACTICAL TIPS FOR WOMEN IN PSYCHIATRY

- Psychiatry is a wonderful field of medicine and well suited for women who want to balance their professional life with their personal life. I have never regretted my decision to pursue psychiatry as a career goal.

- Surround yourself with supportive people. Find a life partner who encourages you to pursue your goals and does not mind getting up in the middle of night to change the dirty diaper and give the bottle to the baby. And if he doesn't know how to do these two essential tasks, teach him.

- Unless you are a superwoman, you cannot submit a grant proposal, treat fifteen patients, teach medical students, and make a finger-licking chicken curry on the same day. Something will have to be put on the back burner sometimes, and only you can decide whether it will be the curry or your lecture for the medical students. Define your priorities and try to stick with them.

- Find mentors. Rather than worrying about whether they have XX or XY chromosomes, look for those who are genuinely interested in helping you navigate through the academic maze and going up the career ladder. Your comfort level with this person is one of the key factors in your learning from him or her. Give back to others what you learn from your mentors and from life. Mentoring others will be one of the most rewarding experiences for you.

- Whether you are a transformational or a participatory leader at work, have moved mountains or have gotten bogged down in bureaucracy, to come home to your family at the end of the day is one of the most satisfying experiences. Have fun with them. Institutional memory is short lived, but your children will remember the time you spent with them forever.

- Remember what Eleanor Roosevelt said: "No one can make you feel inferior without your permission." Do not allow anyone to discriminate against you because of your age, gender, or IMG status. And if you are witness to such behavior, raise your voice to stop it.

- Nurture yourself. Take care of your physical, emotional, and spiritual health.

- Life is short. Roll with the punches. Develop a sense of humor. Learn to laugh at yourself.

References

Akhtar S: Immigration and Identity: Turmoil, Treatment and Transformation. Northvale, NJ, Jason Aronson, 1999

Balon R, Mufti R, Williams W, et al: Possible discrimination in recruitment of psychiatry residents? Am J Psychiatry 154:1608–1609, 1997

Bickel J: Women in Medicine: Getting in, Growing, and Advancing. Thousand Oaks, CA, Sage, 2000

Choudhry UK: Traditional practices of women from India: pregnancy, childbirth, and newborn care. J Obstet Gynecol Neonatal Nurs 26:533–539, 1997

Desai P, Coelho G: Indian immigration in America: some cultural aspects of psychological adaptation, in The New Ethnics: Asian Indians in the United States. Edited by Saran P, Eames E. New York, Praeger, 1980, pp 363–386

Haveliwala YA: Problems of foreign born psychiatrists. Psychiatr Q 51:307–311, 1979

Holroyd E, Katie FK, Chun LS, et al: "Doing the month": an exploration of postpartum practices in Chinese women. Health Care Women Int 18:301–313, 1997

Juthani NV: Challenges faced by international women professionals. Acad Psychiatry 28:347–350, 2004

Kay IT, Sheldon MJ: The people problem in mergers. McKinsey Quarterly 4(Nov):27–37, 2000

Kim-Godwin YS: Postpartum beliefs and practices among non-Western cultures. MCN Am J Matern Child Nurs 28:74–78, 2003

Kupersanin E: Women psychiatrists say mentors key to success. Psychiatr News 36:5, 2001

Lauderdale J: Childbearing and transcultural nursing care issues, in Transcultural Concepts in Nursing Care, 3rd Edition. Edited by Andrews MM, Boyle JS. Philadelphia, PA, Lippincott, 1999, pp 81–106

Levinson DJ: The Seasons of a Woman's Life. New York, Knopf, 1996

Logan J: Mentoring: it's for women, too. Leadership 3:38–39, 1994

Nasir LS: Evidence of discrimination against international medical graduates applying to family practice residency programs. Fam Med 26:625–629, 1994

Phelan ST: Pregnancy during residency: I: the decision "to be or not to be." Obstet Gynecol 72:425–431, 1988

Potter RL: Resident, woman, wife, mother: issues for women in training. J Am Med Womens Assoc 38:98–102, 1983

Rao NR, Kramer M, Saunders R, et al: An annotated bibliography of professional literature on international medical graduates. Acad Psychiatry 31:68–83, 2007

Rodgers C, Kunkel ES, Field HL: Impact of pregnancy during training on a psychiatric resident cohort. J Am Med Womens Assoc 49:49–52, 1994

Shapiro J: Pregnancy during residency: attitudes and policies. J Am Med Womens Assoc 37:96–97, 101–103, 1982

Sood M, Chadda RK: Women in psychiatry: a view from the Indian subcontinent. Indian J Psychiatry 51:199–201, 2009

Stewart DE, Robinson GE: Combining motherhood with psychiatric training and practice. Can J Psych 30:28–34, 1985

Tasman A, Riba M: Strategic issues for the successful merger of residency training programs. Hosp Community Psychiatry 44:981–985, 1993

Young-Shumate L, Kramer T, Beresin E: Pregnancy during graduate medical training. Acad Med 68:792–799, 1993

Chapter 9

Mission Driven and Road Tested

A Career Path in Public Psychiatry

Anita S. Everett, M.D.

IN MANY WAYS I have had an extraordinary career filled with professional adventures. I have done things and been places that few other psychiatrists have. In other ways, I am an ordinary working professional with multiple roles that include psychiatrist, mother, wife, daughter, sister, neighbor, and citizen: the usual stuff that contemporary American lives comprise. It is a tremendous honor to have been asked to participate in a collection of the life stories of professional women. My professional life is not one of laser focus; rather, it is a collection of successive experiences and opportunities centered on the broad area of public service development for persons with serious mental illness.

I think of my own career as including many unusual opportunities and turns that would be difficult to replicate. The following is how a current biographic statement reads:

Dr. Everett is the Section Chief of the Johns Hopkins Bayview Community and General Psychiatry. She is on the faculty of The Johns Hopkins School of Medicine and the Bloomberg School of Public Health, Department of Mental Health. Her current area of research is the health behavior of individuals with long-term mental illnesses. Prior to joining the Johns Hopkins staff, Dr. Everett served as the Chief Medical Advisor to the Federal Substance Abuse and Mental Health Services Administration. There she worked on a number of projects that centered on the promotion of access to quality services and appropriate medications for individuals with mental illness. From 1999 to 2003 she served as the Inspector General to the Office of the Governor in the Department of Mental Health in Virginia. Dr. Everett is a Distinguished Fellow of the American Psychiatric Association and serves on the Board of the American Association of Community Psychiatrists. She is president of the Maryland Psychiatric Society. She is currently engaged in a number of international projects which have included consultation with the Ministries of Health, Department of Mental Health in Iraq and Afghanistan on the implementation of mental health services in these countries.

Early Antecedents

"The network coverage of the assassination and funeral of John F. Kennedy warrants its reputation as the most moving and historic passage in broadcasting history. On Friday 22 November 1963, news bulletins reporting rifle shots during the president's motorcade in Dallas, Texas, broke into normal programming" (Doherty 2011). The solemn funeral procession with a horse-drawn casket moved slowly down Pennsylvania Avenue on our small, square, black-and-white television. I was four years old and living in Huntsville, Alabama, in November of 1963. Our NASA engineer neighbors worked in the space program at Huntsville, which was a Kennedy Administration "New Frontier" project; they came from many different places, including Germany, and most were not native to Alabama. It was hot in the summer and only somewhat less than hot in the winter, but I do have memories of one odd snowfall and of my resourceful mother snowproofing our feet with pieces of plastic and rubber bands around our ankles. My family's first second car was a gray 1964 Volkswagen Beetle (not the VW minibus or camper version that my sister and I lobbied for). The second car meant we did not have to wait while my father closed the department store that he managed in downtown Huntsville in order to grocery shop and run errands. Huntsville provided an early sense of being a part of a small progressive community within a more conservative environment that was periodically a center of national attention during the civil rights movement.

As children, we were isolated from the intense racial situation that existed all over the South and especially in towns like Huntsville. Only recently have I learned that my father was threatened by a phone call in the night, likely from a Ku Klux Klan member, because of his role with other downtown merchants who were considering serving African Americans at department store lunch counters. A common Klan tactic was to threaten the lives of family members of community leaders who might be favorable to these kinds of civil rights for African Americans (Marsh 2001).

Although my father was reared in the Deep South, his family was actually from middle Tennessee, which is culturally influenced by its proximity to Appalachia. His family moved to Mississippi and Alabama in association with the federal public works projects that brought electricity to the rural Deep South. He was recruited into retail management after his service in the Air Force during the Korean War. He met and married my mother, a native Baltimorean, while working in a department store in downtown Baltimore. My father has influenced my career in many direct and indirect ways, not the least of which is having a strong executive work ethic. He worked hard, he was a respected leader in the communities where we lived, and his work was recognized and valued by the company he worked for. When I was thirteen years old, that company went bankrupt. From that point forward, I was interested in a career that would give me a degree of independence.

The Vietnam War touched my family indirectly. A young Walter Cronkite was the evening news reporter on our now color and much bigger console television. One advantage in being in the family of a retail manager is access to the newest appliances. With Cronkite's voice narrating, there were nightly visions of gunfire, smoke, and tired soldiers tramping through a distant jungle. My father, now managing a store in suburban Chattanooga, was president of the shopping center merchants' association and they created a giant Christmas card to send in support of our troops in Nam. As a child, I was fascinated by this giant novelty. To sign the card, one had to walk up steps like the steps from a traveling carnival exhibit. This was on display in the shopping center parking lot, next to the Santa Candy Land Cottage, for several weeks until it was covered with written greetings from people in suburban Chattanooga. Although it was created for the soldiers it was also a show of community support for local military families. I surveyed the increasing density of signatures every morning from the carpool car as we made our way to St. Jude School, which was on a big foothill of red dirt and sporadic grass behind the shopping center. This card symbolized the southern hospitality with which I grew up. Southern hospitality and Catholic educational themes of social justice were part of my foundation. In Chattanooga, my friends' fathers and the carpool drivers' husbands were mostly engineers, this time employed not by NASA but by the Tennessee Valley Authority. The carpool drivers, including my mother, were reading Betty Friedan's controversial work: *The Feminine Mystique* (Friedan 1963). These were overqualified and underpaid chauffeurs, a reality that also would have an impact on our generation of women.

Donny Osmond and the Jackson 5 were in the top 40 on the transistor radio that I had been given as a get-well gift: The first six weeks of sixth grade I was an inpatient on a teaching ward at Henrietta Egleston Hospital for Children in Atlanta, at Emory University. We had moved to northern Georgia and my mother, who was a medical technologist and had trained at a teaching hospital in Baltimore, strongly advocated (more likely demanded) that I be transferred to Emory from the small local hospital where I was first admitted. I had what was determined to be some form of encephalitis that necessitated at least one diagnostic pneumoencephalogram. (Mercifully, this procedure is now obsolete due to computed tomography and magnetic resonance imaging technology.) Several different pediatric subspecialists were involved and each came with an entourage of students and housestaff (male) in short white coats. It was not unusual to be subject four or more times a day to the rounds of various subspecialists. This experience had a powerful impact on my life and on our family. My life was saved as a result of the knowledge and skills of the staff at the teaching hospital.

The hostage crisis in Iran occurred during my college years. I watched the evening accounting of the status of our hostages from the television in my dormitory lobby at the University of Tennessee. It was the first time many of my generation, especially in eastern Tennessee, had thought very seriously about affairs in the Middle East other than issues related directly to President Carter's priority of establishing peace between Israel and Egypt.

Higher Education and Training

The culture in eastern Tennessee is influenced by its proximity to Appalachia. Natives in eastern Tennessee are resilient frontier survivors who have endured many hardships and mastered many skills. Competency in a variety of carpentry, farming, and hunting skills is important for pioneers, and the capacity to work together in small communities is essential for everyone's survival. The culture of middle and eastern Tennessee is not nearly as Deep South southern as is most of Virginia or western Tennessee down toward Memphis. Most of my friends, many of whom were first-generation college students, pursued practical degrees in fields such as engineering, business, nursing, or the newly established field of computer science.

Medical school for me directly followed college. Much of the science content and educational experience were the same as they would be at any medical school. What was different in the small, new medical school in eastern Tennessee that I attended, Quillen College of Medicine at East Tennessee State University, was the freshness of the school. The school was created by legislation in Nashville following the tireless advocacy of community citizens, physicians, and local state legislators. Many of the faculty were hired from established medical schools, while others were borrowed from local universities' basic science departments. Achieving LCME (Liaison Committee on Medical Education) accreditation was in the minds of our faculty. As students we were aware of pending LCME accrediting visits. In putting together the faculty and curriculum, school founders planned for the needs of the local area residents and practicing physicians. Many of the educational experiences were built on the existing local medical infrastructure. I was a member of the third graduating class of the school. As early students we were often welcomed as a physical manifestation of a medical school that was built to provide the area with a needed physician workforce. This was a community medical school that was tied to a clear sense of public service in a medically underserved area.

My medical school provided a balance of respect for medical tradition and openness to progressive ideas. This has been an important influence. Physicians, by nature, are a relatively traditional lot. We follow rules and aspire to classic professional virtues. We are conditioned to be clinically conservative in the treatment of our patients. In leadership roles, particularly in public service where often there are responsibilities for stewardship of public budgets, it is essential to be able to consider new ideas. In a required text for a leadership development course that I participated in much later in my career, I learned the term *outsight* (Kouzes and Posner 2002) In psychiatry we consider insight to be enhanced knowledge of an existing event or behavioral pattern that is augmented by looking inward into one's internal composition and history. Persons make gains in a therapeutic process through incorporating new insight into the origins of a behavior or idea. In contrast, outsight has to do with making gains and moving an organization (or person) forward through looking outward to others' experiences. In *The Leadership Challenge*, Kouzes and Posner (2002) assert that outsight is a critical component of effective leadership. That is, it is essential to be aware of trends and successes of other organizations and industries and be able to incorporate new ideas into an existing organization. This relates to medical school for me, because the new school that I attended was very innovative. In medicine, some practices and services are traditions because they represent the essence of the best way to accomplish a specific goal for an individual or population. Other practices are traditions because they have always been done a particular way, and do not necessarily represent a best practice or the best way to solve a particular clinical or administrative problem. Outsight is an important skill in medical leadership.

Many students choose a medical specialty in the third year of medical school during a series of clinical rotations on different medical services. Several of my clinical rotations were in the Mountain Home VA Medical Center in Tennessee. This was in a previous era in VA medicine. The surgery rotation included patients who waited for as long as six weeks on the inpatient ward to get on the operating room schedule for a hernia repair. Laboratory results often took days to obtain, and medical students quickly learned that this time could be shortened if they ran the tests themselves. (Gloves were not worn for blood drawing and sputum collection, as this was well before the time of HIV and AIDS and the institutionalization of universal precautions for all body fluids.) To get lab results, one called the lab on a telephone and wrote them down. To get X-ray results, a trip to the X-ray file room was made in person; occasionally staff would read a report over the phone. With luck the attendant was there; if he was not there, one found and checked out the film or the report in the film jacket oneself. The wards were large rooms that had an open nursing station at one end. Virtually everyone smoked on the wards: patients, nursing staff, aid staff, and an occasional attending physician. While physician privacy was rare, comradeship and stories of being a soldier during a war were common. It was a different era.

Psychiatry at the VA was in a different building. The rooms there were smaller, usually four patients to a room, and there were also several private rooms. The comfortable, tobacco-saturated day room was generally a convivial place with the types of casual friendships that develop over months of group living. The staff was seasoned in working with a variety of unstable and traumatized patients, but also had a sense of purpose and professionalism in the work they did. I particularly remember a time when we had three patients on the same unit at the same time who all believed they were Jesus Christ, sent to earth with the special mission to save the human race. This was not an uncommon delusion in the Bible Belt. Each of these saviors was so fixed in his delusion that the presence of the two "imposters" was not perceived to be a threat. Every morning the team discussed and prepared for the probability of a confrontation between our three Jesuses. What a fascinating situation! How could three minds falsely believe that they were the son of God? One of the saviors responded within several days to lithium and perphenazine. The other two had a slower course and were on the unit when I rotated off to a different service. We learned from and used the descriptive text of DSM-II (American Psychiatric Association 1968). No one was in a rush to discharge patients. A daily ward census was submitted and it invariably included the names of many patients out on community passes and therapeutic leave. The average length of stay was not a management consideration.

Several months after the psychiatry rotation, I saw one of the two more treatment-resistant Jesuses, who was no longer delusional, in the mall. He darted across the mall concourse to thank me for being part of the team that had facilitated his recovery. He now had a job and his wife had taken him back. It was astonishing to see the difference in his life that the hospitalization had facilitated. Psychiatry was beginning to look like a career that could help people make incredible differences in their lives, with movement from nearly complete disability to being functioning individuals. The order of magnitude associated with restoration of functionality was particularly fascinating to me. This was a great contrast to the often more-incremental differences one could make in working with adults with other chronic disease processes that were common in a VA setting such as obstructive pulmonary disease, heart failure, and diabetes.

The role models in medical school included a wide variety of psychiatry and psychology faculty, mostly men. The psychiatrists at the VA were generally more senior and relaxed with their lives. They were comfortable people, engaging in conversation and very capable of formulating plans for and treating virtually any mental condition or human tragedy that happened to occur among the inpatients. There were also several mentor psychologists who were active participants in the unit and psychiatry rotation. Many of the inpatients had had psychological testing, which was very valuable in diagnostic assessment and treatment planning. Unfortunately, this very useful diagnostic psychological assessment is hardly ever done today.

Women role models were few and far between in this world of medicine in eastern Tennessee in the early 1980s. But my class, the class of 1985, was about one-third women. We would have opportunities to become those successful role models that we had never had. We would become those people, that is, unless we chose the family path, which was of spoken and unspoken concern at this time. Would young female students take up valuable medical school slots, and not increase the physician workforce? Our mothers had read Betty Friedan and had great expectations for their daughters. While my cohort of women was working to learn a challenging profession, the rest of the world was watching. Would women make it as viable professionals, or would this be a short-lived social phase?

Becoming a Psychiatrist

The Challenger space shuttle explosion occurred while I was on a rotation on the Barringer 3 cancer unit at the University of Virginia. As I conducted my early morning prerounds, now in my own resident's short white coat, the image of the flaming rocket seemed to be rerun on every big, square television high on the wall of each semiprivate room. For many of the terminal patients admitted to the Barringer 3 service, it served as a reminder that life can end at any time, that there are no guarantees. For me also it was a reminder: no matter how carefully a life or course of study is planned, there are no guarantees. Between the patients on that unit and the Challenger explosion, I had a personal reckoning with the time and energy I had invested in a professional future. It had become habit to think about the future and not focus on being in the present.

I met my husband, Allen Everett, during my first month in medical school. He was a year ahead of me, and as a second-year student, or MSII, he was very worldly in his knowledge and experience of medical school. In many ways, he has remained ahead of me through clinical rotations, residency, and postgraduate employment. We have been partners throughout our lives and continue to be. His career stability in medical academic research has enabled me to take certain risks with my career that I would not have been able to take had I had the sole responsibility for financial supporting ourselves and our family.

Unlike the progressive, inventive, and fresh Quillen College in Tennessee, our training at the University of Virginia was steeped in tradition. This was a sharp contrast to our innovative little medical school. While Allen was learning pediatrics and then cardiology, I was learning psychiatry and internal medicine. We were on call every third day and sometimes every other day. Occasionally we had every fourth day and, rarely, no-call rotations. As residents, we learned the art of tag-team marriage. We were called *yuppies* (young upwardly mobile professionals) and we were called *dinks* (double income, no kids). With resident-level incomes and medical school debt, however, we did not resonate with the yuppie-dink image (Gianoulis 2002). We lived in and around the world of the hospital; inpatient medicine was our culture for that five-year period of intensive training.

My training world was rich with mentors, several of whom stand out, and virtually no women. The chairmen I worked with were remarkable men with many great attributes. Dr. Wilford Spradlin, chair of the psychiatry department, stimulated a kind of intellectual curiosity that has persisted throughout my life and Dr. Edward W. Hook Jr., head of internal medicine, was an extremely accomplished blue-blooded academic who retained an almost childlike delight in describing the personal histories of patients during his lengthy traditional chair's rounds. Multiple other faculty (virtually all men) served as mentors throughout my training. Clinical psychiatry was commonly practiced during lengthy inpatient admissions at this time, and there was a clear focus on ward milieu and the responsibility of the psychiatrist to establish the milieu. The psychiatrists' tools of the time were the inpatient environment and sometimes (but not always) medications.

The chief resident year is often an important career highlight for those who are fortunate enough to be given that opportunity, as I was. It was a transition in professional identity from that of resident and peer to attending psychiatrist and a different peer group. This was a kind of public expression of trust and confidence in me as a professional that I am deeply grateful to have experienced. Had I not been chief I am fairly certain that I would have had a much quieter clinical career. During my chief year, one of our psychiatry interns became pregnant. There were no written house staff policies on this topic. Historically, special circumstances were dealt with on a case-by-case basis with the chairman; otherwise physicians were expected to be working. The "problem" of pregnant residents was occurring with increasing frequency in other departments as well. Many of this intern's peers openly expressed the concern that it was not fair for them to pull more time on call because she had electively become pregnant. We negotiated a compromise with her classmates so that she had the equivalent number of on-call days, all in advance of her delivery date so that they would not be adversely impacted during her six-week maternity leave. To this day, I don't know whether this was a leadership success (we worked together to engage her peers with a strategy that was fair for all) or a leadership failure in that I did not more strongly advocate for the causes of women professionals who are of child-bearing age. Fortunately the rules are very different now.

When I became pregnant two years later while a junior faculty member, there was no written faculty policy on maternity leave. Although the department chair, my boss, had supported me in taking whatever time I needed, I was pressured to come back to work after a month by a peer who was unhappy with the additional workload he shouldered while I was home with my newborn son. I was too junior in the department of men and the issue was too new for me to know how to ask for coverage for a fixed period of time, and I returned to work after one month on leave. (This was years before the passage of the federal Family and Medical Leave Act which supports a minimal three months of maternity leave.)

Becoming a mother added incredible depth and color to my life. Our little peach-fuzzy-headed boy facilitated a change that was like going from a linear, one-directional world to three dimensions. Ten-hour days in the hospital culture, stimulating as they were, were no longer where my heart was. I needed and wanted predictable time with Sam at home. A faculty position with complex and ongoing expectations for advancement within fixed promotional timeframes was no longer consistent with an optimal balance in life. In addition to family factors, the department itself was changing. The chairman who had originally hired and trained me was leaving, and he took several faculty members with him. In the foreseeable future, there were going to be increased clinical loads for all with very little opportunity for academic success in a department that did not have a tradition of prioritizing early-career academic mentoring. I defected and took a job in a community mental health clinic.

Community Psychiatry and Public Service

From day one, I loved my work as a community psychiatrist at Valley Community Services Board (VCSB) in Staunton, Virginia. The combination of a focus on persons with serious mental illness and practice in a rural area with a great team of dedicated professionals was refreshing. A sense of common purpose, infused with humanitarian values, was common throughout the agency. Time and time again I was personally inspired by the dedication that the staff had to the causes of persons with mental illness. Everyone from receptionist to billing clerk to medical records department staff had a clear sense of the purpose of the agency. It was at this agency in a small community that I began to understand the parts and pieces of a publicly funded mental health care system and how they fit together to create an array of programs that serve local individuals with mental conditions, substance use disorders, and intellectual disabilities. Over time I learned about the local history of most of the services and how they were funded. It was a services system with a fixed geographic catchment area that was small enough to learn about, yet big enough to provide some very effective programs. At VCSB I was able to work with patients in the clinic on an individual level and work on program and staff development on a larger scale.

Early in my tenure at VCSB, a neighboring community psychiatrist recommended I join the American Association of Community Psychiatrists (AACP). I was just learning how to use a personal computer when I became an AACP member and began to receive e-mails that later were organized into a listserver. The AACP correspondence was useful at once; taking part in it provided great support and context for many of the day-to-day challenges that arise in community psychiatric settings.

At VCSB, I was involved with the development of a number of initiatives and programs. These included:

- Regular in-service training for professional development
- Grand rounds presentations on community psychiatry and rehabilitative services at the local university-affiliated state psychiatric hospital

- A specialized treatment program for our patients with severe personality disorders, which became recognized as a regional model for other programs
- Our region's first clozapine clinic[1]
- A clinical elective rotation for physicians in training at the University of Virginia
- Psychiatric services for developmentally disabled (sometimes referred to as *mentally retarded*) patients who were moving into community settings from large institutions as a result of a new state program.

We actively maintained working relationships with local physicians, hospitals, and other public services, particularly the Department of Social Services and the Child Protective Services and Adult Protective Services divisions. We organized a statewide meeting for community psychiatrists so that we could exchange ideas regarding best practices and advocacy.

As we struggled to open our first clozapine clinic, it occurred to us that a visit from the state commissioner might help the decision-makers in Richmond to better understand the realities of persons with treatment-resistant schizophrenia who needed access to this new treatment option. We were hopeful that actually meeting some citizens who might benefit from this new treatment might help to loosen up some funding to provide the medication. After six very busy years at VCSB, I became particularly preoccupied with the adverse impact on our patients and services of a proposed round of state government budget cuts. The proposal was of the type that asked for an analysis regarding the impact of a potential range of cuts, four percent, eight percent, and twelve percent. I saw this as painful rationing for a group of services that were already underresourced in Virginia compared with most other states in the nation. (The funding in other states was an example of outsight [looking outward to others' experiences; see "Higher Education and Training"] that I had gained in part due to the AACP Listserv.) Creating the written impact analysis felt like a game that our leadership had to play. It particularly began to feel weird when I noticed we were happy to think that if we had planned for an eight percent budget reduction, but only had our budget cut by four percent, we would have extra money. Although I had never done anything like it before, I wrote a letter of protest to the governor.

---

[1]Clozapine had recently been approved for use in the United States and was indicated, as it is now, for treating schizophrenia symptoms that have not responded well to other medications. Due to serious potential side effects, its use requires close patient monitoring and frequent laboratory tests.

Our second child was a bright and beautiful daughter. The commute over the mountain to VCSB in Staunton seemed longer, and I wanted to be more accessible to my daughter. Our son had finished the outstanding Montessori preschool program he had attended near my work in Staunton and would be going to a school near where we lived and where my husband worked at the University of Virginia. Our life pattern was changing, VCSB wanted me full-time, I needed to work part-time, and I was becoming a bit demoralized by the state budget reductions. There were many issues for me personally that were associated with a sense of giving up on a cause and leaving the mission-driven work that I had been invested in for years. My decision was fortified by the need to spend more time at home with my young family.

Anticipating that the hours would be more flexible, I accepted a position at a local inpatient unit in a community hospital. My thought: morning rounds started when I got there, not at a set time, and if I efficiently managed my time I could do rounds in the morning and be home in the afternoon with my children. The hoped-for efficiency never really happened. The staff at Crossroads Behavioral Health Services was a wonderful collection of nurses and aides (mostly women) who were truly invested in the community service mission of the hospital and the psychiatric unit. Augusta Health medical center was an extremely well-led and well-managed hospital with many nurse executives in positions of authority. Patients, families, and staff love physicians who spend time with patients. I had been trained to believe and still firmly believe that time spent with patients, with engaged, attentive interactions, is one of our healing tools. This is hard to accomplish in a modern inpatient unit. Sunday morning rounds were my favorite time on the unit. Somehow Sundays are conducive to quiet, quality, uninterrupted and unhurried time with patients. Frequent weekend rounds are not so good for family life, however. The unpredictable pace and schedule of admissions and discharges thwarted my plans to spend afternoons with my children. After several months, and despite the excellent staff, I began to experience compassion fatigue for the first time in my career. I missed the energy I had experienced that was associated with the more comprehensive services and long-term continuity in community psychiatric practice.

An unexpected call from Richmond came at about this time. Apparently the letter of protest I had written to the governor had been received. After several introductions, handshakes, and trips to Richmond, I found myself being invited to become Virginia's first inspector general of the Office of the Governor for the Department of Mental Health, Mental Retardation and Substance Abuse Services (DMHMRSAS). By that time I was experienced in making career moves. By then I was in my third position since completing my residency and my husband was well established in his research career in academic medicine. I decided to take the risk on a low-paying, high-demand, high-profile but potentially high-influence office at the state government level as opposed to maintaining the status quo on an inpatient unit, which was not working well with regards to my goal of increased, predictable time at home with my young family.

What a cool opportunity, I remember thinking, to be able to influence the epicenter of decisions on public mental health, mental retardation, and substance abuse service policy and funding. Reality check: What hope for positive influence could come with a conservative Republican administration in a state that has a tradition of very low funding for mental health services compared with other states? What I learned about then-Governor James Gilmore was that he had personally been to most of the facilities operated by DMH-MRSAS during his term as attorney general. He was very disappointed and maybe even ashamed at the conditions and environment provided to this vulnerable group of citizens of the Commonwealth. He was committed to improving these facilities and I would have the opportunity to contribute to his commitment. Through this position, I learned a great deal about the significance of a governor's support in the state government process.

My service officially began with a press conference. "This is a family-friendly administration, bring your children," the governor's staff advised me. I had already decided my daughter, 18-month-old Margaret, should stay at home; behavior at that age is unpredictable. But how many 9-year-old boys have the opportunity to attend a press conference about their mother that is to be held within the governor's inner office? This was the same governor's office that was designed and used by Thomas Jefferson. There was very little advance notice. I hoped I was on the good side of the karmic debt calculator when I stopped by the Belk department store at 8:30 P.M. on the way home from the hospital, in hopes of finding my son Sam a pair of dress shoes that would fit without the benefit of his trying them on first. I knew he had dress pants that did fit and a jacket we had borrowed from his best friend, Hayes. The press conference was a blur, but the whole event was one of those unforgettable points in time. At the time of the press conference I was 39 years old, had been married to a wonderful man for sixteen years, had two healthy children, a great babysitter, and a golden retriever, and was at the threshold of a new professional adventure. Is this what it felt like if you thought you had it all? This is the point in time that my mother's Betty Friedan generation had hoped would be possible for their daughters. Life looked good, and it was good, but it took tremendous effort to maintain.

The reality behind the vision at that press conference was that our lives took a lot of work and coordination. All working mothers and members of working families know that. Allen and I had always been particularly driven and had a close working relationship based on mutual respect. This has helped us construct the routine parts of our schedule as well as manage and muddle through the typical unexpected things that come up in life as parents, homeowners, and professionals. His career as an academic pediatric subspecialist has been a great complement to the shifting schedules, responsibilities, and demands of my various public service jobs. We work hard and we have had many great and gratifying life experiences with our family and in our professional lives as physicians.

In doing the work to set up the Office of the Inspector General, more than once I had a sense of being called to a mission. I first came to that thought during an interview with a reporter from the *Richmond Times-Dispatch.* The purpose of the interview was to learn how I was going to set up the office, to learn what projects and inspections I was planning to take on, and also to establish rapport with me in case there were anything newsworthy generated from the office in the future. In that interview it came to me that all my past experiences and influences had led to that position. I had a very clear sense that I was in the right place at the right time, poised to set up the office to do the right thing for the thousands of people served by the public mental health system in Virginia. I felt a great relief and I suspect that realization was a way to compartmentalize the ambient stressors associated with the potentially enormous, high-profile task of setting up the office—on a very limited budget, of course, and with the resistance of many who saw no need for the office.

Setting up and running the Office of the Inspector General was an exceptional experience. With lots of luck and guidance, I was able to hire two unusually dedicated staff members and we created a new inspection process. We traveled throughout Virginia day and night to make announced and unannounced inspections of state-operated facilities. Together we completed over eighty inspections in a four-year period and made hundreds of recommendations, each of which we followed through with detailed correction plans and follow-up inspections. Intense effort went into setting up the process and maintaining that pace. We created a credible office that had a significant positive impact on the lives of individuals receiving services in public facilities and services in Virginia. We were purpose driven by the opportunity to do good for persons with mental disabilities. At this level in state government, there are very few physicians to serve as mentors or guides. I am grateful for the friendship of Dr. Harold Carmel, who provided invaluable assistance as an interpreter in the ways of public mental health at the state government level. Many other physicians, staff members, and administrators were exceptionally helpful and patient as we set up our process. A particular source of inspiration for me came from interacting with PAIR, the organization of parents of the resident patients in Virginia's five large state-operated intermediate care facilities for people with developmental disabilities. These parents were passionate in their dedication to their adult children and their concern about the services that were provided for them in these institutions.

The most recent ten years of my professional life have been truly remarkable. When the Office of Inspector General term ended, I joined the federal government as senior medical advisor to the U.S. Department of Health and Human Services' Substance Abuse and Mental Health Services Administration (SAMHSA). This was an adventure from the beginning. This position necessitated our first geographic move in eighteen years. Although my husband describes himself as a trailing spouse, we moved to Maryland as opposed to northern Virginia so that he could continue his research career at Johns Hopkins Children's Center, in the Department of Pediatric Cardiology.

The federal environment in many ways is much more abstract, more thorough, and operates at a slower pace than the state government that I had become familiar with. Although it is also true that there are too few physicians involved at high levels in policy making within the federal government, there are certainly more than in most state governments. During my time at SAMHSA, several of these veterans of federal service reached out to help. I am grateful for the time and sharing of experience I was able to have with Drs. Steven Sharfstein, Mel Haas, Harold Pincus, Darrell Regier, Carol Alter, and many others. At SAMHSA I became involved in many projects including the introduction of the Medicare prescription drug benefit. Although this involved a complex benefit design, I was able to help promote a policy that included mandatory access to all medications for all Medicare beneficiaries in the categories that are often used by psychiatry: antipsychotics, anticonvulsants, and antidepressants.

Through this position, I was able to participate in a series of consultation projects from the U.S. government to the Ministry of Health in Iraq and the Ministry of Public Health in Afghanistan. This consultation involved some invaluable trips to meetings with psychiatrists that were held in Jordan, Egypt, Iraq, and eventually to Afghanistan. What amazing experiences these were! Although by now in the United States it is not unusual for physicians to be women, in Iraq and Afghanistan I felt a renewed sense of duty to be a role model for women and women physicians. In these settings, I have been very aware of being observed in terms of the way I provide lectures, the way I dress, and how I interact with peer professionals, both men and women.

The international exposure in the Middle East and also the experiences I have had in several other, English-speaking countries, helped to shape my ideas regarding the role of psychiatrists in the United States. It has almost become unusual to have a psychiatrist involved in a leadership role in U.S. mental health care systems. The awareness of limited physician participation in leadership in public mental health care processes came to me as I participated in the AACP Listserv while I worked at VCSB as a community psychiatrist. Where were the psychiatrists who advocate for better funding for severely mentally ill individuals? This was further reinforced in a memorable conversation I had with Dr. Jeffrey Geller in Virginia as I was first setting up the Office of the Inspector General. "Where are the psychiatrists?" he asked as we looked around the room of mental health study commission members. There were no psychiatrists appointed to a blue ribbon commission the governor had created to study the current mental health system. The psychiatrists weren't there; they were out practicing in a grossly underfunded fee-for-services setting that did not allow for time to become involved with administration and advocacy.

I am so fortunate to be where I am now, directing a really great community mental health center, the Johns Hopkins Bayview Medical Center. I love my work. It is a mixture of clinical care, administration, teaching, and research. Although I have experienced many events that pull me into awareness of the present and past, I am generally living in the future and thinking forward about the next project. In my current job, I have many opportunities to work on and lead projects that are very stimulating. In the words of my husband, I am a lucky bug.

Summary

In presenting these facets of my professional life, I hope I have provided sufficient background regarding the values, the social mores, and the opportunities that have heavily influenced my professional development as well as the various decisions I have made along the way that have shaped my career. My professional life has been very rich and is very gratifying. It has come at some price, with my children having not had a stay-at-home "helicopter mom" to circle above them. We are a working family and this has had its positives and negatives for all of us. I had long anticipated my fiftieth birthday, in part because my mother was in a particularly challenging time in her life. For me at age fifty, I had been married twenty-five years, had two thriving, flourishing children, and a very rewarding career. I can look back at every decision point and feel right about the choices I made based on what was occurring at the time. I am glad to be a psychiatrist in the twenty-first century.

Practical Tips for Women in Psychiatry

Many of us too often try to make everything all right for our patients, our coworkers, the medical students, the housestaff, our family, and the world. I always post a small copy of the serenity prayer in my office so that I can see it from where I work:

> God grant me the serenity to accept the things I cannot change; courage to change the things I can; and wisdom to know the difference.

In advocacy, in policy, in administration, and with clinical care, I have found this sentiment to be extremely helpful.

References

American Psychiatric Association: Diagnostic and Statistical Manual of Mental Disorders, 2nd Edition. Washington, DC, American Psychiatric Association, 1968

Doherty T: Assassination and Funeral of President John F. Kennedy. Web site of The Museum of Broadcast Communications. Available at: http://www .museum.tv/eotvsection.php?entrycode=kennedyjf. Accessed September 6, 2011.

Friedan B. The Feminine Mystique. New York, WW Norton, 1963

Gianoulis T: Yuppies, in St James Encyclopedia of Pop Culture. Gale Group. January 29, 2002. Available at: http://findarticles.com/p/articles/mi_g1epc/ is_tov/ai_2419101361/. Accessed July 10, 2010.

Kouzes JM, Posner BZ: The Leadership Challenge, 3rd Edition. San Francisco, CA, Jossey-Bass, 2002

Marsh C: The Last Days: A Son's Story of Sin and Segregation at the Dawn of a New South. New York, Basic Books, 2001

Chapter 10

A Community Psychiatrist Straddling Worlds and Bridging Chasms

Annelle B. Primm, M.D., M.P.H.

COMING INTO THE WORLD as a black girl in Switzerland in the mid-twentieth century set the stage for a series of paradoxes revolving around race and gender that would continue throughout my life. One might be curious to know why I, an African American, was born in Switzerland. Because of the limited number of spaces available at that time for African American students, my father, a veteran army officer, was in medical school there. He often tells me that my birth created a spectacle for the hospital staff. They had only witnessed one other black birth at that hospital. Indeed, we were among very few black people who lived in Switzerland in the 1950s.

With French as my first language, I attended a nursery school where I was the only black child. One of my earliest recollections is winning a nationally televised hula hoop contest at three years old, beating my Swiss counterparts, many of them older than I was. Winning this competition made me the center of attention as I had been at the hospital. This would be the case throughout my life.

After my father completed his medical degree, we moved to Long Island, New York, where he practiced general medicine and later anesthesiology. As a youngster, accompanying him regularly on house calls acquainted me with medicine at close hand. Having had this exposure at the impressionable age of seven or eight to my father helping families in crisis instilled in me a desire to be a physician. His subsequent work and leadership in the fields of substance use disorder treatment and HIV infection also had a significant impact on me.

Maternal influences would make a major impression as well. My mother, my maternal aunt, and both of my grandmothers were community leaders and educators. Their academic and social expectations shaped my scholarly and professional choices. Their world, a creation of segregation and the legacy of slavery, gave rise to a cohesive, self-sustaining, and nurturing environment for African Americans. This, of course, for them included all black primary and secondary schools and historically black colleges. Moreover, I remember how my maternal grandmother "took in" and mentored women students at Fayetteville State Teachers College (now Fayetteville State University) in North Carolina.

Once again, I was the only black girl in my primary school on Long Island, and defying the expectations of white teachers, counselors, and parents, I achieved the highest grades. I was studious, athletic, and averse to attention throughout middle and high school in New Rochelle, New York. Nevertheless, I was recognized with an award for leadership in race relations named for slain civil rights worker Michael Schwerner, whose mother taught at my alma mater, New Rochelle High School.

Attending all-female Radcliffe College at age sixteen in the early 1970s instilled in me a sense of responsibility to be a woman leader. There is a long history at Radcliffe of a culture that nurtures excellence in scholarship, social contribution, and leadership among women. The preponderance of female administrators, professors, counselors, and students created an environment that was supportive of women's growth and development and provided a foundation for intellectual, scholarly, and professional achievement. For example, a group of black women undergraduates formed the Association of Black Radcliffe Women, which has grown into a successful organization (renamed the Association of Black Harvard Women when Radcliffe College merged with Harvard University). Many of the women who were part of this group have gone on to professional prominence.

Contemporaneously, African American politicians were achieving local and regional political power. This, along with the civil rights movement, played a significant role in shaping my political consciousness. As a transitional point in history, the totality of events during this period provided me with a larger sense of the need for justice for black people and other disadvantaged groups.

My trajectory toward medicine was surprisingly interrupted during my junior year by the allure of the storm and stress of the business world, especially advertising. On reflection, I recognize that my brief flirtation with business emerged during a time when my mother was very ill with breast cancer. I had taken off the second semester of my junior year at college to help care for her as she received postsurgical radiation and chemotherapy. At that moment, embarking on a career in business had greater appeal than a career in medicine. Not surprisingly, given my experience with my mother, the idea of regularly facing physical suffering and the eventuality of the death of a patient on my watch was undesirable.

My gravitation toward business disturbed my father, who recognized more than I did, at the time, that this decision was more a reaction to my mother's medical crisis than my long-term professional sentiments. For her part, my mother read my response to this crisis as genuine ambivalence rather than a decision made in the immediacy of a critical moment. She encouraged me to pursue whatever profession appealed to me and not feel obligated to continue on the path of a career in medicine.

After my mother's death, maternal responsibility for my two younger sisters, then sixteen and twelve, was a pivotal factor in my life. This commitment made me feel as though I were a parent starting at age nineteen even though I would not give birth until twenty-two years later. Ultimately, my mother's illness and death reawakened my interest in medicine and its psychological aspects. I was accepted to medical school the year after her death but would not embrace psychiatry wholeheartedly until my later years in medical school.

Attending medical school at Howard University in Washington, D.C., a historically black medical school, was an unlikely choice for me as a graduate of an Ivy League college. However, I made this choice, as opposed to attending a majority white institution, in order to receive professional education and training in an institutional environment that I deemed to be more nurturing. I also welcomed the opportunity to go to Howard because both of my parents were graduates of historically black colleges. I came to discover that the experience was particularly validating for me as a black woman who had been educated in majority white schools for most of my life.

The course toward psychiatry was not linear. A long-standing interest in women's health led me to consider obstetrics and gynecology, but the high frequency of cesarean deliveries in medical school quickly turned me away from pursuing that as a specialty. I had been interested in psychiatry since my course in medical school on the subject. It was appealing to me because of the balance of biological and social sciences, appreciation of the life circumstances of the individual, and the complicated relationship between the body and mind. The focus in psychiatry on the social and environmental influences on individuals also resonated with me, given my socially conscious upbringing and membership in an age cohort where societal concerns and activism were common.

My choice to pursue community psychiatry, also known as public psychiatry, is yet another reflection of my commitment to work with underserved and disadvantaged populations. Typically, high proportions of the people served in the public psychiatry realm are low-income and/or from diverse racial and ethnic backgrounds. Historically, psychiatrists have eschewed such demographics, choosing alternatively to situate their practices in areas where they could engage more stable populations that in turn promise higher financial benefits and status. Yet for me, while not offering the same stability and financial gain, public psychiatry provided a different kind of reward in the form of challenging work and the satisfaction of partnering with individuals, families, and communities to improve quality of life. Moreover, this approach is an acknowledgement that the health of the larger society is interrelated with the health of populations living in distressed communities.

Having gone to Howard has turned out to be an important credential in my career. It has become a passport providing entrée into the inner sanctum of black community groups and easy receptivity in engaging diverse communities. Equally important has been my educational experience at Harvard-Radcliffe and The Johns Hopkins University (for my psychiatry residency, fellowship in social and community psychiatry, and master of public health degree), where I became fluent in the customs of that milieu. Possessing multicultural capital positioned me to be a societal broker across different communities. The cultural currency that I earned at Harvard-Radcliffe, Howard, and Johns Hopkins (located in the heart of black Baltimore) situated me uniquely to navigate the jagged cultural terrain of these disparate worlds.

With this transcultural fluency, Baltimore proved to be an ideal working environment for community psychiatry, with its multiethnic population, entrenched ethnic neighborhoods, dense urban poverty, urban redevelopment projects, intense gentrification and its disruption of longstanding social relations, complex urban politics, a large homeless population, and significant problems with drugs and crime. Within this variegated milieu, my experiences as a full-time faculty member in the Department of Psychiatry and Behavioral Sciences at Johns Hopkins include a wide range of roles: clinician; medical educator; researcher in an academic medical center; medical director of a brief-hospitalization unit at a black hospital, a community psychiatry program, an urban-based assertive community treatment program called COSTAR (Community Support Treatment and Rehabilitation), and a service for people with co-occurring substance use disorders and mental illness; and consultant psychiatrist in a primary care clinic, a mobile crisis unit, a peer-run counseling program, and a counseling center at a historically black institution, Morgan State University. I also had opportunities to use my interest in culture to develop educational DVDs about depression in African Americans and older adults of diverse cultural groups (Primm et al. 2002).

Growth and Balance

While this rich context provided me with many opportunities, it also presented myriad tensions, conflicts, and contradictions that had to be negotiated. Without prioritization, discipline, and informed decision making, these opportunities, in the end, could have overwhelmed and subverted the achievement of my initial academic and social goals. As an African American woman community psychiatrist I was straddling multiple worlds. It was a challenge to cope with juggling many institutional roles, expectations of scholarly productivity, and meaningful responses to the needs of community stakeholders. I felt a keen sense of responsibility to give back and be responsive to community needs. This required me to serve as an ambassador and translator between the institution and the community, a role that was over and above the responsibilities of a faculty member. This was a challenge to accomplish while having multiple administrative, teaching, and clinical responsibilities, and community commitments. As a full-time faculty member, the department expected me to not only compete for grants, preferably federally funded grants, but also to be productive as a scholar.

The conventional measurement of academic scholarship is original research and the accumulation of publications in the peer-reviewed literature. Given the multiple demands of my commitment to public psychiatry, I struggled to do research and write papers, as well as to find additional expressions of my scholarly integrity. This expression would hinge on the notion that there are other types of scholarship and different kinds of knowledge and ways of conveying that knowledge. The concept of community-engaged scholarship pertains to the investment of academics, including psychiatrists, in finding ways to tackle real-life problems, through research or the discovery of new information or novel ways to motivate change toward community well-being, in collaboration with community partners (Calleson et al. 2005). For this model, the knowledge should be communicated not only to a professional audience, but also to lay audiences which, in turn, participate in the production and dissemination of knowledge. Scholarly productivity can thus be measured not solely by a publication count, but also by other contributions including audiovisual and interactive programs that have accessibility and utility at the community level. Academic medical institutions have begun to understand the currency and value of a new model of community-related endeavors of faculty members and the responsibilities that those institutions should have in working collaboratively with the distressed communities in their environs.

The question, then, is how did I achieve meaningful balance amid all of these competing expectations and responsibilities? First of all, I recognized that I could not do everything. On the community front, I selectively identified local community leaders, organizations, and projects that were most successful in mental health endeavors and that did not compromise my academic and professional schedule. For example, I collaborated with the congregation of a local church in completing a depression education film project. In the academic realm, I identified professors whose interests were consonant with mine who were able to encourage me and rigorously monitor my progress toward professional goals.

The numerous and complicated demands of academia were deepened by marriage, childbirth, and responsibilities to family. When I first became a mother during my early forties, I worked even harder as a faculty member than I had before my pregnancy. I developed new programs, participated in a fellowship, wrote grants and manuscripts, and wrote and produced two educational videotapes on depression. The only way I was able to do this was to partner with other women faculty and a very bright medical student. We collaborated and shared our expertise and were very productive. But I had motherly duties to attend to as well. Because I was committed to providing my daughter with breast milk, I had to find a space at the hospital where I could privately use a breast pump. I am sure people walking by my office door would hear the whir of the pump and wonder what was going on in there. On occasion, I even had to breast-feed my infant daughter at work. The overriding health benefits outweighed the potential inappropriateness of doing this in the workplace.

I have faced many challenges in striving for balance in my personal and family life and as a psychiatrist. Working in environments where there are a number of problems and a great deal of need, I am compelled to collaborate with psychiatrists and colleagues from other disciplines to solve vexing problems and develop ways to meet unmet needs. The key is not to let this compulsion create undue stress and fatigue. My goal is to have what

I call tempered passion. It is crucial to my well-being to find a middle ground of involvement so as not to overwhelm myself with pressures and frustrations that would compromise the integrity of my familial relationships.

Well-exercised maternal juggling skills were especially necessary when I left the academy to join the executive staff of the American Psychiatric Association (APA) as director of the Office of Minority and National Affairs (OMNA) in the Washington, D.C., area. During this time, I divorced, became a single parent, and commuted from Baltimore as well as traveling extensively on APA business. Necessarily, I had to coordinate child care to fit my schedule and travel itinerary. Nevertheless, feelings of guilt plagued me at times when I had to travel. Now that my daughter is older, our separations are not as painful; however, our time together is still extremely important for purposes of guidance. I look for ways to save time by doing safely more than one thing at a time or batching errands in certain parts of the city. While this is economical from a time perspective, it, too, can contribute to stress. I have had to make a special effort to think through a road map carefully to accomplish a variety of tasks in the shortest and most sensible way possible. This has become an art, a way of life. Fortunately, I was given the flexibility and time that allowed me to reconcile child care and work-related responsibilities.

Having established a functional rhythm, I settled into a manageable and productive work routine. The position gave me an opportunity to carry out on a national level some of the work begun in public psychiatry in Baltimore. With the help of a dedicated and energetic staff and the commitment of APA members, OMNA developed numerous programs and projects geared toward increasing diversity of the psychiatric workforce, exposing and preventing mental health disparities, and facilitating the delivery of quality mental health care for all Americans. Among the many initiatives was a recruitment documentary called *Real Psychiatry: Doctors in Action* (American Psychiatric Association 2004).The film presented psychiatrists of diverse racial and cultural backgrounds and was designed to increase interest in psychiatry. Another film project, titled *Mental Health: A Guide for Latinos and their Families* was culturally tailored for the Hispanic community (American Psychiatric Association, n.d.). Partnering with the American Psychiatric Foundation, we organized a leadership roundtable on women's mental health and produced a monograph, *Women and Mental Health* (American Psychiatric Association 2009). OMNA on Tour, a traveling conference on mental health care disparities, is an educational program customized to the demographics of various cities and regions. These conferences convene community stakeholders to share knowledge and foster collaboration to address issues of racial and ethnic disparities in mental health care. Through another collaborative effort, this one with the National Alliance on Mental Illness (n.d.), OMNA developed a continuing medical education curriculum for primary care practitioners called *In Living Color: Depression Treatment in Primary Care,* to improve the recognition and treatment of depression in racially and culturally diverse populations. These programs and projects have raised the profile of the APA in an unprecedented manner.

With these initiatives and programs we have, in no small part, reshaped the identity of the APA to recognize and address, more forcefully, the sociopsychological needs of an increasingly diverse human landscape. This new maneuverability was nowhere more evident than in our mobilization following the devastating hurricane along the Mississippi and Louisiana coastline in 2005. It was apparent that the immediate trauma of Katrina, the consequence of injury, displacement, and death, would be resolved by the multitude of extragovernmental aid organizations in the weeks and months that followed. But the lasting psychological damage was more attributable to the racism inherent in historical conceptualizations of African Americans. The storm, together with the catastrophic failure of the levee system and the hideous irresponsibility of local, state, and national rescue efforts, revealed the way much of the country views people of African descent.

Hurricane Katrina was the catalyst for one of the more dynamic national projects that I initiated. A group of psychiatrists, allied health professionals, and advocates formed an organization in September 2005, called the All Healers Mental Health Alliance (AHMHA; 2011). AHMHA was created to facilitate culturally appropriate responses to the mental health needs of people of underserved communities affected by disaster. Born out of crisis, this national network has sustained itself through technological innovations to minimize travel and connect members of the group across space. We function essentially as a think tank and a consultation network. In our capacity as a think tank, we explore the discourses of race and tragedy, which in turn inform our policy recommendations and advocacy. As a consultative network, AHMHA provides training, consultation, and emotional support to first responders, a variety of health professionals, faith community leaders, educators, and community health workers on the front lines of disasters. Using state-of-the-art technologies, AHMHA also serves as a clearinghouse for information and provides fact verification, resources, and referral.

An unintended consequence of AHMHA is that it has proved to be nurturing of its participants, providing group mentoring and mutual support, which in turn facilitate individuals' intellectual maturity, reinforce their confidence, and advance leadership opportunities. Through AHMHA,

APA has given me the latitude to do disaster-related work with the program as well as the liberty to explore alternative models. Whereas an office like OMNA would create DVDs, traditional programs, and so forth, AHMHA is different because it marshals the experience of people in various mental health–related occupations to deal with disasters. The leaders of AHMHA, who are primarily black women, have come to the realization that our role is to witness, listen, and facilitate resilience, not only to counter the effects of a given disaster but to thwart the impact of ingrained racism.

Facing Challenges: Lessons Learned

Race, with its overall effect on power relationships, has a far-reaching connection to class and gender. The correlations between race and poverty were revealed to a large extent in the aftermath of Hurricane Katrina. However, the interplay between racism and sexism is particularly vexing given their potency as unchangeable human characteristics (hooks 1981).

Looking back on many of my life experiences, there is a pattern of me in the role of black female, being in a position of "the other" as viewed by those in power. From my birth through early childhood in Europe, I was an exotic spectacle. In grade school, I attended an integrated public elementary school and was an academic standout among white classmates. In academia, I was an ambassador between an ivory tower and an ebony community. Throughout all of these experiences, being and feeling conspicuous as a black female in contrast to those with the most societal power, white males, I felt as if I were under the microscope and subject to the gaze of others unlike me in race and gender.

From my personal perspective as a black woman, gender and race are concomitant identities, inseparable from each other with combined valences of secondary status. The positioning of black women in a negative light was exemplified in a media scandal that led to the firing of Don Imus, a popular talk radio show host, who, while on the air, characterized members of the Rutgers University women's basketball team, dominated by African American women, as "nappy-headed hos." This incident is an example of sexist and racist conceptualizations of black women and how they are viewed by some segments of society regardless of their success.

The way in which black women are viewed contributes to a sense of "double consciousness" which W.E.B. DuBois (1903) wrote about in his book *The Souls of Black Folk.* In interpersonal interactions, my skin color precedes me and has the potential to trigger prejudiced views in people who hold a negative regard for black people.

Several examples from my experience illustrate the commonality of the biased lens through which black women are viewed and at times rendered invisible as unique, legitimate individuals. It was painful for me to be overlooked by a supervisor who sought to give academic advantage over me to a male psychiatrist from Europe while encouraging me to assist him in his research endeavors. My approach to coping with this uncomfortable situation was to contribute to his manuscript and request to be listed as a coauthor on the eventual publication that arose from this work. In several instances, psychiatrist colleagues mistook me for another black woman who was also in a leadership position but who was not a psychiatrist. She had very different facial features and body type and shared only my skin color. The chosen approach to these microaggressions was for me to inform the individuals politely regarding this occurrence of mistaken identity (Pierce 1970). Even with a gentle response, the perpetrators were visibly embarrassed. Another psychiatrist has criticized me for being dressed up all the time. Clearly, he was not conscious of my concern that presenting myself in any other way than professional and well dressed makes me vulnerable to being mistaken for a person of a lower position, which is often the assumption about women of African descent. Two additional examples of how others have viewed me as a black woman in a leadership role were particularly destructive and painful. In both instances, male psychiatrist supervisors proposed that my leadership role be shared with or transferred to nonphysician mental health professionals. These suggestions were insulting and, from my perspective, prompted by a degrading albeit unconscious bias against me as a black woman. Fortunately, my consultation with mentors yielded strategies for counterproposals that allowed me to either maintain my leadership position or make a transition with my status and integrity intact.

My first foray into speaking out in the face of injustice and challenging authority was centered on disparities in the quality of care and staffing for people of color receiving mental health services in an inpatient treatment setting. My questioning of institutional leaders about unjust practices was met with consternation and criticism by my supervisors. Although it was anxiety-provoking to think of losing my job, surviving this conflict gave way to my maintaining good relationships with the individuals in leadership positions, who eventually made changes to rectify the disparities.

In another situation, my questioning of institutional leaders about disparate practices affecting people of color and those living in poverty resulted in my work being scrutinized and my performance questioned by a group of people. This was particularly hurtful because of my lifelong pattern of mediating conflict and maintaining a reputation of competence and excellence. It required me to step outside my comfort zone, of being low-key and avoiding confrontation, to fight back. This was a stressful time, but fortunately through the invaluable support of family and friends I transcended this trauma and returned to equilibrium. In retrospect, this travail was liberating, rendering me more confident and even better positioned to handle other confrontations in the future. Finally, it became clear that it was possible to be a vocal and strong black woman and prevail in the face of institutional power.

Among my lessons learned is that the task for black women in professional and corporate settings where we stand out as anomalies and are the subject of curious gazes is to not become preoccupied with the views of others. We must not let "double consciousness" (DuBois 1903) cloud our judgment and lead us to become paranoid or paralyzed. Instead, we must find ways to cope by engaging in principled action and to recognize that our presence at the table in the rooms of power has value to the people within that organization. Further, if we are leaders, our participation in decision making and advocacy has the potential to affect marginalized populations including our own.

It has been rewarding to mentor women, particularly African American women, early-career academic psychiatrists about how to engage their communities meaningfully and productively and find ways to do research and scholarly writing, as well as make their work and time in the community setting count toward their faculty advancement. This is very important because their presence as women and persons of color in the academic setting not only drives the institution's connection with the community, it also serves as a magnet for women and racially and ethnically diverse medical students, residents, and fellows to come to that institution and pursue careers in the academic realm. The presence of women and members of underrepresented and underserved racial groups in academic institutional environments sends a strong signal that others of the same gender and/or similar background are welcome and that they will be supported so that they can grow and flourish professionally.

I hope that this account of my life experiences from birth to the present has provided an explanation of how the three "yarns" of race, gender, and profession are woven together. To borrow from the poem *Mother to Son* by Langston Hughes (1922/1994), it is true that life for black women psychiatrist leaders is no crystal stair—but we're still climbing, reaching landings, and turning corners. Driven by a social consciousness forged in early childhood and nurtured by my family and many rich experiences, my dream is to continue into my later years finding ways to work collaboratively with like-minded psychiatrists and other mental health professionals and health advocates across cultures to promote mental health and rid the nation and the world of unnecessary suffering and avoidable misery. We must set these goals and invest in sound, relevant programs, services, and preventive measures and formulate appropriate policies that take into account the social determinants of health. Psychiatrists from both genders and all backgrounds can build bridges across the boundaries of difference to provide high-quality, culturally appropriate care to all Americans. Investing in the leadership of more people of color, more women, and black women in particular, will contribute to these goals, all of which are in the nation's compelling interest.

Practical Tips for Women in Psychiatry

My experience suggests several tips for success that will be helpful for women, and in particular women of color, who seek to become psychiatrist leaders.

Having uncompromising *mentors* is invaluable. My mentors have served as cheerleaders who made sure that I did certain things, like getting manuscripts written, submitted, and published in peer-reviewed journals, that would be essential for faculty advancement and positioning for competitive opportunities. I have also been fortunate to have mentors who understood the impact of racism and sexism to help manage conflict and provide decision support at critical stages of my career. Mentors also open doors to strategic experiences and introductions, and provide guidance about when to say *no* and when to stop.

Support for growth is not limited to senior mentors. Connection with *peers* who provide camaraderie and opportunities for collaboration can be helpful in the professional development process. To this end, involvement with like-minded peers in the APA and other organizations has been valuable for me. Seeking membership in organizations that are consonant with one's multiple identities—for me, the Black Psychiatrists of America, the National Medical Association, the Association of Women Psychiatrists, and the American Association of Community Psychiatrists—is a good way to ensure ongoing growth and mutual support. Memberships in and affiliations with these organizations have helped me cope with the periodic frustration that can arise when racism and sexism rear their ugly heads singly or simultaneously. These groups also provide forums for mentoring younger colleagues and those in training, and for celebrating multiple identities.

Another tip for success is to keep in mind that *family* comes first: no matter how important or demanding your job is, your family ties must retain priority. It is also essential to find *balance*—that is, to find ways to do a good job without overdoing and increasing the risk for becoming ill and exhausted. Given the pressures of racism and sexism, one must resist the temptation to go overboard to increase one's certainty of achieving excellence and being well regarded by peers and supervisors. One can achieve balance by building in time for rest, relaxation, and recreation on a regular basis and setting up one's life to ensure that this occurs.

References

All Healers Mental Health Alliance (Web site). 2011. Available at: http://login .npwebsiteservices.com/All_Healers_Mental_Health_ZXRCXS/WhoWeAre .asp. Accessed January 13, 2012.

American Psychiatric Association: Real Psychiatry: Doctors in Action (video). 2004. Available at: http://www.psych.org/share/OMNA/psychiatryvideo .aspx. Accessed January 13, 2012.

American Psychiatric Association: Mental Health: A Guide for Latinos and Their Families (video). n.d. Available at: http://www.psych.org/Share/OMNA/ Latino-Mental-Health-DVD-English.aspx. Accessed January 13, 2012.

American Psychiatric Association: Women's Mental Health (issue paper). 2009. Available at: http://www.psych.org/share/OMNA/Womens-Mental-Health-Issue-Paper.aspx. Accessed January 13, 2012.

Calleson DC, Jordan C, Seifer SD: Community-engaged scholarship: is faculty work in communities a true academic enterprise? Acad Med 80:317–321, 2005

DuBois WEB: The Souls of Black Folk: Essays and Sketches. Chicago, IL, AC Mc-Clurg, 1903

hooks b: Ain't I a Woman: Black Women and Feminism. Boston, MA, South End Press, 1981

Hughes L: Mother to son (1922), in Collected Poems of Langston Hughes. Edited by Rampersad A. New York, Knopf, 1994, p 30

NAMI: In Living Color: Depression Treatment in Primary Care (curriculum). n.d. Available at: http://www.nami.org/Template.cfm?Template=/Content-Management/HTMLDisplay.cfm&ContentID=79294. Accessed January 13, 2012.

Pierce CM: Offensive mechanisms: the vehicle for microaggression, in The Black Seventies. Edited by Barbour FB. Boston, MA, Porter Sargent, 1970, pp 265–282

Primm AB, Cabot D, Pettis J, et al: The acceptability of a culturally-tailored depression education videotape to African Americans. J Natl Med Assoc 94:1007–1016, 2002

Chapter 11

Administration, Advocacy, and Academics

One Woman's Experience

Patricia R. Recupero, J.D., M.D.

I CURRENTLY SERVE AS president and chief executive officer (CEO) of Butler Hospital, a private, nonprofit, academic psychiatric hospital on the east side of Providence, Rhode Island. Since 1847 when it first opened its doors, Butler Hospital has been a facility dedicated to compassion and advocacy for individuals suffering from mental illness. As Butler's first woman president, I feel privileged to be able to follow in the footsteps of Isaac Ray, M.D., Butler's first superintendent and one of the leading founders of modern psychiatry. Dr. Ray felt strongly that hospital administrators should strive to treat fellow physicians as well as psychiatric patients with respect and support (e.g., Ray 1873). Much has changed since the days of Dr. Ray's leadership, but the goal of serving humanity through the provision of humane, compassionate care remains foremost in my mind as psychiatry enters a new era of challenges and opportunity.

In the latter twentieth century, the provision of behavioral health care shifted away from custodial, long-term care to acute care and stabilization.

The understanding and treatment of mental illness has improved dramatically, and demand for psychiatric services has increased. In the twenty-first century, developments in technology and scientific research are rapidly advancing our understanding of the etiology of psychopathology. Quality improvement and evidence-based medicine have become increasingly vital forces in the shaping of psychiatric practice (Morrissey and Goldman 1986; Recupero 2006). At Butler, many of these changes are apparent in the growth of our clinical, translational, and basic science research activities.

Besides serving as a hospital administrator, I have held a number of additional leadership roles within the field of psychiatry. I currently teach as a clinical professor of psychiatry at the Warren Alpert Medical School of Brown University; Butler Hospital is the major affiliated teaching hospital for psychiatry. As an academic psychiatrist, I conduct ongoing research at the juncture of law and mental health, and I maintain an active consulting practice in forensic psychiatry. I am a practicing clinician as well, seeing outpatients. Although wearing so many hats has its challenges, the rewards have been tremendous.

College and Law School

I began my college studies in the mid-1960s with the expectation of pursuing a career in education because it afforded an opportunity to help others in an intellectually stimulating role. Teaching was a vocation that was consistent with the prevailing gender norms and expectations for professionally inclined women at the time. Women were only beginning to enter traditionally male professions in larger numbers, but following gender-conforming roles was still the norm and the expectation. However, I questioned expectations of rigid, stereotyped gender roles and the limitations these assumptions placed on women and society as a whole.

During my college years, I was inspired by the civil rights movement and the dramatic social and political changes taking place at the time. As an undergraduate, I pursued a degree in mathematics, not a traditional field of study for women. Like many others, outside the classroom I felt drawn by the call to rectify discrimination and to fight against injustice. Increasingly I came to view the law as an instrument of social change. In 1964, Congress passed the Civil Rights Act (P.L. 88-352), legislation that represented a sea change in the push for equal rights and justice. As I graduated from college, the legislative changes taking place inspired me to enroll in Boston College Law School. I was optimistic that a career in the legal field would provide an opportunity to effect meaningful change in human rights and civil rights.

During my first year of law school, one of my professors was a young woman whose experience of gender discrimination was telling for the times. Just a few years earlier, prospective employers on Wall Street had told her that they did not hire women, even as secretaries, because the field was so exclusively male. Although the ratio of women entering the legal profession was beginning to increase by the time I entered law school, progress was slow, and female role models were few. The first female Supreme Court justice, Sandra Day O'Connor, was not appointed until 1981. Richard Nixon's explanation for why he did not appoint a woman to the Supreme Court was: "I don't think a woman should be in any government job whatsoever…mainly because they are erratic. And emotional" (quoted in Eagly and Carli 2007, p. 64). I was one of the first women on the national moot court team at my law school, and I worked as an articles editor for the first woman editor-in-chief of the law review. Shortly after my graduation from law school, I began teaching law students, which rekindled my long-standing interest in teaching and education.

Working as an Attorney

I met my husband in law school, and following our graduation we moved to Rhode Island (where he had grown up), and I worked for several years as a litigator, arguing civil and criminal cases. I was admitted to the Massachusetts Bar, was one of the first fifty women admitted to the Bar in Rhode Island, and, in 1975, was admitted to the Federal Bar for the districts of Rhode Island and Massachusetts. As a litigator, I also appeared before the first woman judge in Rhode Island and often took the elevator with the first woman admitted to the Rhode Island Bar. I particularly enjoyed the medical and psychological aspects of some of the cases on which I worked. My first assignment in the Rhode Island Attorney General's office was helping out on an important case in Rhode Island's legal history, *State of Rhode Island v. Johnson* (1979), which led to the adoption of the American Law Institute's test for criminal responsibility, replacing the M'Naghten rule.

From Law to Medicine

Although I found the law intellectually fascinating, the work did not provide me with the opportunities I had sought to be able to effect meaningful social change. I wanted to do more. I began to think about other options to pursue within my community. I had always been fascinated by science and the brain, even from my earliest years as a child. Still driven by intellectual curiosity and a desire to help others, I decided to pursue medicine and enrolled in medical school at Brown University in Providence.

Initially at medical school I was drawn to primary care, but as I learned more about the medical field, I began to realize that psychiatry would present unique opportunities to utilize my legal training in the service of human and civil rights. During the 1960s and 1970s, psychiatry underwent a series of dramatic changes driven, in part, by the civil libertarian reforms that had so intrigued me during my college years. At the time that I chose the specialty of psychiatry, the field was experiencing a shift toward increased emphasis on patient autonomy and dignity and away from the paternalistic model characterized by unchallenged involuntary commitment and long-term custodial care of people with mental illness (Morrissey and Goldman 1986). These trends mirrored my own long-standing interest in working toward equality and human rights.

As a medical student, I was acutely aware of the influence of sexism in the educational system. During my surgery clerkship, female medical students were assigned to the nurses' locker room and given pink scrubs. Male medical students were assigned to the doctors' locker room, given green scrubs, and had access to the phone for dictation of surgical notes. These types of experiences led me to understand that the mentorship of other women in academia and medicine had to be a high priority, and my research work reflects this concern (e.g., Recupero et al. 2004). Unfortunately, discrimination and sexist stereotypes persist in today's world, and gender will remain a significant concern for female psychiatrists in the years to come.

Having worked as an attorney prior to entering medical school, and entering medical school as an older student, I was armed with experience that was very helpful to me throughout my training and subsequent career as a physician. Because of my success as a litigator and the confidence I gained in defending different viewpoints in the courtroom, I had the courage to speak up in class when the professor told a sexist joke. I had already begun to develop leadership skills in college, having served as president of the Student Government Association, and I was able to apply these skills to my role within the Medical Student Senate. Additionally, as an older medical student, I had already achieved some security in my identity as a professional woman, and I knew that my professional identity was not defined exclusively by what happened in my classes. My experience had given me the security and assertiveness to advocate effectively for myself, my colleagues, and, later, my patients.

Mentoring and Leadership in Academic Psychiatry

I graduated from medical school in 1985 and enthusiastically began my residency in psychiatry. My training director, Ronald Wintrob, M.D., has served as a wonderful mentor to me for many years. Following the completion of my residency, and with the support of Dr. Wintrob, I was appointed to the position of associate training director for Brown University's psychiatry residency program, based at Butler Hospital. Looking back on it now, this time was a critical juncture for me, and I am grateful that Dr. Wintrob had faith in my leadership abilities and had taken an interest in my career. Serving as the associate training director allowed me to take on an important leadership role that was still consistent with the traditional gender norms for women and fit well with my long-standing interest in education and teaching. The role felt comfortable in that sense, and I enjoyed being able to help train the next generation of psychiatrists.

Forensic psychiatry was a natural subspecialty for me to pursue, given my background in the law and my interest in civil rights and advocacy. Robert Westlake, M.D., served as another important mentor in my life, helping me to focus my plans on forensic psychiatry and to become involved by submitting a workshop proposal on guardianship to the American Psychiatric Association's annual meeting. Who knew such an opportunity even existed? The American Psychiatric Association and the American Academy of Psychiatry and the Law quickly became important professional "homes" for my interest in research and leadership in forensic psychiatry.

I learned a great deal about management in the health care field from my first mentor in medicine, Wilma Rosen, M.D. Dr. Rosen graduated from medical school in an era in which there were quotas for women and Jewish students. Despite numerous obstacles, she graduated, was elected to the Alpha Omega Alpha honor society, and went on to a successful and rewarding career in psychiatry. To this day, Dr. Rosen continues to be a wonderful mentor and inspiration to me.

Overall, mentorship for women in medicine and the law can be hard to come by. Of particular relevance to my own career path, mentoring has been recognized as a critical factor in psychiatrists' transition from clinical roles to executive leadership (Silver and Marcos 1989). Good mentors can make a tremendously positive impact in a psychiatrist's career development, and I am grateful that I was fortunate enough to have had the support of several wonderful mentors throughout my career. For this reason, serving as a mentor to other early career psychiatrists has been an important priority to me. It has been very rewarding to have been able to enjoy successful work with other women faculty and to work together with them toward academic publications and promotions.

Unconventional approaches to one's career in a particular field, such as selecting a nontraditional field for academic research (in my case, forensic psychiatry as opposed to biological psychiatry), can multiply the difficulties that women ordinarily face in academia. For a career in academic psychiatry, the respect of one's peers and successful publication in peer-reviewed medical journals is typically necessary in order to receive promotions. Although I have achieved a great deal of professional fulfillment today, taking an unconventional approach toward research and publication certainly multiplied the challenges. For example, drafting a model statute is a heavily research-intensive and serious academic pursuit, but most medical journals do not publish this type of work, preferring instead papers written in the traditional scientific method format. Similarly, obtaining grants and funding for a nontraditional research area like forensic psychiatry can be very difficult, which makes the impact of sexism and other hurdles all the more damaging. Although my publications would typically lead to promotion in the academic faculty track, I have had to pursue the clinical faculty track because of the difficulty obtaining grant support for the type of research I pursued.

A desire to rectify the gender inequity in medicine and academia motivated me to serve as the gender equity officer and the sexual harassment officer for Brown University's medical school and has inspired numerous research projects for me. My research on gender has ranged from discrimination and sexual harassment in medical education (e.g., Recupero et al. 2004) to domestic violence (e.g., Heru et al. 2007), and the influence of gender in will contests (research in progress at the time of this writing). Much has changed with respect to these issues in recent years. In the past, domestic violence was treated as a private, personal matter, and police often refused to take women seriously when they called for help or when their safety was at risk. This changed as research revealed the harmful effects that gender subjugation had not only on the women who were the direct victims but also on the family and the community as a whole. The breakdown of gender stereotypes has also revealed that some of the more "benevolent" aspects of these stereotypes are themselves problematic.

When I began my research career, it was widely agreed among feminists in academia that women were almost always the victims in domestic violence and sexual harassment cases and that women in these situations therefore had to be protected from male aggressors. These paternalistic attitudes carried a certain type of sexist beliefs of their own. When my colleagues and I conducted research on the prevalence and nature of domestic violence (now termed *intimate partner violence*) among psychiatric inpatients, we found that much of the violent behavior was bidirectional (Heru et al. 2006). A major consideration as we wrote up the results of our research was the concern that we would run into fierce opposition to this idea from academics who held more traditional feminist beliefs. Clearly, much has changed with respect to gender in academic medicine, and we cannot continue to operate on the basis of sexist assumptions.

Career Development and Advocacy

As well as serving as associate training director for the residency program at Brown, I was invited to serve as Butler Hospital's chief of managed care, organizing the hospital's response to adverse managed care decisions and navigating the appeals process in the early 1990s. My role in this position led to my involvement in a work group to reform managed care in Rhode Island; this marked the beginning of my transition from gender-stereotypical clinical and teaching roles toward a career in management and administration. In support of the work group's efforts, I applied my background in legal research and took on the role of collecting all fifty states' statutes relating to managed care. In the era before easy access to computerized databases and efficient electronic search-and-find tools, this was a daunting task: I spent long hours in the law library and compiled an extensive chart to organize the data.

I am especially proud of my work in drafting one of the most comprehensive utilization review statutes in the nation and working tirelessly to get it passed in Rhode Island. The statute, still in effect as of this writing (Health Care Accessibility and Quality Assurance Act, RI 2010), had what was at the time an innovative structure for external review of denials of care. The statute had several unique features, including strict rules about emergency coverage and requirements for peer-to-peer reviews by specialty (i.e., if a case is in the field of psychiatry, it has to be reviewed by a properly credentialed psychiatrist).

Following my work on the utilization review statute, I joined a team of fellow mental health professionals working together to develop and advocate for a new parity law (Insurance Coverage for Mental Illness and Substance Abuse, R.I. 2010). This statute was designed specifically to address the needs of individuals suffering from mental illness. Since its initial drafting, we have amended and broadened this parity law twice. Getting a parity law passed early in the growing movement toward mental health parity legislation was a very important part of the work that I wanted to pursue and that I found most rewarding. When Congressman Patrick Kennedy took up the parity cause and made it one of his top priorities, we helped him in working toward parity not just in the state of Rhode Island, but throughout the United States.

Looking back on these experiences now, I know that the far-reaching impact of advocacy work has been especially fulfilling for me. As a physician, it is always rewarding to be able to help a patient and to see the patient's symptoms and quality of life improve as a result of your efforts. But advocacy has a much broader and widespread impact! Advocacy provided a way to help large numbers of people and to address major civil rights and human rights issues in general terms rather than focusing merely on one patient at a time. Many physicians do not view themselves as having an advocacy role, but, in fact, doctors can be *very* effective advocates for their patients and for the medical and social needs of society as a whole. In my case, I was fortunate to have been trained initially as an attorney advocate. Combining my experience in law and medicine through advocacy work contributed significantly to my sense of professional fulfillment.

My work in advocacy also served as an introduction to the day-to-day managerial and financial aspects of medicine and showed me more ways in which my background in law and medicine together could be helpful. For a brief period during the mid-1990s, I returned to Boston to work at St. Elizabeth's Medical Center in several administrative roles, and served on several committees. Working in psychiatry in a general hospital system and managing a capitated population were new learning experiences for me. I found that no single aspect of the medical care system can be viewed in isolation. When acting in the capacity of an advocate or leader, one must weigh numerous factors, such as direct cost, human suffering, and system benefits. At St. Elizabeth's, I also served as the director of the Psychiatry Residency Training Program and the vice chair of the Department of Psychiatry. Following my years at St. Elizabeth's, I returned my focus to Rhode Island and began taking on more leadership roles at Butler Hospital and Brown University's medical school.

Around this same time in the 1990s, the American Civil Liberties Union filed suit to challenge questions in the bar admissions process that sought information about applicants' history of mental illness and substance abuse. I was appointed to serve as special master to the Rhode Island Supreme Court, where I was responsible for holding hearings and advising the court with respect to the legality and ethics of the Rhode Island Bar Association's candidate vetting process. I argued in my report that the then-current wording in their questions about mental health and mental health treatments violated the Americans with Disabilities Act. In its finding that the questions were discriminatory and its decision to reform the questions, the court adopted my reasoning (*In re Petition and Questionnaire for Admission to the Rhode Island Bar* RI 1996). Yet again I found great professional satisfaction in combining my legal and medical training in the service of civil rights and equality.

Choosing and Managing a Career as a Physician Executive

Over the years, my career has shifted toward more demanding management and leadership roles in health care. Women executives are still relatively uncommon, and women still must surmount many obstacles in order to achieve meaningful career progress and to gain access to the opportunities that will open doors for them. Typically women have not been afforded venues in which to express leadership characteristics or attributes. As my colleague Alison Heru, M.D., noted (2005, p. 24):

> Traditional gender roles and different socialization patterns are major obstacles for women in attaining leadership positions. Women present themselves more modestly and are less likely to see themselves as qualified for top jobs, even when their credentials are equivalent or superior to [those of] male peers.

Gender stereotypes can pose significant barriers for female academic professionals and psychiatrists. Compared to male psychiatrists, female psychiatrists do not receive the same financial rewards (merit awards, equal pay, etc.) as their male colleagues, and women psychiatrists are not equally represented in academia (Kohen and Arnold 2002). In academia, "women are significantly less likely to be full professors than comparably credentialed men" (Ash et al. 2004, p. 209).

One problem that many women executives have encountered is the prevalent belief that women cannot be effective leaders because the stereotypical "female" social behavior is nurturing and collaborative rather than aggressive and competitive. However, data from recent studies strongly suggest that the aggressive, competitive, "masculine" management style is *not* the surest way to success. As management researcher Jim Collins (2001) noted in his influential book *Good to Great: Why Some Companies Make the Leap...and Others Don't,* the highest-performing and most successful executives often kept a low profile and combined personal humility with a willingness to go to extraordinary lengths to help their companies succeed. Similarly, other researchers have found empirical support for the value of the *transformational* leadership style (characterized by mentoring, inspiring, and empowering others), which is more consistent with prevailing gender stereotypes for women, as opposed to the *transactional* leadership style (characterized by rewarding task-specific performance, correcting poor performance, etc.) that is more commonly associated with male gender stereotypes (Eagly and Carli 2007).

In management, the development of interpersonal communications skills is essential to achieve success with diverse stakeholders. The skills I developed through my clinical training and my work as a psychiatrist regularly come into play in my role as an executive (e.g., consensus building, negotiating between stakeholders with competing interests). I entered leadership roles in psychiatric administration during a time when hospital management roles were beginning to shift back into the hands of physicians and away from non–medically trained managers (Recupero and Rainey 2006). Having a wide variety of interests in reading and a lifelong love of learning has helped significantly in my career as a physician executive. For example, it is important for medical administrators to be familiar with the nursing literature and to understand how nurses perceive themselves and their role in the health care system. It is crucial to understand multiple viewpoints and to be able to merge seemingly unrelated topics in a creative way for the consensus-building process.

A collaborative leadership style can work very well in the context of administration of a psychiatric hospital. In Butler Hospital, as in many other psychiatric hospitals, much of the work is organized around a team. While it is true that in larger, more complex organizations executive leadership is further removed from direct care providers, being able to find common goals and uniting the organization behind a shared ideal can be crucial to the success of the organization. As I noted earlier, one of my most significant mentors in health care management was Dr. Wilma Rosen. Earlier in Dr. Rosen's career, hospital employees had organized a union following a strike. In order to continue helping the hospital to provide high-quality patient care, Dr. Rosen recognized that she had to work *with* the union members after they returned to work rather than against them. As a result of her wisdom, my philosophy has been to try to join the executive management and the union together around a shared motivation to make the hospital a great place to work while providing safe and effective treatment for patients. I was thrilled recently when I learned that the union wanted to form a joint task force with the senior management to explore ways of managing patients' violent behaviors on inpatient units. Through the collaborative leadership model, health care executives can form a powerful alliance with key stakeholders around the shared goal of providing excellent patient care in a safe and well-managed treatment environment.

Nonetheless, as a physician executive, I've found that my experience as a litigator has been especially valuable. Having both clinical and legal training has given me a helpful vantage point for considering some of the major trends and issues in modern health care administration, such as quality improvement, risk management, and regulatory issues. Similarly, the persuasive reasoning on which lawyers rely in arguing a case is directly applicable to roles in management, advocacy, and leadership in medicine. I have not left my legal career behind me; I use my legal training every day in the work that I do as a hospital administrator and psychiatrist. Several years ago, in connection with my role as CEO of Butler Hospital, I pursued a patients' rights case before the Rhode Island Supreme Court, *In re Stephanie B.* (R.I. 2003), resulting in a decision that protects juveniles from arbitrary psychiatric hospitalization. *In re Stephanie B.* involved a cluster of three related cases; without medical testimony, a family court issued an order to prevent the hospital from discharging a patient, despite the absence of medical evidence that continued hospitalization was necessary. Finding that the family court had exceeded its authority, the state supreme court wrote that "Absent a civil certification procedure for a mentally ill child, the family court is without authority to order a child's confinement in a mental health care facility…"(*In re Stephanie B.*, R.I. 2003).

One of the challenges of the role of physician executive is the necessity of grappling with multiple and potentially conflicting ethical codes (Coile 1999). For example, a physician executive must consider the needs of the organization in order to preserve that organization for future patients; to a doctor accustomed to prioritizing the patients' needs above all else, this dilemma can be especially difficult (Recupero and Rainey 2006). In a sense, your "patient" becomes the organization or the system that serves the individual patients. The hospital executive often has to make difficult decisions, knowing that not everyone will be happy with the results. This can be hard for women executives in particular, because many of us were taught as young girls that it is important to please everyone. Others with whom we interact may also behave in accordance with outdated gender stereotypes about women and medicine, such as expecting that we will "cave in" and meet all of their expectations rather than holding our ground when a disagreement occurs. Taking a stand can be very difficult when others adopt a condescending attitude toward us, and it does take a great deal of courage and wisdom to have faith in ourselves and to advocate for ourselves. Remembering our ethical responsibilities and focusing on the eventual outcome rather than individual battles, we can keep our eyes on the end goal in order to resolve even the most challenging dilemmas. Fortunately, recent years have seen a dramatic increase in research and guidance concerning ethical standards and issues for physician executives, including administrators in behavioral health care.

Concluding Thoughts

Today, when I think about practical aspects of the future of health care administration, such as succession planning, I am pleased to reflect that a man and a woman would have an equally good chance at being considered for assuming executive management of our hospital once I am no longer serving as its CEO. This marks a significant change from the way things used to be! When I began my career in health care administration, I was the first female CEO of a hospital in Rhode Island. Today, there are several female executives within my hospital system.

For those who aspire to a career in health care administration or other leadership positions within psychiatry and related fields, cultivating a lifelong interest in learning and maintaining regular continuing education can be extremely beneficial. As Dr. Isaac Ray (1873) noted:

> He [the ideal superintendent], therefore, so orchereth his labors as to reserve some time, even if it be but the smallest fraction of the day, for study and reflection. The more he studies and learns, the more deeply is he impressed with the littleness of his knowledge, and the less is he disposed to indulge in any pride of opinion. While his studies and thoughts are, of necessity, directed chiefly to a special department of the healing art, he is not an indifferent observer of what is passing in the larger field of medical science, and therefore he cultivateth friendly relations with his professional brethren, displayeth an interest in their labors, and endeavoreth to inspire them with an interest in his own.

A lifelong commitment to scholarship, learning, and discourse with fellow professionals strengthens one's knowledge base and develops the skills on which one can draw in future challenges.

Throughout my career, I have found it extremely gratifying to be able to advocate for those who cannot advocate for themselves or who are subjected to discrimination because of stereotyped assumptions. Just as feminists advocated for women during the civil rights movement, mental health professionals today need to advocate for those who face discrimination from the stigma of mental illness. I continue to view advocacy and working toward legislative changes to be an important aspect of my work in forensic psychiatry.

The path toward the top has not been easy, but one of the goals to which I have committed myself is to help remove barriers that may stand in the way of gender equality in the professional world. Certainly, for women in academic psychiatry and related professions today, lacking funding and having difficulty getting work published can make it harder to climb the academic ladder. However, as I have learned through my own experience, if you are passionate enough about your intellectual pursuits and if you are willing to make sacrifices toward those goals, you can still distinguish yourself, achieve advancement, and have a tremendous positive impact on society by sharing your education, training, wisdom, and enthusiasm.

PRACTICAL TIPS FOR WOMEN IN PSYCHIATRY

- Develop your personal strengths and explore your ideals rather than emulating the ways in which another person became successful.

- Join and become active in professional organizations, such as the American Psychiatric Association and the American Medical Association. These organizations can help you to build a network and provide opportunities for you to assume leadership roles.

- Connect with a good mentor and seek out opportunities to be a mentor.

- Keep your eye on the goal, avoid obsessing over minute details, and recognize that in some cases, you cannot please *everyone*.

- Develop active listening skills and a strong interpersonal communication style.

- Speak up when you see discrimination; although things have improved in recent decades, sexism is still a major problem in the workplace. Eagly and Carli (2007) note the example of the recent class-action sex discrimination lawsuit against Wal-Mart in which an executive leadership retreat involved quail hunting and "meetings" held at strip clubs.

- Follow trends and changes in psychiatry and health care as they develop; currently, important trends to watch in psychiatric hospital administration include: health care reform, parity, managed care, access problems, and stigma (Recupero 2006); growth in the importance of technology, quality improvement, and evidence-based medicine (Recupero and Rainey 2006).

- To be a successful physician executive, it is typically necessary to master *several* different leadership styles. For those interested in learning more about this subject, Manya Arond-Thomas, M.D. (2004), describes six different leadership styles (commanding, visionary, affiliative, democratic, pacesetting, and coaching) that are useful in executive-level health care administration; she advocates developing competencies in multiple leadership styles, as different situations call for different styles of leadership.

- When you join an organization, put yourself to work by volunteering to serve on committees or on projects. Do not wait to be asked.

References

Arond-Thomas M: Resilient leadership for challenging times. Physician Exec 30:18–21, 2004

Ash AS, Carr PL, Goldstein R, et al: Compensation and advancement of women in academic medicine: is there equity? Ann Intern Med 141:205–212, 2004

Civil Rights Act of 1964, Pub L 88-352, 78 Stat 241, enacted July 2, 1964

Coile R Jr: Physician executives in the 21st century: new realities, roles, and responsibilities. Physician Exec 25:8–13, 1999

Collins J: Good to Great: Why Some Companies Make the Leap…and Others Don't. New York, HarperCollins, 2001

Eagly AH, Carli LL: Women and the labyrinth of leadership. Harvard Business Review 85(September):62–71, 2007

Health Care Accessibility and Quality Assurance Act, RI Gen Laws §23-17.13-1 et seq (RI, 2010)

Heru AM: Pink-collar medicine. Gender Issues 22:20–34, 2005

Heru AM, Stuart GL, Rainey S, et al: Prevalence and severity of intimate partner violence and associations with family functioning and alcohol abuse in psychiatric inpatients with suicidal intent. J Clin Psychiatry 67:23–29, 2006

Heru AM, Stuart GL, Recupero PR: Family functioning in suicidal inpatients with intimate partner violence. Prim Care Companion J Clin Psychiatry 9:413–418, 2007

In re Petition and Questionnaire for Admission to the Rhode Island Bar, 683 A2d 1333 (RI 1996)

In re Stephanie B, 826 A2d 985 (RI 2003)

Insurance Coverage for Mental Illness and Substance Abuse, RI Gen Laws §27–38.2–1 et seq (RI 2010)

Kohen D, Arnold E: The female psychiatrist: professional, personal, and social issues. Advances in Psychiatric Treatment 8:81–88, 2002

Morrissey JP, Goldman HH: Care and treatment of the mentally ill in the United States: historical developments and reforms. Ann Am Acad Pol Soc Sci 484:12–27, 1986

Ray I: Ideal characters of the officers of a hospital for the insane. Am J Insanity 30:64–83, 1873

Recupero PR: From asylum to neurobiology and behavioral genetics: Butler Hospital today. Med Health RI 89:159–161, 2006

Recupero PR, Rainey SE: The ideal physician executive. Med Health RI 89:232–235, 2006

Recupero PR, Heru AM, Price M, et al: Sexual harassment in medical education: liability and protection. Acad Med 79:817–824, 2004

Silver MA, Marcos LR: The making of the psychiatrist-executive. Am J Psychiatry 146:29–34, 1989

State of Rhode Island v Johnson, 399 A2d 469 (RI 1979)

Chapter 12

Specializing in the Wholly Impossible

Altha J. Stewart, M.D.

MY PROFESSIONAL EXPERIENCES ARE TRULY "the adventures of a woman who specialized in the wholly impossible" (McCluskey 1997, p. 403), a woman who was told as a girl that she could not do things but went on to do those things anyway, and more. I am black, female, a psychiatrist, an administrator, and a consultant, born and raised in the Jim Crow South (before *Brown v. Board of Education* [1954]), to a two-parent, working class household in the city where Dr. Martin Luther King Jr. was assassinated. Most of my life I have been prejudged based on my skin color, my gender, my age, or my southern origins. Although I possess an advanced education, dress and speak well, and introduce myself as *Dr.* Stewart, I usually have to remind others that it's *Dr.* and not *Miss* at least once or twice in new professional settings. And, although it has been many years since I wore a white coat, I can relate to the 2006 article written by a young black female physician titled "My Black Skin Makes My White Coat Vanish" (Lumumba-Kasongo 2006), in which she described her experiences reflecting the frustrating yet prophetic truth in Malcolm X's words (1965, p. 284), "Do you know what white racists call black Ph.D.s? *N****r!*" Her article reminds me of similar experiences during my training in the mid-1970s and how those experiences helped define my career in psychiatry.

It was during my sophomore year of high school that teachers first recognized my interest in and aptitude for science. An advisor recommended I consider volunteering as a candy striper at St. Jude Children's Research Hospital. Although most of my work there was confined to washing test tubes and making deliveries throughout the labs, I was exposed to the world of professional scientists and decided that it was the world I wanted to join. Dr. Carl Johnson, my advisor, did not appear at all surprised as we discussed my future when I proudly informed him that I had decided to become a lab technician and someday work in a place like St. Jude's. His response surprised me, though: "Don't just be the lab tech, go ahead and become a pathologist, then you would *run* the lab." That sounded good to me; I figured it would combine an interest in science with my strong work ethic. Of course, I had no idea at the time that that meant going to medical school, and the other "stuff" that followed.

After spending the last two years of high school at an all-girl Catholic high school where my interest in the sciences was further honed, I was accepted at a local (formerly all-male) Catholic college in Memphis, Christian Brothers University, in the first class that admitted women. Majoring in biology and taking the premed curriculum, I was usually the only black person and frequently the only woman in my classes. During my junior year I became involved in a program sponsored by the local medical school and learned of a summer program for minority students interested in medicine that was held at Harvard University every summer. Again an interested advisor encouraged me to apply, and I was accepted. It was during that summer that I first considered psychiatry. My initial specialty interest had been pathology (related to running the lab) but after finding out that meant spending a lot of time with the dead, I promptly switched to pediatrics, but that too was destined to change.

It was also at the Harvard summer program that I met someone who would play a prominent role in my future career choice, Dr. Alvin Poussaint. He served as a mentor for the program's students and conducted mock medical school interviews, and I was quite impressed that I would be meeting with this man who was a legend in the black community. This predated his days as consultant to *The Cosby Show,* when he entered the public mainstream; back then he was *the* black psychiatrist, whose articles on race, racism, and psychological issues for black folks were published in *Ebony* and helped us understand the psychological aspects of the experiences of most blacks in the post–civil rights era. During my mock interview with him he challenged me to think seriously about the decision to become a doctor. He made it clear that black people needed good doctors and that if I wasn't serious I should get out of the way and let someone who was serious have the spot. No one had ever confronted me in a way that questioned my ability to do what I said I was going to do and I made up my mind that "I'd show him." It was more than a decade later that I finally had the chance to meet with him again and let him know that not only had I been serious, but I was now his colleague and making a name for myself in psychiatry thanks to his words that summer. I went on to graduate from Christian Brothers University, then headed off "up north" to medical school at Temple University in Philadelphia in the mid-1970s.

My decision to enter psychiatry was made during medical school when I had my first clinical experience at Temple, where, as the only medical student rotating at the time, I was given lots of freedom and responsibility by the unit leadership. I only saw one black psychiatrist associated with the program and was so unsure about psychiatry as a career that the only psychiatry residency programs I interviewed for were with Temple University School of Medicine and Hahnemann Medical College; the others were all pediatric programs. When it came time to complete the match form though, I listed only Hahnemann and crossed my fingers. I wanted to go to Hahnemann because they had a core group of black psychiatrists on faculty or otherwise associated with the program to teach, supervise, and mentor me. They recruited me aggressively, introducing me to a dozen or so local psychiatrists that I didn't know existed. I received generous personal and professional support from this local group of black psychiatrists, who met monthly. It helped that Hahnemann also had an excellent community psychiatry program. I've always felt tremendously blessed because over the four years of my residency I had a black supervisor every year and I saw female and male black psychiatrists as clinicians and administrators, giving me a glimpse of what would turn out to be my future.

One of my supervisors, Dr. Earline Houston, happened to be a fellow Memphian (I actually attended college with her sister) and she took me under her wing when she realized I had an interest in administration and leadership. I worked in the community mental health center (CMHC) that she directed and I later completed an administrative elective course at the state hospital where she served as the first female superintendent. She encouraged me to participate in A. K. Rice Institute's group relations training postresidency and a year's course work in organizational management sponsored by the Wharton School of the University of Pennsylvania and La Salle University in Philadelphia. Along with Drs. Alexandra Symonds and Jeanne Spurlock, she encouraged me to challenge the commonly accepted theories regarding women in leadership and provoke discussion about new ones. She even critiqued my first professional presentation, made at a Black Psychiatrists of America Transcultural Psychiatry Conference, titled "African-American Women in Psychiatric Administration," and she encouraged me to continue writing in this area. It also helped that I had mentors and supervisors who "did not look like me" but who respected me enough to accept the fact that my experiences of racism and/or sexism were legitimate. I am fortunate that I didn't have an experience like the one Dr. Vanessa Gamble related in her Health Affairs article (2000), where she described having her perspective on students' reports of racist experiences repeatedly "dismissed" by her white colleagues.

After completing my psychiatric residency at Hahnemann Medical College and Hospital (now Drexel University College of Medicine and Hahnemann University Hospital), I remained in Philadelphia for the next nine years, working first as clinical director of a west Philadelphia methadone maintenance program (where I had my first experience developing new programs) and then as staff psychiatrist at a CMHC to complete my National Health Services Corps loan payback obligation. Later, I was recruited back to the Hahnemann University Hospital to run the short-term acute inpatient unit there. Directing the one unit with only attending physicians was a lot of work but provided a great lesson in leadership. I moved from this position to my first "good government job," serving as medical director of Philadelphia's Office of Mental Health.

When I completed my residency I had no idea I would ultimately wind up as a psychiatric administrator. Like many in my generation, I had assumed that after finishing training I would start a part-time practice, build that practice while working in a CMHC or as a staff psychiatrist in a hospital, and then eventually leave for full-time private practice. In my mind, I envisioned building a practice filled with professional black women clients who would experience psychotherapy with a black woman psychiatrist and be all the better for it. That vision changed when a disagreement with my then-chairman at Hahnemann resulted in my abrupt resignation from the position of director of the inpatient unit, but, as the saying goes, "When one door closes, another opens." Shortly after leaving Hahnemann (for the second time!), I was contacted by the new director of the city's Office of Mental Health and was offered the position of medical director. The position had been abolished by his predecessor, but as part of redesigning the local mental health system he was interested in my joining his team as medical director, providing psychiatric support and oversight.

After a couple of years, I was recruited to New York City and left Philadelphia to see whether I could "make it" working in the largest public mental health system in the country, in the city's Department of Health and Mental Hygiene. Over my almost five years there I served as deputy commissioner of mental health (including a brief stint as commissioner) and also worked as assistant vice president at New York City Health and Hospitals Corporation, responsible for the mental health managed care programs (both appointed positions) during the David Dinkins administration. When he lost his re-election bid, I took a position with the New York State Office of Mental Health as chief executive officer of the Manhattan Children's Psychiatric Center, which turned out to be one of the first hospitals slated for closure following Governor Mario Cuomo's loss in *his* bid for reelection. Fortunately, the director of Philadelphia's mental health system offered me a great opportunity/challenge and I returned to serve as chief executive officer of that city's new Medicaid behavioral health managed care program. My stint in that position resulted in my receiving a call from a headhunter recruiting for the position of executive director of the Detroit-Wayne County Community Mental Health Agency, a $500 million public mental health agency in a city with both funding and political challenges, that was about to undergo a transformation from a traditional fee-for-service system to a managed care system. After three years of battling politics and the system's seeming unwillingness to change, I spent a year with the Wayne State University Physician Group helping to craft the system transformation proposal; then I left the hectic life of government-appointed positions and returned home to Memphis to care for my ailing mother and live a more relaxed life as a consultant.

Not all of my leadership experience was in the academic or governmental arenas. From my days as a Falk fellow of the American Psychiatric Association (APA) during my residency, I have been active in organized psychiatry. Starting as a member of the Committee of Black Psychiatrists, for over 20 years I served on a variety of components including the Council on Social Issues and Public Psychiatry (as chair) and the Presidential Workgroup Regarding Implementing Recommendations of the *Surgeon General's Report on Mental Health: Race, Culture, and Ethnicity* (as co-chair). My APA leadership experiences culminated with my appointment to the Board of Directors of the American Psychiatric Foundation where I served almost eight years, the last four as president. Ironically, it was during a discussion on leadership with several black female early-career psychiatrists that I realized that in addition to there never having been a black president of the APA, I might have been the only black president of any APA subsidiary. I was also privileged to serve as president of both the Association of Women Psychiatrists and the Black Psychiatrists of America.

Looking back on my own experiences, I can vividly remember my first leadership position: chief resident in my residency training program. Descriptions such as "organized," "politically minded," and "problem solver," and statements of how I possessed important traits such as the ability to tolerate the frustrations of dealing with the administration (chairman, training director, attending physicians, and so on), that I was respected by the residents, and that I had a strong interest in group dynamics—all were tossed at me as the reasons I was "perfect" for the job. In addition, faculty support was strong and I first heard that famous line, "It will look good on your CV." I accepted the job, along with the extra $500 per year and the free parking space across from the hospital, and was promptly bitten by the administrative bug. After all, residents didn't make a lot of money and parking was hard to come by, so a parking space near the building and extra money was all it took.

It was during this period that I was selected as a Falk fellow of the APA, which set me firmly on the path to a leadership role in organized psychiatry. At the time, however, I had no idea it was also opening the door to all kinds of other leadership opportunities and that I was, in fact, well on the way to becoming the "mammy" described by Dumas (1979, p. 5) in her article on the dilemmas facing black women in leadership positions. She wrote that this phenomenon has its roots in myths about privileged positions and the role of black women in slavery:

> The mythical image of the strong, powerful, castrating black matriarch pervades contemporary organizations and poses a critical dilemma for black females that makes competition for, and competent performance in, leadership positions at best a costly endeavor. There are increasing efforts to resurrect the black "mammy" in today's ambitious black women who aspire to move up the socioeconomic ladder or into political arenas.

And I didn't know it at the time, but I was about to become one of the "new kinds of people in established professional positions" described by Leggon (1980, p. 190), made possible by a "confluence of unique socio-historical, economic, and psychological factors."

During the early years of my administrative career, most of the literature on psychiatric administration explored the differences between management styles utilized for administrative (nonclinical) versus clinical activities. The leading textbook of the time was *Psychiatric Administration: A Comprehensive Text for the Clinician-Executive,* edited by Talbott and Kaplan (1983). In his foreword, Dr. Melvin Sabshin wrote that psychiatric administration was at a significant crossroads in its historical development. He described the text as "well suited" for encouraging a newer generation of psychiatrists to enter this challenging and important field. He predicted that the text would become a part of the "broad educational activities that affect career choices." He concluded with his "personal delight" at the broadrange description of the diversity of administrative roles. Unfortunately, the mentioned "diversity" of roles did not include diversification of race or gender within the predominantly white male group of administrators.

While there was much attention being paid to the growing field of administrative psychiatry, little attention was being paid to the experiences and problems of minorities in those positions, especially African American women, who were continually confronted with the stereotypes of being too domineering, too aggressive, and unfeminine, and who frequently worked in environments where racist and sexist myths and behaviors clearly prevailed. This was also the time in the early days of affirmative action, when hiring minority women was seen as a plus. Recruiting an African American woman was seen as an advantage because it satisfied organizational requirements to boost both minority and female hiring. Black women were considered double minorities, or "two-fers." However, most evidence in the human resource, personnel, and psychology literature showed that this preferential hiring actually had a negative effect. Colleagues often felt as though African American women were being hired solely because of their racial and gender make-up, not because of their abilities. As a result, African American women hired into these positions often struggled with the perception, whether fair or not, of having a privileged status.

Early on in my career, the primary population with which I worked in my private practice was women, mostly black women, many of whom suffered from depressive disorders. These women, successful professionally in their own right, shared many of the same concerns that the general population had regarding seeking treatment for their psychological distress. I often heard these women describe a variation on remarks reported by Meri Nana-Ama Danquah (1998, pp.19–20*)*, author of *Willow Weep for Me: A Black Woman's Journey Through Depression:* "*Black* women and depression? Isn't that kinda redundant?…When *black* women start going on Prozac, you know the whole world is falling apart." Generally idealized as strong, nurturing caregivers, they were the "fierce angels" described by Sheri Parks (2010), suffering in silence and missing the message of recovery available to others. They believed, as did so many, that black women must be stoic and unflinching in the face of life's worst trials and tribulations. Reaching for help even when sorrow was overflowing was believed to represent weakness.

Delgado et al. (1985, pp. 247–248) described the psychological influences of race and gender on the experiences of African American women professionals as follows: "[W]hile African-American women have been exposed to better administrative positions since the 1960s-initiated affirmative action programs began, they have also faced excessive and undue anxieties in these positions." She described the role of the mother authority figure in the organizational family as follows:

> There is the "good" mother who offers care and protection; the "terrible" mother who is aggressive, devouring, and ensnaring; and finally the "great"

mother who combines all the characteristics of the "good" and "terrible" mothers. In a present-day context, black women are generally taught to strive for being the "good" mother and thus encouraged to subdue the traits inherent in the "terrible" mother. Being seen as a "great" mother carries with it the possibility of taking on some of the qualities desired by men.... [T]he best way for black women to be successful...is to be fully aware of the sexual, racial, and personal conflicts that must be faced in these positions.

Dr. Earline Houston, in an unpublished paper titled "Black Female Clinical Leadership Issues" (E.L. Houston, 1979) reviewed Dr. Otto Kernberg's theories on using a systems approach to understanding the organizational functioning of a psychiatric unit; she used her own experience as an African American female psychiatrist and CMHC medical director to discuss the influence of her multiple status identity on the functioning of the CMHC program.

My efforts in the early days of my administrative experience to find psychiatric literature relevant to my interest in psychiatric administration were largely unsuccessful, primarily because there was not much. Jones et al. in their 1970 article titled "Problems of Black Psychiatric Residents in White Training Institutes" touched on the importance of supervision and mentoring as they described the experiences of five black male psychiatrists. They admitted to a lack of a female perspective in their review as they described events that were perceived as racially influenced. A follow-up paper was presented at the 1986 APA annual meeting, titled "Black Psychiatrists/White Institutes: A 17-Year View." The authors were again forced to admit they could not report on the "special experience of the black female psychiatrist" and that they "recognized the limits imposed by an all-male perspective."

During my residency and early career years, I was fortunate to have been trained by and to have worked with some phenomenal black female psychiatrists who made their mark in administration and served as role models for me, such as Drs. Andrea Delgado and Earline Houston. This early exposure helped me define my leadership style and has served me well in my work in various senior executive positions over the last two decades.

I also searched the psychology and sociology literature, social work resources, and popular literature to understand as much as I could about the personality and developmental issues facing many of my black female patients. Most of what proved helpful was found in the psychology literature. The growing body of black psychology references addressed racially determined issues (related to racism, psychological development, and psychotherapy), and a well-established women's psychology body of references addressed gender-related issues (gender influences in identifying developmental stressors, expression of illnesses, manifestation of symptoms, etc.). There were very few articles, however, exploring the developmental issues facing black women specific to their race *and* gender status. There continues to be a paucity of literature regarding the psychological development issues specific to women of African descent. The pressures of both racism and sexism often conflict in areas of independence, career goals, and personal fulfillment. The combination of issues presented by the *-isms* may result in a general sense of hopelessness, helplessness, and powerlessness for many women of African descent.

Unfortunately, little work has been done related to reformulation of existing psychological theories to provide an analysis from an African-centered perspective. Most clinicians working with ethnic minority patients now recognize that bicultural stress is a legitimate issue and is accompanied by a sense of extra responsibility for maintaining the status level achieved, a sense of pressure to conform to the "norm," and a sense of isolation as individuals try to live between two worlds. Two examples describing bicultural stress in African American women appeared in popular literature. *A Foot in Each World* is a collection of stories by Leanita McClain (1986), who had chronic depression and tragically committed suicide after working her way up the ladder at the *Chicago Tribune.* In a 1980 *Newsweek* column titled "The Middle Class Black's Burden" (McLain 1980), she described her frustration as an upwardly mobile black professional whose success came at the terrible cost of alienation from her own people, writing, "Whites won't believe I remain culturally different, Blacks won't believe I remain culturally the same." Bari-Ellen Roberts (1998) is now famous for her role in the landmark discrimination lawsuit against Texaco in 1994, as recounted in the book *Roberts vs. Texaco: A True Story of Race and Corporate America.* She wrote: "Isolation is surely the most difficult part of being a token black in a hostile, otherwise all-white environment. Because trustworthy sources of information are so limited, you can never be sure of what's going on around you. You feel terribly alone" (p. 121). Stories such as these suggest that we must work to relieve the pressure black women feel to "shift," as described by Jones and Shorter-Gooden (2003) in their book *Shifting: The Double Lives of Black Women in America.*

Another contribution to this area is the book edited by Leslie Jackson and Beverly Greene (2000) titled *Psychotherapy With African American Women: Innovations in Psychodynamic Perspectives and Practice.* The contributors assert that theories and treatment approaches need to be reformulated to acknowledge the effects that racial and class stereotypes, legacies of slavery, present-day racism, African or Caribbean cultural influences, and gender-based maltreatment have on the psychological lives of black women. They recommend that in the therapeutic situation, the emergence of a complex interplay between these factors and the individual black woman's intrapsychic world needs to be encouraged and understood in the context of the therapeutic dyad.

In the mid-1980s, as I worked with mostly black female patients in the CMHC in Philadelphia and later in my private practice, I felt an obligation to understand the cultural influences affecting their lives so I read much of what was in the popular literature of the time. This included black feminist writers such as Michele Wallace, Ntozake Shange, Alice Walker, Gloria Joseph, and bell hooks.

As a medical student on my clinical rotations, I experienced many incidents in which patients were resistant to being treated by an African American. The first time it happened I was hurt, angry, and demoralized because it was an elderly black female patient who didn't believe I was a doctor. It was my first clinical rotation and my first experience with patient care, and as the only medical student on the service at the time I had been given status as a junior intern with my own caseload. I presented cases directly to a renowned local psychiatrist, Dr. O. Spurgeon English, who told me to call him "Spurge," just like one of the boys. I had status and respect, I was on top of the world, and a little old black woman, someone who could have been my grandmother, didn't believe I was responsible for her care and insisted on the "real" doctor—that is, the white male doctor.

Another challenge involves the conflict at the interface of race and gender, which is central to the professional experience of most ambitious African American women. Women are not generally valued for their assertive qualities or managerial styles in the same way that men are, yet they aspire to leadership positions that require these sorts of skills. The dual negative status issues that arise at the intersection of race and gender are not only contradictory, they may also be psychologically damaging. Some of the other challenges faced included:

- Dealing with the *"math of derailment"*—I coined this term to describe how one woman is expected to handle the job of two or three people without being able to hire the requisite number of staff to accomplish the job. For example, one woman manager with more than three distinct roles/responsibility areas may not be authorized to hire one or more assistants (or other administrative support persons) capable, competent, or skilled enough to ensure that she (the manager) performs all the work to her boss's satisfaction.
- *"Hallucinatory whitening"*—Described by Jones et al. (1970), this phenomenon was alluded to much earlier by the father of American psychiatry, Benjamin Rush, who proposed that removing the Negro's blackness would lead to the "oneness of the human race" and would

eliminate the subsequent psychological issues for blacks caused by whites' reactions to blacks (Rush 1799). My own experience with the phenomenon included the typical "I don't think of you as black" comments, as well as later in my career, having a young white male staff member, after watching me handle a management nightmare, "compliment" me by saying "You handled that like a white man." When asked what he meant, he stated that I was decisive and no-nonsense and got the job done. He claimed that the remark was made with "no disrespect intended" but that he'd never had a black manager and had only seen such behavior in white men.

· Negotiating at the interface of racism and sexism when interacting with white women—While conducting research in preparation for delivering the APA Alexandra Symonds Award lecture in 2006, I discovered that in the early days of the women's rights movement, some white suffragists felt that white men were insulting white womanhood by refusing to grant them privileges that were about to be granted to black men. Elizabeth Cady Stanton, along with other white women's rights supporters, did not wish to see the status of black men improved while the status of white women remained the same (Gordon 1997). The records of the 1903 National American Woman Suffrage Association convention include a speech by a southern suffragist, Belle Kearney from Mississippi, urging the enfranchisement of white women on the grounds that it "would insure immediate and durable white supremacy." The historian Rosalyn Terborg-Penn, Ph.D., wrote in her essay "Discrimination Against Afro-American Women in the Women's Movement 1830–1920":

> Discrimination against Afro-American women reformers was the rule rather than the exception within the woman's rights movement from the 1830s to 1920. Although white feminists Susan B. Anthony, Lucy Stone, and some others encouraged black women to join the struggle against sexism during the nineteenth century, antebellum reformers who were involved with women's abolitionist groups as well as women's rights organizations actively discriminated against black women.

I've always considered it to be an advantage professionally that I have been single throughout my career, allowing much flexibility regarding job opportunities, especially those that involve relocation. Living and working in three different major cities over a twelve-year period meant that I was often the "new kid" in a visibly prominent position, and I began each job during a time of transition for the mental health system in that area. To ensure a balance I always tried to get involved with at least one social networking group (e.g., the National Coalition of 100 Black Women) and a local professional group (e.g., the APA District Branch or the local chapter of another organized psychiatry group). Attending governmental, political, and community functions was generally part of my job, so I often attended social and political functions; this afforded me the opportunity to meet and associate with individuals who shared information regarding local leisure and recreational activities (restaurants, jazz clubs, museums, etc.). In the professional arena, I've always tried to include cultural references and symbols in my presentations. I often wonder, when I quote Angelou (Maya), DuBois (W.E.B.), or Hughes (Langston), whether most people in the audience know who these folks are, and if they can appreciate the importance of them in my culture, in the same way that the majority of society does when people quote white authors. We (blacks) often feel that whites don't interest themselves in learning about the nonpathological, nonclinical side of the sociohistorical culture of blacks in America. And we wonder what would happen if more people knew more about Langston Hughes and his writing and the impact that it has on black people. I wonder what impact it would make on the practice of psychiatry, if we could extend cultural understanding to include those things that really matter in the lives of many of the patients for whom we care.

I have been fortunate to have many memorable mentors over the years. During my residency training I was mentored by many faculty members, black and white, female and male, and have remained friends and colleagues with many of those still alive. Drs. Samuel Bullock and Warren Smith, both black psychiatrists and psychoanalysts in Philadelphia in the 1980s, became surrogate fathers to me after the death of my father, as well as supervisors, mentors, and friends. They also helped me understand the relevance of psychoanalytic theory to the black patients I saw in the CMHC. Drs. Earline Houston, Herbert Nickens, and Arlene Bennett were among the others in the Philadelphia area who helped me through the residency and early career years. Other mentors included Drs. Paul Fink and Frank West, who, in addition to helping me professionally, on at least one occasion questioned my date at the psychiatric society summer dance about "his intentions." My relocation to New York City in the early 1990s was sponsored by Dr. Billy Jones; he hired me as his deputy when he served as mental health commissioner and gave me my first opportunity to develop a Medicaid managed behavioral health program, which would become one of my areas of expertise. Other mentors such as Dr. George Gardiner taught me patience, helping me harness and channel the passion for psychiatry into productive actions. Many more, including Drs. Irma Bland, Jeanne Spurlock, Esther Roberts, and June Christmas, were at various points mentors and role models for my career choices.

And there has always been a special place in my heart for the first black women physicians, especially after finding out that the first female doctors in the South were black. Most accounts of women physicians from the nineteenth century have countless references to gender discrimination but relatively few concerning race. For black women physicians the discrimination issue was of course dual, concerning gender and race. Historian Gloria Moldow (1987) noted that black women were a very small part of the corps of practicing women physicians. In the twenty-five years after the Civil War there were 115 black women physicians in the United States, nearly all from an elite black society that developed after the Civil War. Those women, with no family financial support, were helped by the black women's social clubs of the day. Just like today's black women in medicine, these women understood the importance of self-reliance based on a lucrative career.

On my computer screensaver, I keep the engraved image of Rebecca Lee Crumpler (no photograph of her is available), the first black woman to receive a medical degree in the United States (from New England Female Medical College in Boston, in 1864), one year after the signing of the Emancipation Proclamation and fifteen years after Elizabeth Blackwell became the first American woman physician. I also have images—photos—of Rebecca Cole, the second black woman to receive a medical degree in the United States (from Woman's Medical College of Pennsylvania in 1867) and Susan McKinney Steward, the third black woman to receive a medical degree in the United States (from homeopathic New York Medical College for Women in 1870). These images along with that of Solomon Carter Fuller (the first black psychiatrist) and other "first" blacks in medicine are a constant reminder of the legacy passed on to me that I am obligated to pass on to others.

Like most women of color who are in leadership positions or who aspire to leadership positions, I regularly deal with the dual issues of race and gender. Balancing how you are perceived by others with how you perceive yourself in a given situation is a constant balancing act of how to deal with prioritization of these self-identification issues (race vs. gender). And like many black women I've taken a lot of "hits," sometimes from white female colleagues, who believe that gender must be the predominant issue, and sometimes from black males, who believe that race must be the predominant issue. In my experience it means that each day we work to make sure that other people understand, when we emphasize one issue over the other, it's not a slight against either issue—it just depends on the situation. Having the willingness to acknowledge the differences in our realities while being very aware of possible consequences, and taking some calculated risks, is one of the ways that I believe black women (including me) demonstrate their leadership.

PRACTICAL TIPS FOR WOMEN IN PSYCHIATRY

Several years ago the Center for Creative Leadership conducted a study involving professional women and identified the four contradictory sets of expectations that must be reconciled by women if they are to succeed as leaders (Morrison et al. 1987). Although the expectations below do not specifically address racial/ethnic influences, I have often discussed them with groups of women of African descent and have found them to be helpful in understanding the dynamic underlying some of the frustration and anger that I and other black women in leadership positions experience when we find ourselves being viewed through the additional prisms of institutional and individual racism:

- Take risks, but be consistently outstanding.
- Be tough, but don't be macho.
- Be ambitious, but don't expect equal treatment.
- Take responsibility, but follow others' advice.

Along the way I had to learn the difference between a mentor and a sponsor and that being a leader was different from being a manager. And it was important that I understood that my passion for doing the "wholly impossible" often translated into brief tenures in challenging positions. I had to become comfortable being the "change agent" and the "transitional object" in the organization within which I worked. The reality was that I might plan the change but would likely not be around when it really took hold.

Also, I encourage young psychiatrists, especially females, not to confine their choices of mentors, role models, and sponsors to people who look like them. Black women in leadership positions will face a variety of dilemmas and contradictions based on their dual status and must choose their battles wisely. There will be many situations that are either overtly (or covertly) racist or sexist in nature. Responses based on whether the behavior impedes a leader's ability to complete the work task at hand will be more useful than overly sensitive and defensive reactions.

Remember that support networks are important. Do not overlook people outside the field of psychiatry to keep you grounded. It's very important that you maintain an environment where you have supportive family and friends. Absence of these things is what deprives many people of ascending to leadership.

Finally, have a plan: set goals and assess how well you are doing in achieving them. I often have to admit to young psychiatrists that I didn't come into psychiatry with a real career plan. I never applied for a job; things just started to happen. After making the shift to administration, my work at every good job I had was noticed by someone who wanted me to do that for them or their system of care. I learned an awful lot flying by the seat of my pants, so to speak, but I wouldn't suggest that in today's market. I spent my career in a public mental health system that no longer exists. Managed care, draconian budget cuts, stigma and discrimination, restricted scope of practice and formularies, integrated care versus behavioral carve-outs are the issues facing today's young psychiatrists with an interest in being leaders in the field. Having the necessary skill set and being involved with the right mentors and sponsors are key elements in leadership success for the next generation of psychiatric leaders.

Tomorrow's leaders should look for opportunities to obtain formal training in management, finance, and administration. While you don't need an M.B.A., knowledge and skills in those areas will be immensely helpful as you climb the leadership ladder. They are still not part of the curriculum in most general psychiatric residencies, but they are crucial if you aspire to a leadership role.

I believe women who succeed in leadership positions have certain traits in common: toughness; sensitivity; intuitiveness; and the ability to work independently. These women possess a positive self-image and a self-confident manner related to their demonstrated academic achievement and natural ability to engage others. They generally contradict the stereotypes of women in the workplace, being able to maintain a sense of comfort with their femininity while, as Delgado (1985, p. 248) wrote, "proving to the majority culture that they are capable of exercising power and authority." They possess a strong sense of "affiliation" or "belongedness" and accept support from family and others without carrying excessive guilt (i.e., they don't try to be superwomen). And finally, they have demonstrated the ability to work "between two worlds" and manage, rather than be overwhelmed by, the daily challenges they face.

References

Danquah MN: Willow Weep for Me: A Black Woman's Journey Through Depression. New York, One World/Ballantine, 1998

Delgado AK, Griffith EEH, Ruiz P: The black woman mental health executive: problems and perspectives. Adm Ment Health 12:246–251, 1985

Dumas R: Dilemmas of black females in leadership. Journal of Personality and Social Systems 2:3–14, 1979

Gamble VN: Subcutaneous scars. Health Aff (Millwood) 19:164–169, 2000

Gordon AG (ed): Selected Papers of Elizabeth Cady Stanton and Susan B. Anthony. New Brunswick, NJ, Rutgers University Press, 1997

Jackson LC, Greene B (eds): Psychotherapy With African American Women: Innovations in Psychodynamic Perspectives and Practice. New York, Guilford, 2000

Jones C, Shorter-Gooden K: Shifting: The Double Lives of Black Women in America. New York, HarperCollins, 2003

Jones BE, Lightfoot OB, Palmer D, et al: Problems of black psychiatric residents in white training institutes. Am J Psychiatry 127:798–803, 1970

Leggon CB: Black female professionals: dilemmas and contradictions of status, in The Black Woman. Edited by Rodgers-Rose LF. Beverly Hills, CA, Sage, 1980, pp 189–202

Lumumba-Kasongo M: My black skin makes my white coat vanish. Newsweek, April 3, 2006.

McClain L: A Foot in Each World: Essays and Articles. Edited by Page C. Evanston, IL, Northwestern University Press, 1986

McClain L: The middle class Black's burden. My Turn column, Newsweek, October 13, 1980

McCluskey AT: "We specialize in the wholly impossible": black women school founders and their mission. Signs 22:403–426, 1997

Moldow G: Women doctors in gilded-age Washington: race, gender and professionalization. Urbana, IL, University of Illinois Press, 1987

Morrison AM, White RP, Van Velsor E: Executive women: substance plus style. Psychol Today 21:18–26, 1987

Parks S: Fierce Angels: The Strong Black Woman in American Life and Culture. New York, One World/Ballantine, 2010

Roberts B: *Roberts vs. Texaco:* A True Story of Race and Corporate America. New York, Avon Books, 1998

Rush B: Observations intended to favour a supposition that the black color (as it is called) of the Negroes is derived from the leprosy. American Philosophical Society Transactions 4:289–297, 1799

Talbott J, Kaplan S (eds): Psychiatric Administration: A Comprehensive Text for the Clinician-Executive. New York, Grune & Stratton, 1983

Terborg-Penn R, Harley S: The Afro-American Woman: Struggles and Images. Black Classic Press, 1997

X M, with Haley A: The Autobiography of Malcolm X. New York, Grove Press, 1965

Chapter 13

The Challenges of Leadership

A Woman's Perspective

Ann Marie Sullivan, M.D.

I AM CURRENTLY the chief executive officer (CEO) of a large public sector network of two hospitals serving the low-income and medically underserved people in the Queens borough of New York City. When I was asked to write a chapter for this book, I began to ask myself, "How did I get to this position, why did I choose it, and how is it that I have enjoyed the journey so much?" Why public psychiatry and public health care? These are not the most lucrative or glamorous of choices. Public psychiatry is still often seen as second-best. It is not quite as thrilling as research, as intellectually demanding as psychoanalysis, or as rewarding as private practice. The public sector is messy, having to deal with complex and problematic systems, with the failure of our society to deal with poverty, chronic illness, bureaucratic obstacles, and the limited access for so many to the wealth of current psychiatric medical treatments. Many psychiatrists find it overwhelming and mundane. But I find the realm of public psychiatry fascinating and challenging, and hope to explain that view in this chapter.

A second view I would like to present is that of psychiatrist as leader. Surprisingly, our training as psychiatrists teaches us many of the skills a good leader needs, and much of what we do in treating our patients can be effective in leading systems. In the various leadership roles I have held, I depend greatly on my psychiatric training to be effective. Psychiatric training is a primer for leadership; you just need to take the first step.

The third view, which has been so tightly interwoven throughout my career, is that of a woman journeying in this field of medicine while being a wife and mother building a family. Balancing these worlds is a part of life for most women and requires the fine tuning and adjustments that I feel are unique to women. Freud knew that love and work are our challenges over the life journey, and that fulfillment in both is our goal. But how we do it, what we gain and what we lose, is unique to each of us. Here, I would like to describe my choices and struggles—not to say they are the answer, but simply to offer one person's experiences as a starting point for others' discussion.

In this chapter I describe my personal journey, in the hope that it will provide in the telling some food for thought, and a few practical suggestions for other women psychiatrists who are interested in public sector psychiatry, in leadership roles in any area of psychiatry, and in trying to balance love and work along the journey.

Why Public Psychiatry?

When I entered medical school at New York University (NYU) I thought I would be an internist and work in a general adult medical practice. I had always liked the sciences and I imagined that a practice would be something like that of the classic television character Marcus Welby, M.D., a physician with a strong connection to patients, families, and community. My experience in training was different. While I learned a great deal, I found that time was extremely limited when it came to really getting to know my patients, and that much of the work was the interpretation of the technology of medicine. I had never really thought about psychiatry. I had never taken a psychology course in college, and I had never known or even thought much about psychiatrists and what they do.

My last clinical rotation as a third-year medical student was in psychiatry in the adult ward at Bellevue Hospital Center. It was in the "old" Bellevue, with its large wards and many patients with severe chronic mental illness. I enjoyed working there! The patients and their life stories were fascinating; I liked learning about the way patients coped with their illness, the science of the new medications, and the total patient picture I saw through the eyes of my psychoanalytic supervisors. I remember being amazed at the hallucinations patients experienced, at the paranoid structures they used to explain their world, and the intense sadness and hopelessness of depression. I admired how so many of these individuals had managed to thrive in their lives despite their severe problems.

When it came time to choose a residency, I stayed at Bellevue (the main teaching hospital for NYU School of Medicine). It was a fascinating place to learn community psychiatry, and I knew that was what I wanted to study. Community psychiatrists see the whole patient in their life space, with their families and supports, with the problems in their environment, and they work to navigate with patients through their illness to the best recovery each individual can accomplish (Ranz and Mancini 2008). I have always found that process to be exciting and rewarding.

As a resident in psychiatry I enjoyed the challenge of working in systems and being a part of fixing problems when they affected my patients. Many of my classmates found these things frustrating and extraneous to what they were trying to learn. I found it a challenge to understand what my patients needed in the community and to work with staff and patients to meet those needs. "That's the social worker's job" was the usual response to addressing systemic problems, but I always saw that as equally important to my patients as any medication I gave them. In a 2006 survey of psychiatric residency directors, although teaching residents how to navigate systems within their mental health care system (e.g., multidisciplinary team work for patient care) was rated as highly important, understanding and navigating social systems was rated less so, and the importance of learning this across larger systems that affect patients was ranked as almost negligible (Yedidia et al. 2006). This is despite a survey of physician practices that shows an increasing number of psychiatrists in public sector work (Ranz et al. 2006). There still remains a lack of sophistication among psychiatrists about the powerful influence of systems on our patients' care.

In my early years as a psychiatrist, I worked on mobile intervention teams that made home visits to patients and their families. In the same clinic were two patients who were "noncompliant"; that is, they didn't accept the treatment we had to offer the way we offered it. I visited one, a middle-aged woman, whose home was immaculate and who offered us tea. She spoke of her family, and was proud of her home. After our visit, we acknowledged her pride and her successes and she accepted her monthly depot fluphenazine injections. Another was a young woman who lived in the rear room of a filthy row apartment guarded by two pit bulls and an uncle who dealt in drugs. She needed to know we knew how hard her life was, and she too worked with us to take her monthly injections. How we worked with each of these individuals was inextricably woven into their environments, environments I only truly understood when I met them there.

The choice of psychiatry is still an issue for many medical students. The best and brightest are still expected to go into medical or surgical residencies. As recently as a year ago a psychiatry intern on her medical rotation was queried, "You're so smart. Why are you going into psychiatry?" The same bias that society places on mental illness, our own profession places on the choice to work with people with mental illness. The advances in the neurosciences have certainly helped, but the stigma of choosing a public community psychiatry career is still present (Sierles et al. 2003). I still hear some of our colleagues say, with no basis in fact, that those who choose the public sector were not at the top of their class. It is still a sad comment that those who work with the people who have the most serious mental illnesses, sometimes receive the least respect. In surgery, the opposite is true. Is the difference a subtle stigma of our own?

One word of advice that I would offer about life choices is to remain open to possibilities you may never have thought about. Also pay attention to what excites you and interests you as a person. It's OK to value what others may see as not academic enough, or not medical enough, or just too far off the beaten path. As a woman, I think it was easier for me to choose the "unlikely" field of public psychiatry, to actually pay attention to what I was feeling rather than to what was expected of me.

When I graduated from medical school I told my parents that I wanted to become a psychiatrist, and they said "What is that?" When I explained, they were kind but queried, why would I do that after all the hard work of going to medical school? Over time they appreciated my choice, but I think they never really understood why I hadn't become Marcus Welby.

While I have become more knowledgeable about the causes of and cures for mental illness, the very unique experience of each patient in that patient's social and physical environment remains fascinating. As I further understood how systems of care affect our patients and their treatment I began to look to changing those systems to be more effective and to make mental health care more accessible. That led to jobs as clinic administrator, then hospital medical administrator, and finally CEO.

Why Public Sector Leadership?

How to make systems work better: that is a fascinating challenge. And how to make systems work better seemed to me to be very similar to how we help patients be healthier. The skills I learned as a psychiatrist served me well when I needed to understand various issues, engage others in making changes, deal with crises, and get the job done. But I don't think I would have made the move to grow in leadership positions without the mentorship of colleagues who helped me to put interests and ideas into actions. So, I would like to describe with some examples these two points: how my training in psychiatry provided a unique skill set for leadership, and how my mentors were the guides and coaches to developing and acting on those skills.

Listening

The number one skill for a leader is listening to others, really listening. Listening involves a temporary suspension of your own ideas, wishes, and needs in order to hear where the other person is coming from and what they have to say. Women are good listeners. If you watch a mother in the playground talk to her toddler, you see how patient she is in trying to understand what her toddler needs and is trying to say. She speaks at the child's level, tries over and over until she thinks she has it right, and will endlessly respond to queries. She looks for nonverbal cues and responds to needs that aren't spoken.

I learned a lot about listening as a resident, when I took copious process notes of forty-five minute sessions with my patients. In discussions of those sessions with my psychoanalytic supervisor, I learned firsthand how much my supervisor heard that I hadn't, and how we can have different interpretations of the same words. As psychiatrists we are taught to take in all the clues and see the big picture that the patient is trying to show us.

As a leader, you must understand and know as much as possible about the issues and problems you have to deal with, and understand and know as much as possible about the staff and all the players you have to interact with. Listening and reflecting on what they have to say is critical. I learned from my patients, and still do. I learned from my colleagues and staff, and still do. There is no shortcut for listening, as we well know as psychiatrists.

Ability to Be Calm in the Storm

Leadership is "grace under pressure" (Kennedy 1955). Why is that so important? Because a leader needs to be able to pause, think, and begin to see a way out of chaotic situations. A leader needs to help others to pause as well, and make thoughtful decisions. One's self-image should revolve around getting the job done rather than looking good at doing the job.

As a woman I think I found it easier than men do to stop and think, to take the time to discuss and plan. I didn't feel I needed to be immediately decisive in order to prove my worth, or that being thoughtful was a detriment. I think women are less expected to be rushing the charge, and can spend the time to plan the attack, so to speak.

As a psychiatrist, remaining calm in a storm is also critical. We are taught to understand our patients, gather data, and observe and advise with caution, recognizing our limitations in fully understanding all there is to know about our patients. We know how important calmness can be with an agitated patient. We also know when we must act decisively, and take control if necessary, but always return it to the patient as soon as possible.

In an insightful book on President Lincoln's leadership style, Phillips (1992) describes how Lincoln navigated the waters of being decisive while engaging others, keeping a steady course while being flexible, and always being affable even with his enemies. A model leader, Lincoln spent much time understanding people and how to interact with them, and probably would have been a pretty good psychiatrist.

Ability to Engage Others in a Common Goal and Build Consensus

As psychiatrists, we know well that engaging effectively with all of our patients in treatment is step one. We also know that the process is ongoing and requires continuous work to improve. Every form of psychotherapy, whether analytic, behavioral, supportive, or cognitive, offers engagement as step one and continuous improvement as the process. Similarly, when an organizational leader wants to start an initiative or effect change, engagement of his workforce is essential, followed by the work of change.

I have recently become involved in the *lean approach* to management and improvement that was begun by Toyota but has been adapted to health care systems (Fillingham 2008; Koenigsaecker 2009). The two key pillars of this improvement system are: respect for people (which involves having the worker join in designing the improvement or engagement) and a series of processes for continuous organizational improvement that focus on learning new skills to understand and solve problems.

I have been impressed with how many such approaches to working in systems parallel the basic processes of psychotherapy. Systems are composed of human beings and improving systems requires mechanisms that speak to people, engage them, and help them change. As a psychiatrist, to see that unfold can be as rewarding as seeing the improvement in a patient or a family.

Hard Work and Persistence

As premed students, medical students, residents, and then practicing psychiatrists we are no strangers to hard work. The term *workaholic* seems apt. However, persistence is more subtle. Persistence is staying the course, on target, over time, and with a clear goal.

A wonderful story in the Bible describes a woman who goes to a judge for "justice from you against my enemy" (Luke 18:1–8). He refuses her several times but she keeps coming back again and again. Finally he gives her what she asks only because she is so annoying and he realizes she will never stop. The wisdom of this story is to simply not give up if your cause is important enough. And do not be afraid to be that nagging woman who simply won't go away! Sometimes attributes stereotypically applied to us as women seem pejorative, but are actually styles that are effective.

You Only Accomplish What You and Your Team Accomplish Together

In one of the classic books on organizational leadership styles, *Good to Great: Why Some Companies Make the Leap…and Others Don't,* Collins (2001) describes effective leaders as having a healthy dose of humility and a solid understanding that you can accomplish nothing alone. Others have also observed this (ASAE and the Center for Association Leadership 2006; Buckingham and Coffman 1999): Organizations that depend on the charisma of one leader often flounder when that leader leaves; organizations that were built on solid principles and teamwork continue on, because the team was the reason for success.

I learned this lesson well in my work on crisis intervention teams. While I was the titled team leader, I was useless alone. Only with my team of nurses and social workers, and our relationship with the hospital and police backup, could I hope to intervene successfully in any crisis situation. When my hospitals now face financial crises, it is the teamwork of all the staff that makes the difference between moving forward or falling behind.

Teamwork on the inpatient unit, teamwork in the day program, teamwork in the clinic, teamwork on the Assertive Community Treatment team—it goes on and on. Teamwork is the cornerstone of public sector work. And yet in large systems, it is still often undervalued.

An often-quoted saying by Lao Tzu sums up the issue: "Fail to honor people, they fail to honor you. But of a good leader who talks little, when his work is done, his aim fulfilled, they will all say, 'We did this ourselves'" (as quoted in Phillips 1992).

When asked why administration is interesting to a psychiatrist, I often reply "Because it is what we were trained to do." Since complex systems are like the complexity of individuals and families, engaging systems and moving them forward could be called *systems therapy.*

Mentorship

Mentors encouraged me to assume leadership positions. I was the only woman in my psychiatric residency class and the first woman to be chosen as a chief resident in the NYU psychiatric residency program at Bellevue. My training director, Dr. George Ginsberg, gave me the confidence to take on a leadership role for the first time. I found my fellow residents and the leaders of the department surprisingly supportive. A few years after graduating, I was contacted by a former chief resident at Bellevue, Dr. Neal Cohen, about joining him as the associate director at a large community mental health program at Gouverneur Hospital on the Lower East Side in New York City. He had "heard that [I was] a pretty good chief resident" and was interested in community work. Dr. Cohen and my experience at Gouverneur shaped my skills and formed my interest in administration. Dr. Cohen later became the health commissioner of New York City and I learned from him how to lead and how to negotiate the complex waters of systems in that environment. He introduced me to influential leaders in the city and state and helped me make the contacts that are so critical to success.

Also at Gouverneur, I learned from the executive director, Mr. Alan Rosenblut, the front and back office skills of hospital administration. He asked me to assume the role of medical director and supported and tutored me in the transition.

When I graduated, few physicians got a master of business administration or master of public administration degree. I learned by apprenticeship. I was fortunate to have skilled mentors with the interest and the willingness to take the time to teach and support a colleague. I have tried to fulfill that role for others in return. Mentorship is critical as we move along any career path. I often think that if my residency director had not taken a chance on appointing the first woman chief resident, my career may have been very different.

It is important to recognize that mentorship is key to developing leaders, and to ensuring that leadership is open to all with the interest and ability. Our systems of care need to have leadership from all the communities and ethnicities we serve, and mentorship is a key part of enabling such leaders. Women, in particular, often need to be encouraged to take the first step and be mentored to see their potential. Formal programs supported by departmental leadership that are dedicated to advancing women academically actually work (Morahan et al. 2001). More such programs are needed for all underrepresented groups.

Balancing Family and Career

How do you balance career and family? For women, the question often revolves around having and raising children. Can I do both? Can I have the perfect balance? Can I be both the excellent mother and the successful career woman?

My personal answer has been: Yes, I can do both. But no, I can't do it perfectly. Hopefully I can do it well enough. And I definitely can't do it alone. While that may sound simple, it was something I had to learn in order to help myself feel less guilty about my shortcomings as a mom and my limitations in pursuing my career. Balance isn't perfection, but a series of choices.

When I walked into NYU medical school I was one of 10 women in a class of 110. It was 1970 and the women's movement was in full swing. Ten percent women in a nonwomen's medical college was considered revolutionary. Yes, at that time, there were still all-women's medical schools!

When I think of why I chose to go to medical school, at a time when most of the kids on my block in Queens, New York, married and had children at a young age and never went to college, I would say it was my parents. In my high school, which was an all-girls college prep school, most of us did go to college for nursing or teaching but few went to law school or medical school. So why did I? Again, I think it was my parents' influence. I was one of two girls, my sister being three years older, in an Irish-German neighborhood in Queens, New York. Both of my parents were from Queens. My dad never finished high school because he had to work at age fifteen to take care of his mother. My mom graduated from high school and wanted to go to college, but she had to work to take care of herself. My dad taught me to think well of myself, to always do the best I could, that education was a most valuable gift, and that I should pursue my dreams. My mom taught me strength, the value of caring about others, and a love of reading, and she had faith in me. I never recall either of them thinking less of me, or that I could be or do less, because I was a woman. It just wasn't an issue.

When I got to medical school, my experience with professors and peers was more one of curiosity than discrimination. Many professors were surprised at there being women in medicine, but were generally accepting, at least in the cognitive specialties of pediatrics, internal medicine, and psychiatry. Surgery was a different matter, and there women had to prove themselves more directly; my classmates who chose surgery had to be exceptional and tough. In essence, they had to be "man enough" to get through.

I met my husband in medical school and we married when we both were in the second year. Through school and into our residencies we focused on learning and our careers. I knew fellow women students who had children during those years, but I knew I couldn't handle both school and motherhood so we decided to wait until I was finishing my training. Now, many women choose to have children while in training, and that choice is becoming easier.

My first daughter was born at the end of my residency and my husband, who was in a research program at that time, took time off to take care of her. For me, that sharing of the responsibilities over the years has been critical. I had lots of help from spouse and family. I worked close to home when my children were young in order to be able to get home fast in an emergency, spend time at their school events, and be available to help with homework and class projects. I had a full-time caregiver for my child when I worked full-time, plus the help of my mom and dad. It was hectic; I was often tired, and I tried to keep work within the 9 to 5 time frame.

I stopped cooking, didn't spend much time decorating our house, and spent precious weekends with the kids. I read books on how to be a working mom and got tips like: don't make the beds, it's OK; it's OK if meals aren't always on time; it's OK if bedtime isn't always on time; and so forth. Those pieces of advice helped to take the pressure off.

I learned early that I had to make choices. I wasn't the sort of mom who would win the Good Housekeeping seal of approval, and I couldn't work eighty hours a week. I know that my parents' dedication to family taught me how to value family in my choices. Their respect for education and advice to do what I loved got me through years of hard work to become a physician. I know that my husband's support buoyed me through many a difficult day. As my daughters grew up and became more independent, I was able to devote more time to work. My husband made choices about his career that supported our family, too. We both missed opportunities, but we felt that we as a family came first. Again, there were lots of choices that we had to make.

Conclusion

In my current position as CEO for a health care network in Queens, New York, I have had the opportunity to bring to general medical practice much of what I have learned in community psychiatry. The concept of the primary care medical home that is so important in health care reform incorporates in its design the intensive and supportive case management approach that has long been the mainstay of working with individuals with mental illness. When I took the job as CEO, I began a network-wide care management program for patients with chronic medical illness that has had the same positive results as our approach in mental health.

Our assertive community treatment programs, mobile crisis teams, and home-based intervention programs have been shown time and again to be effective in decreasing hospitalizations, increasing patient engagement, and improving quality of life (Dieterich et al. 2010). These concepts are finding their way into medical practice for chronic medical illnesses and I find it exciting to be part of that change.

I have personally had a rewarding career in the public sector. My work with patients has been fascinating. My work with systems of care has been equally gratifying. I hope that more young psychiatrists will pursue this exciting field and experience the same sense of fulfillment that I have found.

PRACTICAL TIPS FOR WOMEN IN PSYCHIATRY

There is no blueprint you can follow. I would recommend considering a few tips I have learned over the years:

- Know you have limits and get lots of help.
- Even though you are a psychiatrist, you don't have all the answers. It's OK to ask for advice.
- You don't have to be a *Good Housekeeping* mom. Be good enough.
- You can make temporary adjustments in your career while your children are young. It may cause some loss of time and advantage, but again that's a choice to consider. For example, bargain for family consideration at your job since you are quite valuable to your employer.
- Be flexible about your time and activities and your expectations. Much of life is unexpected and can't be planned for.
- Lean on family and friends for support.
- Mistakes are OK. That's why we have erasers on pencils.
- Enjoy!!

References

ASAE and the Center for Association Leadership: 7 Measures of Success: What Remarkable Associations Do That Others Don't. Washington, DC, The Center for Leadership, 2006

Buckingham M, Coffman C: First, Break All the Rules: What the World's Greatest Managers Do Differently. New York, Simon & Schuster, 1999

Collins J: Good to Great: Why Some Companies Make the Leap…and Others Don't. New York, HarperCollins, 2001

Dieterich M, Irving C, Park B, et al: Intensive case management for severe mental illness. Cochrane Database of Systematic Reviews 2010, Issue 10. Art. No.: CD007906. DOI:10.1002/14651858.CD007906.pub2.

Fillingham D: Lean Healthcare: Improving the Patient's Experience. Chichester, UK, Kingsham, 2008

Kennedy J: Profiles in Courage. New York, Harper & Row, 1955

Koenigsaecker G: Leading the Lean Enterprise Transformation. New York, Productivity Press, 2009

Morahan PS, Voytko ML, Abbuhl S, et al: Ensuring the success of women faculty at AMCs: lessons learned from the National Centers of Excellence in Women's Health. Acad Med 76:19–31, 2001

Phillips D: Lincoln on Leadership. New York, Hachette Book Group USA, 1992

Ranz JM, Mancini AD: Public psychiatrists' reports of their own recovery-oriented practices. Psychiatr Serv 59:100–104, 2008

Ranz JM, Vergare MJ, Wilk JE, et al: The tipping point from private practice to publicly funded settings for early-and mid-career psychiatrists. Psychiatr Serv 57:1640–1643, 2006

Sierles FS, Yager J, Weissman SH: Recruitment of U.S. medical graduates into psychiatry: reasons for optimism, sources of concern. Acad Psychiatry 27:252–259, 2003

Yedidia M, Gillespie C, Bernstein C: A survey of psychiatric residency directors on current priorities and preparation for public sector care. Psychiatr Serv 57:238–243, 2006

Chapter 14

Having the Courage and Conviction to Succeed

Donna M. Norris, M.D.

I'M JUST A LUCKY SO-AND-SO, a 1945 song with lyrics by Mack David and music by Duke Ellington, was one of my childhood favorites, according to my mother. She humorously compared the dissonance of this tune with our family's stressed economic situation. Nevertheless, the then-popular lyrics were prophetic about my future, filled with special opportunities and a professional career the likes of which I never could have imagined.

I grew up in Columbus, Ohio, a town known for the largest land grant academic center in the state, and attended public secondary schools. I recall my fourth grade teacher asking the class, "What do you want to become when you grow up?" I prepared myself to respond because I knew what I wanted to do. The classmates ahead of me answered with their lists of hopes and aspirations. The teacher nodded her head affirmatively. When my turn to answer came, I responded "I want to become a doctor." The teacher seemed puzzled as she looked directly at me. "Well, you should choose something that is more likely for you, a Negro, to achieve, such as training to become a teacher or a nurse." As other classmates turned to focus their eyes and attention on me, I experienced a mixture of emotions, surprise and embarrassment, to hear my teacher's words. Receiving special attention from the teacher was generally experienced as a good thing, but this felt different. Although I was very much aware of my ethnic identity as a Negro or colored person, as African Americans were called then, and though I lived in a racially segregated part of my city, I had never viewed these factors as limits to my achievement. My shock at hearing these words from my teacher made me question my long-held dream of becoming a physician. My journey towards medicine had begun, and yet, as I would discover later, the skepticism and clear dismissal of these dreams by others as unrealistic goals were similar to the experiences of many other young African Americans, especially women (Spurlock 1999). Additional insights regarding the many challenges faced by women scientists of diverse backgrounds are documented elsewhere (Dickstein and Nadelson 1986; Kirkpatrick 2004; U.S. Department of Health and Human Services 2009).

Where did this idea about medicine come from? My grandmother's brother, "Dr. Joe," was, I discovered years later, not really a physician, but was called *Doctor* as a form of respect. There were no doctors in my family and only one African American general practitioner, Dr. Cox, in my neighborhood. Very few persons of color, including African American physicians, were ever subjects in my schoolbooks. Dr. George Washington Carver, the peanut researcher at Tuskegee Institute, was the lone African American scientist championed in my texts. Other potential African American role models mirrored in the media were those with outstanding careers in music, entertainment, and athletics, positions which only a paucity of African Americans could realistically attain. In my neighborhood, few of my high school classmates attended college. The young women sought jobs and married, and the men obtained blue-collar jobs. I attribute the idea that I could accomplish something so far removed from my environment to the support of my deeply spiritual family, my friends, and my unwillingness to allow others to limit my aspirations.

The Path to Equal Opportunity

"Education and hard work are the keys to opportunity" is a familiar mantra among African Americans, immigrant Americans, and other minority populations who sought to build better lives for themselves and their families in this country. My dream was to pursue a career in pediatric medicine, not psychiatry. In my community, psychiatry was not well respected, and I had never met a psychiatrist until I arrived in medical school. Therefore, I did not consider this field when contemplating my future.

My family, of modest means, worked actively in the church and attained leadership within its nurturing environment. Volunteer service by the church elders, most of whom had little formal education, was valued, and it allowed these men and women to achieve a measure of status and respect within the African American community that was not possible in the outside world (Griffith et al. 1984). It was in this church environment that I received my early religious training and encouragement to take on various leadership roles. My church, similar to others in the community, was also a gathering place for politicians of all racial groups who sought to glean the African American vote before the local, state, and national elections. Politics was a major interest of my family, and particularly so for my grandmother, who volunteered as a poll precinct worker and who took me along to the voting booths as a young child. I did not fully appreciate then that the right to vote was a privilege extended to only a segment of African Americans in this country. These early experiences likely ignited my interest in understanding more about the influence and power of politics in all aspects of American life.

When I graduated from high school, the question was not whether to attend college, but which college and where. By the 1960s, most white-majority colleges accepted a limited number of black students. However, many African American families, mine included, were concerned about these majority educational institutions. Would these schools be fair in the treatment of their children, and could they offer an academic environment in which their children would thrive and be successful? Would these schools provide a caring atmosphere? Although it was more expensive than the state university, my family encouraged me to attend Fisk University, one of the historically black colleges, in Nashville, Tennessee, where I had relatives. At the time I arrived, Nashville, referred to as "the Athens of the South," was still a segregated town beset by sit-ins at the lunch counters and demonstrations at the department stores. The Fisk campus, in contrast, was a bustling educational environment. Although mobility within the city of Nashville was limited, with most student activity constrained physically by the coordinates of the university's property lines, the richness of the liberal arts curriculum offered by a devoted and racially diverse faculty was without boundaries. As students, our education was shepherded by artists-in-residence such as Aaron Douglas, Arna Bontemps, and Robert Hayden, who introduced students to the richness of the Harlem Renaissance period. We were taught a history that included the many important contributions of African Americans to the worlds of science and business and the building of this nation. This history, largely absent or obscured in most written works and unknown by many Americans, utilized African American literature and folk narratives to celebrate the creativity and humanity of a people who had conquered untold obstacles and demonstrated their resilience for life not viewed only through the prism of slavery. Education in historically black colleges and universities occurred during a time of radical change in America. The faculty understood and demanded that students prepare for future leadership roles. Ironically, Fisk University's founding in 1866 was made possible because of the restrictions of segregation. That period predated by 100 years the enactment of new American laws focused on addressing the inequalities of life for African Americans, women, people living in poverty, and other groups.

Whenever perceived injustices occur and seemingly are not readily addressed, I am reminded of the saying that "things are not always fair." When I was applying to medical school, I knew that it would be a long shot, not just because of the academic rigors but also because of my lack of money to afford the tuition. In undergraduate school most of my expenses were paid through scholarships and work-study programs. While many of my college classmates selected one of the two historically African American medical schools in the country, Howard University College of Medicine and Meharry Medical College, I did not have the financial resources to complete the application to attend. For me, the least expensive alternative medical school was The Ohio State University College of Medicine, located in my home state. However, my internist quietly informed me that he was barred from attending this school because of quotas limiting admissions of Jews. Nonetheless, he encouraged me to continue the application process.

As expected, the interviews with the medical school admissions committee were stressful. They inquired about my motivation for a medical career and my personal life plans. One member suggested that if admitted, I would take up a slot for a man, who, he noted, would likely have a longer and more productive career. I never forgot this admissions committee experience, and I reflect on it whenever interviewing others for positions of leadership. It was challenging to keep my spirits up as other classmates received their notices of acceptance before me. Then, my acceptance letter arrived and I eagerly began to plan for my medical studies. I needed to find a way to finance my extended education. I applied and was named one of the two semifinalists for a privately funded scholarship. Although told that my academics and interviews were superior to those of my male classmate, I was informed that he would receive the grant because he was male. Today, few would be so bold as to verbalize such flagrant gender bias.

My arrival at medical school was a major cultural change for me, and in looking back I believe that it was also a cultural shock for many of my classmates. The shock for me related to the lack of diversity, and for others, it was, perhaps, the *presence* of diversity. This was a historic class for the school, including the largest number of women—thirteen, less than 10% of the freshman class. These women quickly formed a solid bond, which rivaled that of the male-only fraternities in the school. Four other women and I rented a house together, established study groups, and stuck together throughout our school tenure. Initially, I did not fully appreciate that many of my medical school classmates were limited in their life experience with women and others of diverse minority, cultural, and ethnic groups. Later, some shared with me that they had never attended school with nor had they ever personally known a Negro person. For many, their world—education, religious life, housing, and socialization—was separate and segregated in different respects than my life.

In contrast, knowledge of majority cultures as well as those of other minority groups had shaped my life experiences since early childhood. I did not realize how rare it was to have African Americans in this medical school, but I knew that others had come before me. Colonel Clotilde Bowen, M.D., a career Air Force psychiatrist, introduced herself to me at an American Psychiatric Association (APA) annual meeting and informed me that she was the first African American to graduate from The Ohio State University College of Medicine and that I was the second, twenty years later. The college was founded in 1870.

There was so much to learn: the sciences and the complexity of disease processes, the scientific and medical terminology, medicine's hierarchy (interns lower than residents; medical students the lowest of all), the cultural dimensions of the patients and my fellow classmates, and how I fit into this complex schema. Early on, I noticed that things that were funny to me did not strike the same humorous note with my classmates. I truly missed my college friends, with whom I was so in tune that we could just give a look and understand each other without any verbal explanation. Humor can be an adaptive response to manage anxiety situations, but I also observed another side of "humor," not funny but hurtful and demeaning, that was often shared in the closed group between physicians and students. Their jokes were often at the expense of illiterate and economically disadvantaged patients regarding their particular cultural practices. I reflected on my position as having a foot in both worlds but without much power in either. There were many valuable lessons learned in those days about how to manage myself within the differential power setting of being an "only one" in a group: the only woman, the only African American. At that time, the women's liberation movement was gaining momentum, but there was little in the literature about negotiating these challenges. Now, a rich body of scientific work written by women is available regarding the dynamics of working in predominantly male groups (Gilligan 1982/2003; Roeske 1973; Spurlock 1995).

Several life experiences stand out as important in focusing my interests in psychiatry and in learning more about human behavior and personality development. As a medical student, I worked with a patient on the consultation-liaison psychiatry service who had attempted suicide by handgun and sustained injuries that left her unable to pursue her vocation. Severely depressed and hopeless about the future, she faced a life of blindness following her suicide attempt. The therapeutic challenge was to build a bridge of hope for the future. Following this work, my supervisor strongly urged that I consider a career in psychiatry. This encouragement was the beginning of my interest in psychiatry. In another example of a motivating factor, a young woman whom I knew well in childhood developed a serious mental illness and used a handgun to kill her teenaged stepchild. She was committed to a mental hospital and died at a relatively young age in the institution. These experiences inspired me to gain more understanding of psychiatric illnesses and their treatments.

Training, Marriage, and Family

Socially, medical school offered me little time for dating, but fortunately a Fisk classmate and I continued our friendship from college. During medical school we married, but our marital life was soon interrupted when he was drafted into the Army. Over the next year, he moved to different bases until he reached officer training school. In those early years there was always a lack of synchrony to our professional training schedules. As I completed my internship in Ohio he was assigned to an Army research laboratory in Massachusetts, and I joined him there. Finally we had an opportunity to live in one place together for longer than a few months, and I was successful in obtaining a psychiatric residency position at Boston University.

My husband and I began our first full year of living together in Boston: he as an officer in a research military installation and I as a resident in psychiatry. It was an interesting time of transition. When we arrived in Boston, the community was a hotbed of anger, violence, and tumultuous upheaval punctuated with street demonstrations aimed against court-ordered busing to desegregate public schools. In a personal communication with a professional colleague active in Boston, she recalled that many leaders in the mental health community were silent regarding any potential effects on the mental health of children and families and/or any impact of the violence and threats of violence present within the town and the schools. The town of Boston was split on the issue of busing, and this crisis affected everyone, including patients.

I settled into my residency. On the hospital inpatient wards, I learned that word of my pending arrival had preceded me. The paraprofessional staff soon noted their disappointment that I did not arrive with a large Afro hairstyle and ready to challenge the hospital unit management. My arrival occurred during a period in psychiatry in which there was strong advocacy for shared decision-making and responsibility regarding patient care (Caplan 1969). I was accustomed to the medical model in which the doctor was in charge; this was a another transition for me. The new model did not seem to hold as strongly when unit crises occurred; at these times, the doctor was called to take charge. During these training years, I learned a tremendous amount about dynamic psychiatry, transference, and countertransference, and I observed the impact of staff feelings on the therapeutic milieu and the treatment of patients.

In that first year, my psychiatric inpatient caseload included many seriously and persistently mentally ill persons; some of these inpatient relationships continued throughout my entire adult psychiatric training. Another challenging factor surfaced with my first pregnancy. As is common for young women early in their careers, I worried about the timeliness of this decision, managing a new baby, a new full-time residency, and helping to financially and emotionally support my husband, who was beginning his first year in dental school. While I anticipated that patients might have difficulty with change, I spent less time considering staff's concerns. Yet it was from the staff group that I heard the most grumbling. One staff member anticipated resultant problems with my health and suggested that I would become incapacitated and depart the unit suddenly, leaving behind an unmanageable patient group. Significantly, while some patients experienced ambivalence about my pregnancy when they considered their own separation from or loss of their children (often due to their mental illnesses), most, even those with psychotic illnesses, demonstrated appropriate responses. My supervisors were very supportive and advised, "Go have your baby and enjoy yourself." Although all of my adult training was overseen by men, these supervisors had a supportive perspective on the importance of balancing career and family life. And today, the young women I meet as they are completing their residency training still express the universal concerns about starting a family and its the impact on their career progression, just as did I and my peers. I offer the same advice that I was given: Go and enjoy your pregnancy and your baby. This is an important developmental stage for women, one that should not be diminished because of career advancement worries.

Once my husband completed his military service obligation, he began a long period of training in dentistry, public health, and oral surgery. Looking back, one of the most important factors for our successful management of this period was that we maintained our sense of humor even when our plans went awry, which was often. Our children, our extended families,

and my husband and I enjoyed good health, which allowed allowed flexibility regarding any unforeseen changes. Serious illnesses for any of us, including our parents, would have made our lives much more difficult,
especially considering our seventy-mile roundtrip travel to work each day.
We used the travel time to teach our young daughter her multiplication ta-
bles, nursery rhymes, and family stories. Even with our complicated schedules, there was a bonding time for family.

Mentorship From Many

My mentors are numerous and include women and men from all ethnic,
cultural, and racial groups and backgrounds from across the spectrum of
the medical profession, not limited to psychiatry. When I met Department
Chair Dr. Julius Richmond in my interview for a residency position in the
child psychiatry program at Judge Baker Guidance Center/Children's
Hospital Boston, I was "great with child." Dr. Richmond became my mentor and led by example, as his life exemplified a commitment of service to
children and families and to improving community-based health care. Although not a psychiatrist, he had already served as a medical school dean
in Syracuse and as the first national director of the Head Start program.
"Julie," as he was affectionately known (although I never could make myself call him that in person), encouraged my involvement in organized
American psychiatry. Within months of my arrival in the child psychiatry
residency, he informed me that he had written a letter of support for me to
become a Falk fellow. This fellowship program was the predecessor of the
American Psychiatric Association (APA) leadership programs for residents. Dr. Richmond quickly added that he did not know whether I would
get it, but he wanted me to look out for a possible invitation. I did not realize it then, but there were few occasions when his recommendations did
not achieve their purpose. Dr. Richmond and I maintained a friendship for
more than thirty years, and when I became the first African American and
the first woman to be speaker of the Assembly of the APA, I invited him
and he came to Washington, D.C., to address the assembly. By that time,
he had already served as the assistant secretary of health and as Surgeon
General of the United States. During the late 1990s, American medicine
was engaged in bitter struggles with managed care and was attempting to
negotiate the various definitions of what represented quality medical care.
In his address to the APA Assembly, Dr. Richmond implored the assembly
to keep the interests of patients first regardless of the surfacing economic
challenges of managed care and other cost-containing measures that might
follow.

Another mentor, Dr. Carol Nadelson, whom I met when I began my fellowship in child psychiatry, took an active interest in my career and in me personally. She became the first woman president of the APA and encouraged my involvement in committees within the Massachusetts Psychiatric Society and the Harvard Medical School. As others may agree regarding volunteer work in organized medical groups, some committees are considered "plums" and participation is highly competitive, while others are less valued. Nevertheless, committee involvement offers opportunities to engage in focused work with professional colleagues, to learn new material, and to develop close personal and professional relationships. I was thrilled to be involved in these professional activities.

Boston is an extraordinary place of academic excellence and the home to many world-renowned universities, hospitals, and leaders in psychiatric medicine such as Drs. Bernard Bandler, Evoleen Rexford, James Carter, and Bill Malamud, whom I met during my Boston University training program. And I discovered that there was a core group of African American clinical and academic scholars in the greater Boston area that included Drs. Chester Pierce, Francis Bonner, Charles Pinderhughes, Alvin Poussaint, Anne Bell, Dorthea Simmons, Irving Allen, and Orlando Lightfoot Jr. In the 1970s, they inaugurated the Black Psychiatrists' Forum of Greater Boston, which monitored many African American psychiatric residents who trained in the local community. Our discussions were wide-ranging and included clinical case studies, the local impact of sociopolitical forces of busing, the special challenges of African Americans training in majority medical institutions, and the changing roles of minority leadership in the emerging community mental health centers in the United States (Jones et al. 1970). Deriving its roots from the national organization of the Black Psychiatrists of America, the forum focused on improving the mental health of black Americans and others living in poverty. As a young resident, I appreciated the richness of their contributions to psychiatric education in general and their influences on my early knowledge of the profession. For example, Chester Pierce (1970), coining the term *microaggressions,* gave content and context to the psychological understanding of the behavioral dynamics in power relationships.

Within the APA, the Falk fellowship, funded by the Falk foundation, offered opportunities to develop personal mentorship with the national leaders in psychiatry and to participate with them in important work projects. Also, I learned about the competitive nature of the group, of which most were men. Some mentored me and were generous in sharing their expertise, insights, and knowledge about organizational politics and power dynamics, which were transferable to my work with other medical groups.

Training for Leadership

My first position in the APA Assembly was as deputy minority representative for the Caucus of Black Psychiatrists. The caucus idea was an excellent concept to build training venues for potential leaders in the field who were outside of the mainstream of organized psychiatry. Since its inception, the APA Assembly, viewed by many as the representative governance body of the membership, consisted predominantly of white men. In the late 1960s and 1970s, there were calls from the members that the assembly become more representative of the entire membership. The caucus process established increased representation from subspecialty organizations as well as minority/underrepresented groups. Nevertheless, change rarely occurs in a vacuum or without consequences. Some members of the Assembly openly expressed disgruntlement and doubts regarding the worthiness of these new groups of women and other underrepresented groups to be included in the assembly's governance structure. A few psychiatrists noted their own hard struggles to achieve positions within the Assembly in contrast to these "new" groups of members who, in their view, seemingly skipped the bottom rungs on the ladder to leadership. Years later, some publicly acknowledged their appreciation of the many contributions that these new groups made in the work of the association.

As I worked more closely with the APA, I met another person who would play an important role in my life, Dr. Jeanne Spurlock, the Deputy Medical Director of the American Psychiatric Association's Office of Minority/National Affairs. She was feisty and outspoken about psychiatric concerns and other critical national issues facing women, children, and other minority and underrepresented groups. I was in awe of her commanding presence and stature as she eloquently eloquently advocated for these patient populations and the profession. Modeling other women coauthors, I asked and Jeanne agreed to co-author several papers about African American children. Over the years, we developed a close friendship, shared a room together at psychiatric meetings and talked late into the night about psychiatric concerns affecting the profession. I often wished that I had tape-recorded our communications. Our last work focused on her book *Black Psychiatrists and American Psychiatry* (Spurlock 1999). Although I was aware that she was editing a book about the history of black psychiatrists in American psychiatry, we had not discussed her vision for the final work. One afternoon as we sat down to dinner in her home, I noticed that Jeanne was distracted and seemed very concerned about completing this book task. I had no experience writing books, but I volunteered to help and she accepted. Later that evening I began to work on my portion of the manuscript; I had no idea that this would be our final collaboration. Other colleagues who were fortunate to have shared a personal relationship with Jeanne Spurlock understand that she quickly became a confidant and a member of one's family. She developed a friendship with my children and knew them well enough that my daughter lived with "Aunt Jeanne" for six weeks during her summer job placement in Washington, D.C. The collegial and personal nature of the relationships we shared, fostered through APA committee activities, provided another valued dimension to my work in psychiatry. I continue to miss the lively discussions and debates with Jeanne.

When I began child psychiatry training, a supervisor suggested that I develop an area of clinical expertise. Since my academic placement utilized the juvenile courts and it appeared from my limited experience that there were significant numbers of minorities in the system as offenders, but few among the professional groups, it seemed important to consider this work setting as an opportunity. Dr. Tom Gutheil, another important mentor, encouraged me to join his forensic study group and the parent group, the American Academy of Psychiatry and the Law. This began an active collaboration with him and other colleagues engaged in clinical and research work in forensic psychiatry.

While my husband was a full-time dental student, I was the primary financial support of the family. As such, I combined teaching residents and treating children and families in an academic center with work in court settings and other areas in public psychiatry, and maintained a small private practice.

Recognizing the growing interest within African American communities in access to professional expertise regarding psychiatric care, there were more requests for presentations than I could fulfill. This allowed me to share these additional opportunities with my colleagues, who were well aware of the shortage of psychiatrists, and particularly of African American psychiatrists. I sought to optimize my effectiveness as a professional by gaining experience in many areas, including teaching, consultation, group work, and forensic psychiatry. In addition, I continued my volunteer work with professional and community-based organizations, which ultimately led to additional and unexpected leadership opportunities.

In my first campaign for district branch office within the Massachusetts Psychiatric Society, I lost by a small margin. Prior to this election, I was informed that campaigning was not permitted; however, since my opponent had done so, I was offered the position of chair of the Legislative Committee. As a new chair with little experience but major responsibilities, I sought out and encouraged society members to join me on the committee. Our work led to the society's first successful state legislation, which clarified the circumstances under which psychiatrists may legally breach patient confidentiality, and led to further opportunities for leadership advancement. With these achievements, leaders in the state legislature with whom I had worked nominated me for various gubernatorial appointments, including appointments to the Board of Registration in Medicine and other boards. These were not positions that I sought or even knew were possible, but were the result of my advocacy and demonstrated ability to work collegially with other health professionals and members of the state legislature. Attaining such a positive outcome of legislation as we did was a major achievement for the society and demonstrated to some member critics that it could be worthwhile to work with our state legislators on initiatives that benefit patient care.

Sometimes mentors chose to work with me, and at other times I sought them. I asked Dr. Charles Pinderhughes to be my supervisor because he demonstrated a keen intelligence and articulated an understanding of the world within his framework of psychoanalysis. Long after the completion of my training, we had a conversation in a New Orleans airport while waiting for a plane to Boston. He had been successful in APA politics and was the first African American elected to the APA Board of Trustees. As we discussed my active involvement in the APA, he encouraged me to pursue the challenges to maximize my involvement in the organization. Recalling an earlier talk with Dr. Nancy Roeske, a leader in the first APA Women's Caucus, Pinderhughes noted her discussion with him about her own political ambitions. He reported that Dr. Roeske, a leader in psychiatric education and a spokesperson on issues affecting women patients and women psychiatrists, had decided to delay running for higher APA office until a later time in her career. However, he stated that she never had that opportunity again because of serious health concerns. Dr. Pinderhughes strongly urged that I accept opportunities when they presented themselves, because the future was not guaranteed. Keeping this advice in mind, and with the encouragement of my many psychiatric colleagues, I again sought and achieved elective offices over the years, as an Area I trustee on the APA Board of Trustees and as APA secretary-treasurer.

In the latter role, I served as chair of the task force that vetted participants who would work on DSM-5. The APA Board of Trustees demanded the most rigorous disclosure of interests and affiliations for this DSM-5 group that were ever required by the association, and by doing so the board placed the APA's actions significantly ahead in the field of psychiatry and many other areas of medicine. The disclosure rules placed strict limitations regarding acceptable reimbursement for work as directors, advisory board members, or speaker's bureau members, and/or being stockholders of pharmaceutical companies or companies that make medical devices. I completed this work and my term as secretary-treasurer and ran for APA president-elect. I lost this election, but was encouraged by colleagues throughout the country to run a second time. Some supporters related my subsequent loss of that election in part to my earlier role as chair of the Task Force to Review Disclosures and Interests of DSM-5 Nominees. In retrospect, I believe that APA members would have benefited from more information about this new vetting process prior to its initiation.

The APA was out in front of many medical organizations on these concerns. Subsequently, many academic centers, the U.S. Congress and federal institutions, and journal editorial boards investigated conflicts of interest among medical and scientific faculties and responded with the institution of new and more stringent rules. These changes have had a profound influence on the field of medicine and have engendered revisions in the relationships between academic institutions throughout the United States and the industry. Such policies were established to regain the public trust that suffered erosion by the revelations of questionable practices such as withholding all study results (positive and negative), ghostwriting, and significant financial and other types of reimbursement to physicians and other interested parties that, whether intentional or not, raised questions of conflicting allegiances (Colen 2010; Freedman et al. 2006; Massachusetts Medical Society Committee on Publications 2011).

My campaigns for the national office of president-elect of the APA were exciting and at the same time quite daunting experiences. I enjoyed meeting APA members from across the country and engaging them in discussion regarding their hopes for improving the profession, enhancing the scientific knowledge base, and improving patient care as well as addressing concerns of the profession. Several aspects of the elections process were troubling and relate to the enormous time needed to mount a campaign, the persistence of campaign irregularities, and violations with little redress. Some APA members believe that the election guidelines have no teeth and that the Elections Committee has little power to enforce the rules, since the campaign is run as a polite agreement between candidates without real sanctions. In retrospect, one of my major concerns is that as the United States moved toward greater comprehensive health care system reform, the vast majority of APA members were not engaged in our elections process through which they could communicate with leadership.

Within the APA, my leadership opportunities have included service on more than thirty components and as chair of the APA Membership Committee, vice chair of the Joint Commission on Government Relations, and secretary of American Psychiatric Publishing, and I am currently a member of the Executive Committee of the newly created American Psychiatric Foundation Board of Directors and the chairperson of the Massachusetts Ethics Committee.

My involvement in organized medicine encompasses work within my subspecialty interest of child and forensic psychiatry and with state medical organizations. In April 2010, I completed my term as president of the Norfolk District Medical Society, a division of the Massachusetts Medical Society with more than 3,500 members. I have been a member of the Massachusetts delegation to the American Medical Association, and at the time of this writing I serve as a member of the Massachusetts House of Delegates, the Massachusetts Medical Society's Finance Committee, and the society's Committee on Professional Liability.

Within the Massachusetts medical, educational, and community arenas, my opportunities to serve have included gubernatorial appointments to the Children's Trust Fund, the Board of Registration in Medicine, and the Board of Trustees of the University of Massachusetts–Lowell. During the sexual abuse scandal involving the Catholic clergy in Massachusetts, I served as a member of the Cardinal's Commission for the Protection of Children, which was charged with recommending policy revisions and planning for the implementation of educational programs for the protection of children. Currently, I am Chairperson of the Board of Trustees of Regis College in Weston, Massachusetts, and a director of a medical liability insurance company.

The Totality of Life

My husband and I have two children. In their infancy, our primary concerns were that we have excellent child care at whatever cost and that our children have basic math and reading skills prior to entering public schools. My husband and I are products of public education and believe in this system. We live in a community now more diverse than when we moved here. The most important stabilizing factors were that our children were healthy and that we had a strong and supportive family network, which included my mother who would travel from Ohio to assist us when needed. She also accompanied me to several APA meetings with my daughter. Following their retirement, my parents moved to Massachusetts and were very supportive, which permitted me the flexibility to engage in many professional activities without compromising our family life. We lived in close proximity for over twenty-seven years.

My personal life and professional career activities are interwoven and demanding, and periodically some aspect requires my complete attention. This was particularly true when my parents' health began to fail and they both died within the same year. Although I had written about separation and loss and had assisted my patients in managing this process, it was very difficult for me as my parents aged with failing health. Significantly, these family crises were managed with the support of other family members, friends, and professional colleagues who offered personal insights regarding the particular coping mechanisms used in addressing these challenges. We are a close family and frequently spend time traveling on vacations together. Some may think that our lives appear charmed, but there continue to be significant sacrifices. Our daughter is an emergency medicine physician and is completing her work on an executive master of business administration (MBA) degree. Our son has an MBA and a master's degree in finance and works in business. As my husband solidified his academic career in dental education as an oral and maxillofacial surgeon, he moved into administration leadership. He is now retired after serving sixteen years as Dean of Tufts University School of Dental Medicine.

In addition to my professional and leadership activities, I have a role as the spouse of the dean. This has permitted us to develop friendships with a very generous alumnae group, to meet national and international leaders in education, in government, and in entertainment and sports, and to travel throughout the world. Priorities for my husband and me include being supportive of each other in our careers and our family, which now includes our daughter-in-law who is pursuing her interest in medicine. These shared opportunities have broadened our views of the world and enriched our life experiences. Growing up in communities with limited access to health care and upward mobility for African Americans, we value the benefits of education for all and understand the personal sacrifices needed to succeed. With these ideas in mind, we endowed a prize fund at the dental school to recognize a senior dental student who has excelled academically and has consistently displayed professionalism and strength of character while managing and balancing challenging personal responsibilities. Expressing our commitment to diversity, an endowment was established to support the Tufts Chapter of the Student National Dental Association.

Developing a Leadership Style

In May 2010, the APA's Committee of Black Psychiatrists honored me as the Solomon Carter Fuller Award recipient, which required a lecture presentation at the APA annual meeting. In preparation for this lecture, I interviewed leading African American and white American psychiatrists regarding their perspectives on racism in American psychiatry and the sociopolitical changes that have occurred occurred before and since the life of the first African American psychiatrist, Dr. Solomon Carter Fuller (Norris 2010). One member of this distinguished group noted that although there has been great progress in this country, "race is one of the most important issues…facing the world as we enter the twenty-first century" (A. Stone, 2010).

With respect to African Americans and leadership, the historical fact of slavery adds additional complexities to how our voices are heard and understood (DuBois 1903; White 1985). These experiences are unique and should be understood in the context of an important history that is a powerful reminder of the realities of life for African American women in American society. This chapter started with the lyrics of a song and a review of the importance of having a wonderful extended family who enabled me to seize the opportunities presented, to accept and manage the challenges that might seem beyond my grasp, and to understand that the world, while not always fair, can be a place of excitement and learning and holds a treasure of life experiences.

When I began my career, I had no idea what my potential would be. As opportunities presented, I tried to maximize them and to not become discouraged when the outcome was not exactly as I had planned. With each new experience, I always gained personally regardless of the outcome. I never wanted to look back and regret that I had limited myself by my fear of the unknown. Success requires the courage to take risks. I believe that medicine is a wonderful profession, one that requires very hard work but presents unique opportunities to serve others for a lifetime in so many different ways.

Practical Tips for Women in Psychiatry

- Leaders are not preordained. Most leaders must develop their skills to lead effectively. Leadership is earned through the respect of others and a strong work ethic, and is gained with appropriate performance and vision. Listen to and value each person's contribution and recognize that tasks, even if they appear menial, may be opportunities to gain important expertise and may represent a foundation for future work.

- Look for guiding principles that keep the group moving forward and deter stagnation.

- Seek to build consensus and, when possible, demonstrate growth of all members of the group. Be aware that all group members may not be uniformly supportive of the mission, but work toward consensus.

- Leadership is not always "safe." If you are afraid to take risks or to face failure, then you will fail to be a strong leader and will hold back on your full commitment to the tasks. Make every experience you choose to accept work for you.

- Learn to communicate effectively to enhance the potential for positive results. Create an atmosphere of welcome.

- Consider group dynamics and alliances. Some women have observed that (perhaps because of their softer voices) they may not be heard or paid attention to by the men in a group. Or when leading a meeting, they have noticed a man in the meeting reiterating the same talking points in a later discussion and being credited for their ideas. Other women express reluctance to rehash old material or to keep attention centered on points that do not seem to move the discussion forward— a common challenge for women and other group members who do not have readily identified allies in the group. It may be helpful to review the group dynamics with a trusted colleague to accurately assess one's own role in the group. Otherwise, one may find that self-evaluation of the process is inaccurate.

- Recognize that humor can be a key tool with which to enhance communication, and is especially useful to deflect interpersonal strain between individual members.

- Maintain honest and ethical dealings with others and seek to include individuals who are positive, who are hard-working, and who share the group's values.

- Develop your mentoring skills. Share your experiences and encourage others to excel and to dare to become leaders. Their successes will reflect positively on themselves and on your mentorship.

References

Caplan RB: Psychiatry and Community in Nineteenth Century America: The Recurring Concern With Environment in the Prevention and Treatment of Mental Disorder. New York, Basic Books, 1969

Colen BD: University adopts faculty financial conflict of interest policies. July 21, 2010. Available at: http://news.harvard.edu/gazette/story/2010/07/university-adopts-faculty-financial-conflict-of-interest-policies. Accessed September 13, 2011.

David M (lyricist), Ellington D (composer): I'm Just a Lucky So-and-So. 1945.

Dickstein LJ, Nadelson CC (eds): Women Physicians in Leadership Roles. Washington, DC, American Psychiatric Press, 1986

DuBois WEB: The Souls of Black Folk: Essays and Sketches. Chicago, IL, AC McClurg, 1903

Freedman R, Lewis DA, Michels R, et al: Conflict of interest, round 2. Am J Psychiatry 163:1481–1483, 2006

Gilligan C: In a Different Voice: Psychological Theory and Women's Development. Harvard University Press, Cambridge, MA, 1982 (first edition)/2003 (most recent edition)

Griffith EE, Young JL, Smith DL: An analysis of the therapeutic elements in a black church service. Hosp Community Psychiatry 35:464–469, 1984

Jones BE, Lightfoot OB, Palmer D, et al: Problems of black psychiatric residents in white training institutes. Am J Psychiatry 127:798–803, 1970

Kirkpatrick M: The feminization of psychiatry?: some ruminations. J Am Acad Psychoanal Dyn Psychiatry 32: 201–212, 2004

Massachusetts Medical Society Committee on Publications: Conflict of interest policy. Journal Watch (n.d. [no date given]). Available at: www.jwatch.org/misc/conflict.dtl. Accessed September 12, 2011.

Norris DM: Solomon Carter Fuller: what would he say about racial politics in American psychiatry today? Lecture presented at the annual meeting of the American Psychiatric Association, New Orleans, LA, May 2010

Pierce CM: Offensive mechanisms: the vehicle for microaggression, in The Black Seventies. Edited by Barbour FB. Boston, MA, Porter Sargent, 1970, pp 265–282

Roeske N: Women in psychiatry: past and present areas of concern. Am J Psychiatry 130:1127–1131, 1973

Spurlock J: Multiple roles of women and role strain. Health Care Women Int 16:501–508, 1995

Spurlock J (ed): Black Psychiatrists and American Psychiatry. Washington, DC, American Psychiatric Association, 1999

US Department of Health and Human Services: Women in Science at the National Institutes of Health, 2007–2008. Bethesda, MD, Office of Research on Women's Health, National Institutes of Health, 2009. Available at: http://orwh.od.nih.gov/pubs/pubs_list.html#wis. Accessed September 23, 2011.

White DG: Ar'n't I a Woman?: Female Slaves in the Plantation South. New York, WW Norton, 1985

Chapter 15

Army Psychiatrist

Elspeth Cameron Ritchie, M.D., M.P.H.

I HAVE NOW BEEN AN ARMY PSYCHIATRIST for twenty-four years, and a colonel for the last six. However, I never expected to have a career as a soldier.

Growing up in Washington, D.C., I joined the protests against the Vietnam War and tried to levitate the Pentagon. When I was an undergraduate at Harvard University, I double majored in biology and folklore and mythology, but was not going to be a doctor. I was going to be an anthropologist or a botanist. I took a semester off to join my father in Malaysia, where he was working to develop the country in a sustainable way, and studied different patterns of gardening among Malays, Chinese, and Indians. When I returned to Harvard, I wrote my thesis on the use of medicinal plants by shamans, focusing on hallucinogenic ones. Many of our psychiatric medications are derived from or related to botanicals. In retrospect, this was a perfect lead-in to being an Army psychiatrist, traveling to Korea, Somalia, Cuba, and Iraq, as well as tending my gardens.

I applied to graduate school to pursue a degree in anthropology. Life shapes plans. My father, who had worked in economic development all of my life, was laid off during my sophomore year at Harvard and was without a job for several years. I contemplated life after college as an anthropologist or botanist, but going to graduate school would cost money we did not have.

So I worked for two years, first for a television program producer who went bankrupt, then researching books about the human body for *U.S. News and World Report.* I realized you don't make much money being a writer, especially an unpublished one. So, I applied to medical school, having fortunately taken all the required premed courses, although not with very good grades in calculus or inorganic chemistry. (Botany and folklore were all A's.)

Medical School: My Path to the Army

After acceptance to the two most expensive medical schools in the country, George Washington University School of Medicine and Health Sciences and Georgetown University School of Medicine (I applied to those schools because I had grown up in D.C.), I moved back to Cambridge to earn money, washing dishes at Casablanca restaurant in Harvard Square and running pigeon experiments in the B.F. Skinner laboratory at Harvard University. When the pigeons escaped, I chased them around William James Hall with a net.

The federal so-called HEAL loans (Health Education Assistance Loans) had an exorbitant level of interest. I applied to the Army and Air Force for scholarships. The Air Force lost some of my medical records—my Pap smear—and the scholarship from the Army came through first. So I raised my right hand up to be a soldier and went to medical school at George Washington University.

Medical school at George Washington was far less exciting than college. Too much memorization; how many muscles and which ones make the thumb move? My fellow students were anxious about their loans. I was very glad I had the Army scholarship, but thought I would only serve the four years owed after residency, then be out.

Like so many others who go into psychiatry I vacillated in medical school: internal medicine, neurology, infectious diseases, surgery, or psychiatry? I really liked surgery, the concrete actions of taking out sutures, and quickly curing a problem. But what we read in psychiatry was so much more interesting than reading about antibiotics for the variety of infectious diseases. And I got headaches looking through a microscope.

A psychiatry internship and residency followed at Walter Reed Army Medical Center. I had made the right choice; I loved it. Walter Reed had a great faculty, fascinating patients, and solid fellow residents.

Division Psychiatrist and Beyond

I shipped out for my first years of Army obligation, initially as the division psychiatrist at the Second Infantry Division (2ID) next to the demilitarized zone (DMZ) in Korea. Camp Casey was practically on the DMZ, and full of testosterone, both from the threat from North Korea and from having thousands of men in a foreign land. I played down being a Yankee and an Ivy League grad, and learned to "hang" on the division runs. As the first female 2ID psychiatrist, I lived in a glass bowl.

Saddam Hussein invaded Kuwait four days after I arrived. Promptly the eyes of the world turned to Iraq. This provided a perfect time for North Korea to invade South Korea. We called ourselves *speed bumps* and the soldiers back in Seoul *REMFs* (*rear-echelon motherf*****s*). We were "stop-lossed" so no one could leave, and soldiers doubled up in their barracks. Soldiers fretted, worrying that they were losing all the glory of actual combat.

Demands for my services were high, as soldiers were bored and worried about their marriages back home. I used to say, "If I sent everyone home who was worried about their wives leaving them, we would not have a division here."

After a year, it was back to the inpatient psychiatry ward at Walter Reed. After another year, I volunteered to join Operation Restore Hope in Somalia. We went over in the first week of the humanitarian assistance mission, which turned very quickly into low-grade but dangerous combat. I was in a combat stress unit, driving around the country to do assessments and provide therapy; bringing Prozac, Haldol, and Benadryl in little ziplock bags.

A young female aid worker was ambushed. Four service members were blown up. A Marine shot himself in the stadium. The demand for my services increased. But the United States turned the mission over to the United Nations, and we left. A few hours after that, the infamous Black Hawk Down incident happened.

After another year on the inpatient psychiatry ward, I next had a forensic psychiatry fellowship at Walter Reed, when that program was just beginning. We worked in a criminal psychiatry hospital in Maryland, at the Behavioral Science Unit at the Federal Bureau of Investigation, and learned about courts-martial expert testimony. Then came another utilization tour, this time at the 121st Hospital in Seoul (as a REMF); and then back again to running the inpatient psychiatry ward at Walter Reed.

The Army is incredibly varied: giving therapy in a snow-covered tent in the mountains of Korea; or in the back of a pick-up truck in Mogadishu; or interviewing a recently returned prisoner of war in Seoul. My urges to leave the Army then and now were all centered on my children: my daughter Jessie, now thirteen years old, and my son Lyell, now eleven. Bottom line: the Army kept offering me more interesting opportunities every time I thought about leaving.

9/11 and the Long War

My life was tremendously changed by the terrorist attacks of 9/11, as has been true for many of us. On September 10, 2001, I was in the Pentagon all day. The morning of 9/11, I was at the Navy's Bureau of Medicine and Surgery, in a meeting about optimal facilities for breast-feeding. The phone calls came in about the attacks in New York. We went outside to get better reception for our cell phones. There I watched across the Potomac River the plume of smoke rise right after the plane hit the Pentagon.

I have ever since regretted my next decision. I was in a skirt and heels. I thought that I should go back home and change into BDUs (battle dress uniform) so I could help carry stretchers into Walter Reed. However, almost no casualties ended up at Walter Reed. The good part was that we developed the plan to provide mental health care to the Pentagon personnel. This eventually morphed into a very active program to provide outreach and education, known as Operation Solace. (However, I have avoided skirts and heels since then and love to wear combat boots.)

I was lucky. When my children were small, after four more years at Walter Reed, I negotiated a four-year stint at the Department of Defense Office of the Assistant Secretary of Defense/Health Affairs working on mental health policy and women's health issues. After that, I was offered the then-new disaster psychiatry fellowship at the Uniformed Services University of the Health Sciences, where I earned a master of public health degree. I have found this to be an incredibly useful degree in my present job, which involves applying lessons learned from research to policy.

I was then selected to be the psychiatry consultant to the Army surgeon general, a position that involves doing assignments and deciding policy on psychiatric issues. I was the first female selected for that job.

What I did not do, because of my husband and children, was to accept positions that would require relocating to other forts around the country. I managed to juggle marriage, motherhood, and the increasing responsibilities of my positions, partly by staying in the D.C. area. However, I knew that in order to make the rank of general officer, one would have to be willing to move. So I forewent the fast track (I thought) and concentrated on being a good psychiatrist, writing, and teaching.

After four years at the Department of Defense Health Affairs and the two-year fellowship in disaster psychiatry at the Uniformed Services University of the Health Sciences, I have now been at the U.S. Army Office of the Surgeon General, in northern Virginia, for five years, working on mental health policy for soldiers and families. My current job title is Director of the Behavioral Health Proponency, which essentially means handling all mental health policy for the Army.

The Dark Side

We have now been at war for ten years. It has been a tremendously interesting and difficult period, with the wars in Iraq and Afghanistan. The Walter Reed scandal in 2007 over care for wounded warriors and similar media outrage over the care of veterans have also shaped my work.

Actually, many scandals have been a major influence. The question of suicidal gestures among detainees is one. I went down to Guantanamo Bay, Cuba, in 2002, when the Maryland sniper was wreaking havoc in the neighborhoods near my home in Silver Spring. There in Cuba I reviewed all the suicidal gestures among the detainees and recommended many basic changes, including promoting more privileges for those who did not throw feces at the guards.

The question of abuse of detainees led us to develop the behavioral science consultation policies. Although controversial in the American Psychiatric Association and the media, I continue to believe that psychologists and forensic psychiatrists can contribute in a very positive way to legal, safe, and effective interrogation.

I later reviewed the care of both soldiers and detainees in Iraq in 2004. Providers there were hampered by a lack of resources to do a good job in caring for either soldiers or detainees. Both improved, partly because of our yearly assessments by the Mental Health Advisory Teams (MHATs). I have been involved directly or indirectly with all the MHAT teams between 2003 and 2009. In 2007 we also flew to the combat theater and did an assessment of the increasing number of suicides there, and recommended multiple improvements. (I take partial credit for the relative decrease in suicides in the military theater.)

The number of suicides in the Army overall has continued to rise. We held conferences and beat the drums on recommendations to decrease suicides. It is not an easy task, and there are no easy solutions. The Army Suicide Prevention Task Force in March 2009 developed over 160 recommendations. Fortunately, they had the authority of the vice chief of staff of the Army behind them, which ensured their implementation, and suicides finally seem to be declining.

Another scandal was over accusations that the Army was discharging soldiers for having been diagnosed with personality disorders but who, in actuality, had posttraumatic stress disorder (PTSD) or a traumatic brain injury (TBI). We revised our procedures to ensure that all these recommendations were carefully reviewed. I have now been responsible for a variety of policies to ensure that soldiers are screened for PTSD and TBI prior to discharge from the Army.

Back in 2007, I was an Army of one doing mental health work, and the Medical Command chief of staff asked, "What would happen if Col. Ritchie was hit by a bus?" Since then, numerous other organizations have been formed to tackle the problems of PTSD and suicide in the Army. They include the Defense Centers of Excellence, Comprehensive Soldier Fitness, and various campaign plans. This is both good and bad. There are so many general officers with bright ideas (GOBIs) that it takes all of our energies to keep up with new initiatives. Nonetheless, access to care has dramatically improved; quality of care has improved, and we do excessive screening for PTSD and TBIs. However, while we talk about decreasing stigma, I believe that we still have too many policies that add to the reluctance of soldiers to seek help. I call these my "rocks" and have been dedicated to resolving them, with only partial success so far.

Despite the controversies, it has been a wonderful career, and I would not consider trading my experiences for a minute. It has involved lots of trips, including three to Iraq and four to Guantanamo Bay, Cuba, and many to various Army installations to look at issues around suicide and behavioral health.

The Fort Hood shooting in November 2009, though, was extremely difficult. To have one of your own do the mass killings, and to have every radio show talk about the Army psychiatrist shooter, has taken a real toll on not only me, but every Army psychiatrist. I found myself simultaneously responding to the shooting incident by helping to develop a Fort Hood plan to respond to a mass casualty, and being the subject of inquiry as to whether I or other Army psychiatrists should have known about the shooter's murderous tendencies.

Now we are asked to develop a simple self-report screen for violence, obviously an unattainable goal. It is similar to numerous other unrealistic requests to screen incoming recruits for the likelihood of developing PTSD in response to combat or suicide many years later. This is an ongoing issue and will not be resolved soon.

I have been fortunate in having many senior Army leaders who have taken an interest in my career. However, none were women. There are still too few senior women in the Army.

The outside world focuses on "military" sexual assault. In my experience, although sexual harassment and assault do occur, they are probably no more common than in the civilian world. The Army has really tried to discourage these behaviors.

Much more problematic for many Army women is how to juggle the demands of being a mother and a wife and being deployed. While I have managed to do this, it has not been easy. In the Army, you need to move around taking command jobs in order to be promoted. I chose not to do that, since I wanted to have a stable home life. As a result, I expect my final rank to be colonel, which is not a bad final rank.

There are few women who have taken my career path. I was the first female division psychiatrist for the 2ID, and the first female psychiatry consultant to the Army surgeon general. Nearly all of my contemporaries left the Army when they had children. Few female general officers have children.

I wonder now whether I should have chosen to go into command, since my female contemporaries who have no children have been picked up to be general officers. But I cannot and do not regret being a mother or my choice to stay centered around my family and tend my garden. I have over 130 publications, mainly in the areas of forensic psychiatry, disaster psychiatry, suicide, ethics, military combat and operational psychiatry, and women's health issues. Recent major publications include the textbook *Interventions Following Mass Violence and Disasters: Strategies for Mental Health Practice* (Ritchie et al. 2006) and *Humanitarian Assistance and Health Diplomacy: Military-Civilian Partnership in the 2004 Tsunami Aftermath*, published as a journal supplement (Ritchie 2006). My 47-chapter *Combat and Operational Behavioral Health* textbook, which I worked on for four years, was finally published in August 2011. I do need to circle back and publish on the topic of female soldiers, as not nearly enough has been written about them.

I have also published poetry over the years. Most of my poems have reflected the experiences of soldiers, and some focus on gardens. Often they are intertwined. Both involve life and death, whether from jumping off a hooch barracks in Camp Casey, facing bullets in Mogadishu, or yanking weeds. I am not a prolific poet. But I take satisfaction in knowing that many of my poems have been reprinted, often numerous times. I published a collection of my poetry, *Tearing Through the Moon,* in 2010.

What are my lessons learned to transmit to others? Obviously I have been happy in my career as an Army psychiatrist and would urge others to consider it. I do not think it is easy, however, to balance being a wife, mother, soldier, and psychiatrist. Nevertheless, I have done it—and I also keep offering peas and lettuce from my garden.

References

Ritchie EC: Humanitarian assistance and health diplomacy: military-civilian partnership in the 2004 tsunami aftermath. Mil Med 171(suppl 10), Feb 2006

Ritchie EC: Tearing Through the Moon: Poetry and Prose of an Army Psychiatrist. Washington, DC, Wineberry Press, 2010

Ritchie EC (ed): Combat and Operational Behavioral Health: Textbook of Military Medicine. Washington, DC, Office of the Surgeon General, U.S. Department of the Army and Borden Institute, 2011

Ritchie EC, Hoge CW (eds): The mental health response to the 9/11 attack on the Pentagon. Mil Med 167(suppl 9), Sept 2002

Ritchie EC, Friedman MJ, Watson PJ (eds): Interventions Following Mass Violence and Disasters: Strategies for Mental Health Practice. New York, Guilford, 2006

Chapter 16

A *Serendipitous Career*

From Cowboy to Out Lesbian Faculty Psychiatrist

Ellen Haller, M.D.

ON JUNE 30, 1988, I graduated from the University of California, San Francisco (UCSF) psychiatry residency program. The very next day, I began a full-time faculty position working on the same inpatient unit where I'd just completed a senior resident rotation. As a brand new inpatient attending physician, I never imagined that I would transition, nine years later, to become the director of a women's mental health outpatient program followed by being named, six years later, director of the UCSF Adult Psychiatry Clinic. And I certainly would have been shocked as a newly minted assistant professor back in 1988 if told that I'd be appointed director of the General Adult Psychiatry Residency Training Program in my nineteenth year on the faculty. But that is exactly what happened.... Each of these career transitions was completely unanticipated and serendipitous, and each leadership position has had its significant challenges, immense excitements, and deeply gratifying moments.

I had come out as a lesbian during residency, and although lesbian, gay, bisexual, and transgender (LGBT) issues have not been the focus of my psychiatric career, as I've advanced to these increasingly broad and visible leadership roles, being out of the closet has turned out to be an asset to my career. When my department chair asked me to develop a women's mental health clinic, he said that he hoped it would have outreach to the lesbian community as one of its missions. In addition, my visibility as an out faculty member has demonstrated to students and residents that being out is not necessarily an obstacle to advancement. LGBT trainees have frequently met with me to discuss their professional development, and it has been a complete joy to see them thrive as their own careers have progressed.

Outside of my active and demanding professional life, I have a wonderful spouse, an M.D./Ph.D. who is also on the UCSF School of Medicine faculty but in a different department. We've been a couple for twenty-five years, and I'm thrilled that we became legally married in 2008 in California. As two very busy academicians (she runs an active basic science laboratory and is also a division chief in her department), we wondered how we could successfully balance our careers with raising a child, yet we clearly wanted to become moms. Ultimately, we decided to coparent with a gay couple in a long-term relationship whom we knew very well because one of the men had been in my residency class. On occasion they'd been asked by women to be sperm donors, but they wanted to be dads, not donors. When we approached them about possibly coparenting a child together, they were ecstatic. My spouse gave birth, and from the start all four of us have been very proud and active parents raising our now fifteen-year-old son.

The Path

So, how did all this happen? How did I end up as the director of residency training and as an out lesbian psychiatrist? A happy tomboy who loved to pretend I was living in the Wild West of the 1800s during my childhood, I also developed a passionate interest in sports as I grew older, both as a fan and as an athlete. Consequently, as a young child, I had two career goals in mind: first, to become a cowboy (a costume worn many, many years in a row for Halloween) or second, to become a sports medicine doctor. Math and science were favorite subjects in school from the beginning, and as I gradually realized that becoming a cowboy wasn't all that realistic, I settled for plan B, becoming a doctor. Sports medicine seemed like a great idea, even though I didn't truly understand exactly what that meant.

Throughout college, I knew that I was headed to medical school, but psychiatry was nowhere in the picture. Then, as a medical student, psychiatry remained out of the picture while I contemplated different careers. The sports medicine idea faded away once I realized that orthopedics was not the area I wanted to work in. I considered a number of different specialties, but ultimately I chose obstetrics and gynecology due to its combination of surgery and medicine and the opportunity for longitudinal patient relationships. With applications complete, letters of recommendation requested, and the dean's letter written, becoming an ob-gyn was my planned career path.

Then, in the beginning of my fourth year of medical school during an obstetrics subinternship at a large academic medical center, I had a sudden crisis of identity because of an incident one night while on call. My on-call schedule was every other night, and late one night a patient was admitted in the middle stages of labor. A highly educated and sophisticated woman, she'd read multiple books about labor and brought with her a very well thought-out and detailed labor plan. However, as the night unfolded, her plan collapsed. She began to develop failure to progress in her labor, and the infant began to show signs of mild fetal distress. The resident and I attempted to manage her distress while waiting for the attending physician to come in to supervise a cesarean delivery. During the wait, in the setting of intense pain coupled with utter exhaustion and severe disappointment about not having "a natural delivery," the patient began yelling repeatedly, "I don't care, I don't care…just get it the f*** out of me!" She also swore at her husband and talked about the pain not being worth it. Ultimately, she had an uncomplicated cesarean delivery and gave birth to a healthy baby.

The next morning, I was responsible for checking her vital signs, pain level, fundus level, and wound as part of my prerounds on the team's patients. When I entered her room, she looked intensely sad and did not want to talk about her baby. In the context of prerounds, I had only a few minutes to speak with her, but in that short time I could tell that she felt horribly guilty about what she had said the night before and that her guilt was affecting her bonding with her infant. I hated being so rushed but had to leave to see several other patients after just a brief conversation. Later that day, I spoke with her in more depth and noted that the very act of talking about what had happened helped relieve her feelings.

Participating in this patient's care was a transformative moment for me. On arriving home in my exhausted, postcall state at the end of the next day, I realized that I didn't want to spend just five minutes with patients when they were emotionally distressed; I didn't want to check only their vital signs, lab results, and physical findings. After that night I noticed that when on call in labor and delivery, I hoped and wished for quiet nights with very few laboring patients, and I began to realize that although I enjoyed ob-gyn thoroughly, I didn't love it. Recognizing that having such an attitude as a student was a problem, I listened to the little internal voice that began to say "maybe ob-gyn isn't the right choice after all."

Suddenly, as a fourth-year medical student, I had no clear path to follow and no clue what specialty to pursue. I stared at the table of contents in the book listing all residency programs in the United States (this was long before the Internet existed) and methodically thought about each and every specialty from anesthesia to vascular surgery. Gradually, with much family support and a course of brief psychotherapy at the student health clinic where I was doing the subinternship, what I loved about being a doctor dawned on me. It wasn't figuring out why someone had a low potassium level or where the cancer had spread or how to manage an infection or why an antihypertensive regimen wasn't working. Rather, it was that I loved having time with patients, getting to know them; hearing their concerns, conflicts, joys, and heartbreaks, and helping them emotionally cope with whatever was going on medically. "Oh," I said, "psychiatry...who knew?" After finally figuring out that psychiatry was where I belonged, I've never regretted my decision for even a nanosecond. Psychiatry is home.

Women's Mental Health

I didn't think my identity as a woman influenced my work at all, but then, in 1997, I was tasked with starting a new outpatient women's mental health clinic and needed a crash course in the subject. As I read and attended talks about postpartum depression, perimenopausal mental health issues, the relational theory of women's psychology, intimate partner violence, and the use of medications during pregnancy (to name just some of the topics), I became increasingly fascinated with the topic of women's mental health. My growing interest and expertise in women's mental health also involved learning about lesbian mental health. Despite being a lesbian, I hadn't previously read about lesbian identity development or mental health issues in any significant depth. I began to give talks on women's mental health and lesbian mental health to a wide variety of audiences including trainees and general practitioners. I also presented at meetings of professional organizations such as the American Psychiatric Association and found that there was a significant and growing interest in these topics.

The more I read, the more I recognized how being a woman had influenced my own development and career. I had a different leadership style than my male peers had, I related differently to trainees, and I became more aware of often being the only woman or one of the few women in a committee meeting or on a planning group. Additionally, as I learned more about lesbian mental health and became more involved in the organization the Association of Gay and Lesbian Psychiatrists, I developed a much more conscious awareness of the impact of homophobia on many gay individuals' mental health. Overall, becoming a specialist in women's mental health led to a more conscious awareness of myself as a woman and as a member of a minority, and that awareness has helped me subsequently in my clinical work and as an educator.

The Challenge of Juggling

This path, however, has not always been easy. The greatest professional challenge I've faced has been coping with the multiple and heavy responsibilities of being a faculty member, particularly since becoming the director of the UCSF psychiatry residency program in 2007. Being a clinician, administrator, teacher, researcher, and contributing citizen of the department as well as being active in various professional organizations means always having an impossibly long to-do list. In recent years I've had to accept a new reality of pretty much always having far too many balls in the air, but a colleague's wise words have been very helpful. She advised that I focus on knowing which of these balls I can afford to drop because they will bounce as opposed to which ones I simply must keep in the air because, if dropped, they will break. But she made it clear that given the vast size of the to-do list, some balls will, inevitably, get dropped. This metaphor has been extremely helpful, and although I still feel overwhelmed frequently, taking a brief time-out to imagine some bouncing balls is usually wonderfully restorative. In addition, learning to delegate and staying as physically active as I can have been important coping mechanisms.

The Dance of Work-Life Balance

Regarding the issue of balancing professional life and personal life, I have two major areas to discuss. The first pertains to being a parent and an academic, and the second is about being a lesbian. Compared to many of my faculty peers, the balance of my professional and personal lives seems a bit easier for me thanks to my family's unique structure. Since our son was a newborn, my spouse and I have coparented our son with his two dads, and he spends about half of his time in each household. We live only five minutes away from each other, and on the three nights per week that he is with his dads, my spouse and I typically work late. Then, on the four nights that he's at our home, we are able to really be present for him, although now that he's fifteen years old he happily spends most of each evening in his room doing homework while simultaneously instant-messaging his friends. He wants little to do with us directly, as is true for most kids his age. (He still does check in with us now and then, and we playfully tease him that we'll tell his friends that he actually *does* talk to his parents….) Although we are active parents only about half of each week, the balance of professional and personal life is still challenging. This is due to the multiple responsibilities we carry, and the fact that working most nights and much of each weekend is a routine part of our lives. Happily, because of our co-parenting arrangement, neither of us ever feels burnt-out as moms and the balance of our professional and personal lives feels pretty manageable.

The other aspect of the work and personal life balance for me has to do with being a lesbian. Here, it's not about the number of hours spent doing work or doing family activities, but rather the unique issues raised by being in a sexual minority myself and treating patients, some of whom are also lesbian and most of whom are not. Throughout my career, some lesbian patients have known of my orientation from the beginning of our work together because the person who referred them had told them. During the course of my work with some others, I have disclosed my orientation when it was clinically appropriate to do so because it was helpful to the patient, particularly if they asked me directly. However, I've also had some patients for whom I did not believe my disclosure would be helpful.

Many, if not most, lesbian patients would prefer to work with a lesbian therapist, so the potential for seeing patients in social situations is high. And, although San Francisco is a major city with a large LGBT population and many activities for the community, I have had the occasional experience of running into patients at social events of various types. Sometimes I've been with my family and sometimes not. For all therapist-patient relationships, inadvertent contact outside the office may raise complex issues and is always grist for the mill. On the few occasions when it has happened in my career, I've always gained a deeper appreciation of the patient's dynamic issues as we've explored the incident in therapy. All therapists have similarly complex work to do in therapy if they run into a patient when they are out with their family. However, the professional-personal balance issue does have some unique attributes for an LGBT therapist. The potential shared experience of negative consequences due to one's sexual minority status may affect the therapist-patient relationship, and overall, maintaining strict boundaries is critically important due to the small size of the LGBT community.

Homophobia's Impact and Coming Out

Happily (and luckily), I have not experienced overt sexism or homophobia in my career to date. I feel very fortunate to live in San Francisco and to work for an institution that offers fully equal benefits (including retirement benefits) to same-sex couples. Unfortunately, such equal benefits are not yet commonplace, and many same-sex partnered people are simply not eligible for equal pension or health benefits compared to their heterosexual peers. Given the current absence of social security benefits for all same-sex couples (even those legally married in their state), having access to benefits from the workplace plays a key role in feeling valued and equal to one's peers with respect to financial well-being.

Although I haven't experienced it directly myself, lesbian, gay, and bisexual (LGB) physicians have reported ostracism and harassment by colleagues, and prejudice against LGB physicians has been described in several published studies (Brogan et al. 1999; Prichard et al. 1988; Rose 1994). (I use *LGB* here because there are no data at all about the experiences of transgender doctors.) A 1993 survey of lesbian doctors found that 41% reported harassment at some point in their life, including 18% during residency and 19% during practice (Brogan et al. 1999).

As with all invisible minorities (as opposed to being a person of color or having a physical disability), LGBT people can choose to conceal their minority status, and although doing so can shield individuals from discrimination and harassment, it has its costs. For example, if not out about sexual orientation, a gay person needs to continually struggle with decisions such as whether to bring one's same-sex partner to the office party, whether to have a photo on one's desk, or how to answer when coworkers ask seemingly innocuous questions such as "What did you do this weekend?" (Burke and White 2001; Druzin et al. 1998; Risdon et al. 2000). In addition, the absence of one's true self at work can lead to tension between being honest and true to oneself and risking negative consequences. The constant vigilance needed if one is not out takes its toll, and closeted LGB physicians appear to suffer more stress than those who are not closeted (Henry 1994; Risdon et al. 2000). On the other hand, one needs to be very cognizant of the potential negative consequences of being out, for example, the potential to lose one's job if in the military under the so-called *Don't ask, don't tell* policy that was in effect for seventeen years until late 2011. In addition, as there is currently no national law protecting against discrimination in the workplace on the basis of sexual orientation, a physician could potentially have no legal recourse should he or she experience a truly negative outcome of being out at work (Oriel et al. 1996; Ramos et al. 1998).

I struggled with whether to disclose my orientation during residency. I was anxious about the reactions of faculty and the training director, but felt very comfortable with my peers. Ultimately, I decided to not talk directly about it, but I did bring my partner to the graduation ceremony and party, and I was relieved when my caseload supervisor's reaction was a warm "Hello, nice to meet you" when I introduced her. Again, being in San Francisco helped, as did having gay and lesbian colleagues in my residency class.

One concept that isn't commonly known by heterosexual people is that of *internalized homophobia*. This refers to individuals viewing themselves negatively (and often being unaware of it) as a result of absorbing all the multiple negative messages heard about gay people. Examples include: "All gay people are promiscuous…All gay people have AIDS… There's no way you can have a committed relationship if you're gay… All lesbians hate men…Gay people are mentally ill…You'll never be happy if you're a lesbian…." Because internalized homophobia is often fairly subtle and may even occur unconsciously, it can have a pernicious effect on one's mental health. Physicians are not immune to internalized homophobia, and an individual in the process of coming out can benefit greatly from learning about the huge diversity of the LGBT community and about the fact that these stereotypical views are simply not true.

When I first came out, I worried about what it meant for my identity as a woman and also about its impact on my family relationships. I carried assumptions that many lesbians hated men and didn't want to associate with them in any way, but I also knew that that didn't apply to me. Talking with other LGBT people challenged my assumptions, and I learned that the community is just as diverse as the heterosexual community. Over time, the internalized homophobia gradually dissipated.

LGBT people are commonly stereotyped, and the negative stereotypes are often fueled by provocative images (such as photographs in most newspapers the day after pride celebrations that typically focus on people dressed in leather or men in drag). Society is full of negative messages about LGBT people, both explicit and subtle, and while growing up such messages are unavoidable. Because of these negative stereotypes and because of internalized homophobia, having positive role models is critically important, particularly for students and residents (Risdon et al. 2000). During my coming out as a second-year psychiatry resident, I was very lucky to have some gay and lesbian friends who were incredibly supportive, and I also knew of some gay faculty. Throughout my career, I've been firmly committed to being available as a resource for LGBT students or residents. Having out faculty as role models can be extremely reassuring for a vulnerable trainee struggling during the coming-out process, coping with rejection from family, friends, or others, or dealing with their own internalized homophobia.

Unique Impact of LGBT Physicians

In contrast to the potential negative consequences of being a lesbian, gay, bisexual, or transgender physician—such as discrimination, internalized homophobia, transphobia, or having to hide one's true identity—Cathy Risdon and her colleagues have written about the potential positive impact of being a physician who is a member of a stigmatized minority group

(Risdon et al. 2000). Being an outsider may enrich one's capacities to be an effective clinician through enhanced ability to connect to others from a variety of minority groups. LGBT doctors may have enhanced recognition of patients who are experiencing inner conflicts and may use inclusive language more routinely. In addition, such physicians may have a heightened understanding of the impact of biases in patient care and of the health care disparities experienced by members of minority groups (Risdon et al. 2000). These positive points resonate with my experience in clinical work; however, I'm fully aware that there is much I do not know about what it's like to be, for example, a person of color or someone with a disability. In my clinical work and when teaching students and residents about cultural competence, I try to be open to the uniqueness of each individual's experience and to learning as much as possible from those experiences.

Practical Tips for Women in Psychiatry

As I reflect on my career to date, it's clear that I would never be where I am today were it not for a wonderful mix of mentors who have provided unending support, encouragement, and nudging. These mentors, including both women and men, gay and straight, have taught me invaluable lessons, including those listed below.

- It's OK and can be very important to say *no* sometimes when asked to take on new responsibilities.
- As a very busy person, actively pursuing opportunities that grab one's interest rather than saying *yes* to all opportunities is critically important to avoid burnout.
- Take credit when it's due, but also be sure to give credit to others, particularly for group successes.
- Seek out mentors.
- Be a mentor.
- Publish and give presentations (and, once created, repeat presentations to as many audiences as possible).
- Become active in professional organizations.
- Periodically take on new challenges and experiences.
- Seek out role models. If you are a member of a minority group because of your ethnicity, race, disability, sexual orientation, gender identity, age, nationality, language capabilities, culture, or any other factor, you have the potential to contribute richly to the field of psychiatry, but you also have the potential of facing discrimination and of having to cope with stereotyping. Role models can help!

- If LGBT, gain comfort in being out professionally and in being a role model to others.

- Embrace a more feminine leadership style, if that's what comes naturally to you.

- Having a collaborative style of leadership can help with success. It can be complicated and time-consuming, however; it also can greatly facilitate change processes.

- Emulate leadership styles from leaders you admire and avoid the mistakes observed in others.

- Aspiring to a psychiatric career means that you need to be self-aware and reflective, develop a network of supportive colleagues, take care of yourself in whatever way you need to do so (e.g., eating well, exercising, being in psychotherapy, getting massages), find your niche within the field, and be comfortable with the possibility of working in different aspects of the field throughout your career (e.g., switching from inpatient work to outpatient work and/or to a leadership position).

Overall, my career has been totally serendipitous, but it's been a joyful and exciting journey, and it has also been tremendously gratifying, particularly to see trainees develop into superlative clinicians and leaders in their own right. So, strap on your seatbelts, enjoy your own journeys, and remember to give back; it has been a pleasure for me.

References

Brogan DJ, Frank E, Elon L, et al: Harassment of lesbians as medical students and physicians. JAMA 282:1290–1292, 1999

Burke BP, White JC: Wellbeing of gay, lesbian, and bisexual doctors. BMJ 322:422–425, 2001

Henry WA III: Pride and prejudice. Time magazine, June 27, 1994, pp 54–59

Oriel KA, Madlon-Kay DJ, Govaker D, et al: Gay and lesbian physicians in training: family practice program directors' attitudes and students' perceptions of bias. Fam Med 28:720–725, 1996

Prichard JG, Dial LK, Holloway RL, et al: Attitudes of family medicine residents toward homosexuality. J Fam Pract 27:673–679, 1988

Ramos MM, Tilez CM, Palley RB, et al: Attitudes of physicians practicing in New Mexico toward gay men and lesbians in the profession. Acad Med 73:436–438, 1998

Risdon C, Cook D, Willms D: Gay and lesbian physicians in training: a qualitative study. CMAJ 162:331–334, 2000

Rose L: Homophobia among doctors. BMJ 308:586–587, 1994

Chapter 17

Another Immigrant's Tale

So Near and Yet So Far

Geetha Jayaram, M.D., M.B.A.

I WAS THE FIRST BORN and the only girl in a sibship of five children, and I was the first granddaughter. In a culture that prized women who were pulchritudinous and educated in dance and music (Nidel 2011), but did not always encourage them to be highly educated in academics, my father strongly supported education among women. Brilliant, a businessman, an erudite polyglot, he took a keen interest in his children's education. He was a strict disciplinarian, and he required us to excel in our studies. One memory that stands out for me is that he would not sign my report card if I was second in my class.

My mother was the much-adored woman of our family—she was beautiful and college educated, and spoke and wrote several languages. What I most sought to emulate, however, was her high regard for all human beings, her nonjudgmental acceptance of all who came to our home, the generosity and kindness that are remembered by anyone who knew her. As a psychiatrist, I think of her when encountering a difficult patient who needs understanding and empathy.

My father was a religious man who devoted an hour or so to prayer daily. Hindu households have a private area or shrine for daily prayers (Dasa 2007). Hinduism pervaded all aspects of our lives as children, from the way meals were prepared to gathering flowers from the garden for daily prayers to helping my mother or grandmother in the kitchen for the meals that were served three times a day. My mother and grandmothers were excellent cooks; my mother learned baking, canning and preserving, made her own wine, grew her own roses, and cultivated new flower colors by grafting. As a girl I was assigned to help my mother, and I developed a close bond with her. I learned the benefits of extended family, working with others in a cohesive fashion.

My paternal grandmother was a disciplined, bright woman who had taught herself English. She often told me stories about the trials and tribulations of women who had to bear many children and hope that some might make it to adulthood. Indeed, she herself had lost seven children to childhood infectious diseases. She spoke highly of a British-trained nurse who was brought in by my international-businessman grandfather to assist her in childbirth, which was conducted at home. As a child I contracted chicken pox, whooping cough, and diphtheria, those being the days before vaccination. There were many trips to the doctor with my father, and injections of antibiotics were routine. The doctor, our family friend, praised me for not crying when I was given an injection. I can vividly recall the antiseptic smell of his office.

Stories about Mahatma Gandhi were told and retold. Simplicity and frugality were espoused as virtues. I won essay competitions as a teenager for an analysis of Gandhi's books, including *My Experiments With Truth* (Gandhi 1927/1929). I struggled with what "Truth" he really meant.

Stories of rationing and the lack of food, supplies, and newsprint in the postwar depression era were all told at mealtimes or when we accompanied the adults in our family on road trips. Education abroad was seen as a panacea for all that was lacking in India and was an aspiration of many. Doctors who had completed a postgraduate education in England or the United States proudly proclaimed it on signs at their offices. Those doctors were sought after more than those trained in the country, regardless of applicability to the local circumstances.

Early Education and Influences

I was sent to a private convent school and taught by Irish nuns who were attentive and exacting teachers. Needless to say, the instruction was in excellent English, placing me at an advantage in learning medicine but at a relative disadvantage in not learning enough about the pre-British culture of India. The teaching was broad-based, exposing us to the history of India, Britain, and the United States. Books were our path to the rest of the world. I was a voracious reader, consuming the material faster than my English literature teachers could make the books available. The education system was patterned after the British system, offering courses that were in rigid combinations of science or the liberal arts, not permitting a synthesis of subjects.

The nuns at school were protective, not permitting behavior that they saw as flamboyant or too liberal. At home as well I was protected, because girls raised in a proper Brahmin family did not stay out late or go about unaccompanied by an elder or a male companion, such as my brothers. Although we were educated in the English system, we read all the American classics, as well as comics about heroes of the Wild West, the Gold Rush, and the wars fought over land in America; we embraced Dean Martin, Cliff Richards, and Bobby Darin, and later the Beatles, the Rolling Stones, and the Beach Boys. My father played Indian film music at home and we were forbidden to listen to pop music, but we did anyway when he was not home. Reading books like *Giant, The Virginian,* and scores of others prepared me to acculturate in the United States in ways that were not easy for some of my immigrant colleagues. Many years later, when I looked at the list of books assigned for reading in my daughter's Gifted and Talented program, I noticed I had read twenty-three of the twenty-five books. I managed to read J. D. Salinger that year at my children's recommendation.

My paternal grandfather and my father were philanthropists. Besides donating funds, my father, who was a scrupulously honest Rotarian (Rotary International 2011), raised our awareness of those who were downtrodden, and he and my mother opened our home to poor or sick relatives. We as children were included in caring for them. We all had tasks assigned to us; we were treated fairly and expected to accommodate those less fortunate. During Indian festivals, we were taught to give gifts to children in slum areas before we could enjoy our own. On one road trip, our father took us to see the site of a mental asylum. I recall seeing the chains that were used to control the people with mental illness. He deplored the poor treatment they received.

I had wanted to be a physician since the age of thirteen. Having read books that extolled the virtues of life-saving procedures and discoveries in medicine led by Western researchers like the "Big Four" of Johns Hopkins (Johns Hopkins Medicine 2011), and having loved the biological sciences, this seemed like a natural course to me. Books were made available to me that were beyond the reach of the average family, since there were no public libraries, television broadcasts, or radio broadcasts available. I finished my bachelor's degree from National College, Bangalore, as an outstanding student, majoring in botany, zoology, and chemistry and being ranked among the top ten in the state in some subjects, at the age of eighteen.

Education in Medical School and Beyond

Medicine in the postindependence climate of India suffered from the contradictions involved in two very different systems of medicine: the western way, and medical practice indigenous to India—homeopathy, Ayurveda, and other practices. I obtained admission to two medical schools in Bangalore, but I was persuaded to attend the private Catholic school that taught western medicine, one that was reputed to be excellent and that required its students to pass an entrance exam for acceptance. I was one of a minority of girls in a class of sixty-five students. Our preclinical courses were taught by a devoted group of professors who had traveled abroad, had worked in the United States or England, and were able to foster enthusiasm and interest. The United States was by then noted to be at the forefront of medical prowess, the epitome of medical advancement.

We heard about The Johns Hopkins University School of Medicine and read publications by leading researchers from Hopkins. We heard that classes were small and involved hands-on training with patients, a departure from the old lecture format. From the start, talented women were permitted to enroll, overcoming a prohibition that many older schools held for decades. Medical research by both faculty and students was fostered as part of the educational process and as integral to patient care. The "clinician-scientist" had become a Johns Hopkins hallmark (Johns Hopkins Medicine 2011). This greatly appealed to me.

Immigration to the United States

I was married in the last year of medical school to my engineer husband. I wanted to go to the United States for two main reasons. First, medicine was at its best there. Resources to recognize, treat, and prevent illness and suffering were less advanced in India at the time. Second, we could raise our children as we thought fit in the United States. I had my daughter before finishing medical school. Simultaneously, the Carter administration decided to "import" physicians to meet the demand for them, and taking and passing the Educational Commission for Foreign Medical Graduates exams permitted us to get permanent resident status. I traveled to Paris to take the exam and passed. We were given six weeks to prepare to leave India, then the Carter administration decided to end this immigration policy, requiring us to be in the United States by January 9, 1977 (AMA-IMG 2010; Educational Commission for Foreign Medical Graduates 2011). I had to travel without my family, find a job and a place to live, and then sponsor my family to live in the United States.

Internship and Residency

The first available position was an internship in psychiatry. I had experience as a senior house officer in internal medicine, which helped me a great deal in breezing through another (and to me, unnecessary) rotating internship. During the internship I encountered prejudices about my level of education and shock on the part of a male superior when I easily solved the electrocardiogram quizzes posted for the third-year medical residents! He asked me what on earth I was doing in psychiatry. Because I was alone for several months before my husband and daughter joined me, men tried to date me, and some male supervisors made sexually inappropriate remarks.

Seeking a site for my residency, I applied to Johns Hopkins in response to an advertisement in a journal for residencies in internal medicine and psychiatry. Once I interviewed for the internal medicine residency, it became apparent that with being on call every other day, I would be able to see my twenty-month-old daughter only for a few hours every second day or so, and I most likely would not be emotionally available to her as needed. I had no ties to Baltimore and no family members to help at the time. The psychiatry residency seemed more appealing; the interviews were more warm and welcoming. The residency was demanding because there was no cap on the number of hours worked, but the orderliness, the high expectations, and the drive that I was taught helped me to finish my residency with pride at a world-class institution.

I took my board exams with little time for preparation. My mother came during my residency to stay with me for a few months to help with my daughter. She died two years later. My husband worked in other states, driving long distances to see us on weekends. I traded working weekdays for working on weekends, which was welcomed by my fellow residents. I was determined to avoid having a stranger as a babysitter for my child. Being a psychiatry resident made me acutely aware of the need for safe and solicitous parenting of our children, as did my culture.

The chairman of my department at Johns Hopkins, Dr. Paul McHugh, was an outstanding teacher, a brilliant diagnostician, and fair and principled in his treatment of residents. I am to this day grateful to this man, who is a wonderful example of nondiscriminatory treatment of women and immigrants. His book *The Perspectives of Psychiatry,* cowritten with Dr. Phillip R. Slavney (McHugh and Slavney 1998), paved the way in offering a solution to understanding and diagnosing psychiatric conditions in which chaos reigns. As a woman, I have been treated with nothing but respect and dignity at this institution. Paul made me one of the first women chief residents, recognized my administrative abilities, and later placed me in charge of a community psychiatry clinic when I was in my early thirties.

Meanwhile, despite this support, as a young mother who wanted to raise another child, I found that there was no place in the work setting that would accommodate my needs. I remember answering a survey that the institution sent around to estimate the need for a day care facility. Nothing came of it. Women did not dare get pregnant during their residencies. In fact, some were asked to resign and reapply if they requested a leave of absence. A senior woman in my department, when I approached her in an effort to change the rules, told me that she had had an abortion, and so should the women who wanted to work in such a competitive setting. Other women told me not to make noise. Nonetheless, on one occasion, I stood up in a faculty meeting to protest dress codes made for women faculty by people who never consulted any woman physician in drafting the codes. I argued about job sharing for women who wanted to raise a family and were willing to split job responsibilities without asking for benefits(!). To this day, we have failed to accomplish this task. Many law firms have allowed this arrangement for years. Bright and capable women who would otherwise pursue academics opt out because of rigid and uncompromising policies.

In the mid-1990s, Linda Fried and others first published their work outlining the process for retaining women faculty and promoting them (Fried et al. 1996). Since that publication, there has been an effort made to support women, train them, and address issues of relevance to women, such as salary equity (Domenici et al. 2011). More work remains to be done.

Early Employment

Soon after my residency, I worked in a state setting as medical director of the Prince George's County (Maryland) Department of Mental Health, for several community psychiatry clinics. This was during an economic downturn in the early 1980s. There was no fellowship offered to me, my husband was laid off, I had planned to have a second child, my mother died, and we needed to help family members financially, so I had no choice but to work. I was given full-time benefits, advanced pregnancy leave, and flexible hours for a job of seventeen and one-half hours of work per week. The health officer, who was a woman, understood my needs, supported me, and deeply appreciated the reforms that I brought about in the system. Productivity and quality of care increased, physicians were hired, and they formed a network that helped cover for each other in six community mental health centers. This break from academics enabled me to devote precious time to my children. I took breaks in the summer by accumulating my compensatory time, something unheard of in academia.

I returned to academics at Johns Hopkins once my son entered school. I had chosen to work with people with severe mental illness and people living in poverty in urban Baltimore. I found the work extremely gratifying, as I still do. Dr. McHugh kept requesting me to return full time to Johns Hopkins to run the community psychiatry clinic, which I did once my son was in school six years later.

With the help of dedicated colleagues, the clinic, which had not passed state inspection earlier, did so without a hitch under my guidance; we won a gold medal at the Hospital and Community Psychiatry Institute at Philadelphia for a program in community psychiatry and were recognized for our comprehensive array of services ("Gold Award" 1989).

However, my academic career suffered, and I spent long hours at work away from my children. This dilemma haunts many accomplished and capable young women who struggle with these choices to this day. I could not attend to my private patients' needs in the clinic setting. I was constantly interrupted during therapy sessions. I asked for a change in my job description, having felt burned-out with the effort of rescuing the clinic. I was appointed physician advisor in a limited full-time capacity and codirector of an inpatient community psychiatry unit, and this enabled me to make an arrangement to keep my practice separate and to devote more time to my academic endeavors. My challenge has been to work smart, not just work hard.

In directing the inpatient unit and as physician advisor for the hospital's psychiatry department, I have played a singular and pivotal role in advancing quality of care. I work with other advisors in other departments to decrease adverse events, promote quality, and teach multidisciplinary techniques to avoid mishaps or lapses in care. As a woman, my tone may be more conciliatory; I network well, and I am not intimidating in my approach. However, I have been selected less often to represent a mainstream group, I have not been mentored in my area, and I have needed to find my own way in a pioneering effort. My upbringing and Indian background do not lend themselves to being aggressive; aggressiveness can be seen as pushy and demanding. The obstacles to advancement are subtle, but persistent.

Leadership and Advocacy

I have now been recognized and acknowledged as a leader in patient safety in the country and abroad, being invited to lecture on how to protect our patients. I have taught other physician advisors in many hospitals. I have pioneered incorporating scientific endeavor in an area never researched in psychiatry. I continue to chair the Patient Safety Committee for the American Psychiatric Association. My handbook coauthored with Al Herzog, a fantastic mentor, has had close to eighty downloads in a year from the American Psychiatric Association (APA) website (Jayaram and Herzog 2008).

During my years of community psychiatry leadership, I began noting the needs of people with severe mental illness in securing medical care, necessary living arrangements, or funds for survival. This paved the way to my working pro bono on scores of committees such as the Disabled Persons Review Boards of Baltimore, Howard, and Prince George's counties, being appointed by the county executives or governor at the time. I did not realize that this would not promote my academic standing. Nevertheless, humanitarian work is gratifying and an end in itself, not a means for academic recognition. During many of these hours of endeavors, dedicated women were my companions—social workers, nurses, outreach personnel. To this day, I remain friends with many of them.

Believing in advocacy for our patients and for our profession, I have served on scores of committees at the Maryland Psychiatric Society and the APA. I was made a distinguished fellow in my thirties, an honor bestowed by one of my male colleagues. This did not necessarily favor academic success, but it helped me network with great women outside of my institution who were encouraging, many of whom have written chapters in this book. I need to mention Dr. Leah Dickstein, a phenomenal woman who sought me out at every meeting to inquire about my progress; Dr. Donna Norris, who involved me in writing this book; Dr. Annelle Primm, who has guided minority fellows in working with me; and many others to whom I am grateful. Dr. Paul Appelbaum asked me to be the chair of the Scientific Program Committee for the APA annual meeting, as did Drs. Marcia Goin and Michelle Riba. We offered a fantastic array of programs with excellent scientific content. We had the highest attendance ever in the history of the APA for those years, 2003 and 2004. For the next year, I wanted to give a chance to lead to Dr. Marian (Mimi) Butterfield, who had been diagnosed with cancer. We helped her complete the task of the scientific program chair—and although she succumbed to the illness, she fought it bravely. The sisterhood of the Association of Women Psychiatrists stood behind her (Association of Women Psychiatrists 2011).

As I gained experience in administration and teaching, so did I as a Rotarian. Twelve years ago I worked with women in my profession and my club members to raise funds to develop and provide mental health care services to indigent women in rural southern India. Rotarians in India helped manage the implementation of services with my alma mater, St. John's Medical College. Today, thanks to Rotary International and the passionate female case workers that we have trained, comprehensive medical and psychiatric services are available to women and children in 187 villages. I am grateful for the privilege of giving back to my home country. Numerous challenges we faced in care delivery are particular to the ethnic groups and the economic and cultural circumstances of care. They are described in several papers that have been published (Isaacs et al. 2006; Srinivasan et al. 2006; Wasan et al. 2009).

Support Going Forward

Although I worked hard to further my professional goals, I could not have done so without the help of my family in spirit and in accommodating my absences. My husband grew up with accomplished sisters and supported my endeavors, always told me to fight for my rights, and never stood in the way of my professional goals. My children as adults are invaluable to me in their honest appraisal of my endeavors. There were tough times, both financially and in the family. We lost our parents when we were fairly young, so our children did not have the privilege of growing up with grandparents. I lost a younger brother to cancer, and my chairman, Dr. McHugh, was very supportive during my grieving. We siblings paid my brother's hospital bills, which were immense. I was criminally assaulted in San Francisco during an APA meeting in 2003, sustaining severe injuries. Ironically, the assailant was a severely mentally ill homeless man. The poor structure of public sector psychiatry and the neglect of continued care of people with severe mental illness became a much-debated topic in the public arena for several weeks. I suffered from excruciating pain from cervical cord bleeding and it took several months of diligent support from my family, support from my departmental colleagues, and neurosurgery at Johns Hopkins to recover almost all of my physical abilities. This interrupted my career, but highlighted what was important in my life—my family, and the ability to love and forgive others. I was more determined to be an advocate for people with severe mental illness. My colleagues from the APA and friends were remarkably supportive and kind during my recovery. My academic advancement was stalled during these times, but I became stronger in the process. It meant postponing, not giving up, some of my goals.

My work brought me recognition and awards from both academic and nonacademic institutions. Consistent daily exercise and yoga gave me energy. I have worked with several South Asian and other associations to volunteer my services in helping patients. I have taught and mentored hundreds of students (both medical and nonmedical), residents, and junior faculty who have advanced in their careers and become administrators and researchers. I was recently nominated from three zones of Rotary International (hundreds of clubs) for a global humanitarian award, a singular honor for my work in mental health for the indigent.

Being an immigrant means you lose some of your identity, your support systems, confidantes within your family, and the shared experience of milestones in your lives. As you grow to love the country you chose to embrace, you inevitably find yourself disenfranchised from the cultural network of women you grew up with, the loving aunts and female cousins with whom you celebrated holidays. I miss the poignancy of the fragrances and colors of my native culture, the spirituality that is part of the fabric of life, and the support of extended family. As a woman psychiatrist, in visiting my home town, I am accosted by the downtrodden plight of many women who are subservient, suffer from anxiety and depression, and remain mutely tolerant of inequities in their lives. There is much to be done and much to be learned.

As a young girl, I saw America as the land of intellectual freedom, of great choices and great acceptance of those who are different, a land rich in industry and the search for scientific progress and exactitude. I am truly grateful to this country that has welcomed and received so many as its own.

PRACTICAL TIPS FOR WOMEN IN PSYCHIATRY

Here is what I would impart to younger women:

- Choose your career path and never diverge from it—find mentors, both men and women, who will guide you, are genuinely interested, and are willing to give you the time needed.

- Don't fall prey to someone else's ambitions, be it man or woman. Ask yourself how accepting a proffered responsibility will expand your horizons, create an impact in your career, or help with your focus. I lost precious time helping others without a thought of increased income or academic advancement. You can help others once you have succeeded in establishing your direction first.

- Your children need you as infants and elementary school students. There is no better guidance than that which comes from parents. Dr. McHugh once said to me that it was women like me who should have more children. I understand that statement better now than when it was made to me. I would say the same to you. I also willingly took on tasks he assigned to me and did not ask the questions: What about my career? How will this job help me? Will I make academic gains in the process? Looking back, I should have declined some of them. They did not help my research focus.

- Find gratification in something you do. A job is different than a calling. Look for your calling. Find a way to give back to society. There is no better reward, spiritual or intellectual. Find a way to advocate for yourself, your patients, and your profession.

- Never stop addressing inequities in the workforce. Good teamwork means recognizing the contributions made by both genders, our sons and our daughters. Acknowledge the work of other women. Teach your sons to admire and respect both men and women alike. They will be rewarded for it in their lives. Support younger women, and assist them when you can. The world will be a better place for it.

References

American Medical Association International Medical Graduates (AMA-IMG) Section Governing Council: International medical graduates in American medicine: contemporary challenges and opportunities. Position paper. January 2010. Available at: http://www.ama-assn.org/ama1/pub/upload/mm/18/img-workforce-paper.pdf. Accessed September 23, 2011.

Association of Women Psychiatrists. Available at: http://www.womenpsych.org/links.html. Accessed September 8, 2011.

Dasa SN: Ganga Flows West: The Essentials of Modern Hinduism. Sanskrit Religions Institute, 2007. Available at: http://www.sanskrit.org/www/Hindu%20Primer/HinduPrimerCover.html. Accessed October 7, 2011.

Dominici F, Busch-Vishniac I, Landau B, et al: Women in academic leadership: analysis of root causes of under-representation. Available at: http://www.biostat.jhsph.edu/~fdominic/NIHwomen/extra1/rootCauses.doc. Accessed September 23, 2011.

Educational Commission for Foreign Medical Graduates: Certification. Available at: http://www.ecfmg.org/cert/certfact.html. Accessed September 5, 2010.

Fried L, Fracomano C, McDonald SM, et al: Career development for women in academic medicine: multiple interventions in a department of medicine. JAMA 276:898–905, 1996

Gandhi MK: My Experiments With Truth. Edited by Trust N. Ahmedabad. Vol 1, 602 pp, 1927; Vol 2, 608 pp, 1929

Isaacs AN, Srinivasan K, Neerakkal I, et al: Initiating a community mental health programme in rural Karnataka. Indian J Community Med 31:86–87, 2006

Jayaram G, Herzog A (eds): SAFE MD: Practical Applications and Approaches to Safe Psychiatric Practice. American Psychiatric Association Committee on Patient Safety, 2008. Available at: http://psych.org/Departments/QIPS/Downloads/SAFEMD.aspx. Accessed January 18, 2012.

Johns Hopkins Medicine: Revolution in American medicine. Available at: http://www.hopkinsmedicine.org/about/history/history3.html. Accessed September 23, 2011.

McHugh PR, Slavney PR: Perspectives in Psychiatry, 2nd Edition. Baltimore, MD, Johns Hopkins University Press, 1998. Available at: http://jhupbooks.press.jhu.edu. Accessed October 7, 2011.

Nidel RO: Music, classical music. World music: the basics. Available at: http://en.wikipedia.org/wiki/Indian_classical_music. Accessed November 1, 2011.

Rotary International. Web site. Available at: http://www.rotary.org/en/Members/Pages/ridefault.aspx. Accessed November 1, 2011.

Srinivasan K, Isaacs A, Thomas T, et al: Outcomes of common mental disorders in southern rural India. Indian Journal of Social Psychiatry 22:110–115, 2006

Wasan AJ, Neufeld K, Jayaram G: Practice patterns and treatment choices among psychiatrists in New Delhi, India: a qualitative and quantitative study. Soc Psychiatry Psychiatr Epidemiol 44:109–119, 2009

Chapter 18

Receiving Effective Support While Making Culture and Language Changes

Esperanza Díaz, M.D.

ESPERANZA MEANS HOPE IN SPANISH. I like telling people what it means and asking them to repeat it. It makes me believe for a brief moment that they speak Spanish. Some people say it is the perfect name for a psychiatrist, and I have adopted it as my main goal in teaching. As psychiatrists, we have to inspire and give hope overall.

My mother was very proud of me. She would introduce me by saying "This is my daughter, Dr. Díaz." I graduated from the Pontificia Universidad Javeriana in Bogotá, Colombia, in South America with a medical doctor degree. The Colombian government asks all medical graduates to serve in rural areas as part of the requirement to get a Colombian medical license. I fulfilled my requirement, too. Around the end of that commitment I met a Colombian man in New York City. After he asked me to marry him almost right away, we continued our courtship by letters and phone calls and he visited me in Bogotá about five times during the following year. We say that we got married to get to know each other. But after thirty years we still have not finished learning about each other.

My husband was very supportive, so our plans were made around my professional career. He could stay in the United States or go back to Colombia. If I were to able to validate my license and work as a medical doctor, we would stay in the United States. If I had not been able to practice as an M.D., we would have gone back to Colombia. He was working as a psychotherapist in a hospital in central Connecticut, Meriden-Wallingford Hospital. I moved to Meriden, Connecticut.

My primary language is Spanish. My parents enrolled me in a Catholic school, where I remained until high school graduation. I started to learn English in kindergarten. Despite twelve years of English lessons we were not forced to speak it, so I was able to read and comprehend English but did not speak it fluently, though I created the illusion of speaking fluently. So it was a shock to find out the real truth when I arrived in Connecticut. I could not understand what they were saying, I could not think in English, and it was going to take a long time for me to learn these skills. The process of adjusting to a new culture is not simple (Akhtar 1994). I feared telephones, and I think that for a while I was phobic. While I prepared for my validating exams (for certification by the Educational Commission for Foreign Medical Graduates [ECFMG]), I also realized I did not know how to cook! I discovered the famous chef Julia Child on the public television network. I learned English and cooking from Julia and also learned English during my own psychoanalysis.

There was no doubt I would become a physician. My mother said I knew it since I was two years old. Perhaps from the special attention she gave to physical ailments that now I would call somatic concerns, she probably reinforced her wish. So thanks to somatic concerns and mother's wishes, I am a doctor. I did not know back then what my choice of specialty would be.

When I learned that I was accepted at the Javeriana University medical school as one of the top ten, my joy was surpassed by the worry of how was I going to pay for it. A private university with steep costs was not in my family's budget. My parents were ready to help as much as they could and I had a special reassurance from my mom because she knew better how to save money. I applied for government loans to the Colombian Institute of Educational Credit and Technical Studies Abroad (ICETEX), to partly pay for my medical education. Thanks to my family and those loans I was able to complete my medical education.

I knew I was not going to be an orthopedic surgeon. While I was fine in most of the surgeries, if they started to use the electric saw to cut bone,

I would pass out. Perhaps I would have overcome this, but having had to leave the surgical suite twice, it was too embarrassing for me to try again. But I like surgical specialties, so along with my hobby of miniature collections I found ophthalmology to my liking. I was interested in it as I moved to the United States. I obtained a letter of recommendation from a famous ophthalmologist who practiced in Colombia at the time, José Barraquer, M.D. That opened the door to some talks I had with the head of ophthalmology at Yale University. They offered me a preresidency fellowship with no pay. I was excited about it, but did not accept the offer because I became pregnant with my first child; they did not want me then and I did not think it would be wise to pursue the ophthalmology fellowship. Yet I still collect miniatures and I still am particularly concerned about ocular side effects from psychotropics, frequently finding that eyedrops do not make it to the medication formulary lists.

Being pregnant was a joy with some minor side effects. I was tired and sleepy preparing for the ECFMG exams but I had what I never had had before, time at home. That period in my life was special. I was learning English, cooking, and attending a course to prepare for the exams. I was also able to travel with my husband, who in his early youth had a travel agency. This was a real treat, and later on with our children it was unique to have him prepare a trip especially for us. We visited places, mainly in Europe, that we read about with the children from library books. These were unforgettable times for all of us.

Giving birth was a life-changing experience. My husband and I prepared for labor with the Lamaze course (Scott and Rose 1976). We went further; my husband used hypnotic suggestions to deal with my labor pains. I did not need any pain medicine or analgesics until the very end, and we had a beautiful baby boy. I had a normal delivery, but my baby was born with a diaphragmatic hernia that ruptured into his lungs. He went into cardiac arrest two hours after his birth. Nothing could have prepared me for that.

He was resuscitated and placed on life supports. Then I met John Seashore, M.D., a neonatology pediatric surgeon who intervened (Seashore 1978). I can never forget him. Tall, blond, blue eyed, he reminded me of my grandfather. I could not understand him well but, with my husband, I understood the plan. My baby went into surgery at Yale–New Haven Hospital a few hours after his birth. The surgery went well, but it was shocking to see my baby in an incubator with chest tubes on both sides. Slowly, he woke up and the supports were removed. He recuperated well, with scars to prove the ordeal. We went on to have a second baby boy, who was born healthy and had no complications. I was an only child, and I never wanted to have just one child. Our children are a joy.

During the time I prepared for validating my degree, I also attended some lectures and conferences related to my husband's profession of psychiatric social work. My parents, who had immigrated to the United States, helped me with child care and supported my career. We went to a conference with Salvador Minuchin, M.D., about family therapy. I met many people in the social work profession, as well as his colleagues and coworkers, among whom some were psychiatrists. I got curious about psychiatry and liked it. It made sense to have a profession with no surgical schedules, so I decided to apply and ended up finishing a psychiatry residency at Yale University.

During residency at various sites in Connecticut, I went through my acculturation in America at an accelerated rate. I was struggling with the English language and the fact that medicine in America was practiced very differently than in Colombia. Being an intern again was an opportunity to learn not only medicine but also the culture. I remember fondly Eleanor Stutz, M.D., who offered me her friendship and support as I was dealing with residency. Being able to share coffee or lunch with a fellow resident was just great. I admired all the attending physicians and wished to become like them. I discovered I really liked psychotherapy and had the opportunity to learn it. I volunteered to present psychotherapy process notes, and to my surprise, it went well. I spent my last year of residency at Yale Health (a not-for-profit, physician-led health plan that operates a medical center on the Yale campus). I greatly enjoyed engaging in psychotherapy with the student population.

My first job after residency was at Meriden-Wallingford Hospital in central Connecticut, where I started a program for people with mental illness who had spent many years in the state psychiatric hospital. We could consider that still deinstitutionalization. I worked with a great multidisciplinary team and had fun creating a partial hospital for these patients. I had less than a full-time job in order to have some time for myself and the children, to arrive home early enough to be there when my two boys came back from school. At some point, I decided to go back to some of my interests that I'd left unfinished after graduating from residency. I was influenced by my training at Yale and decided to start training in psychoanalysis.

Psychoanalytic training is an intense process that requires time, commitment, and money. I was accepted at the Western New England Institute for Psychoanalysis. It was all well worth it. I had exceptional supervisors: Samuel Ritvo, M.D., Albert Solnit, M.D., Rosemary Balsam, M.D., Sidney Phillips, M.D., and many others. Understanding myself, my decisions, and my choices became a lot easier, and I gained a new perspective that made life fun and more productive. Understanding my patients and staff in the light of the psychoanalytic training has proven useful. My colleagues seek me out to deal with difficult personalities and staff issues.

The work in the community was going well, but then something un-expected happened. A psychiatrist friend of my husband, Alberto Fergu-son, M.D., asked me if I could introduce him to John Strauss, M.D., at Yale. Dr. Ferguson, of Bogotá, Colombia, is the founder and organizer of a program geared to the homeless people with mental illness in that city. The program is called FUNGRATA (Fundación Granja Taller de Asistencia Colombiana) and is based on his own theory about rehabilitation, in which work is the motivating force. Patients are engaged on the city streets fol-lowing a special engagement without causing resistance. When they feel ready, they are invited to join the program, located on the outside of the city on a quasi-farm, where they can stay or leave at their leisure. Alberto wanted an evaluation of the program and wanted John Strauss to lead it with a visit there. John did not have time to do it, but he said that if I would evaluate the program he would serve as a consultant. I had never done any work like that before, but the idea of learning to do health services research sounded appealing.

I jumped into this new project, still working as a community psychia-trist, meeting frequently with John to develop an evaluation plan and pre-pare for the visit. He connected me with Janis J. Jenkins, Ph.D., an anthropologist at Case Western Reserve University at that time. The plan was to do a mixed-methods evaluation, with a quantitative part using some instruments on symptoms and diagnosis, and a qualitative part including some interviews to understand the therapeutic action of the program (Diaz et al. 2004a). Qualitative research was certainly a novelty for me at that time. I was taking it all in with energetic curiosity and a fascination with learning to do research. This was a turning point in my career.

I decided I wanted to return to Yale School of Medicine's Department of Psychiatry to learn more about research and to become a faculty mem-ber. I applied for a job with a faculty appointment. I chose the Connecticut Mental Health Center (CMHC; a collaborative endeavor of the Yale De-partment of Psychiatry and the Connecticut Department of Mental Health and Addiction Services), where John Strauss was and where I had been as a resident. I did say to my interviewers that I wanted to learn research and become successful on an academic path. I also told them that I knew the difficulties women and minorities have succeeding in academia so I needed their support. Jeanne Steiner, D.O., and William Sledge, M.D., hired me.

I entered as an associate unit chief on one of the inpatient units at CMHC. I discovered that my leadership skills were fine, even great, and that I liked teaching and was good at it. The positive feedback I got from John Strauss about my evaluation, from Richard Belitsky, M.D. (currently dean for education at Yale School of Medicine) about teaching, and from other attending physicians, students, and residents about my job, was a motivating force to continue. Michael Sernyak, M.D., the unit chief, was extremely supportive. He connected me with Scott Woods, M.D., who was doing studies on the newest atypical antipsychotic medications. He suggested that I work on the part related to medication adherence, and helped me with my writing, library searches, and reading and interpreting the literature. Through his mentorship and commitment to my success, I obtained my first grant, a NARSAD award (from the National Alliance for Research on Schizophrenia and Depression, now called the Brain and Behavior Research Foundation) to conduct research on treatment adherence among schizophrenic patients (Diaz et al. 2001a; Diaz et al. 2004b). Scott allowed me to use his team, so I had a statistician and research assistants to support the work. We had regular research meetings with his staff and one-on-one meetings to review my work. I felt I was part of a research team, which was very encouraging. If I had planned this project without support, I would not have gotten anywhere.

The clock kept ticking. Two years had passed, and somebody else thought of my upcoming review for promotion. Robert Rosenheck, M.D., professor of psychiatry and epidemiology, a famous, respected mental health services researcher talked to me about doing research with the Latino population. He thought I needed to create a niche in the department, and suggested Latino services. I had been working tangentially with the Hispanic Clinic at CMHC, but had never thought of doing research there, yet Dr. Rosenheck encouraged me to try. He supported a survey of the needs and services of this first Hispanic clinic in the country. We planned the survey (Diaz et al. 2001b), and translated it; he even invited an expert in Latino mental health research, Javier Escobar, M.D., former chair of psychiatry for the University of Connecticut. This was fortuitous because I knew Dr. Escobar was also a Colombian and very supportive of Latino researchers achieving success in America.

I kept working on my research. There was an announcement for a National Institute of Mental Health (NIMH) grant related to adherence to medications and services research. I embarked on this new initiative, proposing a medication adherence research project focused on Latinos with a quantitative part and a qualitative part. I remember well that the most important aspects of the grant writing process were the development of the hypothesis and writing clear, specific aims. This was a K23 grant to provide training and support for a research plan. Both Bob Rosenheck and Scott Woods helped greatly, making suggestions to create an appropriate research plan. When I got my scores from the grant review, I hid for two days, sometimes crying. I thought I had gotten the worst score. In fact, I had gotten the best. I mistakenly thought that a higher score was more favorable! My misunderstanding was rectified when Scott showed excitement about the results. He said that in that round of proposals my grant should have been the best reviewed. He said that was Bob's doing, but I thought it was due to Bob's and Scott's and everybody else's efforts including my own. I do not recall why, but somehow Howard Zonana, M.D., who was covering for the head of CMHC, asked one of the editors of the center to help me by editing the grant for correct English. To this day, I think this was very effective aid that made my plan more understandable and contributed to the exceptional score. I do not recall asking for all of this help, but somehow I received it, and I will always be grateful.

The month prior to the grant's submission deadline, I was dealing with my father who was gravely ill and in an intensive care unit. My father was always a hard worker, dutiful and ready to help others. I felt that putting forth great effort to submit the grant was what I needed to do then. He would have been pleased. I remember going back and forth from the intensive care unit to my office to keep working on the grant proposal. Some people said, "You need to take time for yourself." I said, " Yes, but I need to keep my focus on my goal." My father died one week before I sent the grant application. Fortunately, it had been nearly finished at around the time he became critically ill, and it was at that stage that Bob Rosenheck had suggested that I "leave for a while," so that when I came back to the grant proposal I would be more effective in criticizing it.

My Aunt Inesita used to say to me, "You do so well, everything you wish comes true!" So, I got all I wanted, but I was too busy. I was finishing psychoanalytic training and had to start taking courses in the Department of Epidemiology and Public Health. I spent long nights writing papers and learned about SAS statistical software; I loved methodology, but did not do well in epidemiology. Humans have their limits. My husband deserves an award for the patience and support he gave me.

Equipped with an NIMH training grant proposal with a great score, I was a minority woman and a psychiatrist working on health services for the Latino population. I dutifully attended to my research plan and my courses. I met with mentors, collected data, and analyzed it with help from both Bob and Scott. The qualitative data analysis was entered into ATLAS.Ti, a software program to manage qualitative data. I could do analyses for many more moons. Throughout this period, I kept meeting Latino researchers through Javier Escobar and the mental health services researchers (Diaz et al. 2005).

John Krystal, M.D., our current Yale psychiatry department chair, holds a yearly conference in collaboration with NAMI, the National Association on Mental Illness. This conference educates the public about the latest advances in psychiatric treatment and is always a success. One day in the cafeteria line, he was talking about the conference and asked how to go about organizing such a conference for the Spanish-speaking community. He asked me, "Would you be interested?" I knew the great need for Hispanics to be educated about mental health treatments. I said yes. He said, "You have all my support, and I will put you in contact with the key people." We decided to move forward with this idea.

It was the first conference in New Haven in Spanish informing the public about the advances in mental health research. I chaired the conference. We met for six months, planning and organizing to address barriers to access such as language, cultural sensitivity, transportation, and child care. The results were amazing; we expected perhaps fifty people, and 450 people attended the program. We owed it to teamwork with NAMI and the State of Connecticut mental health department, represented by Jose Ortiz; to the Hispanic Clinic and the CMHC team; and of course to John Krystal (Katz 2001).

Five years of the grant had passed. I had not succeeded yet in obtaining an R01 grant from NIMH. I had tried twice and decided to make a third attempt some other time. I was feeling the need to explore other grounds. Nobody asked me to leave Yale, but I chose to work for two and a half years at Robert Wood Johnson Medical School (the University of Medicine and Dentistry of New Jersey) in Piscataway, New Jersey, with Javier Escobar, who was now the department of psychiatry chair. He wanted me to organize a clinic for the Latinos in New Jersey and to work on Latino health research. I worked on two studies: diagnosis in Latinos and somatization. It was a great experience.

It was challenging to develop a clinic for Latinos in New Jersey, but we did. This was one of the personal successes that I savor the most. This was my first time as a psychiatrist away from Connecticut and Yale. I learned about other styles and ways of treatment. I appreciated the clinicians' dedication to their work and understood their challenges. I admired how Dr. Escobar had gathered successful researchers for his department; I taught medical students, residents, and staff. It was a great opportunity. We founded Clínica Latina in New Brunswick and Newark. We also started *Cultural Rounds in Mental Health,* a monthly community conference opened to the local clinicians to learn about issues of Latino mental health. We started a Latino internship track for Latino psychologists from Rutgers, the State University of New Jersey. I also worked on several research projects related to somatization and diagnosis in different ethnicities (Diaz et al. 2009).

I found that I missed Connecticut, and one day Luis M. Añez Nava, Psy.D., called me from Yale. They were starting an expansion of the Hispanic Clinic to include primary care and wanted me back. Jeanne Steiner,

D.O., medical director of CMHC, said "We are recruiting you back." When I left Yale, Steve Bunney, M.D., the Yale psychiatry department chair, had said to me "Think carefully before you make your decision to go; there will always be somebody who wants to recruit you." But I left. I thought I needed to at the time. I never thought I would come back.

Since returning to the Yale Department of Psychiatry, I have been the medical director of the Hispanic Clinic and the Connecticut Latino Behavioral Health System. I am now one of the associate directors of the Yale psychiatry residency program. When Robert Rohrbaugh, M.D., residency director, asked me to join his team, I wondered whether this would be the right job for me, even though it is an honor. This is a visible position that makes me a little uneasy. I continued my other duties in the clinic, with some time set aside for the educational part. Now I will have to publish on education.

It is easy to train someone when the trainee is responsive and very accomplished. The real success is to train somebody who is challenging. I am trying to embrace that challenge. Many experiences make this opportunity appealing to me: my own struggle of having a medical degree from abroad; being so self-conscious about my accent; being a mother of a child born with medical problems. My experiences as a psychiatrist in the community serving seriously mentally ill patients have created in me an urgency to pass on this experience and to educate trainees to understand that patient care is not optimal, that health disparities exist, and that we need to continue research to understand biology and how best to provide health care services.

As a psychiatrist, being who I am influenced my work greatly. I am an immigrant in this country, where I speak English as opposed to my native language of Spanish. I have seen poverty and struggles of people trying to make it in life with their families and children. I am a woman, the first to be a physician in my family. My biggest challenge has been to overcome my own doubts. My own psychoanalytic process, my husband and family, my mentors, my teachers, and positive results from successful endeavors have all helped me to progress. I have been rejected by a training program because I was pregnant; some supervisors gave me a hard time because of my accent; and sometimes patients were biased against me. But I chose not to give much energy to those occurrences. I hope I am not blind to my own weaknesses and faults. Fortunately, I have enough people around whom I can trust who will tell me if I am admiring myself too much. Developing such a circle of individuals is important as you go forward in your career.

As I watched my mother extinguished by dementia and old age, I became more attuned to how ephemeral we are. My mother died in September 2008. My journey with her health problems is probably an experience to share so others can benefit from what I learned. But it is still too raw, my grief is too present. My parents are buried in New Haven, Connecticut. They said their happiest times were in New Haven because of me, my husband, and their grandchildren. They never regretted having immigrated to the United States. But once my father told me, as he was healing from a cardiac procedure: "Daughter, you have to do something for patients who cannot understand English. It is difficult when you are ill in the hospital."

Balancing a professional and personal life with this career is not easy unless you have a partner who supports you in your efforts to succeed. I trust my husband's intuitions; he allows me to be as independent as I want while allowing me to be dependent on him when needed. I think we understand each other. I am not perfect and he is not perfect. He has been a partner in raising children, as well as in planning finances. He has been a true partner in life.

My leadership style revolves around the assumption that all work should be done as a team. I expect collaboration. Being a leader places you in the spotlight. It helps immensely to have endured and overcome challenging circumstances, because those experiences help you to be more attuned to others' struggles. Learning to manage disappointments is crucial. I learned to be positive and to be hopeful at the most difficult times.

PRACTICAL TIPS FOR WOMEN IN PSYCHIATRY

My practical tips to women aspiring to psychiatric careers are the tips I live by myself:

- Take advantage of your strengths and overcome weaknesses.
- Continue to be curious about the brain and human behavior.
- Continue to learn from others, and find a mentor.
- Get feedback about your performance.
- Persist despite failure. Use failure as your motivation to forge ahead.
- Be positive and always give *esperanza*—that is, hope.

References

Akhtar S: A third individuation: immigration, identity, and the psychoanalytic process. J Am Psychoanal Assoc 43:1051–1079, 1994

Diaz E, Levine HB, Sullivan MC, et al: Use of the Medication Event Monitoring System to estimate medication compliance in patients with schizophrenia. J Psychiatry Neurosci 26:325–329, 2001a

Diaz E, Prigerson H, Desai R, et al: Perceived needs and service use of Spanish speaking monolingual patients followed at a Hispanic clinic. Community Ment Health J 37:335–346, 2001b

Diaz E, Fergusson A, Strauss JS: Innovative Care for the Homeless Mentally Ill in Bogota, Colombia, in Schizophrenia, Culture and Subjectivity: The Edge of Experience. Edited by Jenkins JH, Barrett RJ. New York, Cambridge University Press, 2004a, pp 219–237

Diaz E, Neuse E, Sullivan MC, et al: Adherence to conventional and atypical antipsychotics after hospital discharge. J Clin Psychiatry 65:354–360, 2004b

Diaz E, Woods SW, Rosenheck RA: Effects of ethnicity on psychotropic medication adherence. Community Ment Health J 41:521–537, 2005

Diaz E, Miskemen T, Vega WA, et al: Inconsistencies in diagnosis and symptoms among bilingual and English-speaking Latinos and Euro-Americans. Psychiatr Serv 60:1379–1382, 2009

Katz D: Language barriers: Hispanics have limited access to mental health care. New Haven Register, November 8, 2001, p C18

Scott JR, Rose NB: Effects of psychoprophylaxis (Lamaze preparation) on labor and delivery in primiparas. N Engl J Med 294:1205–1207, 1976

Seashore JG: Congenital abdominal wall defects. Clin Perinatol 5:61–77, 1978

Chapter 19

Unexpected Adventures Behind the Walls

Cassandra F. Newkirk, M.D., M.B.A.

MY LIFE HAS BEEN ONE OF ADVENTURE, doing things differently and taking chances. Whether behind the walls of prisons throughout the United States or behind the scenes of major corporations, I have worked as a staff psychiatrist in some, evaluated services and managed staff in others. My mother worked as an elementary school teacher, not taking overt chances herself but encouraging the children she taught (although not necessarily her own children) to expand their worlds. My father moved from teaching to administration, a change similar in nature to my having moved from the traditional practice of psychiatry (office and hospital based) to working in different venues such as jails and prisons and then ending up in administration full time. My brother has been the "settled" child, more like my dad, and I have been the adventuresome one, more like the people I envisioned that my parents wanted to be. They were both born and raised in the rural south during the 1920s to hardworking, African American farmers and laborers, and they shielded us as best they could from much of the racial discrimination prevalent during our childhoods.

Beginnings

How did I become interested in medicine? In high school I was interested in biomedical engineering because it sounded different and I fancied myself interested in all things technical. I volunteered at the local hospital as a candy striper during my junior and senior years of high school and enjoyed the experience immensely. The world of medicine was of interest to me; I was thinking not about being a physician, but about perhaps going into some other area of medical support, though I was unclear about what occupation. Upon reflection, the doctor who delivered me was African American and my parents took me to him for medical care until I left home for college, but I had never met a woman physician of any nationality, so it did not cross my mind that I could become a physician. The guidance counselor at school did not think I would do well at all in college even though I was an honor student. Nevertheless, I persisted, and matriculated at Duke University in Durham, North Carolina, in 1970.

I was educated in the public school system of North Carolina, and studying at Duke did not come easily; I came to realize that whereas I had not had to study very much in high school, in college it was absolutely necessary. Elementary school was uneventful except that we moved from one small town to a smaller one when I was in fourth grade, in order for my father to become the principal of a high school instead of the smaller elementary school where he had been principal for several years. At that time my parents began building a home in a small city; once it was completed, we commuted on Friday nights to our city home and returned to the rural home and school on Sunday evenings. Interestingly, my life at the moment involves my commuting between my job in Florida and my home in New Jersey, where my husband lives and works—history truly does tend to repeat itself.

My brother and I were the "principal's kids," which led to everyone knowing who we were but at times made for awkward social situations. Our mother was a teacher at the same school , so it was natural that others thought we were given good grades rather than earning them. I was a happy kid when my father and mother were able to find jobs close enough for us to move to the city home permanently. Dilemmas arose because we were not allowed to go to the city schools but, again, had to go to the school where our parents worked. My brother and I finally prevailed, and our parents allowed us to go to the city schools in Wilmington, North Carolina. To our dismay, my brother and I discovered that the new teachers thought we were academically behind because we were transferring in from rural schools and there was a perception that the city schools had much more rigorous curriculums. It is worth noting that all of the schools in my life, including this one, were segregated schools which only African Americans attended. I was placed in regular classes in the ninth grade and was bored, finding the work very easy. My algebra teacher is the one I remember who encouraged me the most and gave me extra work to do. She was my first mentor.

High School

In 1967 I entered high school. The late 1960s were the height of the civil rights movement in the South, and I found myself in the midst of a cultural change. Although the rulings in the landmark U.S. Supreme Court case of Brown v. Board of Education was handed down in 1954, integration of most of the public schools in the southern United States did not begin until several years later. The year 1957 marked the beginning of federally mandated integration of public schools with the integration of Little Rock Central High School in Arkansas, and the Little Rock Nine. Though I was only four years old at the time, this incident had a profound effect on the lives of millions of people. In North Carolina, it was the time of voluntary integration of the public schools, when African American students could choose to go to schools from which we had previously been barred. I do not remember how the decision was made within my family that I would attend the white school for my tenth-grade year. I joined the band and found it boring, since the music they played was not what I was used to, but I stayed in the band and joined the orchestra as well. I learned to play the oboe in addition to the clarinet. It was clarinet in the marching band and oboe in the orchestra. I was the only oboe player in the orchestra, and I recently came across a newspaper article saved by my mother that featured me in the city paper as being one of only two oboe players at the time in the entire school system. In my junior year, I ran for vice president of the senior class and won and was inducted into the honor society. In spite of all this, my guidance counselor still did not think I was college material. Luckily for me, as both of my parents had master's degrees, not going to college was not an option.

My senior year was one of turmoil, filled with lots of racial tension throughout the city. In 1969 all of the public schools in Wilmington, North Carolina, were forcibly integrated. The African American schools were closed and became a part of history. Because of the suddenness of this situation, many of us felt as though a part of our community's culture had been lost. I had looked forward to the social life of high school with familiar friends from my neighborhood. Instead, functions at the newly integrated schools were open to all students, but most of us felt uncomfortable socializing with people with whom we were unfamiliar and who, as a group, had been quite hostile toward people of color. I therefore seldom ventured out socially with classmates. Because of the racial unrest in the city, my parents were afraid to allow us to go to any social functions. To try to compensate, my mother joined an African American social group for professionals with hopes of providing us with other social outlets. This did not make me more comfortable to any great extent, so the social butterfly I was not. I was more content to stay at home and read than to go out with friends.

The erroneous assumption that all African American schools were inferior led to their being closed with little or no planning or evaluation prior to making such a major change. What was lacking was appropriate allocation of tax dollars for African American public schools. Many African American teachers lost their jobs, although most were transferred to other schools. The school in which my parents worked was spared because it was relatively new. Located in another county, their school remained open and white children and teachers were assigned to it.

Thus began my senior year, one year after the death of Dr. Martin Luther King Jr., with the country awash in unrest. I participated in meetings regarding proposed school boycotts by African American students because of the way we were being treated in the newly integrated schools. All of this was new, exciting, and frightening. What stands out most as I recall that period is that my parents did not participate overtly, but I did. It was a time of growing pride in being an African American, but also one of uncertainty about the future.

Church played a major role in my life growing up and was a major part of my social upbringing. My parents were active in the Baptist church and wherever we moved, the family joined a local church. Churches I attended were havens for me socially and I participated in them as much as I could. They were also places where I learned about the political issues of the times and the teachings of Dr. Martin Luther King Jr. While I was in college, church continued to be a social outlet, as it did upon my move to Atlanta to do my residency training. Within a short period after moving to Atlanta I attended and joined Central United Methodist Church; it was pastored at the time by Dr. Joseph Lowery, who was then president of the Southern Christian Leadership Conference and had been a trusted confidant of Dr. King.

College

When I arrived at Duke University in the fall of 1970, I was still seriously considering studying biomedical engineering, and the civil rights movement in the South was in full swing. Admission to the school of engineering at Duke was not automatic, as one had to apply to the school of engineering during their freshman year. After arriving on campus I became caught up in civil rights issues along with other students, and I was talking to peers who were interested in political science so they could apply to law school, or who were premed majors planning to go to medical school. No one was interested in engineering. I was also swept along in trying to find out how I fit into this very diverse group of students. Looking back, I realize I was usually in the forefront of doing things differently, and I learned to just do them and tell my parents later. This practice continues with my mother, who is now ninety-two years old and who at times just shakes her head at my adventures. I appreciate now more than ever that my parents were concerned about my well-being and were therefore afraid that my participating in activities with diverse groups of people would bring harm to me, as had so often happened to African Americans in the past. I appreciate it now that their world of growing up in the rural and segregated South did not afford them the opportunities that were opening up for me as integration progressed.

I ended up majoring in Black Studies and also took all of the premed requisite courses. Black Studies allowed me to explore black history and other areas to which I had never been exposed, broadening my horizons and giving me a depth of understanding of American history from a different perspective. It was a time of increasing anger at the injustices that had been and still were occurring to people of color in this country, but it was also a time of hope that things were changing. The very fact that I and others of color were admitted to Duke in greater numbers than previously was a big change in itself. Subconsciously, my being there created its own stress and anxiety because of the need to succeed and not disappoint my parents—and to prove my guidance counselor wrong.

Many of the Black Studies courses were taught by professors from the Duke Divinity School; they were a fascinating combination of traditional sciences and courses exploring the world of religion and its impact on the African American community. I met my first African American scholars, my instructors, who challenged us to read the great African American writers such as Frederick Douglass, W.E.B. DuBois, James Baldwin, and Frantz Fanon. These professors and the authors to whom I was exposed lifted me to another plane and opened up the possibilities that I could do and be anything to which I put my mind. DuBois (1903) spoke of his wish to be an American *and* a Negro, which is the essence of what I and many others were looking for during those times. Thoughts such as these, from early twentieth century writings by DuBois and others, kept me going. There were such courses and instructors at Duke at that time because students who preceded me made demands that African American studies become a part of the curriculum and accessible to all students.

My interest in engineering waned as I met other African American students who were focused on becoming physicians, many of them women who believed that they could accomplish this. An older cousin of mine was admitted to Duke's medical school while I was an undergraduate, and that also helped solidify my goal to enter medical school.

Although there were support systems at Duke, I found it extremely difficult to navigate the academic and social issues, and I managed to lose some of my motivation and focus. I had a very slow social life and was disappointed in this because high school had also been a time of few social outlets. I graduated from Duke but was not admitted to medical school immediately. All of these circumstances took their toll on my self-esteem. I stayed home with my parents for six months and reflected and weighed my options. Restrategizing, I attended North Carolina Agricultural and Technical State University, a historically black college, where my brother was a freshman; I took more science courses and found my self-esteem again. One of life's lessons from this experience was to persist in my goals no matter how I felt. It is through the failures that we often learn the most valuable lessons. I reapplied to medical schools as well as schools of public health and was accepted to several.

Medical School

I entered medical school in 1974 at the University of North Carolina at Chapel Hill. During the summer prior to the first year I had the opportunity to participate in a program geared toward African American and other minority students entering medical school. For several weeks prior to the beginning of the first year, I lived on campus and went to classes, bonding with many of the other incoming freshmen. There, I met another group of mentors who were students who had just completed their first year of medical school. The majority in this support system were African American women. They reached out and never let go. I continue many of those friendships to this day, including one of my best friends. Though medical school had a much more rigorous curriculum than undergraduate school, I had matured, and I utilized my support systems to a much greater extent than in undergraduate school. There are always those willing to help us, but one must be willing to ask for help and then accept it.

It was during medical school that I first became acutely aware of the differences in the way men and women were treated, especially in highly skilled professional arenas. My awareness regarding women's rights was heightened during this time, when much attention was being drawn to the rights or lack of rights of African Americans in general. In those days there were many fewer women in medical school classes than men, and we learned to keep quiet in public forums because medicine had been a male-dominated profession for so many years. Many of us did discuss these issues with other women, but there were few women faculty members to go to for advice. The first woman attending physician I encountered was a psychiatrist; I was awestruck and found it fascinating to listen to and learn from her. I often wonder now if this is why I eventually chose psychiatry as my specialty. There were very few women instructors during the first two years of didactics in medical school. It was noted by everyone, though, that the number of women in our class was one of the highest the school had ever experienced, and the number of women was projected to grow. This awareness that the face of medicine was changing provided some comfort. As an African American woman, I found it hard to discern whether others' behaviors toward me were secondary to the fact that I am African American or to the fact that I am a woman.

During my third year of medical school I had the opportunity to do my ob-gyn rotation at Meharry Medical College in Nashville. Meharry was founded in 1876 as a part of Central Tennessee College. It was chartered as a medical school in 1915 and was the first medical school in the South that admitted African Americans. I had wanted to attend Meharry because a maternal aunt had worked as lead surgical nurse there for many years and I remembered the fond stories she would tell with such pride about working there and the wonderful physicians with whom she worked. I remember her talking about Dr. Lloyd Elam, who was a psychiatrist and was named president of Meharry in 1968, becoming the second African American president of the college since its inception. It was long after my aunt passed away that I finally met Dr. Elam. He became one of the elders that I looked up to and listened to, heeding his advice until his death in 2008. My rotation at Meharry was a wonderful experience because so many of the faculty and students remembered my aunt. Meharry did not have the financial resources that the University of North Carolina had, but the atmosphere of support and camaraderie more than compensated for its limited resources. Here I was, again being given a boost to my self-esteem and seeing several African American women physicians to use as role models. Though there were some women faculty members at the University of North Carolina, none looked like me. I cherished the time spent at Meharry and was appreciative that the University of North Carolina was open to allowing students to choose diverse experiences in their formative years before this notion became popular.

Residency

I started medical school thinking about pursuing a primary care practice, but during my third year I began to think of other options. I enjoyed pediatrics and psychiatry and thought I would do a pediatrics internship. I decided I wanted to go to Howard University to experience training at a predominantly African American institution. Howard University College of Medicine was established in 1867 in Washington, D.C., as a training institution for newly freed slaves as well as a place to provide much-needed medical care. I was matched at Howard for an internship in pediatrics and although I enjoyed pediatrics, I decided that the mothers needed help and that I would train to become a child psychiatrist. Since the department of psychiatry at Howard was going through a transition at that time I looked at Emory University in Atlanta and was accepted as a postgraduate year 2 (PGY2) student in the psychiatry program. I mentioned to a nurse that I would be leaving Washington for Atlanta and had to find a place to stay. She knew of a woman who was also moving to Atlanta and needed a place to stay. We met and decided we would look for a place together. We ended up renting Congressman John Lewis's house in Atlanta, as he was moving his family to Washington, where he was going to work as the director of ACTION (the federal volunteer agency comprising Volunteers in Service to America, the Peace Corps, and National Senior Service), under President Jimmy Carter. Meeting Congressman Lewis and his family was another one of those awe-inspiring moments given that he was one of the foremost organizers and leaders of the civil rights movement in the South (Biography of John Lewis 2011). Atlanta was a booming city and Grady Memorial Hospital (affiliated with Emory University School of Medicine) was a perfect place to train, as it was an extremely busy teaching hospital.

When I moved to Atlanta in 1979, it was exciting and fun, with lots of things to explore, and very welcoming to an African American young professional like me. It was also a city that had very strong roots in the civil rights movement. Upon entering the residency program I found I was the only African American resident in my year, which was a change for me. There were a few African American residents in the classes ahead of and behind mine. I soon discovered that no one remembered whether or not, up until that point, an African American woman had completed the psychiatry residency program at Emory. I found the environment nurturing, so I focused little on this issue.

I continued to have an interest in child psychiatry until I was exposed to forensic psychiatry by Dr. Jonas Robitscher, one of the lecturers during my PGY2 rotations. He was very well known in the field of forensic psychiatry and brought the subject alive for me. He died in 1981 during the time that I was doing extra work in this area, during my PGY4 rotation, so I never had a chance to work with him. Shortly after he passed on, several forensic psychiatrists in Atlanta formed the Robitscher Society and met regularly for dinner and discussion of forensic topics of interest. In this way, I got to learn of his work from those whom he had mentored in the Emory University community.

Part of our scut work as PGY2s was to perform preliminary competency evaluations on detainees from the Fulton County Jail one day each week. This was my initial exposure to persons living with mental illnesses who were behind bars. I found the entire field of forensic psychiatry to be intriguing and began to ask questions about how to specialize in this area. I met another forensic psychiatrist, Dr. Lloyd Baccus, a part-time faculty member who was assigned to the Psychiatry and Law Service to perform the responsibility-to-stand-trial evaluations of detainees for whom the Fulton County courts had ordered this evaluation. Lloyd became a friend and mentor during my PGY4 year; I did a preceptorship with him, performing competency and responsibility evaluations at the jail and then going to court with him to testify. There were only a few forensic psychiatry fellowship programs in existence in 1981, and the advice I was given by senior faculty was to get experience. I eventually became board certified in forensic psychiatry via examination.

I decided not to pursue a child psychiatry fellowship but to focus on forensic psychiatry instead. I was named chief resident for the 1981–1982 year. I held this position while I did my preceptorship with Dr. Baccus. This was my first opportunity to test my skills as a leader. My mentor during that experience was Dr. Dewitt Alfred, who was one of the professors who taught me several lessons about the practice of psychiatry. Emory had a very eclectic training program and I remember many of us complaining about all the traveling we had to do, between the teaching hospitals, Grady Memorial Hospital and Emory University Hospital, and to private practitioners' offices for some of our supervision. This running around actually served us all very well as we entered the real world of practice. When I complained to Dr. Alfred about this, he told me that it was not good to put all your eggs in one basket. I heard him then and have followed that advice ever since. It has benefited me; I was then and still continue to be open to new and different venues of service and practice. Dr. Alfred allowed me to develop my own leadership style during that year. My job was to be the liaison between the faculty and the residents, and in this capacity I began to learn some of the politics of medicine. Dr. Alfred encouraged me to make decisions on my own but to keep him informed. I thoroughly enjoyed the job and have found myself in several leadership roles since.

Dr. Alfred was responsible for introducing me to the world of methadone detoxification and maintenance. There was a methadone clinic on the ground floor of the building that housed the community mental health center where the Emory psychiatry residents did some of their rotations. Many of the people addicted to heroin were also living with a major mental illness. I was able to treat their mental illness and prescribe the methadone, and the social workers in the clinic helped them with supportive therapy, housing, and other basic needs. (Almost twenty years later, while working as the mental health services director for the Philadelphia Prison System, I was able to build on this experience and work with a consultant to establish a methadone detoxification program at the Philadelphia Prison System.) It was during this time of working with those who were addicted to opiates that I learned to become comfortable with people living by their wits and surviving on the street, or, as we might term them, *master manipulators.* I have always remembered that my patients with addiction taught me valuable lessons about human nature that have been priceless in honing my skills to work with incarcerated persons. I was trained in an academic setting about the attributes of addicted behavior but no formal education is as valuable as working with people where they are and how they are. During my fourth year of residency training, I was required to facilitate a group therapy experience for the entire year with concomitant supervision. I chose to work with a group of people in the methadone maintenance program who had become addicted iatrogenically as a result of some medical illness for which they had been prescribed opiates for medicinal purposes. This was one of the most rewarding and eye-opening experiences of my training. Most of the group members were incapacitated by their addictions, people who had been working but who fell prey to drug use that had all started innocently enough. What was most startling was the lack of sensitivity to the addictive nature of the medication, usually opiate analgesics, that had been prescribed for legitimate pain with little attention paid to their inherent addictive properties.

Private Practice

Once I had completed my residency program, I started my private practice by sharing office space with an established psychiatrist. Along with seeing patients for general psychotherapy and medication monitoring, I worked part-time at the Fulton County Jail and a state prison in Atlanta. Both of these jobs were interesting and provided me with guaranteed income as I began my practice. I initially considered both of these jobs as temporary while I built my private practice. The job at the jail also entailed some administrative work that required me to oversee the mental health services with the guidance of a private company that was providing medical and mental health services at the jail. I enjoyed the work immensely and stayed at the jail and the prison for several years. One of my most memorable experiences at the jail involved my being terminated from the position at the jail by the private company in 1982 because I stood my ground on an ethical issue. I have never regretted that decision. I was devastated at the time but sought advice and support from mentors and friends. I was hired by the same company some fifteen years later to again provide mental health services to inmates in a correctional setting. This experience solidified wisdom taught to me by my parents that my reputation is essential to retain.

At the same time that I was establishing my private practice, in 1981, Morehouse School of Medicine became an independently chartered medical school, becoming the first medical school established at a historically black college during the twentieth century (Morehouse School of Medicine 2011). Dr. Alfred was named chair of the Department of Psychiatry and asked whether I was interested in being an instructor. I was thrilled to be a part of a brand-new medical school. My primary role was to teach basic psychiatry to first- and second-year students and to mentor as many students as possible. I also kept an affiliation with Emory, primarily working on the Psychiatry and Law Service performing court-ordered evaluations, and supervising residents and students who had an interest in forensic psychiatry. During the years that I worked on that service several of the students or residents decided to pursue forensic psychiatry fellowships. I stay in touch with many of them who are now in practice, just as I stay in touch with my mentors. Some of my mentors have passed on (Drs. Alfred, Baccus, and Elam), but the lessons learned and the wisdom they shared will never go away. There has been a comfort in knowing that what was passed on to me, I, too, must pass on to others. As I grow older I have begun to reach out to support high school students who have an interest in medicine. It remains quite amazing that though we are a "wired" world and have information at our fingertips, it takes the human element of compassion and concern to guide those coming behind us to show them where to look or else they run the risk of looking in all the wrong places. Mentors are what Napoleon Hill (1938/2008) would call a mastermind group, which is utilized to share ideas and to explore options for success as well as to plan and analyze processes that have worked and those that have not led to successes. Now again I find myself a part of a newly established medical school, as I have recently become a part-time faculty member at Florida International University's Herbert Wertheim College of Medicine in Miami. The first class entered the college in August 2009 and I again have the opportunity to mentor young doctors. This is the first new medical school to be established in the United States since Morehouse School of Medicine was chartered in 1981.

My private practice consisted of an eclectic mix of practice settings, including seeing patients in the office, being on the staff of at least one or two private psychiatric facilities at any given time, and working several hours a week at a jail, prison, juvenile detention facility, or other public psychiatric facility as well as part-time teaching at Emory and Morehouse Schools of Medicine. Over the years, I worked at a Job Corps site, a community mental health center, and three different county jails and for a while I worked with the counseling service at Spelman College, one of the most prestigious historically black colleges for women. I enjoyed doing these part-time jobs primarily because they provided me with different venues as well as a steady and guaranteed income. When I began to practice, payment for private patients was primarily via traditional insurance plans, which tended to pay eighty to ninety percent of charges for psychotherapy, including medication monitoring. During the early 1990s, managed care organizations began to flourish and provider panels (networks) were the norm. This was a major change for me and my colleagues. By this time, I was practicing with a multidisciplinary group of mental health care providers, all of us sharing the office expenses but maintaining our individual practices. Managed care wreaked havoc on our practices. As one of the few in the group who had several part-time jobs outside of the office, I set the example for my colleagues to follow as managed care took hold in Atlanta. Our expenses increased but payment for services decreased, and the paperwork and justifications required were ever-increasing.

I also accepted forensic psychiatry cases dealing primarily with issues of criminal responsibility. At times I also took civil cases relating to mental pain and suffering. After I had been in practice a few years, Dr. Baccus began to refer prison litigation cases to me. I was usually accepted by the attorneys as an expert based on the referral from Dr. Baccus, as he had established himself in this area of expertise over several years. During the span of twenty years, I built my own reputation, being one of only a few African American women engaged as an expert in prison litigation cases. My work as a staff psychiatrist in several correctional settings gave me credibility with attorneys when it came to understanding what mental health services were needed by those living behind the walls. I learned much from the attorneys that I worked with over the years as well as from Dr. Baccus, who continued to be my mentor. I worked for plaintiffs as well as defendants who were often in prison or jail systems that allegedly were not providing constitutional levels of care.

During my psychiatry residency program, I was introduced to the world of guild societies. Several of the Emory faculty members were involved in the Georgia Psychiatric Physicians Association and encouraged the trainees to participate. I did, and attended my first American Psychiatric Association meeting the spring of my PGY4 year. I remember it being in Canada, and I was amazed at how many psychiatrists were gathered in one location. Shortly after beginning private practice, I was introduced to correctional health care meetings and groups and joined those as well. Because of my experience working in jails and prisons, I participated in accreditation surveys by the Georgia State Medical Association on behalf of the National Commission on Correctional Health Care, which began as a program established by the American Medical Association. I was fascinated by the information to be learned in the worlds of psychiatry and corrections, and volunteered for committees on both at the state level. I enjoyed the networking and the learning as well as the travel. I eventually began presenting at conferences, primarily on correctional mental health issues, which was a way for me to live and work in both worlds. As the deinstitutionalization of the state psychiatric hospitals around the country progressed, with more and more people being discharged into their home communities with few resources following them, the number of people living with mental illness within the criminal justice system continued to rise. Because of my work inside as well as outside of the correctional environment, I have been able to present a unique perspective on the issues facing those who serve this population as well as the persons served.

The road to leadership roles for me was one of volunteering for committees, which led to nominations for board seats and eventually to larger, elected positions with more responsibility. I have served on the boards of several organizations including the Georgia Psychiatric Physicians Association, the American Correctional Health Services Association, and the Black Psychiatrists of America. I eventually was elected to the presidency of all three of these organizations over the past twenty years. It is much easier being a member of a board or committee than leading a volunteer organization. One of the lessons I've learned is that only a few people end up doing most of the work. Though the memberships and boards make decisions as to what will be done, it is the president to whom it falls to make things happen. It has been much easier to motivate those whom I supervise at work than to motivate committee members because, although all are participants presumably because they want to be, the consequences associated with not following through with commitments are vastly different.

While working as a staff psychiatrist at a women's prison in the Georgia Department of Corrections, I was asked to become the mental health director for the entire system. Because of consequences of a lawsuit at one of the women's prisons surrounding issues of inadequate physical and mental health care as well as allegations of sexual abuse, the state agency chose a new commissioner of the system, Dr. Allen Ault, who reorganized the health divisions of the department. Dr. Ault and I met while he was working as a consultant to the administration. When he was named commissioner, he asked me to take the job as mental health director. In this position I was responsible for overseeing all of the mental health services for the entire department, which consisted of some 33,000 inmates at that time. Several months later, Dr. Ault appointed me Deputy Commissioner of Offender Services, which involved the oversight of several areas of services including mental health, substance abuse, counseling, education, recreation, and chaplaincy. Each division had its own chief, and Dr. Ault was the mentor extraordinaire. He trusted all of us to do our jobs well, but he was always available to help if we needed it. He was and still is an excellent teacher and friend. He empowered us to make decisions and in a manner that was very similar to Dr. Alfred's, as he was always encouraging us to do more.

Dr. Ault also taught me to continue in my other pursuits and interests, since no one job or position was ever guaranteed. I heeded his advice and continued to participate in national meetings, committees, and a few litigation cases when there was no conflict of interest. The commissioner served at the pleasure of the governor, and my position was appointed by the commissioner. When the politics of the governor changed, so did our jobs. We were all asked to resign, which was a new experience for me, but that is how it is with appointed positions. Dr. Ault had been in this position before, in Georgia and other states, and thus understood the politics very well. The experience was invaluable. I never closed my private practice and continued to see patients some evenings and on weekends because of Dr. Ault's advice.

At the time I began working at the women's prison, I was also asked to serve on a women's advisory group for the Substance Abuse and Mental Health Services Administration. It was within that work group of advocates, mental health professionals, and survivors of physical and psychological abuse that I first came face to face with outspoken women who had been in mental health systems around the country. It was from this group of brave women that I became more sensitized and aware of the damage that many of us in psychiatry had probably naively perpetrated in the name of treatment. Some of the most blatant ways that many men and women were retraumatized in psychiatric facilities were through the use of seclusion and restraints in the names of treatment. These were often the same methods by which many people had been abused previously in their lives. During this time, I realized that I knew very little about the impact of trauma on the lives of the people whom I had been treating. This group, combined with my contact with the women behind the walls of the prison where I was now working, gave me another opportunity to learn about psychiatry and treatment options in practical ways so I could be more helpful to those whom I served. I discovered that working with women offenders was much more rewarding than my previous experiences with men. These experiences prepared me for later opportunities in my professional career as well.

Though I left the Georgia Department of Corrections fourteen years ago, I have never severed ties with many of my former colleagues and friends. Dr. Ault remains my mentor and friend, as have many others. The corrections component of the criminal justice system provided me with an opportunity to grow to a much greater depth and expand my horizons by putting my psychiatric and leadership skills to work in a very unique environment. Health care and mental health care are necessities in this environment, although, as we like to say, medicine is a guest in the house of corrections, where safety and security come first. I learned to respect the inmates as people who were often victims themselves even though they may have been the perpetrators of violent crimes. I learned to listen to their stories and treat their mental illnesses as I did for those in my private practice. The biopsychosocial issues with which offenders live tend to be much more complex than those that my private patients experience, but not any less important. I also had to come to terms with my own thoughts regarding the death penalty. I was the psychiatrist assigned to death row in the Georgia Department of Corrections and my job was to treat those living with psychiatric symptoms. For the majority of the time I was assigned to this area, there was a moratorium on the death penalty and therefore there were no executions. At some point, Georgia resumed carrying out the death penalty, and I soon left this service. I came to personally oppose the death penalty, as I was exposed to so many people who were victims of adverse circumstances who had often perpetrated crimes because many of their issues were never dealt with prior to something terrible happening. Some of the men on death row with whom I worked had their sentences commuted to life in prison because new evidence was presented. I do believe there are some people who should never be released from prison.

During my last year at the Department of Corrections, I began to date a man living in New Jersey. We had first met while freshmen in college on one of my trips to visit relatives in New Jersey. We did not keep in touch, but it was on another trip to visit the same relatives that we met again, then started dating and were married eighteen months later in 1996. We dated long-distance and it was during this time that I was relieved of my duties as Deputy Commissioner at the Georgia Department of Corrections. I had several options as to what to do including whether to rebuild my private practice, find another full-time salaried position, or move to New Jersey. We decided to marry, and because he had children living in New Jersey and I had no relatives in Atlanta we made the decision that I would move to New Jersey. It is interesting to note that I had dated some prior to meeting my husband David again, but the older I got, the less time it took me to decide whether a relationship was serious. We married at my parents' home in Wilmington, North Carolina, because my father had Alzheimer's disease and Parkinson's disease. History was repeating itself again: my mother too had been married in her parents' home in 1951.

I continued to do some consulting work on prison cases throughout the country, and after getting my New Jersey medical license I worked part-time at a women's prison, for the same company that had terminated my employment at the Fulton County Jail in 1982 because I would not do some things they had wanted me to do. I honed my skills in working with women offenders as a staff psychiatrist, but found myself once again in the middle of a consent order secondary to litigation to improve the medical and mental health services throughout the Department of Corrections. The issues were similar to those involved in the lawsuit mentioned above in the Georgia Department of Corrections.

In 2000, I was offered the job as mental health services director for the Philadelphia Prison System, which was a 7,000-bed jail complex. Again, I was working for a private provider of health care services in correctional systems. I was in a leadership role again, which I enjoyed. It was in this role that I was asked to oversee budgets, monitor the costs of the psychotropic medications that the psychiatrists were prescribing, and strategize how to provide more services for less money. It was then that I decided I needed to learn more about the business of medicine. I ended up obtaining a master of business administration degree in health care administration over the next few years. The coursework was mostly online, with students from throughout the United States with varied backgrounds. It was a wonderful opportunity to learn from each others' experiences. In all my classes, I was almost always the only health care provider working in a correctional setting. With each class I took, I was able to immediately apply the new skills learned in my work. We were actually encouraged to use our work issues for class projects. What a different world from that of the science of medicine! Now when I talk to young physicians, I encourage them to consider business courses prior to leaving school, as the world of medicine plays a pivotal role in our country's economy.

After almost three years in Philadelphia, I was asked to take the job of mental health director at Rikers Island penitentiary in New York City. There were ten jails compared to the five in Philadelphia, twice as many detainees, and about three times the mental health staff to oversee. I was responsible for being the liaison between the jail's chief and my supervisor with the company providing the health care services (the same one as in Philadelphia), and also between them and the oversight group monitoring the contract for the City of New York. It was similar to the responsibilities I had in Georgia and in Philadelphia, but with very different politics. One of the most prudent lessons that I learned working in management positions in correctional settings, whether for a governmental agency or a private company, was that you must navigate the politics. You only learn this by being mentored and watching how others play the game. Working at Rikers Island gave me the confidence to believe that I could probably work in just about any setting and succeed. Learning to navigate around

New York City was also an accomplishment, and not nearly as intimidating as it sounds.

Though I enjoyed the work at Rikers, I had a five-hour roundtrip commute each day from my home in central New Jersey. I finally had to acknowledge that this was exhausting, leaving me little time for family or friends. I did not overtly seek other jobs but did begin thinking seriously about needing to make a change. I received a call at my office from a gentleman looking for someone to lead a newly created division of correctional mental health services at another private company, GEO Care, Inc. I went to the interview and got the job, which required me to move to Florida to work at the corporate headquarters. My husband was not ready to leave his home state but encouraged me to take the job anyway. We laugh at times now because just as we had a long-distance courtship, so goes the marriage now. It is a little easier because we both travel for our jobs, but this is not for everyone. We have no young children, which makes such an arrangement feasible.

I have worked for GEO Care for the last five years. I have been able to utilize almost all the skills I have learned over the years from my many varied jobs. Because the company is continuing to branch out into diversified areas of corrections and behavioral health care, the networking skills I've developed over the years have been very useful. I am now the vice president of correctional mental health services and chief medical officer. I am busier than in previous jobs but travel a lot for work, which I enjoy. I am active in the psychiatric and correctional organizations as well as being responsible for setting up academic relationships with several of the universities in Florida and other states where we have facilities.

I am in a place now that is fulfilling, though I cannot say that about all of my endeavors. As I am asked to write book chapters, edit books, and lecture, I accept the challenges because this keeps me learning. Thirty-two years ago when I completed medical school, I did not see myself doing any of the things I am doing now. The world of medicine is so different now than it was then, and I am sure it will continue to change. Technology has drastically changed how we perform our jobs as clinicians as well as how we communicate professionally and personally. One of my most significant attributes is being one who loves adventure and things that are different. My husband laughs and often tells me that being around me is a never-ending adventure because most times I do not really know where I will end up. I have developed an abiding faith that I will always end up where God wants me to be and that it will occur when the time is right. It has been a remarkable journey thus far, as almost all of the adventures in my professional and personal life have come to me; I have not really sought them other than by venturing out and allowing myself to be open to new possibilities.

Practical Tips for Women in Psychiatry

- Listen to your family, patients, and mentors—they are your teachers.
- Follow your heart.
- Find a mentor.
- Always be humble.
- Life is an adventure.

References

Biography of John Lewis. Available at: http://johnlewis.house.gov/index.php ?option=com_content&task=view&id=17&Itemid=31. Accessed September 10, 2011.

Brown v Board of Education (1954): About the case (n.d.). Available at: http:// brownvboard.org/content/about-brown-v-board. Accessed December 4, 2011.

DuBois WEB: The Souls of Black Folk: Essays and Sketches. Chicago, IL, AC Mc-Clurg, 1903. Available at: www.bartleby.com/114/. Accessed September 23, 2011.

Hill N: Think and Grow Rich (1938). Radford, VA, Wilder Publications, 2008.

Morehouse School of Medicine. Website. Available at: www.msm.edu/ about_us.aspx. Accessed September 23, 2011.

Chapter 20

My Partly Planned Journey

What Has Worked for Me

Gail E. Robinson, M.D.

UP UNTIL THE AGE OF TEN, I wanted to be an actress. Around the age of ten I decided that becoming an actress was not feasible. Probably because my mother, who was a nurse at the time, had always wanted to be a doctor, I instead set my sights on being a doctor and never thought about the goal of being an actress again. Currently I am a full professor at the University of Toronto in the department of psychiatry, with a cross-appointment to the department of obstetrics and gynecology. I was the founding codirector of the University of Toronto Women's Mental Health Program and currently serve as director of the Women's Mental Health Clinic at the University Health Network at Toronto General Hospital. I have been active in various professional organizations and have been on the board of several community organizations.

All of this is quite ironic to me because, like many women, I did not set out with these as clear goals in sight. In fact, I distinctly remember saying in my first or second year of psychiatry residency that psychiatry was a great career because you could work part-time and earn $35,000 a year. At that time, that seemed a very generous sum of money, although I am sure it certainly dates me now.

After completing a year as chief resident, I was encouraged to apply for a fellowship in community psychiatry. I had no idea what to do after that and so was pleased to be asked to stay on as a staff psychiatrist at the hospital in which I had spent my last three years of training. I had not asked for this job but was happy not to have to think about where to go next, and so I became a psychiatrist in an academic setting at a major university-affiliated teaching hospital.

Despite not having really planned this early phase of my career, I have learned some things that I believe have been helpful for me in my career and may be useful for other women seeking leadership positions in psychiatry.

Children and the Tenure Clock

I have two daughters, born within the first five years of my completing my residency. Fortunately, the University of Toronto's Department of Psychiatry does not have a tenure clock. I was therefore able to gradually start writing papers, the first when I was pregnant with my first daughter. Had I had the same pressure on me that women have in U.S. universities, many of which require promotion to associate professor within six or seven years or you're out, I am not sure how I would have handled it (Yedidia and Bickel 2001). That is not to say that there were not pressures associated with having a family and a career (Carr et al. 1998; Levinson et al. 1989).

After each girl was born, I took off only one month. Some of that was vacation time. I never even asked for more but was sure that if I did, I would lose all credibility as someone interested in an academic career. Now, in Canada, women routinely take six to twelve months off after having a baby. I did start to take two half-days off each week and rigidly stuck to this system for many years. I used this time to be with my children, run errands, or even go for a massage. It helped to make the career-family tension easier.

The other major advantage I had was finding an excellent nanny. She was a genuine English nanny, with many years of being "in service," as she would say. She had worked as a live-in nanny all her life but was eager to have her own place now, and coincidentally lived only a 15-minute walk away. This worked for us because we were not sure we were comfortable having someone in the house all the time: with two busy careers, we relished our privacy. Ms. Blake (Nursie) was well known in the community, and we were very lucky to get her. She was totally reliable and a combination of Dr. Spock and Mary Poppins. She was with us for 14 years, which allowed our children the type of total stability that is rare and could never have been accomplished with a series of au pairs changing every year.

It took me a little while to take full advantage of this wonderful care. We had set Nursie's hours as ending at 6 P.M. I suffered through many evenings of anxiously fighting rush-hour traffic, worrying about being late, until it occurred to me that if we had her leave at 6:30, life would become far less stressful.

I coped with any sense of missing early milestones by deciding that my children didn't accomplish anything until I had seen them do it. If Nursie said they had taken their first step or said their first word, in my mind it didn't happen until they did it in front of me. In this way, I never felt a rivalry with Nursie or jealousy of the time she was able to spend with the children. As well, we became very family-centric. Weekends were spent with the girls, and we socialized less with friends.

As Nursie got older, we got an auxiliary nanny, Corinne, who came in the afternoon to shorten Nursie's work day. This nanny had the added qualification of being able to drive, which was important because we had entered into the stage of after-school lessons and events. All in all, these two wonderful women made a huge contribution to my career.

Find a Mentor

Some years ago, a new psychiatrist-in-chief started in our department, and he was interviewing all of the staff to get a sense of who they were and what their potential was. By that time I had been working in our university-affiliated hospital for about ten years and had published a few papers. I had been in charge of our community psychiatry program and then the outpatient program, neither of them very large at the time. In meeting with the chief, I recall saying that I thought I was a good clinician and a good teacher but that I had no experience in research. He asked whether, if I had some support, I might be interested in applying for research grants.

This marked the beginning of a complete change in my career. Previously, no chief had taken any special interest in developing my career. I did write a grant proposal, aimed at supporting development of a women's mental health program with research into aspects of the psychological consequences of obstetrical and gynecological situations. With the grant support and without the benefit of any specific research training, I became a "researcher" as well as a clinician and teacher. I discovered that I had very good ideas about what sort of research would be of value in looking at women's mental health issues, and it was possible to hire people who understood the technical aspects of statistical analysis. I began to obtain grants, which led to writing many papers. It was fortunate timing, because it was in that period that the department started to take on a more academic tone. Instead of being one of the clinician teachers, I began to be seen as more of an academic, something I had never actually envisioned for myself.

I am not suggesting that the only way to get ahead academically is to do research. Nor do I think this is the best way to become a researcher, and I would certainly recommend getting training before embarking on such a route. I report all of this to stress the importance of finding a mentor, as others have emphasized (Fried et al. 1996; Levinson et al. 1991; Osborn et al. 1992; Yedidia and Bickel 2001). A lot has been written and said in terms of the value of a mentor. It is also important to add that there are many different kinds of mentors and mentors do not necessary last a lifetime (Levinson et al. 1991). This mentor I found in the chief psychiatrist was an essential part of my shifting gears into a much more academic framework.

Many women look for mentors who can advise them about how to do such things as combining a career and family. I have acted as a role model to others myself, helping sort out the conflicts that arise when combining career and family. This is, however, only one kind of mentor, and it is important for women to realize that a man can be a mentor in advising them about specific career moves and opportunities (Hamel et al. 2006). The psychiatrist-in-chief was a specific type of mentor for me, and the mentorship did not last forever. He was very vital to me for many years but later, in fact, he became rather a disappointment as my goals began to conflict with his. Nevertheless, I will always value his input for he played a key role in my progress and development as a psychiatrist and leader.

Find a Special Area of Interest

After I graduated from my residency, a group of women and I began to realize we had not received any specific teaching about women's mental health and the kinds of issues that might be important to women. This all occurred in the early 1980s, when this area was a new field of endeavor. The study of women's mental health involves psychiatric conditions that are unique to women or that present differently in women, as well as looking at the role of women in society and how that might affect them both generally and in terms of psychiatric disorders. We worked together to set up a 12-week, after-hours elective course in women's mental health. The course gave an overview of women's development and examined specific issues in psychiatry and sociocultural issues that are of importance to women.

We collected evaluations during the course. I took these to our central Postgraduate Education Committee to show them the very good ratings we had received and emphasized to them that this was information that was missing in their usual teaching. They allowed us to have one special half-day symposium concerning women's mental health. We, then, went on to lobby for even more time in the central curriculum and were given two half-days. In 1990, my mentor, who was then chair of the department, had decided to set up a number of priority programs for the Department of Psychiatry at the University of Toronto. He encouraged us to submit a proposal concerning women's mental health. One of my colleagues, Dr. Donna Stewart, and I did send in a proposal, and it was accepted. Donna and I became the founding codirectors of the University of Toronto Women's Mental Health Program. This was the first such program in Canada and one of the first in North America.

Establishing this program was not easy. We had to fight against the impression that we were anti-male "bra burners" who just wanted to talk about the victimization of women. We had to establish that this was a legitimate field of study by obtaining grants and writing papers. We set up teaching courses so that all of the residents would receive this information as part of the regular curriculum rather than as an elective. Our involvement with other university departments and Canadian provincial and federal governments was essential in terms of setting policies concerning the welfare of women in the community.

These difficult but groundbreaking opportunities highlight the benefit of being able to find and develop a new field (De Angelis 2000). We were able to get recognition for the work that we were doing because it was not in competition with anybody else in our department. I was able to become an instant expert in this area on our faculty because only a handful of us were looking at these issues. This also led to my having important leadership roles in the department in terms of setting curricula for the residents and establishing policies such as antiharassment policies between students and staff and leading task forces on issues such as improving the recruitment, retention, and promotion of women in academic psychiatry.

A second opportunity for innovative work came in the early 1990s. Because of my work in women's mental health, I was invited to be on a city task force, Public Violence Against Women and Children. I led the subcommittee on support services. This committee made recommendations about setting up a rape crisis center in hospitals and advocating for specially trained police officers to deal with sexual assaults. I was a founding member of the Metropolitan Action Committee on Public Violence Against Women and Children (METRAC). This was an organization that did not offer direct services but instead looked at working with government, courts, and schools to change attitudes and policies concerning violence against women.

In the early 1990s an interesting case came before the discipline committee to the College of Physicians and Surgeons of Ontario (CPSO). A
doctor (not a psychiatrist) was practicing a form of psychotherapy called
bonding therapy. This involved treating the patient like a child and having
the therapist play the role of a parent. In this particular case, the young
woman was on her knees being hugged to the groin area of the therapist.
There was a difference in testimony between the patient and the therapist
as to whether or not the therapist was wearing clothes.

As was their custom, the CPSO committee looked for someone else in
the city who was experienced in bonding therapy and asked that person to
come to testify as to whether or not this was appropriate. This physician, of
course, said that the therapy was perfectly fine. The results of this disciplinary investigation hit the newspapers. In their wisdom, the public saw this
case and laughed, realizing that the rationalization that this was a form of
therapy was just that—a rationalization. The CPSO committee felt quite
embarrassed about what had happened. At that time, METRAC presented
them with a white paper suggesting that there were numerous possible
cases of abuse of patients by physicians that the college was ignoring or dis-
missing. We were asked to present an information and teaching symposium
to the college staff and their lawyers. Out of that grew the CPSO Task Force
on Sexual Abuse of Patients. This group traveled around Ontario and held
hearings. They found a large number of women who had either never for-
mally complained about their abusive doctor or who had had their complaints dismissed by the college. CPSO then established guidelines about
relationships between physicians and patients, setting up appropriate
boundaries. As a result of the various complaints that had come forward,
there were many cases to be heard by the discipline committee. I became
the first expert witness engaged by the college to testify at these hearings to
help the disciplinary committee understand why sexual relationships between a doctor and a patient represented an abuse of power.

Although there was already some discussion of these kinds of boundary violations in the United States, this was the first time that it had been
publicly discussed in Canada. I became a frequent expert witness at CPSO
as well as many other professional colleges, including those for occupational therapists, physical therapists, laboratory technicians, massage therapists, social workers, nurses, and many others of the twenty-two regulated
health professions. Also, I was asked to testify in court as an expert witness
concerning this kind of abuse occurring not only with health care professionals but between lawyers and their clients, teachers and their students,
and clergy and their parishioners. This led me down another path, embarking in an area that was not well known in Canada, of conducting educational sessions and setting policies and guidelines for health professions

with the government, several university faculties of medicine, and various professional colleges.

The expert witness work about boundary violations later extended to testifying about adult consequences of childhood sexual abuse. I have since gone on to carry out assessments of the consequences of childhood abuse for members of native populations who were sent to residential treatment programs as children, where they were abused emotionally, physically, and sexually.

Acquire Special Skills

It is common for women working in a department to be assigned to committees that organize the social outings or have functions that do not have much clout either in terms of increasing one's status in the department or academic future (Yedidia and Bickel 2001). There are very few men who would ever agree to be on the social committee. One way of being recognized in the department is to acquire skills normally assumed to be those belonging to men.

In my department we have a partnership to which all of the psychiatrists belong. Many years ago I became the chair of the management committee for this partnership. The result is that for thirty years I have been managing the financial business of this large partnership, now including forty-six full-time psychiatrists and another thirty part-time psychiatrists. As well as making decisions about the departmental budget, I determine what each individual psychiatrist's monthly pay will be, based on their billings and other sources such as honoraria and university salaries, and when to increase or decrease it or hand out advance profit checks. Each year, I run the annual partnership meeting during which time I review the audited statements for the past year. I can see many eyes glaze over as some of my partners either don't know how to read a financial statement or have no understanding of the business side of our profession. As a result, I receive a great deal of respect. Having this role also gives me a position on the executive committee of my department and, therefore, a voice in decisions that are made for the department of psychiatry.

Become an Advocate

Just after I delivered my first child, a social worker on my team came to see me with a *Ms.* magazine. In this magazine they described the establishment of a rape crisis center. At that time I was practicing community psychiatry and we decided that we would establish the first such center in Canada. This was a very interesting process. First, we dealt with a group of women who appeared in army boots, jeans, and no makeup and saw us as sellouts to the establishment rather than as women who were being successful in a largely male world. Fortunately, we were able to shift gears and team up with a group of women from the criminal justice program at the University of Toronto.

I set up information sessions for women who worked at the center, informing them about the physical and psychological consequences of sexual assault and how to deal with survivors. Because survivors of sexual assault would initially come to the emergency department of my hospital, I also had to provide training to the emergency staff so that they would be more understanding of and receptive to these women when the police brought them to our hospital. I had to combat some rather strange attitudes such as that of the medical director of the hospital, who asked "What if the rapists get mad at us for bringing these women here?"

We were able to get this crisis center up and running. It was a result of my work in this area that I was asked to be on the Metro Toronto Task Force on Public Violence Against Women and Children and chair the implementation subcommittee. Out of that grew the establishment of METRAC and my work on their board, and then as chair of the board for many years. In my role there, I was asked to work with groups and consult with the government when rape laws were changed in Canada such that no meant no—when drunkenness was dismissed as a defense for attacking and sexually assaulting women, and when defense attorneys started to seek access to the victim's medical records in order to try to discredit the victim. The government's initial response was to say that when the defense sought records, they would first be given to a judge to review and assess whether there was any value or merit in their being used for the defense. I was asked to give training sessions to the judges in order to make them aware of the nature of psychiatric records. It was important that they realize that the record was not a police report, but instead a document containing a combination of the patient's words and the therapist's interpretation. In addition, it was important for the judges to understand that patients typically speak about feeling guilty and blaming themselves for being in the wrong place at the wrong time or for being too friendly to someone they met in a bar. In order for the judge to properly assess whether the record should be handed over to the defense, it was important that they be able to put any of these types of comments in perspective. My work in areas of violence against women also led me to be invited to join the board of the YWCA Toronto and eventually become chair of the board of that organization.

As well, I was asked to speak to the special sexual assault investigators of the Toronto Police Service. I spoke to them about the types of presentations that women might have who had been sexually assaulted and discussed with them ways of approaching different types of victims. As a result, I was invited to join the police Sexual Assault Advisory Council. I remain on this council, which has a goal of helping women learn how to prevent sexual assault, improve the police response to victims, and make it easier for the victim to negotiate the legal system if she does complain to the police.

This type of work, as well as my work with women who are victims of either childhood sexual assault or assault by authority figures, has been personally satisfying. It also has given me a status both within the profession and in the community and a reputation as someone who strongly advocates for women. Not everyone is interested in being an outspoken advocate, yet being involved in some sort of charitable cause or community endeavor can be gratifying and emotionally rewarding, and establishes one as a leader in the community.

Deal With Your Insecurities

Many women struggle with an impostor complex. They constantly feel that they have fooled the world into thinking they are competent and that at any moment they will be exposed. They attribute their success to luck rather than skills. This makes them hesitate to try to assume any leadership positions because they feel they do not have the qualities to take on such roles (Yedidia and Bickel 2001) The irony is that when they look around at the men in leadership positions, the women are often very good at identifying the weaknesses displayed by the men. It is quite a fascinating mental trick to simultaneously realize that many of the men she knows are incompetent or imperfect in various ways and yet believe that there is no way that she could take on a leadership role and do any better.

Women also often worry far too much about what everyone thinks about them. They are afraid that they will not be liked if they speak up, have strong opinions, or assume leadership roles. They have a conversational style that is self-defeating; that is, they raise their voice at the end of sentences, which makes them sound unsure, and they apologize too frequently (Tannen 1994). The reality is that the only way to never offend people is to appear like bland wallpaper that disappears into the background. I have been fortunate in that I have never hesitated to speak up and voice my opinions.

I also learned a very valuable lesson from karate, which I continue to study. In karate terms, the message is that I know I can hurt you so I do not have to fight with you to prove that I can walk away. In psychological terms, it means that I know who I am and what my strengths are. If other people want to spend their time trying to undercut me or talk about me that is their problem, not my problem. This does not mean that I or any woman should be insensitive to getting along with other people, trying to include people and form a consensus. It does mean, however, that you stop losing sleep and burning up energy over people who really don't want to work with you but who are just intent on trying to sabotage you.

Push for Promotion

Although my chief kept talking about my promotion to full professor, it seemed as though the criteria kept expanding. He would say I'd be promoted after publishing "two more papers," but, two or three papers later he would still be saying the same thing. I decided that I needed to take things into my control.

I researched the best way to present my information to the promotion committee. I spoke with people who had outlined ideal résumés and indicated what supporting documents could be included. Developing these documents involved many hours and hard work. Now I advise young women to keep files on teaching, residents/medical students/fellows they have supervised, and all evaluations they have ever received. For my documentation I had to comb through all of my files to find this type of information. I eventually assembled a résumé and teaching dossier that others later used as models. I went forward with supported strength in teaching, research, and creative professional development (including having established the Women's Mental Health Program) and easily got promoted. Had I just listened to my male chief, this probably wouldn't have happened until many years later.

Insist on Fair Income

In my department, the staff has two main sources of income, fees from the government insurance plan (the Ontario Health Insurance Plan [OHIP]) for seeing patients and a stipend from the university for teaching. Initially, in my naivety, I accepted the university money that was allotted to me. The finances of each member of our psychiatric partnership were not known to others. As I became more financially savvy, I began to insist that the finances be disclosed to all the partners. When this happened, I was shocked to see that I was getting less university money than anyone in the department, even those junior to me.

I was outraged. I was initially told that it was because I was taking two half-days off (did I neglect to mention I was the only female on staff?). I asserted that this might reduce my personal OHIP income if I saw fewer patients, but that I was still carrying a full teaching load. My chief reluctantly acknowledged this but said that the university stipends had already been allotted for the year so there was nothing to be done. I then called the chair of psychiatry, who agreed with my stand but said the university money was allotted to the individual departments and they decided how to dispense it. Back I went to my chief. I told him that if the university money had been allotted, he would have to give me extra funds out of the partnership money until the next year.

I won my fight, but it taught me several things. Sexism is alive and well; I fully believe they took advantage of my position as the only woman in the department and someone who was trying in a small way to balance career and family (Ash et al. 2004; DesRoches et al. 2010). I also learned to become better at negotiating money up front and realized the necessity of finding out what others are paid in order to successfully negotiate. I learned to be smarter about asserting my rights and not just accepting the fantasy that others would look after me.

Find Support

Given that women are still in the minority in most settings and leadership positions, it is very important to be able to find support. There is a kind of support in joining with and confiding in other women that is different from career mentoring. These are the people who can tell you about their own experiences dealing with colleagues or trying to cope with career and family conflicts. These are the people who can encourage you when you are feeling low and about to give up rather than continuing to assert yourself and fight for your rights and position. Sometimes these colleagues are in your own setting. Sometimes they are mentors that you can find in various outside organizations (Levinson et al. 1991; Yedidia and Bickel 2001). I have been very fortunate to connect with several women who held strong leadership positions. They have been encouraging and supportive and over the years have helped me to develop strategies to deal with career-family conflicts, departmental politics, and my own insecurities.

Maintain Sanity

Although it is challenging and rewarding to try to take on leadership positions it can also be stressful and draining, especially in psychiatry as we deal with patients who are unhappy and looking to us to heal them. We often sit for many hours on end speaking to people who feel hopeless and helpless. It is, therefore, essential that we find some ways to balance our lives. Without this balance we will either get discouraged and drop out, start drinking too much or abusing other substances, or become depressed ourselves.

I have always been very inspired by my family. I spend as much time as I can with my two daughters and have recently had the unexpected joy of having a grandson. I have always kept active in things very different from my work. For many years I performed in community theatre. For the past fourteen years I have gone to karate training three or four times a week. Not only has this ensured a degree of fitness, it has been a wonderful distraction. If work issues are still on your mind, punching a bag or pad can certainly help to get rid of the tension. There is no one thing that works for every woman, but it is important that there be some time for you in the day; otherwise you will get burnt out.

Conclusion

In summary, looking back on my career, there are some things that I have done well and others that I have not done so well. As is typical of many women, I did not have a five-year plan on which I kept focus. My career came as rather a surprise to me. I did not set out to have the type of roles that I eventually gained. I have, however, always felt comfortable in speaking up and making my opinions clear. I was able to capitalize on opportunities as they came along. For the most part, I have not let my insecurities overwhelm me, but have pushed ahead rather than letting myself be convinced that I was incapable of taking on a leadership position. This does not mean that things were always sunny. Sometimes, I have felt overwhelmed and wondered, as my daughter once asked, why I was willing to "do homework my whole life." However, for the most part this has been a gratifying, challenging, and exciting life. I hope that some of the pointers I have shared will be of help as guidance for a desirable career.

References

Ash AS, Carr PL, Goldstein R, Friedman RH: Compensation and advancement of women in academic medicine: is there equity? Ann Intern Med 141:205–212, 2004

Carr PL, Ash AS, Friedman RH, et al: Relation of family responsibilities and gender to the productivity and career satisfaction of medical faculty. Ann Intern Med 129:532–538, 1998

De Angelis CD: Women in academic medicine: new insights, same sad news. N Engl J Med 342:426–427, 2000

DesRoches CM, Zinner DE, Rao SR, et al: Activities, productivity, and compensation of men and women in the life sciences. Acad Med 85:631–639, 2010

Fried LP, Francomano CA, MacDonald SM, et al: Career development for women in academic medicine: multiple interventions in a department of medicine. JAMA 276:898–905, 1996

Hamel MB, Ingelfinger JR, Phimister E, et al: Women in academic medicine—progress and challenges. N Engl J Med 355:310–312, 2006

Levinson W, Tolle SW, Lewis C: Women in academic medicine: combining career and family. N Engl J Med 321:1511–1517, 1989

Levinson W, Kaufman K, Clark B, et al: Mentors and role models for women in academic medicine. West J Med 154:423–426, 1991

Osborn EH, Ernster VL, Martin JB: Women's attitudes towards careers in academic medicine at the University of California, San Francisco. Acad Med 67:59–62, 1992

Tannen D: Talking From 9 to 5: How Women's and Men's Conversational Styles Affect Who Gets Heard, Who Gets Credit, and What Gets Done at Work. New York, W Morrow, 1994

Yedidia MJ, Bickel J: Why aren't there more women leaders in academic medicine?: the views of clinical department chairs. Acad Med 76:453–465, 2001

Chapter 21

Centering

Mary Jane England, M.D.
with M. J. Doherty, Ph.D.

"KNOWING YOU, MOM, who would have thought you'd take the college coed and build athletic fields?"

So said my son Thomas, a teacher and then a second-year medical student, to me, a child and adolescent psychiatrist and then president of Regis College, a Catholic women's college in greater Boston and my alma mater. An ardent women's advocate and a person only remotely interested in sports, I had just announced that, after ten years, I'd be stepping down from the presidency and returning to various endeavors in medicine and public health.

"But," he continued, "like the other things you've done at Regis, it's student centered, and I'm not surprised."

"Centered," I mused; student centered, patient centered, and family centered. Centering has been my striving as an educator, woman psychiatrist, public administrator, mother, grandmother. It's the art of situating myself in relation to others, the environment, the world; it's identifying the essential, responding as needed to what presents itself, letting go of what is not essential, and moving forward. Over a lifetime, *centering* names my struggle to strengthen families, including my own; to open the societal circle to women and minorities; to address health care failures and gaps; to bring higher education into twenty-first century realities; and to build better policies and practices and more inclusive systems. For me personally, centering integrates feelings with discipline to create a particular sensibility with an emphasis on productivity and pragmatism.

Writing personally about it, however, presents a challenge. Doing so seems counterintuitive to the very psychiatric training that formed me, the science and evidence-based reasoning that certainly demands consciousness, but also affective reticence and restraint. I reflect further that a life of tragic loss and conflict, as the protagonist overcomes difficulties (or not), with all the attending lamentation, probably makes a more engaging story than my relatively stable and happy life. My life is not one of loss and conflict. Lamentation has never been my style. Rather, science honed my judgment from my student days, along with the disciplined time management that many laboratory courses demanded. I learned the value of transparency—being who you say you are—as well as the appropriateness of a strong boundary between private life and public life. Evidence-based decisions became a habit, a characteristic of everything I did. Not letting go, when the evidence declared one should, was clearly a waste of time. Yet even psychiatrists have their life stories, and because of scientific and affective discipline, the best psychiatrists know the inner pulse of their feelings and can sanction, reject, or share them without getting caught in dangerous transferences and countertransferences or other kinds of emotional wheel spinning in relationships.

So my story is relatively simple. If, as Sigmund Freud taught, love and work center our lives, love and work have constituted my life, with my three children being the exemplars and work the narrative thread. The two have always, it seems, gone together. Science has been the underpinning of my career, and love freed me to work, giving me the opportunity to work in ways that many women lack.

Origins

From the beginning I had wonderful models in the women around me. The strength and independence of my mother, Anna Fahey Regan from Bangor, Maine, a nurse manager of the Florence Crittenton House (a home for unwed mothers in Boston) and later at Massachusetts General Hospital, and the independence and intellectual excellence of the Sisters of St. Joseph of Boston, teaching me from grammar school at St. Columbkille's through Mt. St. Joseph Academy and through Regis, the college they founded and staffed, made me a confident and articulate person.

As I began medical school thinking I'd become an obstetrician and gynecologist, there was an awareness of the value of a broad, interdisciplinary education for psychiatrists, a desire to move psychiatry more into the public sphere, and a feeling that psychiatry "should expand its boundaries to a wider field of social interventions" (Scully et al. 2000, p. 128). Mine was a generation pursuing social justice. We were drawn to the possibilities of social intervention. The rapid advance of psychosocial knowledge in the cause of helping society made me think about approaching women, children, and families through psychiatry rather than gynecology.

The extremely talented women professors of child and adolescent psychiatry at Boston University School of Medicine in the early 1960s modeled the possibility for me and confirmed my change in direction: I would become a psychiatrist. Evoleen Rexford, Susanne van Ameringen, and Eleanor Pavenstedt offered some of the best courses at the school. A cadre of peers—women medical students in psychiatry and now lifelong professional companions and friends, including Nina Auerbach, Judith Borit, and Cynthia Rose—reinforced my choice. We entered and pursued psychiatry *together*. At that time, the school of thought in which we were trained was psychoanalytic psychotherapy (Freudian), but with Erik Erikson's influence, and there was also a shift from the psychoanalytic perspective to that of community mental health.

In the late twentieth century, most psychiatrists were men who, like other groups of men, tended to form closed rather than open groups. So the politics of being a woman entering psychiatry was never easy, but the arena of the struggle and *when* that struggle would manifest, could shift. In my life, the gender question emerged only in midcareer. At the beginning, psychiatry was even opening up to Catholics. Only once, when I was interviewing for a psychiatric residency, was my religion challenged. An interviewer asked whether I could, as a Catholic, be a psychiatrist. My commitment to women, children, families, and social justice, however, was consistent with both Catholic teaching and sound mental health principles, and I was always transparent about my faith and practice, including sending my own children to parish schools and Catholic colleges.

Personally, the change of professional direction to psychiatry marked the first major opening of the circle of my adult awareness, and I was affirmed in it by the remarkable men in my life, starting with my father, Thomas Regan, a Boston police officer who supported the idea I could do anything I wanted and could do no wrong. During medical school, I married Robert England, a cardiologist, and went with him on various internships and residencies from Boston to Hong Kong, to San Francisco, and back to Boston again. A Jew and a Catholic, we immediately started our own family. I had three great children born fairly close together: Alexandra, Kara, and Thomas. They are all grown up now and I am the grandmother to Alexandra's Sara and Ben.

Early in my career in Boston and San Francisco I had gotten to know the psychiatrist Bill Goldman and his wife Riese, a psychologist. Bill has been my mentor for decades, and the three of us were close friends. Each of us understood that life is mobile and requires all human beings to discern what to keep and what to let go as one moves along. As Rilke once noted, "the transformed speaks only to relinquishers" (Rilke 1996, p. 127). Whatever within us refuses to let go, when letting go is necessary, paralyzes. At decisive moments in life, the Goldmans and I have been able to relinquish, to discern what to let go of and what to keep.

Social Change

Ours was also a generation forged in the civil rights and peace movements to take down barriers to human achievement and the common good. We sought social change and believed we could achieve it. During numerous Boston demonstrations in the 1960s, we Boston University medical students and residents—women and men alike—wore our whites and stethoscopes and stood on street corners to constitute a medical presence and prevent unnecessary brutality. We women students did not feel forced into an "either-or" stance, marriage *or* medical career, even though we worked twice as hard to advance, and three times as hard as we married, bore children, and balanced our family relationships with our careers. Dedicated to the profession, it would even be a while before we recognized how much we would have to take on with the barriers to women in the profession, especially the economic denigration of being paid less for the same or more work.

At the outset of my career, I was neither involved in nor caught by any gender question as such. True, the particular challenges I faced as a physician, wife, and mother were to stay balanced, focused, and centered. However, the challenges themselves helped me shape certain patterns for a career that would embrace a widening and increasingly inclusive open circle.

In a way, social change does not really begin until it affects one personally. Established on the gifts of life, we were a family that also began to know the fragility of things human, the need we human beings have for one another, and some tragic loss. During my internship, I had to have an emergency tracheotomy because of staph pneumonia. Bob saw me through. My father passed away in 1965. My mother was diagnosed with colon cancer in 1966 but kept working as a nurse at Massachusetts General Hospital. In 1969, following the completion of my child and adolescent psychiatry residency, I was named Director of Psychiatry at St. Elizabeth's Hospital in Brighton, not far from my home. As a family, we lived with my mother in my parent's house, also in Brighton, firmly embedded in the local Catholic parish, St. Columbkille's. The three of us medical professionals—my mother, Bob, and I—alternated shifts and were engaged together in rearing the three kids. "It takes a village." The neighborhood knew and liked the two docs and the nurse-grandmother living in their midst. We held open house for family and friends, friends of our children, neighbors, local clergy, and other physicians. The neighborhood formed a kind of clan.

In this strongly supportive context, being pragmatic by nature helped me advance professionally. For example, inserted into the neighborhood, seeing local patients in the clinic, I recognized that strength-building in whole families offered a better option for children and adolescents than individual treatment alone. This was my own experience, too.

I lost both my parents before I was thirty-five. I felt the loss of my mother on Easter in 1972 most acutely. She was an integral part of our family, and her death represented a genuine social change for me. Besides my bereavement and grief, my mother's death required me to let go of one role and embrace another. It asked me to move both closer to home and farther out professionally as I began a truly community-based practice. In 1972, I became Director of Clinical Psychiatry for the Brighton-Allston Mental Health Clinic, which we were able to locate on the first floor of the St. Columbkille's convent at the invitation of the Sisters of St. Joseph, only two blocks away from our house. At more or less the same time, again not far from my own Brighton neighborhood, I became a consultant to the marriage tribunal at the chancery in the Archdiocese of Boston. Father Dennis Burns had been college chaplain when I was a student at Regis; he was now the canon lawyer heading up the marriage tribunal. He recognized that women professionals needed to be involved in reviewing cases, determining whether there was cause for marriage annulment, that is, a broken contract, or one inadequately made to begin with, and asked me and other women psychiatrists to consult.

The first real pattern to emerge, then, in my effort to center—it emerged both through growth and through loss—was a social and relational one focused on children, couples, families, the neighborhood, the religious community, and the work of gathering us all together for the sake of our children's good health. This pattern determined my whole career.

Mobility and Stability Are the Same Thing

Of course, things did not stand still; neither could I. During the 1970s, this child and adolescent psychiatrist actually began moving into public administration and social activism. My career took off—in place, as it were.

The reality was, for my family's sake, I needed to stay put and not uproot everyone to take opportunities nationally. My career had to advance locally, if it were going to advance at all, while I centered on my family, as women do. No career decision for women is without reference to that personal life or without cost. But this same situation gave me the courage to take some risks and to move out of narrow definitions of my professional life. The result was that, between 1974 and 1983, when the feminist world movement also took off, I assumed a new major position almost every three years, marking a period of rapid career advancement that consumed most of my energy. In this sense my career narrative *is* my life narrative.

First, I was asked in 1974 to move beyond the world of hospital and clinic and apply my thinking in the Massachusetts Department of Mental Health, in Boston, as Director of Planning and Manpower for Children's Services. Bill Goldman came from San Francisco to become commissioner of the Massachusetts Department of Mental Health simultaneously, so I had professional support as I directed the development of statewide child and adolescent mental health services (institutional and community based), including policy and program development, as well as conducting budget preparation, training, and human resource development.

I began to think about the challenge of systems: How does one devise systems for delivery of care without relinquishing the strength of family and community? In the 1970s psychiatry as a whole was involved in a major cultural shift away from huge institutions (the remote castles for the insane, whether for children, youth, the elderly, or the mentally ill) toward smaller community-based enterprises like my original neighborhood clinic. Accomplishing such a shift on the large scale of whole states and across the nation was truly daunting. But life did not let me off the hook; evidently the challenge of systems was a problem I was called to solve or, at least, contribute to solving. It became a second centering pattern in my career.

Rather than immediately imposing a theoretical, top-down solution, I worked from the ground up and got to know an expanding neighborhood—all of greater Boston—by becoming an active participant in Action for Boston Community Development (ABCD), part of the national antipoverty program, coming out of the Office of Economic Opportunity. ABCD was reimagining Boston by bringing different local communities into the discussion, challenging existent barriers of race and ethnicity and emphasizing, rather, the common theme: *neighborhood.* Between 1971 and 1976, I was a member of the ABCD Board of Directors, serving as its president from 1973 to 1975, and simultaneously serving as a member of the advisory group of the Citywide Coordinating Council, advising Judge W. Arthur Garrity Jr. on Boston school desegregation (1975–1976). I also worked with Catholic Charities of the Archdiocese of Boston, as an incorporator from 1976 to 1979 and, a decade later, as a member of its Board of Trustees (1985–1987). Striving for peace in the 1960s, we in Boston were striving for racial and gender equality and desegregation in the 1970s and 1980s.

In 1976, with community-based evidence and community service fully engaging me, I became an associate commissioner in the Massachusetts Department of Mental Health. In that role, I directed a $400 million mental health and mental retardation agency with 20,000 employees, nine state hospitals, and six state schools. Responsibilities also included managing the operations of seven regions in the Commonwealth with a total of forty-one catchment areas, to provide comprehensive community mental health and mental retardation services. The job gave me an extraordinary opportunity to see how locked-in we had become in service delivery. The system kept growing in an institutional way, but without necessarily achieving better results. I was convinced we had to move from a closed to a more open system by developing a community-based system from the ground up.

During that time, and for the next decade, I also became a National Institute of Mental Health (NIMH) Human Resources Policy Committee consultant. During the 1980s, I was chair of that committee, which was charged with developing national policy for NIMH regarding states' mental health human resources. The blessing in this work was the nationwide collaboration of professionals. We were all facing, and all struggling to solve, similar problems.

A third centering pattern developed, therefore, as I learned the ramifications of health care and social services delivery in the public domain. Both in my home state and nationally, an understanding of politics and budget was crucial to the advancement of delivery of care in any public health system. In both the Massachusetts Department of Mental Health and the NIMH committee, I must have been voicing my discontent with what currently existed and my sense that a new model was needed, because I got the chance to build an entirely new state agency.

In 1979 I was named the first commissioner of a new state agency in Massachusetts, the Department of Social Services (DSS) which I had helped design and implement. I had mastered the politics, at least for the time being, and had the necessary budget. DSS took over service delivery from the Department of Public Welfare and decentralized it, ensuring citizen involvement and improving the quality of services. Although I was now directing a $210 million social services agency with 2,500 employees spread over 54 areas in regional offices with over 120 contracts, my team and I had constructed it all as a family-, community-, and neighborhood-based enterprise. In the course of making this shift, we also developed social services and child welfare policy for the Commonwealth. Those four years were an opportunity to recreate the system, making it new and fresh. My team in the central office on Causeway Street in Boston's North End was young and dedicated. With the fervor of missionaries to a foreign land, we all worked long hours and had the motivating conviction that we were saving children. Governor Ed King was in full support of what we were doing; he trusted my leadership.

Between the idea and the reality, however, falls the shadow of politics. In the next election, a new governor came in. Faced with his own political challenge to balance the state budget, Governor Mike Dukakis cut the budget of the fairly new DSS, and with that, cut the spirit of possibility in the agency. There was no way the Commonwealth of Massachusetts could achieve and sustain a family- and community-based social services enterprise without having the budget to support the more visionary model we had devised. With the budget cut, we began experiencing the problems that understaffing brought: overworked social workers and more families in need than we had workers to see. The tragic loss of a child's life, precisely because our budget and the staffing it supported had been undercut, marked the end of the new delivery system we had designed and implemented, and my role as commissioner.

DSS, conceived along certain lines, has never been able to realize its potential. Rather, the Commonwealth has continued to contract work out to multiple agencies. Child and family services have become as fragmented and noncollaborative as groups of nongovernmental agencies in the third world, with the result that, as recently as 2008, the current Massachusetts governor, Deval Patrick, named a statewide Child Advocate to try to bring unity into the system.

The shadows that challenged this bright and positive agency and the expanding circle of my career during these years were also personal, involving a betrayal of trust and the anxiety that followed. In 1984, twenty-three years into our marriage, Bob and I parted, and I experienced months of anxiety. Everyone, woman or man, has to balance career and personal life—but successful women professionals inevitably testify to the reality of a social undertow pulling us one way or the other, or demanding we pay a price for having both.

The Larger Society and Public Administration: From Academe to the National Health Policy Debate

My experiences in public administration had summoned me in 1983 to the John F. Kennedy School of Government at Harvard University as Associate

Dean and Director of the Lucius N. Littauer Master in Public Administration Program. There, I directed a graduate professional education program for 250 midcareer professionals from the United States and abroad, developing and implementing the program's marketing strategies. Simultaneously, I represented the university at all levels of government (federal, state, and local) and managed professional, technical, and support staff in the Kennedy School of Government. As an academic administrator I also represented the Kennedy School in other schools and divisions within the university, developing funding for and implementing the Women's Leadership Program with full-tuition fellowships. The Kennedy School experience, which was wonderfully affirming and supportive, enabled me to formalize and intellectualize what I had learned and experienced as good practice; teaching and leading others into public administration, I recognized how much I had become a skillful public administrator. While there, I reinvented myself and became an active participant in the American Society for Public Administration and in the National Academy of Public Administration.

The sequence of events during this time, from 1983 to 1987—from the letting go of DSS before it could fulfill its potential, to the move to the Kennedy School, and through the break-up of my marriage in 1984, when my youngest child was in high school—pushed me more fully, with both painful lessons learned and a new, joyful consciousness, into an even wider horizon. I was the sole breadwinner. As love and work continued to center my life, the 1980s and '90s saw me discovering a new balance of those two powers and having the freedom to do so. To start with, because my personal circumstances had changed, I was literally freer to move around the country, to become more fully engaged with professional organizations, and to take on roles of national leadership.

Through the American Medical Women's Association (AMWA), I met American Psychiatric Association (APA) leaders Dr. Carol Nadelson and Dr. Leah Dickstein. They became my role models in organized psychiatry. During the 1980s the inequality of women and minorities was a major focus of the work at AMWA. As I emerged into leadership positions and saw how gender injustice affected women professionals, the issue became real for me, too. In 1985, in my mid-forties, I became president of AMWA, another affirming experience, as women medical professionals worked together on issues of gender equality in the strongly emerging world movement of feminism. Once again, the combination of evidence gathering, incisive decision-making, letting go, moving forward, and taking some risks to broaden my professional base worked for me.

In 1987, twenty-three years after I received my M.D., my youngest child left for college and my career took me out of Massachusetts for the first time, to become vice president of medical services in the Group Department of the Prudential Insurance Company of America in Roseland, New Jersey. As I had learned public administration by doing it, I learned about insurance and private finance from the ground up, developing mental health policy and coordinating mental health quality assurance for the managed care networks in the Prudential health care system. I also oversaw risk management for six regional offices; organized and implemented mental health training programs for regional and local staff; and represented Prudential in psychiatric and other medical organizations locally and nationally.

The next year, 1988, the Robert Wood Johnson (RWJ) Foundation appointed me program director for its Mental Health Services Program for Youth, charging me to develop a 25 million dollar grant program to fund comprehensive home- and community-based services for youths with mental disorders in twenty states. I became a national advisor providing technical assistance to state and local governments, academic institutions, and independent service providers regarding systems development and financing. The RWJ Foundation financially supported twenty percent of my time and staffing needs in an arrangement we worked out with Prudential.

The RWJ Foundation project continued and came with me when I left Prudential in 1990 to enter yet another domain of business as president of the Washington Business Group on Health (WBGH; now called the National Business Group on Health), a nonprofit health policy research and education organization whose membership represents Fortune 500 companies and large public employers. I represented the RWJ Foundation and the WBGH initiatives to national child advocacy and interest groups. At WBGH, I was asked to oversee the development of national health system reform policies, to represent large employers in the national health system reform debate, and to oversee the development and operation of grants and programs in the following areas: health and productivity; organized systems of care; innovations and performance measurement; aging; disability management; worksite accommodations to comply with the Americans With Disabilities Act for people with psychiatric disabilities; prevention; worksite health promotion; depression awareness, recognition, and treatment (D/ART) at the worksite; and special populations under managed competition.

I spent a decade in Washington, D.C., where work and play blend and the day's office hours merge into the evening's social events, all the time representing the community of employers from all segments of American industry at meetings of national organizations, health care providers, unions, consumers, governmental agencies, and representatives of electronic and print media. Almost without my realizing it, two decades of career moves that expanded my horizons from medicine and psychiatry to public administration, insurance, and business had put me in a position to have a voice on national health care reform.

National Policy-Making and the Fight for Quality and Parity

The relative stability of my years in Washington was important because the 1990s were an extraordinarily busy period in my personal life. Typically, I was still doing the balancing act that family demands but this time with my grown children participating from different points of the compass. We were all over the country and parts of the world. Kara was finishing law school at Boston College. Thomas had taken his Master of Arts in Teaching degree at Boston University and was teaching in Venezuela, and later in New York City. In the spring and summer of 1997, I had a prefabricated house set up on family property in Cape Cod so a suitable place would be available for my daughter Alexandra's wedding that October. Alexandra had returned from Peace Corps service in Latin America and was marrying another corpsman from Boston who had served in Mali. With my career well established, I was also freer to undertake forms of volunteer service. Two forms of service in the 1990s—leadership in the APA and membership on the Mental Health Task Force at The Carter Center—actually shaped what would become the next circle of my professional endeavors, namely the developing national conversation on mental health care parity and health care reform.

Early in the decade I had become involved in national APA leadership, first serving two terms as treasurer, then becoming APA president. In 1994–1995, when I decided to enter the race to become APA president, the gender question was front and center. Further, there was misunderstanding about my efforts to comprehend, and, if necessary, reinvent systems of care and health care delivery in the managed care realm. Since I, a woman psychiatrist advancing in APA leadership, happened also to be a professional whose work with systems had informed me about managed care, the gender politics of my election became mixed up in the minds of my opponents with emerging patterns of managed care that seemed to threaten psychiatrists' livelihood.

Initially, the race for APA president was polite and professional, but within a short time, the election process became quite contentious. There were several attacks against me, and I was publicly called the "Queen of Managed Care." Colleagues approached me during the race to tell me I had to learn quickly to talk about my accomplishments and to not hesitate. I did. That helped my campaign and I won the election.

I probably won as much, if not more, for another reason, however. My campaign had built a coalition of women, minorities, and young psychiatrists. It was time to open the closed group of senior men who ran the APA to a new generation of leaders. When I won I made sure that fifty percent of the leadership of the APA included women, minorities, and young psychiatrists. This made a substantive political and professional change in the APA, a lasting contribution to American psychiatry, since those new leaders have since assumed major posts in the field across the United States. One example will illustrate. Not long after I became APA president, I was asked to visit South Africa, a country that was trying to heal from apartheid. Having consulted with officials there a few times, I had established a relationship with a child psychologist in the government who became a member of the Truth and Reconciliation Commission. Later, I brought three women psychiatric residents with me to South Africa, and they ultimately served the Truth and Reconciliation Commission in various capacities. Those two trips have had long-range and positive consequences.

Opening doors and introducing others into larger realms of our profession was probably an aspect of the educator in me, and I was soon asked to do something similar in Washington. While still at WBGH in D.C., and working on the RWJ Foundation project through 1997, I was also called on by various agencies of the U.S. government to join study and action groups addressing health policy. As a physician trained as a psychiatrist, experienced in both public administration and the workings of insurance and business, I was able to offer a rich perspective on health care issues facing our country. Between 1996 and 2001, I worked on the Task Force on Community Preventive Services and chaired the depression chapter workgroup for the Centers for Disease Control and Prevention. At the same time, I joined the national advisory council of NIMH in the Department of Health and Human Services (DHHS) and chaired two task forces, one on child mental health research, the other on parity of mental health care. The DHHS Substance Abuse and Mental Health Services Administration (SAMHSA) also involved me as a member of their National Advisory Council and as chair of the Committee on Standards and Performance Measures (1994–1997).

Having become a member of the National Academy of Public Administration in 1987, I emerged in the academy's leadership throughout the 1990s, becoming vice president in 1998. That year, I was also invited to join Rosalynn Carter's Task Force on Mental Health at The Carter Center, which had been founded in 1982 to advance human rights and alleviate human suffering. During the 1990s, the APA was struggling with major changes in mental health care delivery. Rosalynn was aware of the need for better mental health services across a broad spectrum of society and was involving professionals nationally in thinking through how to reinvent the system. Concerned about the lasting stigma of mental illness, she developed and conducted academic symposia, journalism programs, and educational programs to inform the general public; she drew on national and international experts to formulate better mental health care policies and practices; and she made the Task Force on Mental Health a national voice on mental health parity in health care. I found myself working within both governmental groups and private research and advocacy groups on mental health parity. Mrs. Carter has recently published a book reflecting her more than thirty-five years of advocacy, in which she shows how far we have come since the 1970s, and how far we have to go (Carter 2010).

By 1998 quality-of-care issues were coming to the fore across all divisions of medicine. President Clinton's 1996 Advisory Commission on Consumer Protection and Quality in the Health Care Industry envisioned creation of a private sector entity (a *Quality Forum*) to bring health care stakeholder sectors together to standardize health care performance measures and norms and, in 1998, the White House convened a Quality Forum Planning Committee on which I served for two years. The mantra of the Quality Forum as an organization of organizations was that quality improvement required a systematic approach.

In 1999, the Institute of Medicine (IOM) and National Research Council of the National Academies had taken up consideration of the quality chasm and began to produce a series of study reports. The first was *To Err Is Human* (Kohn et al. 2000), with recognition of the scope of medical error in the United States. *Crossing the Quality Chasm—A New Health System for the 21st Century,* appeared in 2001 (Committee on Quality of Health Care in America), followed by studies on leadership, the fostering of rapid advances in health care, priority areas for national action, health professions education, the work environment of nurses, patient safety, and rural health. In 2005, I chaired the IOM national committee that prepared and issued *Improving the Quality of Health Care for Mental and Substance-Use Conditions* in the quality chasm series (Committee on Crossing the Quality Chasm 2006).[1] The editors of the American Catholic weekly magazine *America* asked me to write an article on health care reform. I did, arguing that American health care could not be fixed piecemeal, that a new system was needed (England 2007). Already working with IOM's Board on Chil-

---

[1]Subsequently, *Healing Body and Mind: A Critical Issue for Health Care Reform,* by Roger Kathol, M.D., and Suzanne Gatteau (2007), carried our published report's findings to a different level of communication in a narrative filled with stories of patients and a vision of change.

dren, Youth, and Families, in 2007 and 2008 I also chaired the committee that resulted in *Depression in Parents, Parenting, and Children: Opportunities to Improve Identification, Treatment and Prevention* (England and Sim 2009).

The push to achieve mental health parity and to carry through on national health care reform was on, and parity would succeed first. New Mexico's Senator Pete Domenici had introduced the first bill to require insurance companies to provide parity between mental health and other medical benefits in 1996, but his bill, which passed and was signed into law, did not provide full parity. Domenici and Massachusetts Senator Edward M. Kennedy and Connecticut Senator Chris Dodd continued working to require full parity and close loopholes. They tried in 2004 and did not succeed. As the nation prepared to elect a new president in 2008, we learned that the lion of American health care reform, Senator Ted Kennedy, had been diagnosed with brain cancer. That autumn, fighting two wars and challenged by major financial scandals, the United States had also begun to enter "the Great Recession." Congress geared up to pass a $700 billion financial bailout plan to boost the struggling economy, and Dodd and friends attached mental health parity legislation. Thus, on the wheels of the bailout, mental health parity passed after twelve years of struggle.

The first year of office for the new president, Barack Obama, was consumed by the struggle toward health care reform and the ongoing financial bailout. Senator Kennedy passed away in August 2009, and the president resolved to get health care reform legislation passed. The question of providing health care to all Americans was historically deep, at least a century old. Politically, the active quest for health care reform had begun in the 1930s. Finally, in December 2009, on Christmas Eve, the Senate passed the bill; in March 2010, the House passed it.

Returning to Boston

Meanwhile, as we had crossed into the new century and the struggles for health care quality and mental health parity had heated up in the national health care reform debate, I had come full circle, returning to Boston to become president of my alma mater, Regis College, in July 2001. I had returned in order to give back and I had, in a sense, now become the "mother superior." Regis had provided me with a superb education as a young woman; now I was in a position to help and had the skills to translate Regis into the twenty-first century as it strove to meet the needs of increasingly diverse student populations. Both of my daughters had also established themselves back in the Boston area, and after a sojourn teaching in the Bahamas and in Turkey, my son would soon follow suit. We were all centering homeward.

The next circle of my career in psychiatry and public administration, including my work with IOM, continued with my efforts to save the college that had formed me. Regis needed to escape the downward spiral of an increasing financial deficit. Technology—e-mail, conference calls, the fax machine, and the BlackBerry—effectively enabled all of this work to go on simultaneously, just as informatics was gradually changing health care records and delivery, making the patient the center of her or his own medical home.

At the college, disciplines of mind that I had first cultivated when I was a student there guided me, now proven through experience. Evidence and evidence-based decisions were paramount. I immediately began to collect data on prospective students, current undergraduates, and graduate students as well as the numbers associated with enrollment. We developed team leadership and co-responsibility on my administrative council, where the chief financial officer and the chief academic officer, the enrollment and marketing vice president and the vice president of student life, could all meet face to face. We conducted major research, environmental scans, and feasibility studies; we examined trends, assessed strengths, and shaped evidence-based decisions. We became increasingly student centered. What did they need and what must the college provide so they can go where they need to go?

The school year of 2001 began with the attacks on the World Trade Center and the Pentagon on September 11, and Americans were reeling with shock. As the news reached me and my administrative council that morning, parents had begun calling the president's office about coming from various points in New England to get their daughters. My pragmatism rose to the surface and I said, "No. Leave them here. They are safer here." Indeed, in the morning hours of Tuesday, September 11, when no one knew quite what was going on, the town of Weston, where Regis is located, declared the college a local emergency center. The town did this not only because of the supply of food and water there but because of the network of underground tunnels linking several buildings. The campus was a natural civil defense site. The world had changed, and on September 12 my message to the campus went up on the Regis Web site:

> Today and in the months to come we assert more firmly our educational mission, our commitment to understand, to teach, to act, to seek the deeper wisdom of faith and knowledge.... Our preparation for the new world that has overtaken us is actually already in place. It is underway in our classrooms and in our campus life as Regis women carry intellectual discipline and human kindness to the larger community across bridges developing under our feet.... To build and not destroy, to send forth and not hold back, to move to the next integration....

Less than six months after September 11, the clerical sexual abuse scandal and crisis overtook Boston's Roman Catholic Archdiocese, and I was asked in February 2002 to serve on the Cardinal's Commission for the Protection of Children and to help reform some administrative practices in my church. I persuaded my friend Dr. Donna Norris, especially with her experience in forensic psychiatry, to join the commission. With a dozen other professionals drawn from education, psychology, sociology, social work, law, and medicine, we worked steadily to help the Archdiocese formulate better policies to protect children, prevent abuse, and shape a more transparent, responsive, and responsible direction for the church itself. In the media turbulence of the year that followed I found myself saying that the Catholic church of Boston needed a saint to lead it out of the management and communications mess the crisis had become, that transparency was more than a communications issue; it was also a matter of truth.

Both events and their fallout—September 11 and the church crisis—reinforced my conviction of the value of Regis College as it educates women and teaches a global peace-making perspective. If anything proved the need for contemporary American academe to become truly student centered, the campus massacre at Virginia Tech (Virginia Polytechnic Institute and State University) on April 16, 2007, did. At the time the APA issued a response explaining, once again, how important it is to have appropriate campus systems in place to help at-risk students. Fortunately, the value system of the Sisters of St. Joseph of Boston had made the Regis campus inclusive; our student life professionals had such systems in place. As both a psychiatrist and a college president, I was asked to give the keynote address at a state-wide conference bringing counseling, student life, academic, and security interests together to make sure Massachusetts campuses were safe. On April 28 of that year, *The Boston Herald* published an op-ed piece (England 2010) in which I wrote:

> Socially, we've learned a lot about mainstreaming and community-based care of the mentally ill. Politically, we value parity in mental health coverage in health care. But we're weak on operation, on implementing the better systems we devise.... The depressed student who goes to the infirmary for a flu shot should also be able to have his depression recognized on the spot and access counseling without it being a big deal. The professor worried over a student's substance addiction should be able to feel confident that someone is defining suitable boundaries and monitoring a treatment plan that empowers the student himself to be co-responsible.... But, ultimately, human beings exercising good judgment must conduct the conversation, direct the systems, and interpret the outcomes. Clear communication is vital. Using our wits together benefits everyone.... Education—for all of us— is still about the relationship of thought to action.

Evidence-based research had also taught that to survive meaningfully in the twenty-first century, Regis College needed to grow. We recognized that our students are looking for professional success in a region increasingly focused on biotechnology, science, and health, and this told us how to grow. The master's degree was becoming the entry-level degree to the job market; some professions needed the doctorate. We dug in our heels to do some strength-building on campus and to reestablish the college's niche in higher education in Boston.

Systemic and structural transformation is slow, never fast enough; once again the art of successful change seemed to depend on the science of knowing what to keep and what to let go of, having the courage to relinquish and move forward, including the freedom to self-assess and take risks. Building a new infrastructure at Regis has not brought me the adulation of the faculty, but it has launched a new stability for the college in what is substantially a biotech, medical, and university hub. In the past decade we built on the strength of our graduate programs in nursing; strengthened the core curriculum; positioned our undergraduate liberal arts programs to provide opportunities for professional success; made a smooth transition to undergraduate coeducation; articulated learning agreements with other colleges; identified two schools within the one college, now named the *School of Liberal Arts, Education and Social Sciences* and the *School of Nursing, Science and Health Professions*; mapped out interdisciplinary pathways to help guide contemporary graduates and undergraduates toward their professional goals; launched our first doctoral program; and, yes, built a superb athletic center and fields. Team leadership extended to our Board of Trustees, and through some difficult decisions the board members stepped up to the major issues facing Regis and partnered with us to take radical and imaginative actions to save this institution. Having worked with Dr. Donna Norris on the Catholic church crisis in 2002, I was very pleased when she later joined the Regis College Board of Trustees and became an active participant in the strength-building of this college. Step by step in the past decade, successful deficit reduction while sustaining academic quality has supported Regis's meaningful continuation into the twenty-first century. Teamwork has enabled the college to move from turnaround to transformation, giving Regis a twenty-first century presence in greater Boston's competitive higher education environment. (Regis College even became one of the institutions portrayed as a model in Terrence MacTaggart's *Academic Turnarounds: Restoring Vitality to Challenged American Colleges and Universities* [MacTaggart 2007, pp. 27–30].)

With a rigorous decade of transition at Regis now over, it is also time to pass the torch to new leaders who will carry the college toward its full century in 2027. I have stepped away from the Regis presidency as of June

2011, but will continue pursuing my longstanding interests in health policy and psychiatry in different forums. For example, the implementation of the 2006 IOM study on improving health care for mental health and substance-use conditions (Committee on Crossing the Quality Chasm 2006) has already involved me in the Advancing Care Together (ACT) program, working with Larry Green, M.D., Professor of Family Medicine at the University of Colorado and an IOM member.

Similarly, the passage of mental health parity legislation by Congress has also required the preparation of avenues of implementation, beginning with needed changes in the health care professional curriculum. For instance, this past year, it was a privilege for me to work with U.S. Representative Patrick Kennedy (D-RI) and his staff on that issue. On May 25, 2010, Congressman Kennedy and Congressman John Sullivan (R-OK) introduced legislation to form the Council on Integration of Health Care Education. The bill would also create grants to implement the council's recommendations. According to IOM, integrated training can greatly increase the degree to which medical and other health professionals screen and treat patients for mental health and substance use disorders. At the time the legislation was introduced, Representative Kennedy explained:

> With the extension of mental health parity protections in health care reform legislation and the inclusion of mental health and substance use services in the essential benefits package, it is more important than ever that health care and behavioral health providers have the tools they need to recognize, screen, refer, and treat patients with these illnesses. The Council on Integration of Health Care Education would bring together experts in the field to produce recommendations on exactly what secondary education and continuing education should include as far as curriculum regarding mental health and substance use. The incorporation of these recommendations into education and continuing education will ultimately lead to better outcomes for patients.[2]

So my work continues, carrying through on the different challenges that confront education, health care, and humanity.

---

[2]Laurel Havas, M.P.P., Legislative Director in Representative Kennedy's office, forwarded me the press release on May 26, 2010. Two days later, on May 28, Representative Kennedy also introduced legislation to reauthorize SAMHSA. Established in 1992, SAMHSA is tasked with targeting services to the millions who fail to receive the substance abuse or mental health services they need, and to translate research in these fields into more effective prevention and treatment strategies. As this book goes to print, however, the legislation to form the Council on Integration of Health Care Education has not been brought to a vote in Congress.

Human Issues and Human Change: Haiti's Lesson

Centering is the pragmatic advice I pass on to other women professionals, no matter their field of endeavor and no matter the opposition they may encounter. As for identifying what really does matter, that is something you must decide and then be passionate about. Dr. Arthur Kleinman (2006, p. 232) puts the challenge very clearly in his book *What Really Matters: Living a Moral Life Amidst Uncertainty and Danger*, when he writes, "as troubling and uncertain as it is to come to terms with what matters in the actual conditions of our worlds and our lives, I have come to believe that this is the way to be authentic and useful in crafting a life." It takes courage to identify what really matters, and it takes courage to change—and time—but don't be afraid to broaden your professional horizons; even become an agent of change. For me the passion was family, women, children, and social intervention by thinking through systems, identifying broken systems, and helping to create new systems. For you, it may be something else. Whatever the center of your circle is, both family and the world will be part of its circumference.

About five months after Haiti was struck by a devastating earthquake in January 2010, I visited the country with the dean and several faculty members of the Regis College School of Nursing, Sciences and Health Professions. Regis has had a collaborative relationship with the Haitian Ministry of Health and the main university in Port-au-Prince since 2008 to "educate the educators" in nursing and help Haiti build its human infrastructure in the nursing profession, with all of the continuity and self-empowerment that implies. Before the earthquake we had already brought Haitian officials and a number of Haitian students to Boston. After the earthquake, when more than ninety student nurses and their professor were killed outright on January 12, we worked with and through the non-profit organization Partners in Health to reestablish our connections and offer moral support until such time as we, and they, could resume our Haiti Project. We went to Haiti in June 2010 to reconnect and reaffirm existing partnerships and to create new ones, against the tide of destruction.

In so many ways, as someone who has spent her career in thinking through systems, identifying broken systems, and helping to create new systems, I found the visit to post-earthquake Haiti constituted a living image of fragmentation at every level, fragmentation defying even the worst imagination. What I also found, however, was terrific strength and courage, "grace under fire," in Haitian people. From these perspectives, the same human issues emerge as the obstacles, and the same human virtues as the disciplines needed for change. That is Haiti's lesson for us all.

Applying the fundamental rule of community-based action

Dr. Paul Farmer, the charismatic founder of Boston-based Partners in Health, and Loune Viaud, director of operations and strategic planning for Zanmi Lasante, the Haitian sister organization to Partners in Health, testified at the U.S. Congress on July 27, 2010, as reported by Stephen Smith (2010) in *The Boston Globe*. Farmer and Viaud emphasized that the Haitians and Haitian government—not outside agencies—must map out and direct the course of recovery in that earthquake-destroyed country. The rest of us, in Viaud's words, must support "the capacity and the leadership of both the Haitian government and Haitian communities…, deferring to the experiences of Haitians and guaranteeing our participation in the rebuilding of our country."

Several universities exist in Haiti, public and private. Numerous aid agencies from other countries have had a presence there for decades, and *a fortiori* after the earthquake, but few, if any, actively join forces to collaborate with each other for the common good. Resources, funding sources, and national origins often keep the nongovernmental organizations in relatively separate silos. The Regis Haiti Project requires collaboration; our team has been applying the fundamental rule, if you will, of community-based action: What do Haitian nursing faculty and the Haitian Ministry of Health want for their country as it rebuilds? (See box; Smith 2010.) With those insights taking the lead, we met together on this trip with representatives of the Haitian government, private and public universities, and nongovernmental agencies to stimulate collaboration and a truly Haitian initiative on this one project. This, too, is a way of centering—this time on Haiti and what the Haitians desire. With that in focus, I am confident constructive change will come.

As for my family, my children are now fully accomplished adults who are well launched on their own careers. Alexandra, a mother of two, completed the work for a master's degree in public health several years ago, then decided to earn a master's degree in nursing, and is now a licensed nurse practitioner working in a neighborhood health center in Boston. She and her Peace Corps husband ultimately want to return to the third world in some capacity as a team. Their children, Sara and Ben, are in grammar school. My daughter Kara, having earned her law degree at Boston College, chose a career in law enforcement. She is now a Massachusetts State Police trooper working on domestic violence issues out of the office of the district attorney in Middlesex County. My son Thomas is in his third year of medical school at Boston University School of Medicine. We are together in Boston, our conversations rich with knowledge of and concern for the world. This is perhaps the deepest centering of all.

References

Carter R: Within Our Reach: Ending the Mental Health Crisis. New York, Rodale, 2010

Committee on Crossing the Quality Chasm: Improving the Quality of Health Care for Mental and Substance-Use Conditions. Washington, DC, National Academies Press, 2006. Available at: http://www.nap.edu/openbook.php?isbn=0309100445. Accessed September 5, 2011.

Committee on Quality of Health Care in America: Crossing the Quality Chasm— A New Health System for the 21st Century. Washington, DC, National Academies Press, 2001. Available at: http://www.nap.edu/openbook.php?isbn=0309072808. Accessed September 5, 2011.

England MJ: Diagnosing U.S. Health Care. America: The National Catholic Weekly. December 3, 2007

England MJ: Lessons amid VT tragedy (editorial). The Boston Herald, April 28, 2010

England MJ, Sim LJ (eds); Committee on Depression, Parenting Practices, and the Healthy Development of Children: Depression in Parents, Parenting, and Children: Opportunities to Improve Identification, Treatment, and Prevention. Washington, DC, National Academies Press, 2009. Available at: http://www.nap.edu/openbook.php?record_id=12565. Accessed September 5, 2011.

Kathol R, Gatteau S: Healing Body and Mind: A Critical Issue for Health Care Reform. Westport, CT, Praeger, 2007

Kleinman A: What Really Matters: Living a Moral Life Amidst Uncertainty and Danger. New York, Oxford University Press, 2006

Kohn LT, Corrigan JM, Donaldson MS (eds); Committee on Quality of Health Care in America: To Err Is Human: Building a Safer Health Care System. Washington, DC, National Academies Press, 2000. Available at: http://www.nap.edu/openbook.php?isbn=0309068371. Accessed September 5, 2011.

MacTaggart T: Academic Turnarounds: Restoring Vitality to Challenged American Colleges and Universities. Westport, CT, Praeger, 2007

Rilke RM: Uncollected Poems, Bilingual Edition. Translated by Snow E. New York, Farrar, Straus & Giroux, 1996

Scully JH, Robinowitz C, Shore JH: Psychiatric education after World War II, in American Psychiatry After World War II, 1944–1994. Edited by Menninger R, Nemiah JC. Washington, DC, American Psychiatric Press, 2000, pp 124–151

Smith S: Haitian government must lead recovery, Farmer tells Congress, in The Boston Globe, July 27, 2010. Available at: http://www.boston.com/news/health/blog/2010/07/haitian_governm.html. Accessed September 4, 2011.

Index